1

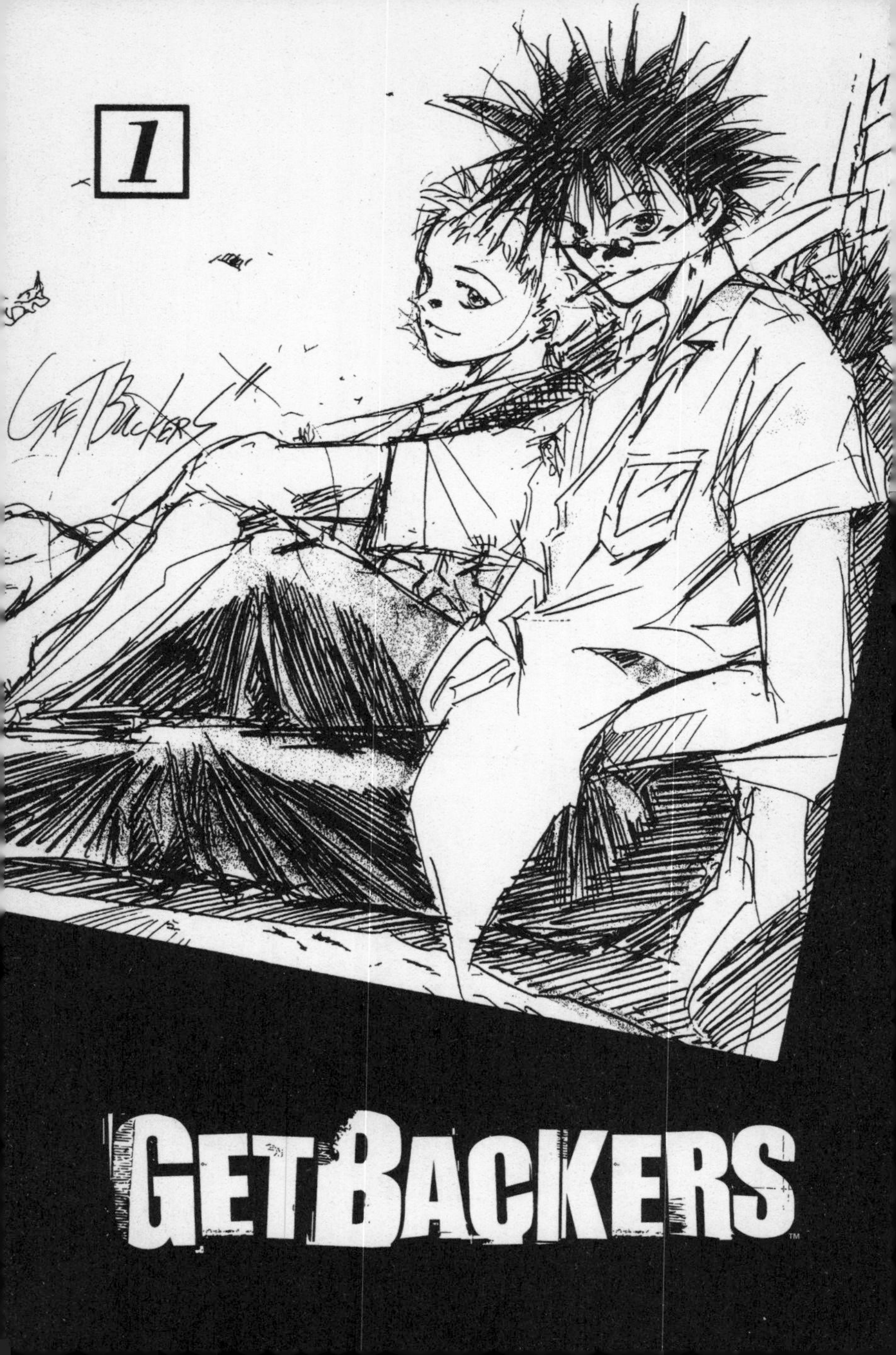
GetBackers

GETBACKERS™

GETBACKERS™

Volume 1

Art by Rando Ayamine
Story by Yuya Aoki

HAMBURG // LONDON // LOS ANGELES // TOKYO

GetBackers Vol. 1
Written by Yuya Aoki
Illustrated by Rando Ayamine

Translation - Egan Loo
English Adaptation - Ryan Shankel
Associate Editors - Alexis Kirsch and Peter Ahlstrom
Retouch and Lettering - Jose Macasocol, Jr
Production Artist - Bowen Park
Cover Design - Patrick Hook

Editor - Luis Reyes
Digital Imaging Manager - Chris Buford
Managing Editor - Lindsey Johnston
Editor-in-Chief - Rob Tokar
VP of Production - Ron Klamert
Publisher - Mike Kiley
President and C.O.O. - John Parker
C.E.O. and Chief Creative Officer - Stuart Levy

A  Manga

TOKYOPOP Inc.
5900 Wilshire Blvd. Suite 2000
Los Angeles, CA 90036

E-mail: info@TOKYOPOP.com
Come visit us online at www.TOKYOPOP.com

ISBN: 1-59182-633-0

First TOKYOPOP printing: February 2004
10 9 8 7 6 5 4
Printed in the USA

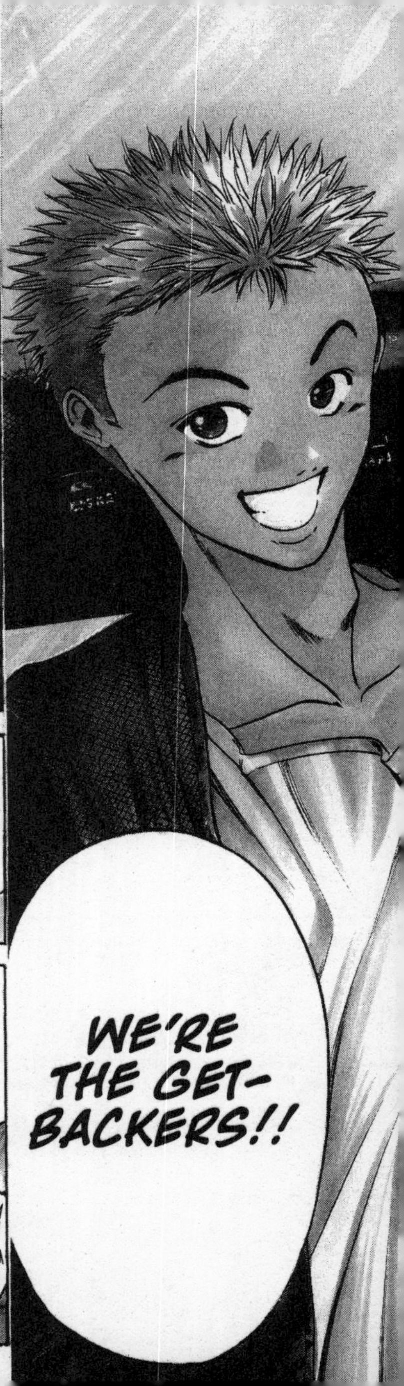
WE'RE THE GET-BACKERS!!

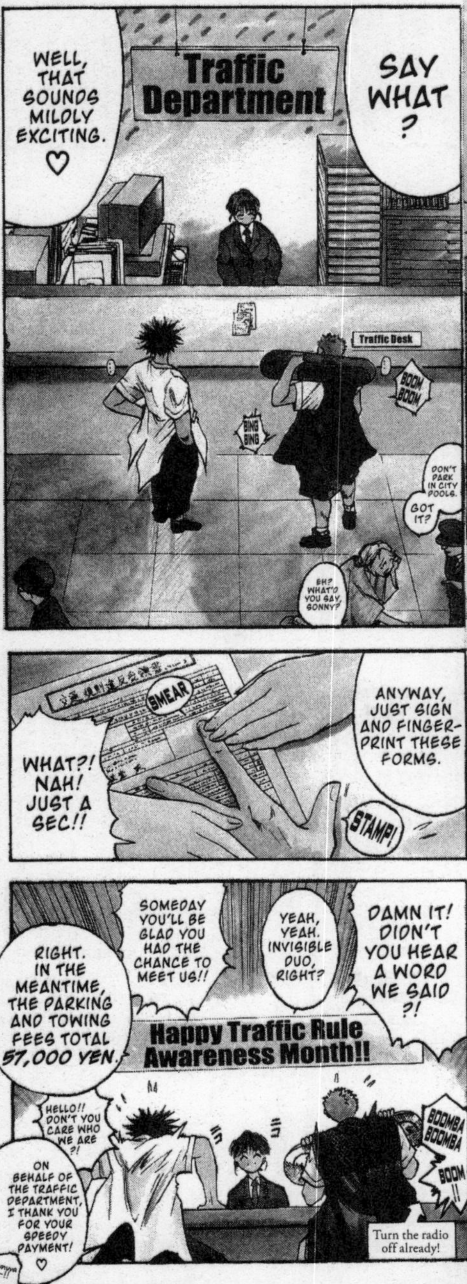
Traffic Department
WELL, THAT SOUNDS MILDLY EXCITING. ♡
SAY WHAT ?
Traffic Desk
...
...
BOOM BOOM
BING BING
DON'T PARK IN CITY POOLS.
GOT IT?
EH? WHAT'D YOU SAY, SONNY?
ANYWAY, JUST SIGN AND FINGER-PRINT THESE FORMS.
SMEAR
STAMP!
WHAT?! NAH! JUST A SEC!!
DAMN IT! DIDN'T YOU HEAR A WORD WE SAID ?!
YEAH, YEAH. INVISIBLE DUO, RIGHT?
SOMEDAY YOU'LL BE GLAD YOU HAD THE CHANCE TO MEET US!!
RIGHT. IN THE MEANTIME, THE PARKING AND TOWING FEES TOTAL 57,000 YEN.
Happy Traffic Rule Awareness Month!!
BOOMBA BOOMBA
BOOM !!
HELLO!! DON'T YOU CARE WHO WE ARE ?!
ON BEHALF OF THE TRAFFIC DEPARTMENT, I THANK YOU FOR YOUR SPEEDY PAYMENT! ♡
Turn the radio off already!

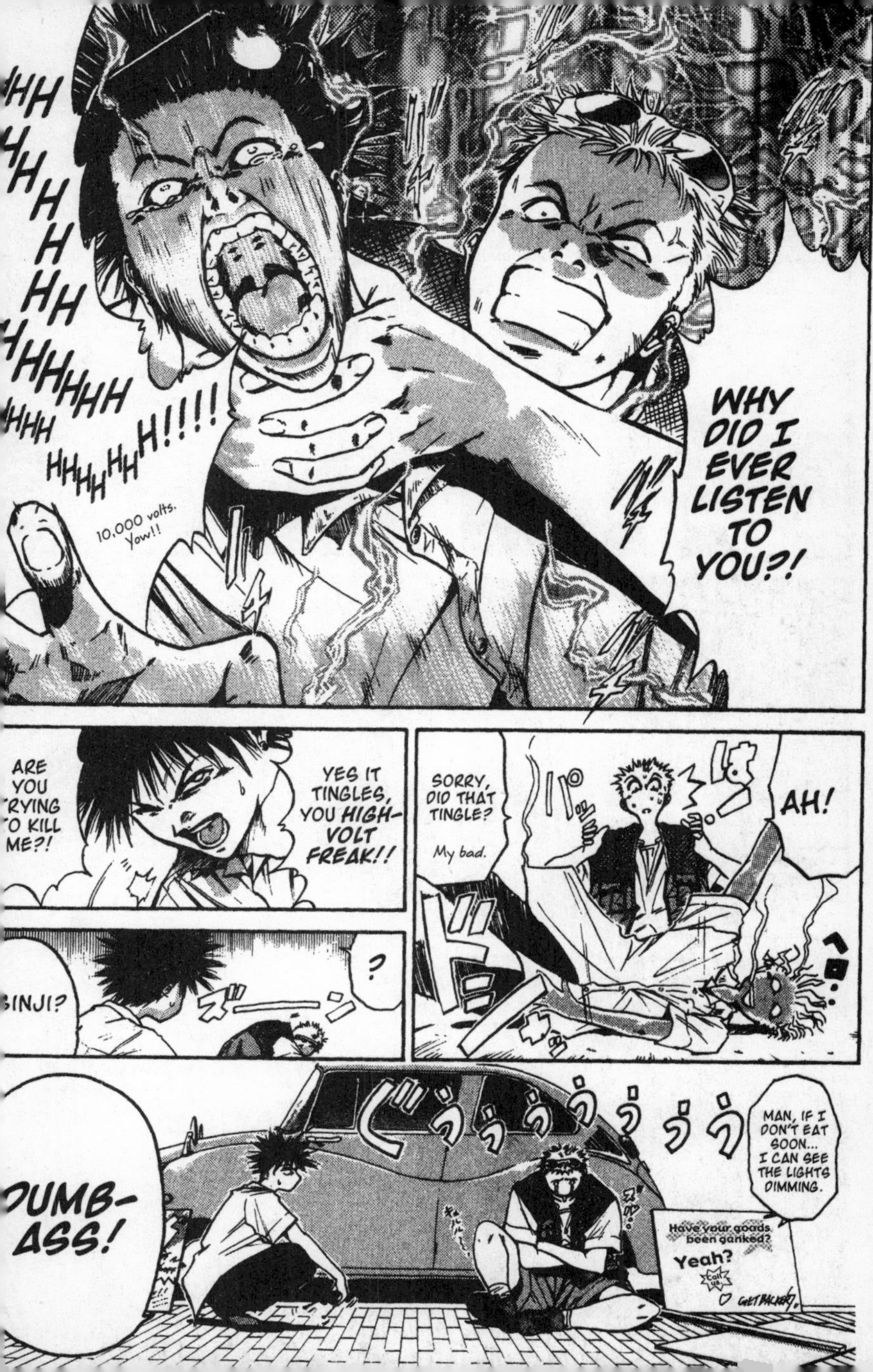
WHY DID I EVER LISTEN TO YOU?!
HHHHHHHHHHHHHHHHHHHHHHHHH!!!!!
10,000 volts. Yow!!
AH!
SORRY, DID THAT TINGLE?
My bad.
YES IT TINGLES, YOU HIGH-VOLT FREAK!!
ARE YOU RYING O KILL ME?!
?
INJI?
MAN, IF I DON'T EAT SOON... I CAN SEE THE LIGHTS DIMMING.
Have your goods been ganked?
Yeah?
GET BACKERS
OUMB-ASS!

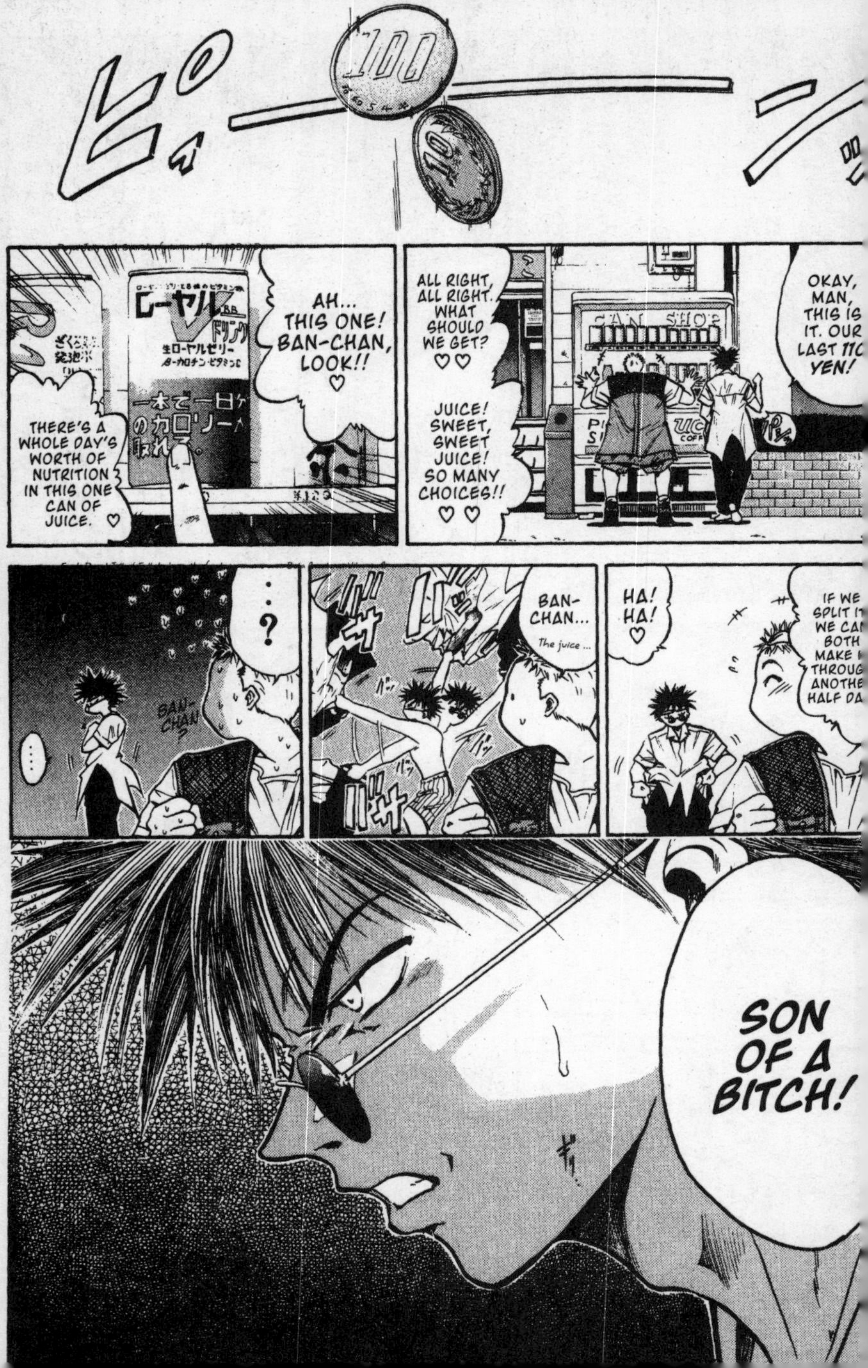
OKAY, MAN, THIS IS IT. OUR LAST 11C YEN!
ALL RIGHT, ALL RIGHT. WHAT SHOULD WE GET? ♡♡
JUICE! SWEET, SWEET JUICE! SO MANY CHOICES!! ♡♡
AH... THIS ONE! BAN-CHAN, LOOK!! ♡
ローヤルV ドリンク
生ローヤルゼリー
THERE'S A WHOLE DAY'S WORTH OF NUTRITION IN THIS ONE CAN OF JUICE. ♡
IF WE SPLIT I WE CA BOTH MAKE I THROUG ANOTHE HALF DA
HA! HA! ♡
BAN-CHAN...
The juice ...
...?
BAN-CHAN?
....
SON OF A BITCH!

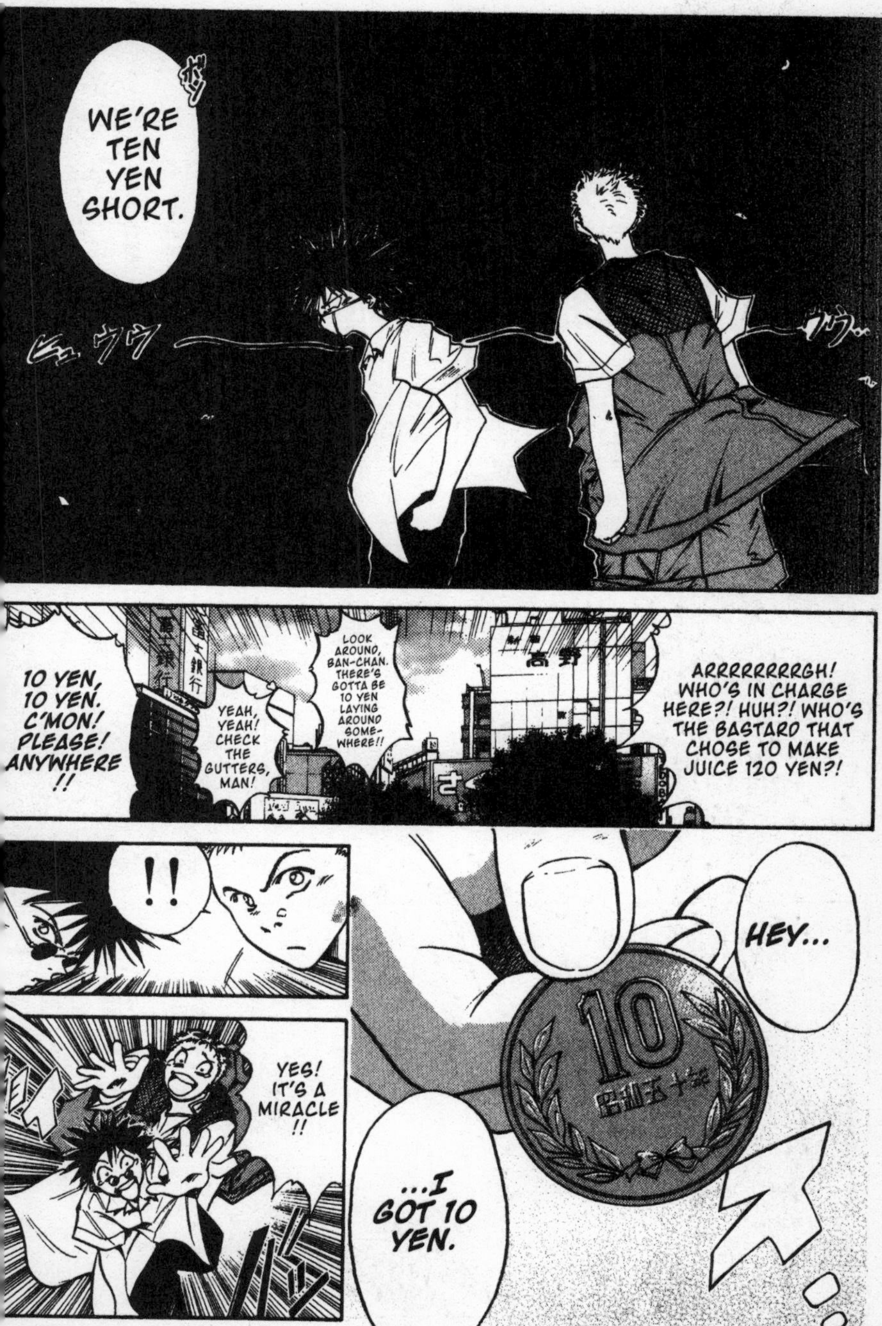
WE'RE TEN YEN SHORT.
ARRRRRRRRGH! WHO'S IN CHARGE HERE?! HUH?! WHO'S THE BASTARD THAT CHOSE TO MAKE JUICE 120 YEN?!
LOOK AROUND, BAN-CHAN. THERE'S GOTTA BE 10 YEN LAYING AROUND SOME-WHERE!!
YEAH, YEAH! CHECK THE GUTTERS, MAN!
10 YEN, 10 YEN. C'MON! PLEASE! ANYWHERE !!
HEY...
...I GOT 10 YEN.
!!
YES! IT'S A MIRACLE !!

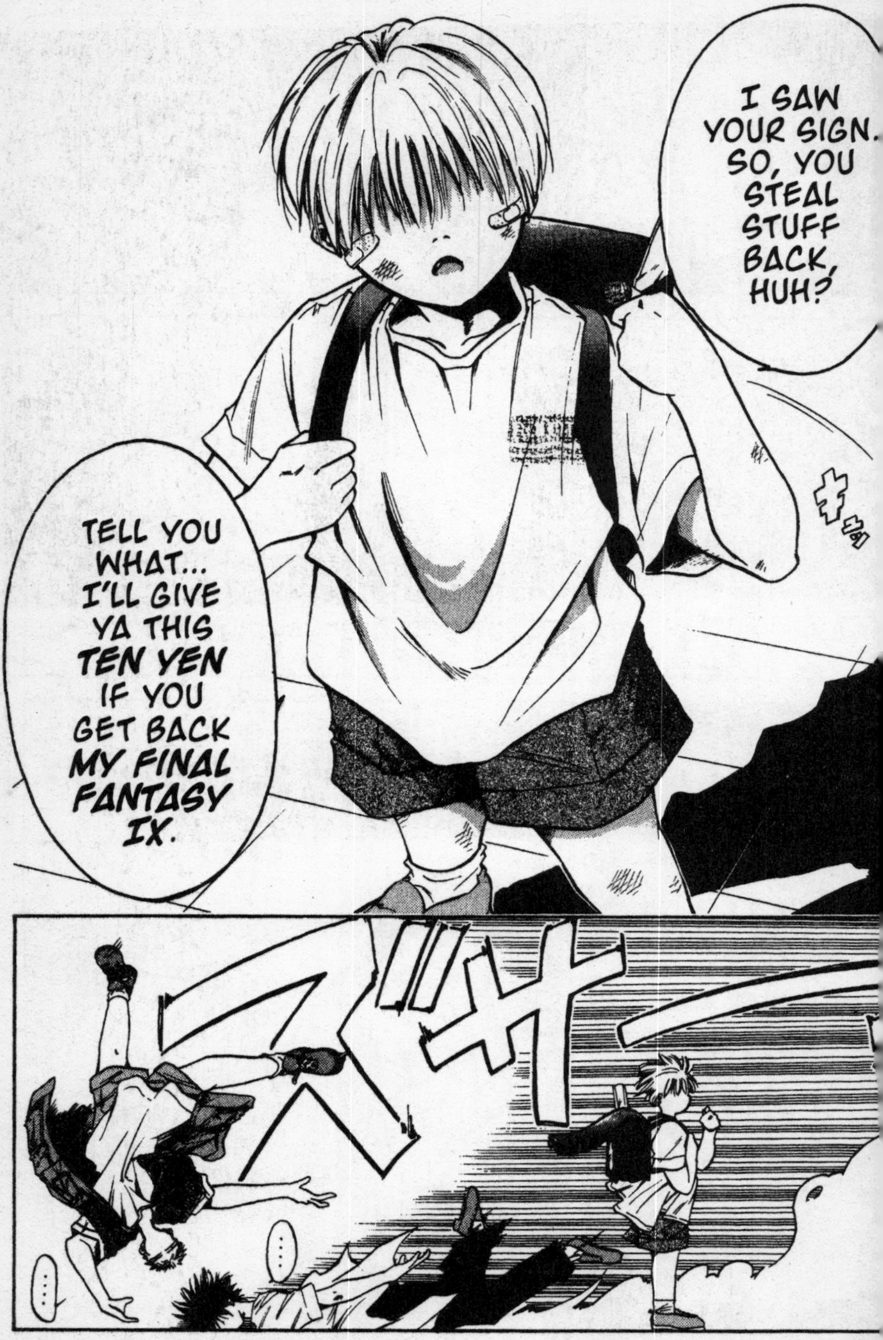
I SAW YOUR SIGN. SO, YOU STEAL STUFF BACK, HUH?
TELL YOU WHAT... I'LL GIVE YA THIS TEN YEN IF YOU GET BACK MY FINAL FANTASY IX.
...
....

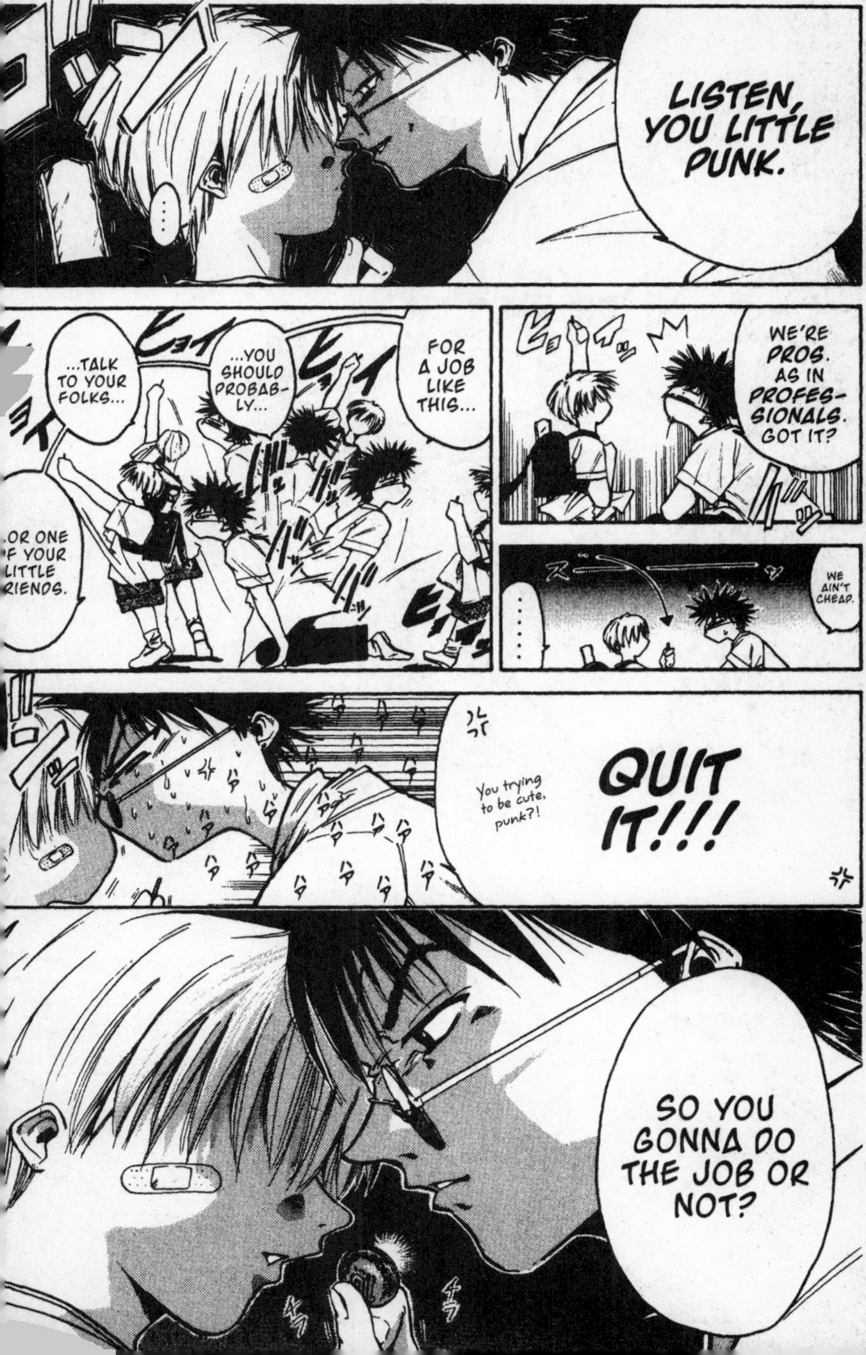
LISTEN, YOU LITTLE PUNK.
...
WE'RE PROS. AS IN PROFES-SIONALS. GOT IT?
WE AIN'T CHEAP.
......
FOR A JOB LIKE THIS...
...YOU SHOULD PROBAB-LY...
...TALK TO YOUR FOLKS...
..OR ONE OF YOUR LITTLE FRIENDS.
QUIT IT!!!
You trying to be cute, punk?!
SO YOU GONNA DO THE JOB OR NOT?

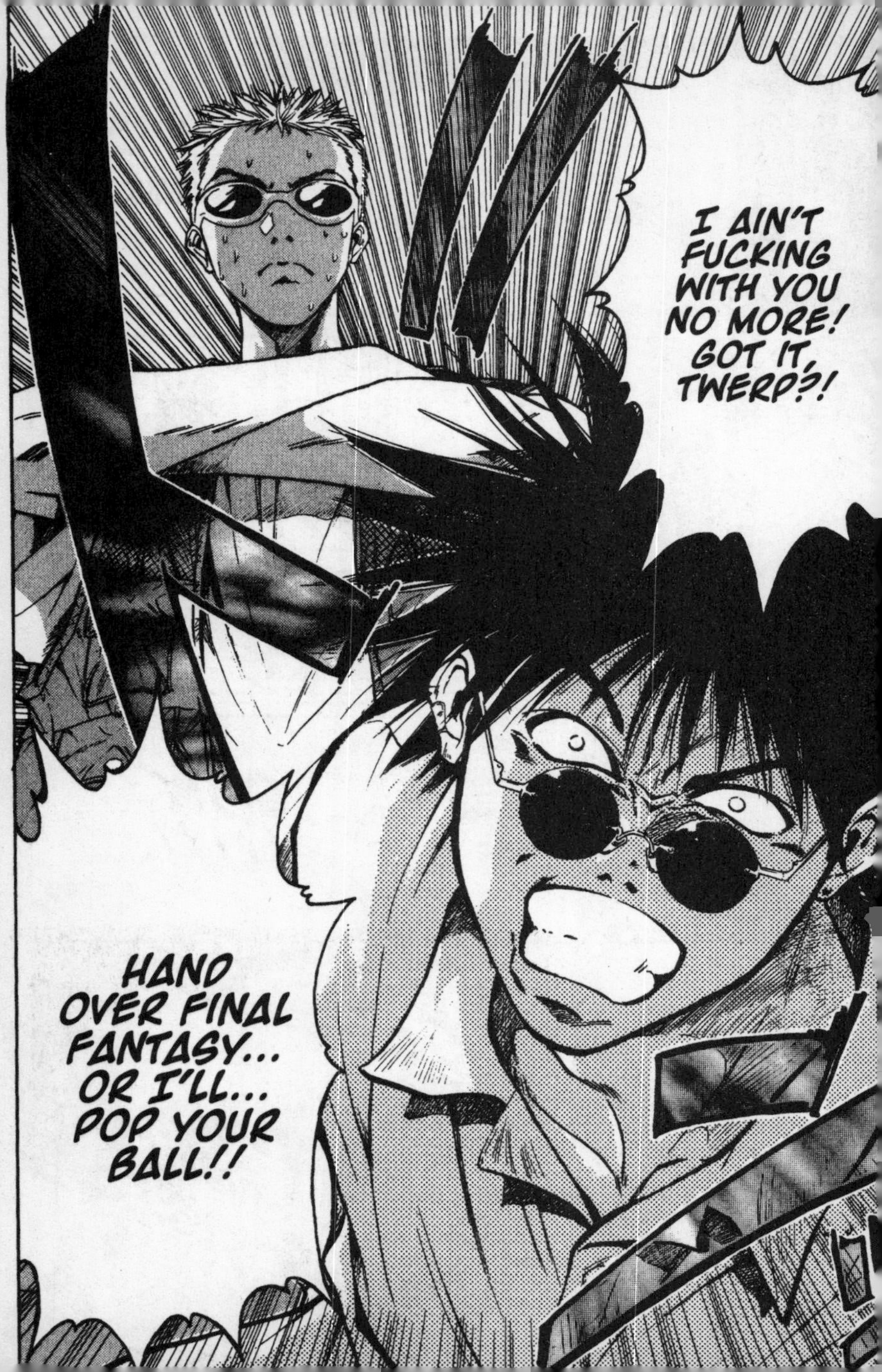
I AIN'T FUCKING WITH YOU NO MORE! GOT IT, TWERP?!
HAND OVER FINAL FANTASY... OR I'LL... POP YOUR BALL!!

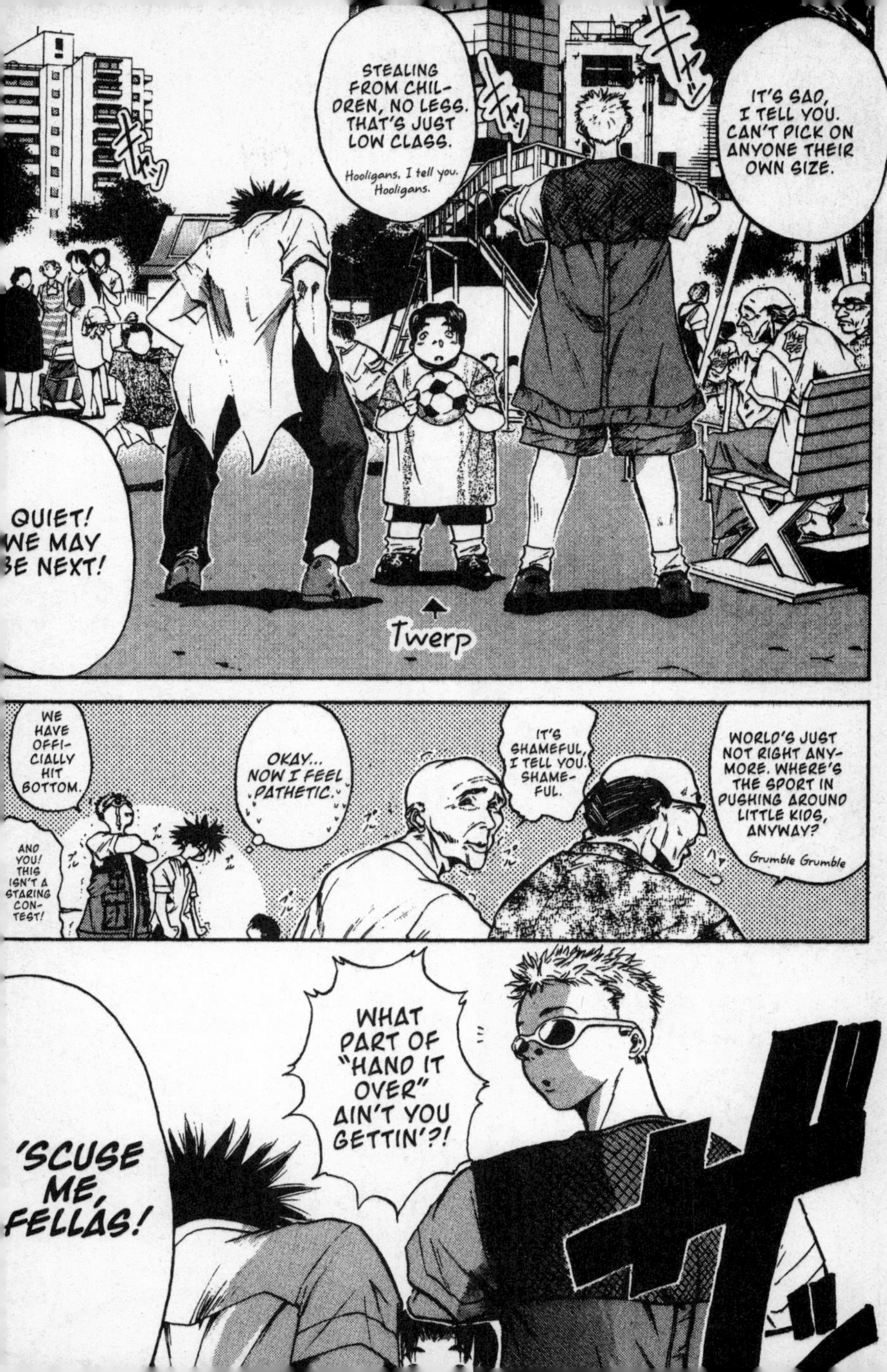
IT'S SAD, I TELL YOU. CAN'T PICK ON ANYONE THEIR OWN SIZE.
STEALING FROM CHIL-DREN, NO LESS. THAT'S JUST LOW CLASS.
Hooligans, I tell you. Hooligans.
QUIET! WE MAY BE NEXT!
Twerp
WORLD'S JUST NOT RIGHT ANY-MORE. WHERE'S THE SPORT IN PUSHING AROUND LITTLE KIDS, ANYWAY?
Grumble Grumble
IT'S SHAMEFUL, I TELL YOU. SHAME-FUL.
OKAY... NOW I FEEL PATHETIC.
WE HAVE OFFI-CIALLY HIT BOTTOM.
AND YOU! THIS ISN'T A STARING CON-TEST!
WHAT PART OF "HAND IT OVER" AIN'T YOU GETTIN'?!
'SCUSE ME, FELLAS!

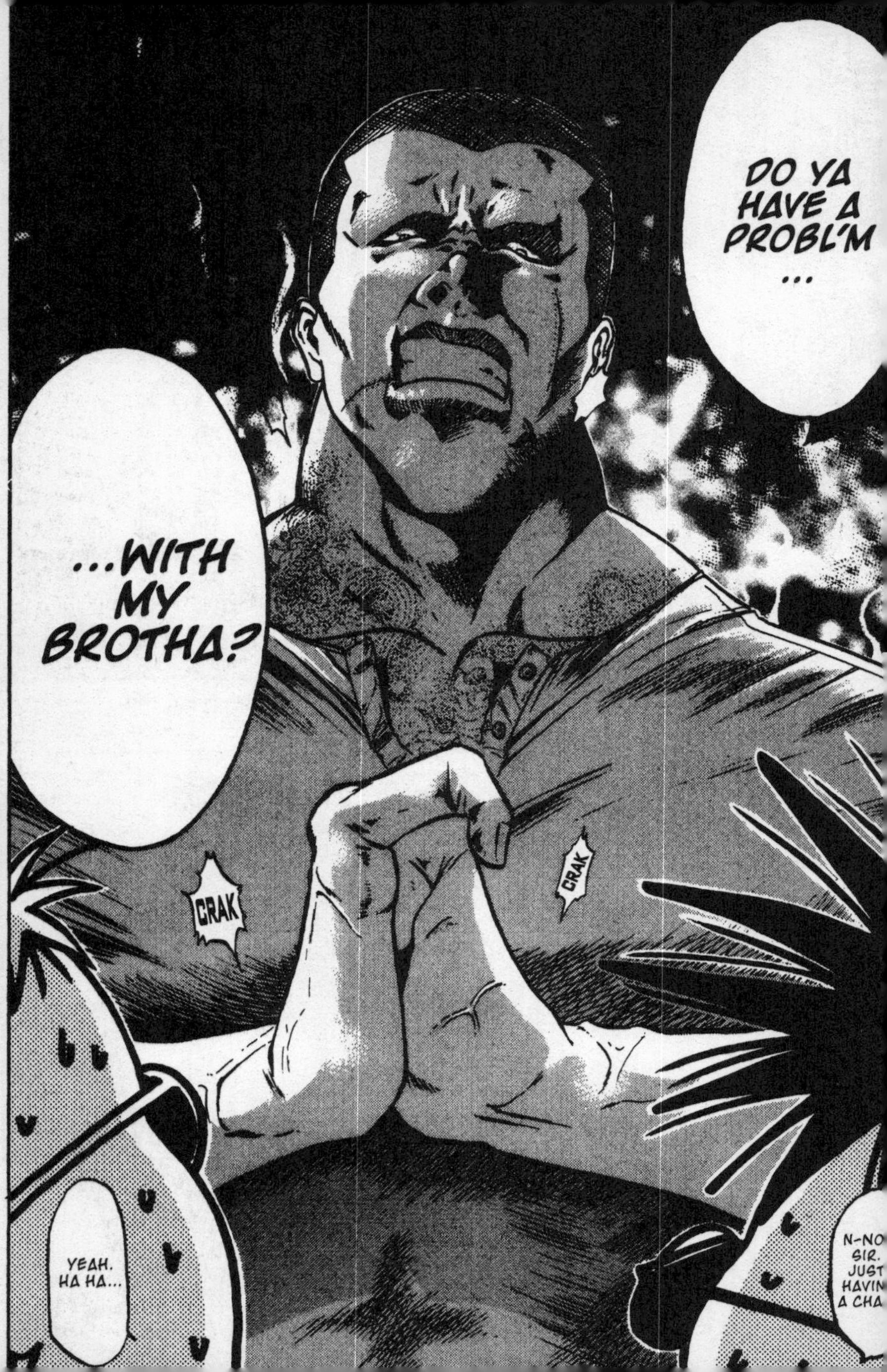
DO YA HAVE A PROBL'M ...
...WITH MY BROTHA?
CRAK
CRAK
N-NO SIR. JUST HAVIN A CHA
YEAH. HA HA...

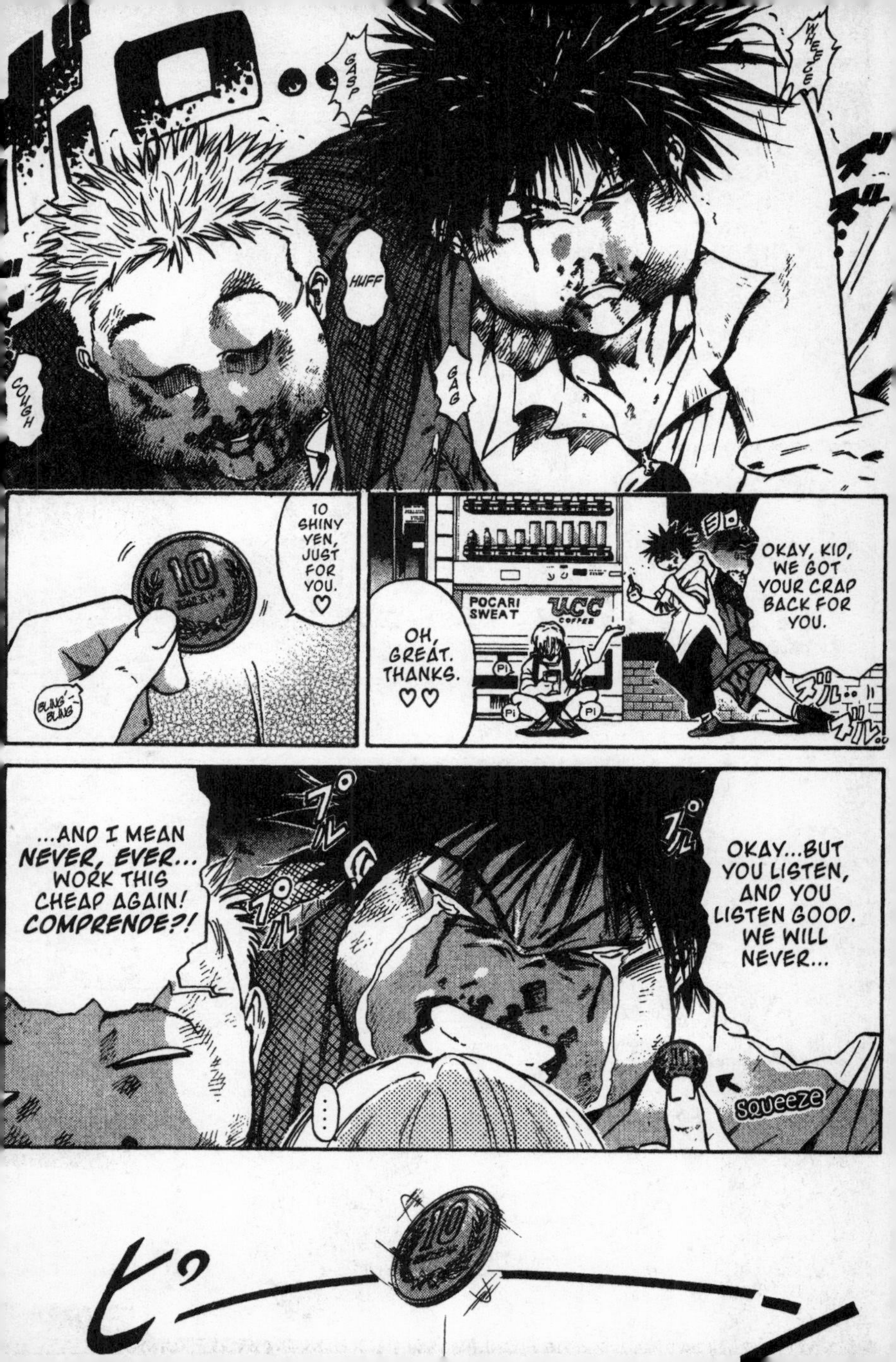
WHEEZE
GASP
HUFF
GAG
COUGH
OKAY, KID, WE GOT YOUR CRAP BACK FOR YOU.
OH, GREAT. THANKS. ♡♡
POCARI SWEAT
UCC COFFEE
PI
PI
PI
10 SHINY YEN, JUST FOR YOU. ♡
BLING BLING
OKAY...BUT YOU LISTEN, AND YOU LISTEN GOOD. WE WILL NEVER...
...AND I MEAN NEVER, EVER... WORK THIS CHEAP AGAIN! COMPRENDE?!
SQUEEZE
....

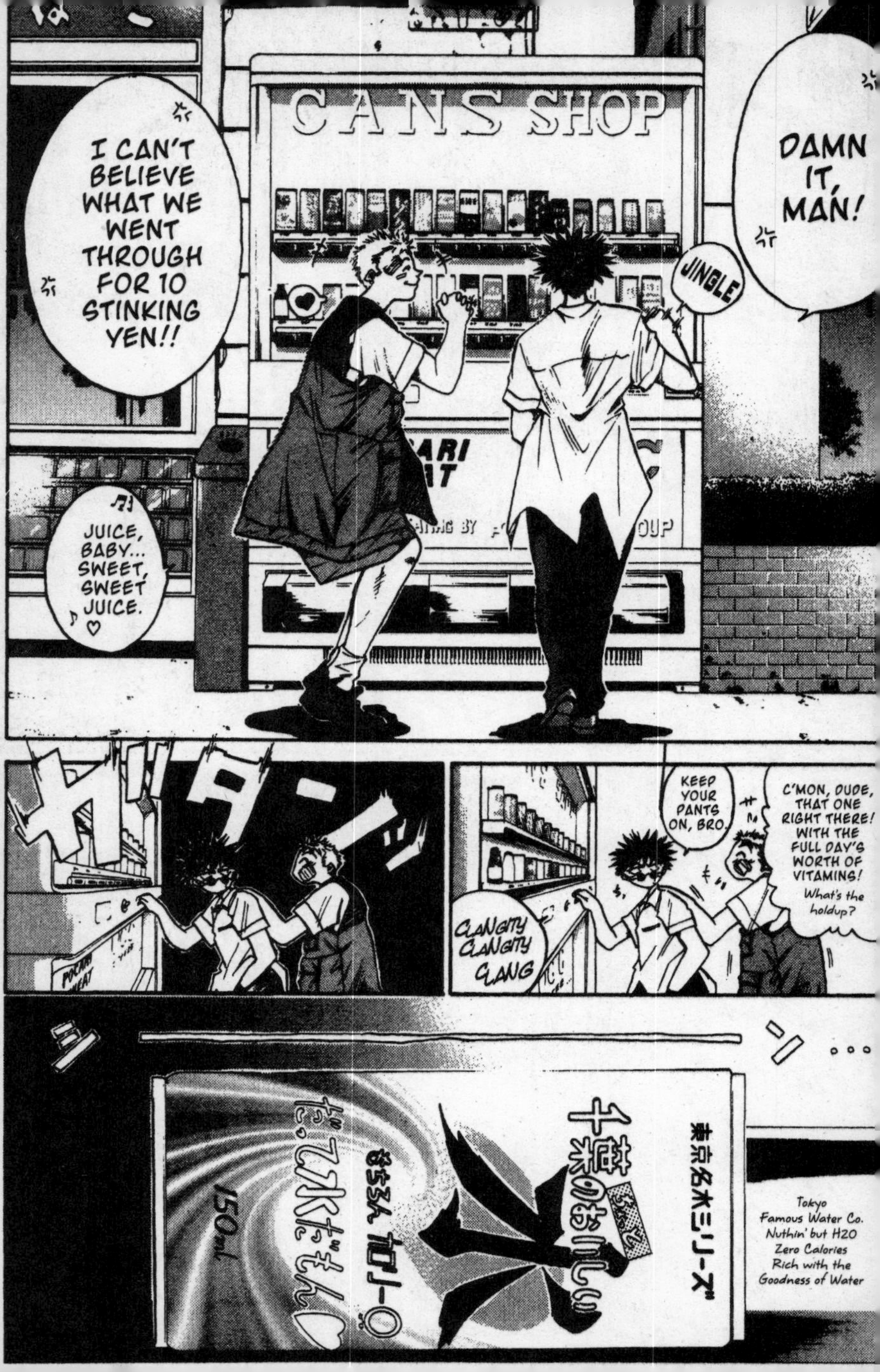

CANS SHOP
DAMN IT, MAN!
JINGLE
I CAN'T BELIEVE WHAT WE WENT THROUGH FOR 10 STINKING YEN!!
JUICE, BABY... SWEET, SWEET JUICE. ♪ ♡
C'MON, DUDE, THAT ONE RIGHT THERE! WITH THE FULL DAY'S WORTH OF VITAMINS! What's the holdup?
KEEP YOUR PANTS ON, BRO.
CLANGITY CLANGITY CLANG
東京名水シリーズ
150ml
Tokyo Famous Water Co. Nuthin' but H2O Zero Calories Rich with the Goodness of Water

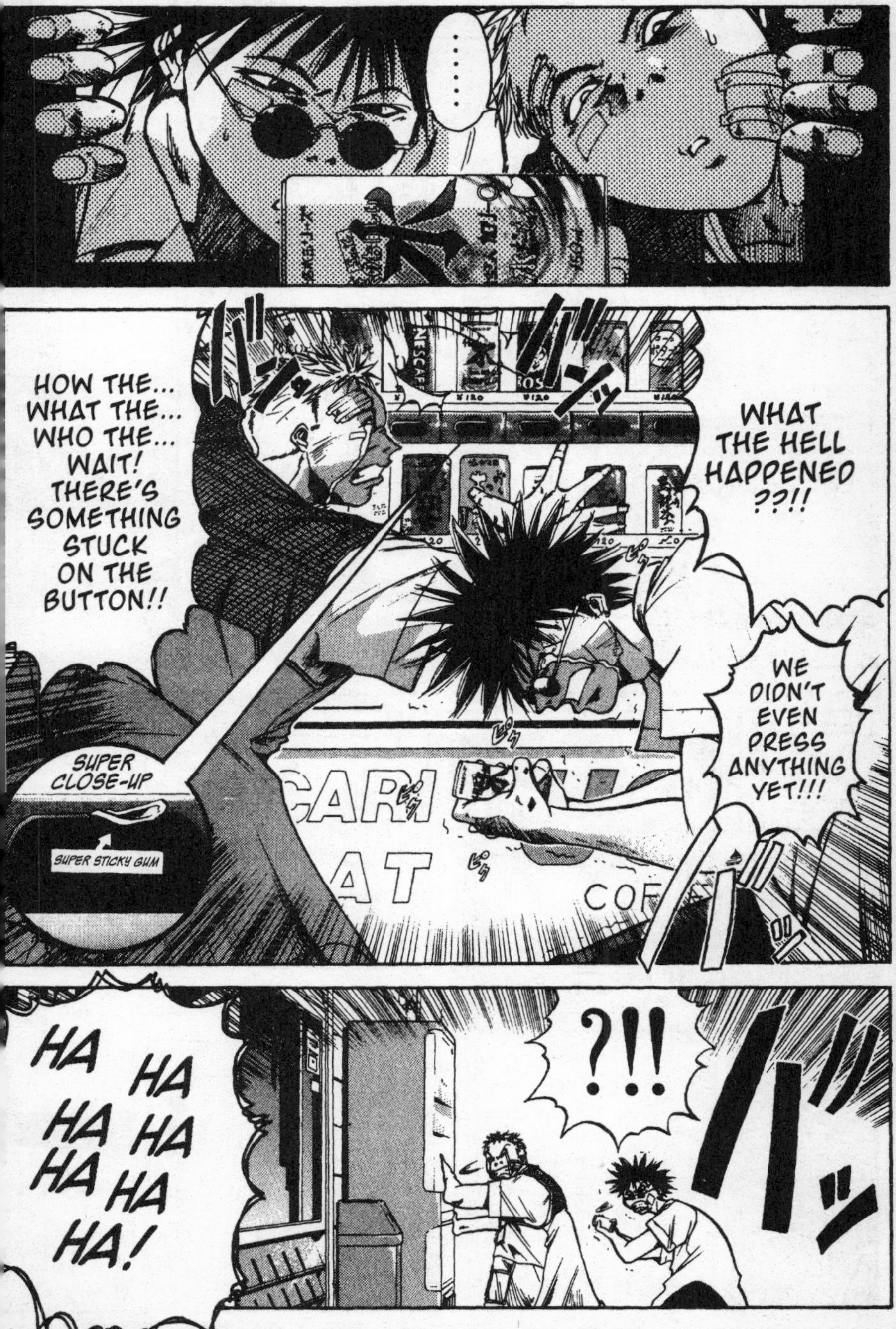
......
WHAT THE HELL HAPPENED ??!!
HOW THE... WHAT THE... WHO THE... WAIT! THERE'S SOMETHING STUCK ON THE BUTTON!!
WE DIDN'T EVEN PRESS ANYTHING YET!!!
SUPER CLOSE-UP
SUPER STICKY GUM
?!!
HA HA HA HA HA HA HA HA!

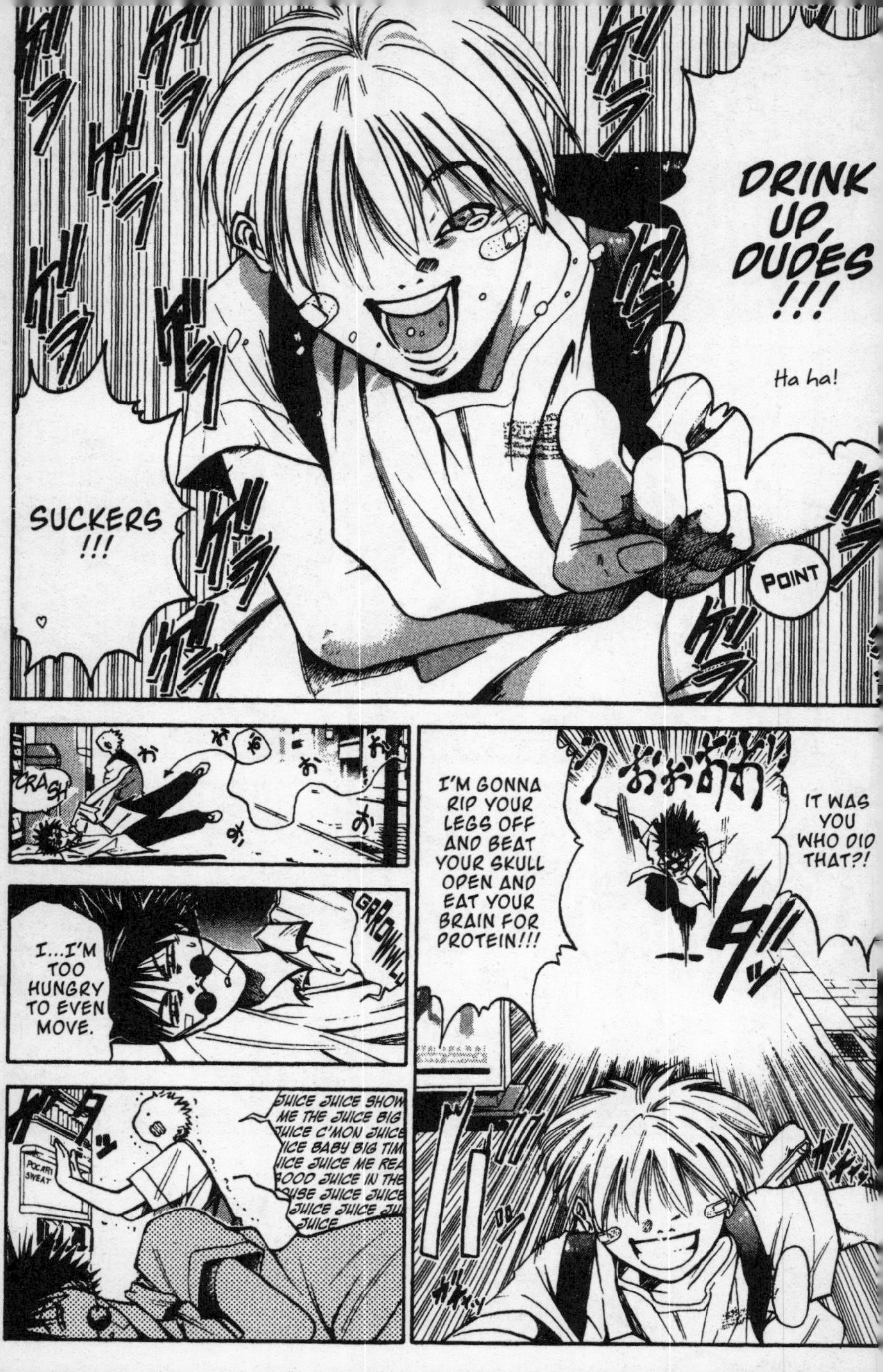
DRINK UP, DUDES!!!
Ha ha!
POINT
SUCKERS!!!
♡
IT WAS YOU WHO DID THAT?!
I'M GONNA RIP YOUR LEGS OFF AND BEAT YOUR SKULL OPEN AND EAT YOUR BRAIN FOR PROTEIN!!!
CRASH
GROWL
I...I'M TOO HUNGRY TO EVEN MOVE.
POCARI SWEAT
JUICE JUICE SHOW ME THE JUICE BIG JUICE C'MON JUICE ICE BABY BIG TIM ICE JUICE ME REA OOD JUICE IN THE USE JUICE JUICE JUICE JUICE JU JUICE

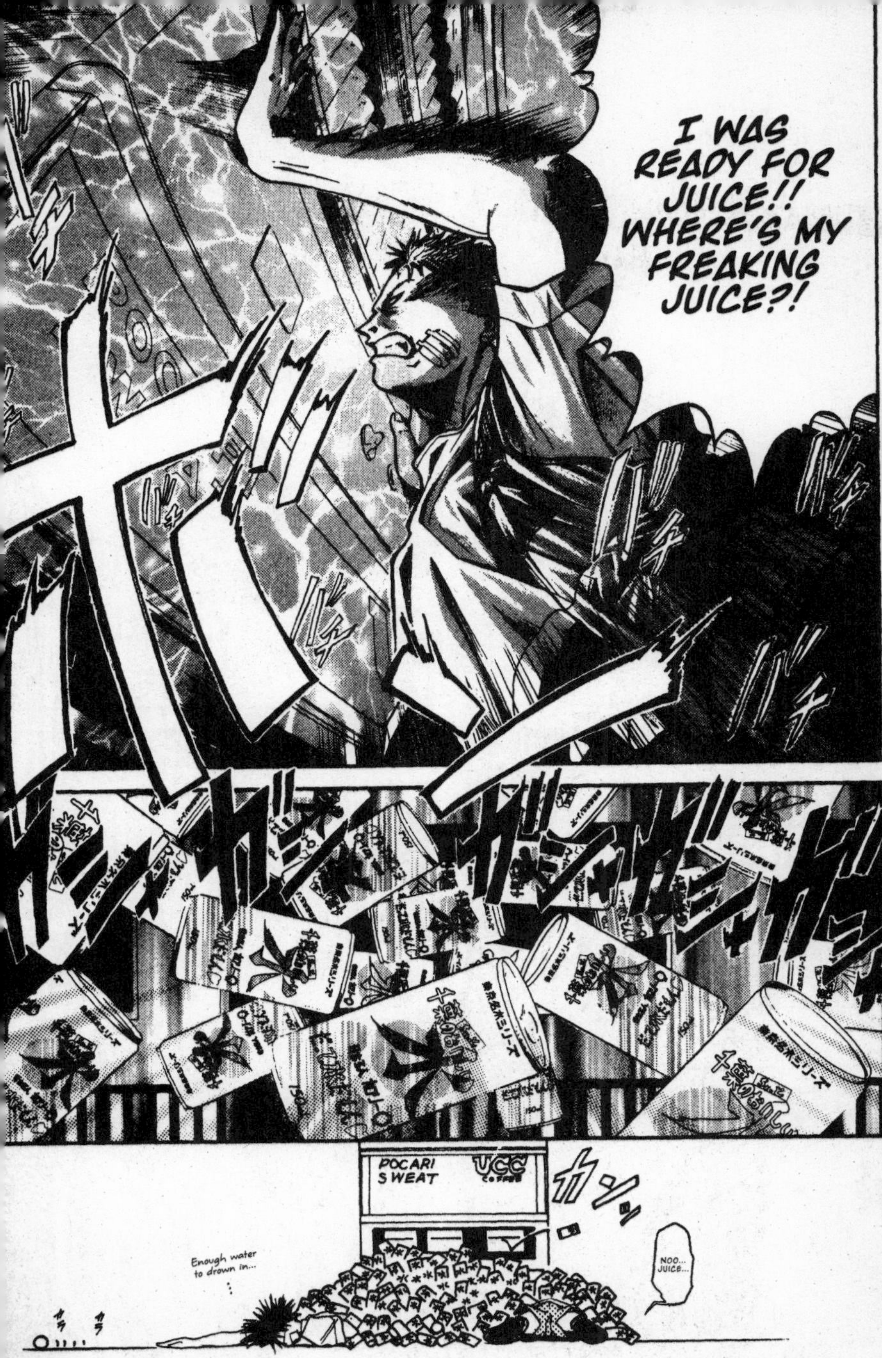
I WAS READY FOR JUICE!! WHERE'S MY FREAKING JUICE?!
POCARI SWEAT
UCC
NOO... JUICE...
Enough water to drown in...

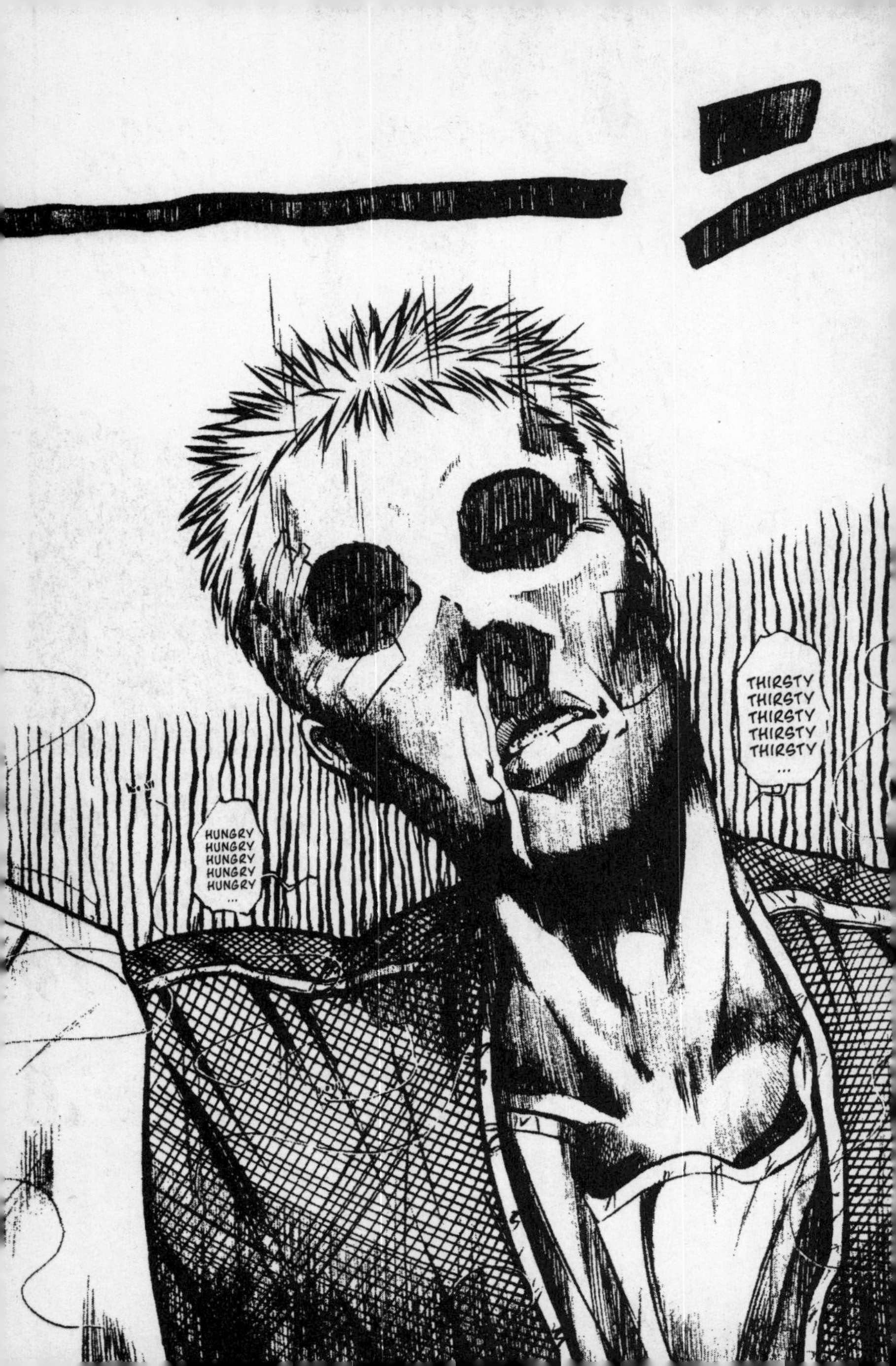
THIRSTY THIRSTY THIRSTY THIRSTY THIRSTY ...
HUNGRY HUNGRY HUNGRY HUNGRY HUNGRY ...

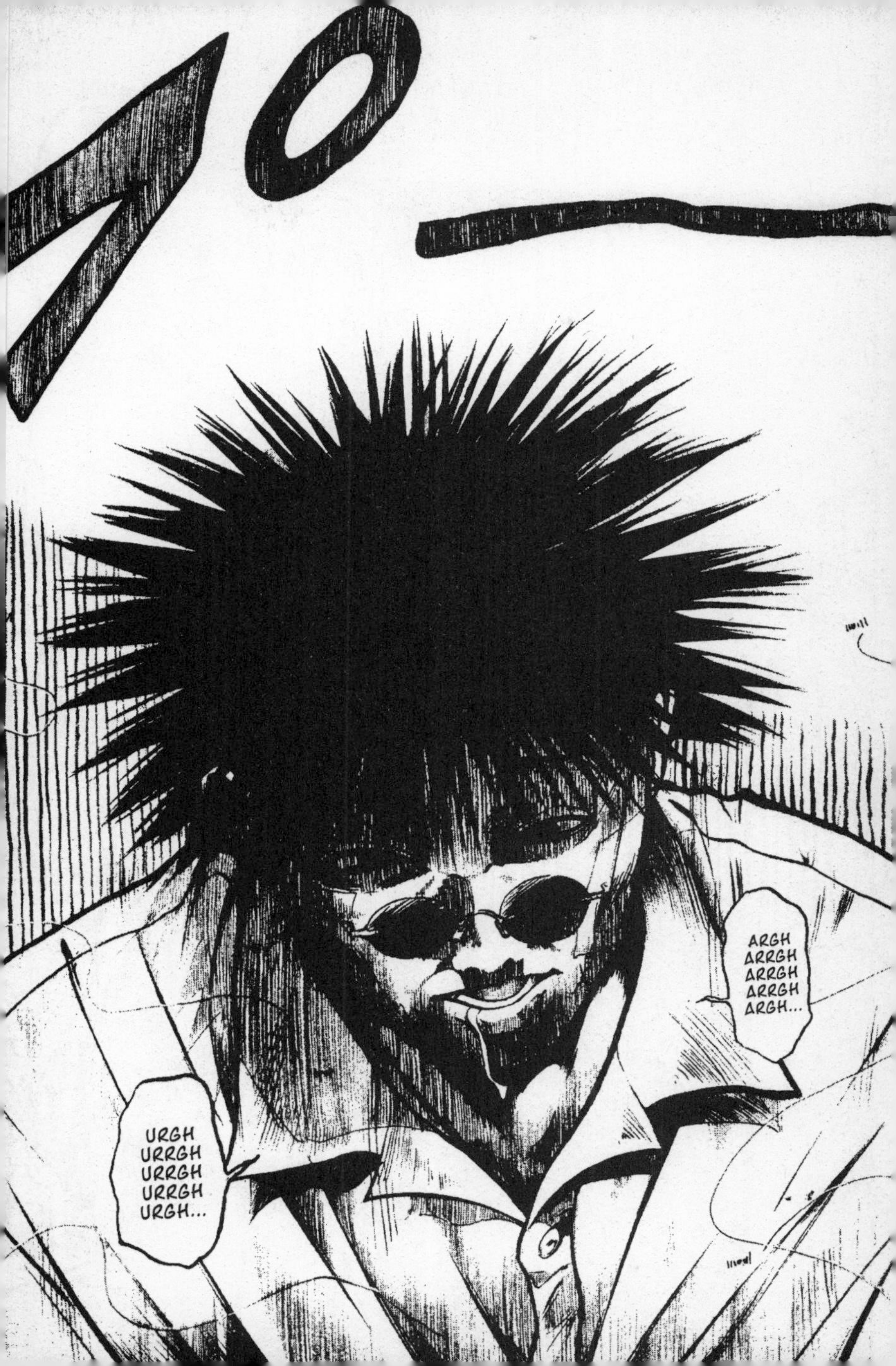
ARGH ARRGH ARRGH ARRGH ARGH...
URGH URRGH URRGH URRGH URGH...

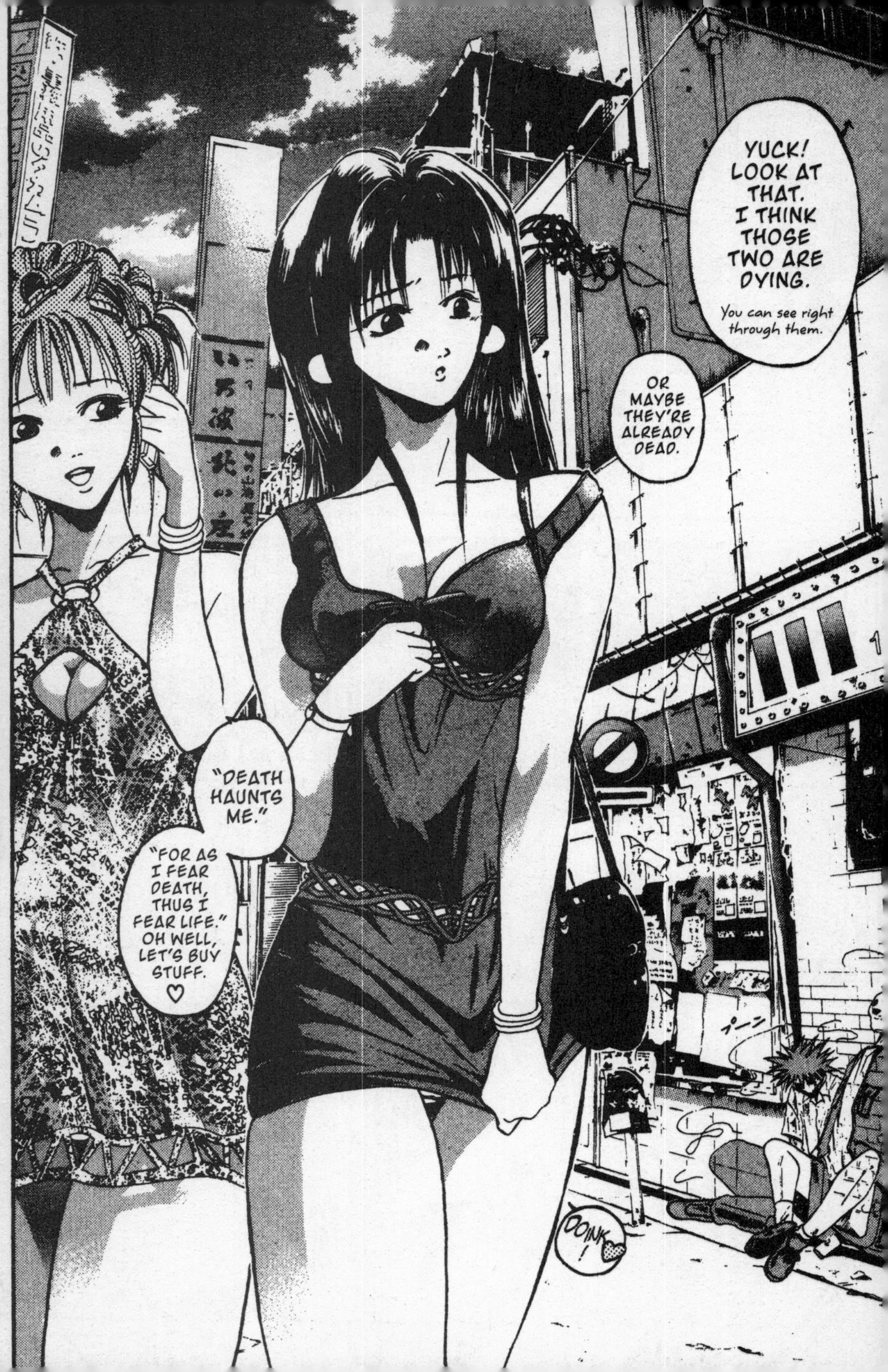
YUCK! LOOK AT THAT. I THINK THOSE TWO ARE DYING.
You can see right through them.
OR MAYBE THEY'RE ALREADY DEAD.
"DEATH HAUNTS ME."
"FOR AS I FEAR DEATH, THUS I FEAR LIFE." OH WELL, LET'S BUY STUFF. ♡
DOINK!

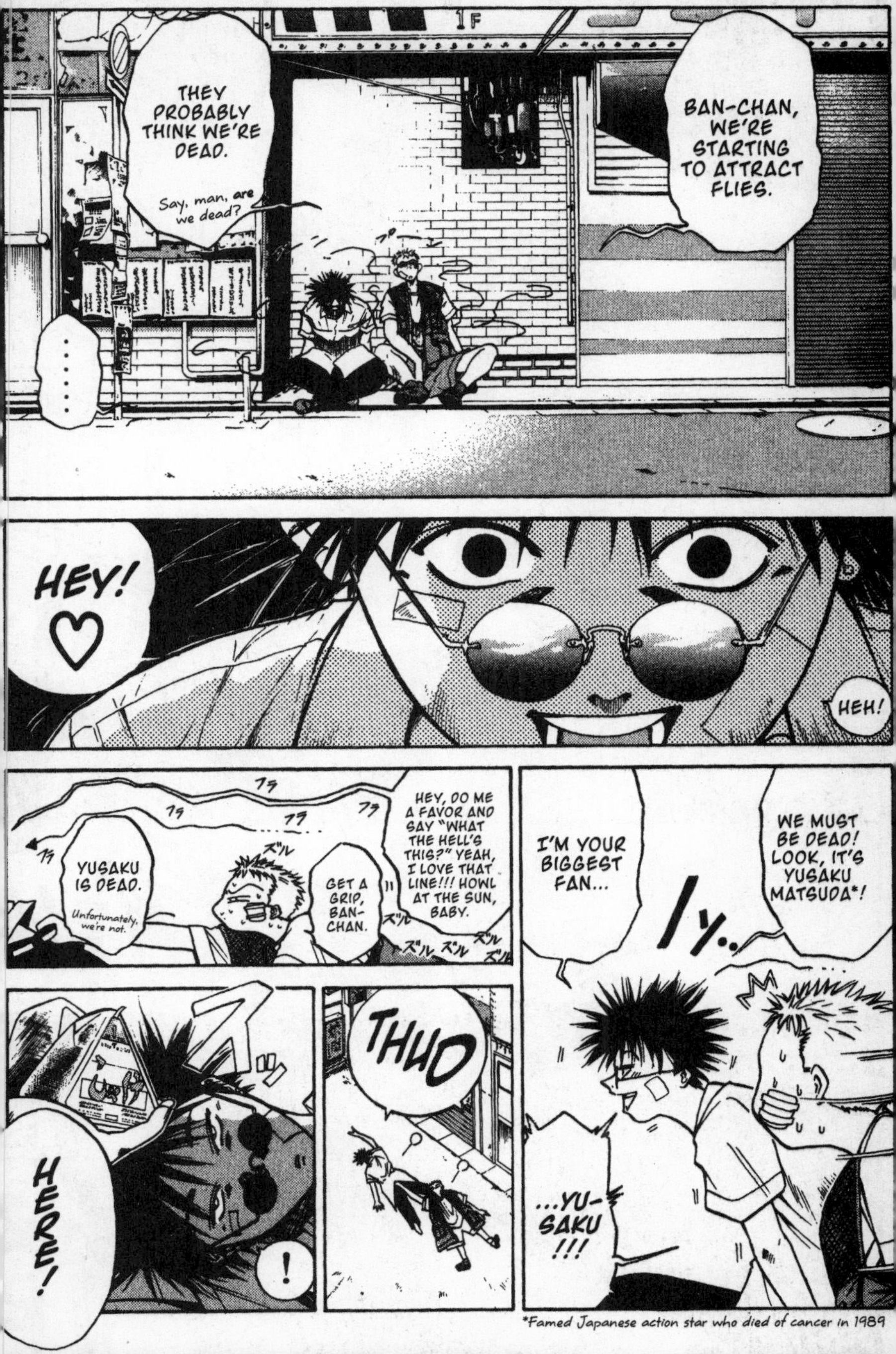
BAN-CHAN, WE'RE STARTING TO ATTRACT FLIES.
THEY PROBABLY THINK WE'RE DEAD.
Say, man, are we dead?
......
HEY! ♡
HEH!
WE MUST BE DEAD! LOOK, IT'S YUSAKU MATSUDA*!
I'M YOUR BIGGEST FAN...
...
...YU-SAKU !!!
HEY, DO ME A FAVOR AND SAY "WHAT THE HELL'S THIS?" YEAH, I LOVE THAT LINE!!! HOWL AT THE SUN, BABY.
GET A GRIP, BAN-CHAN.
YUSAKU IS DEAD.
Unfortunately, we're not.
THUD
HERE!
!

*Famed Japanese action star who died of cancer in 1989

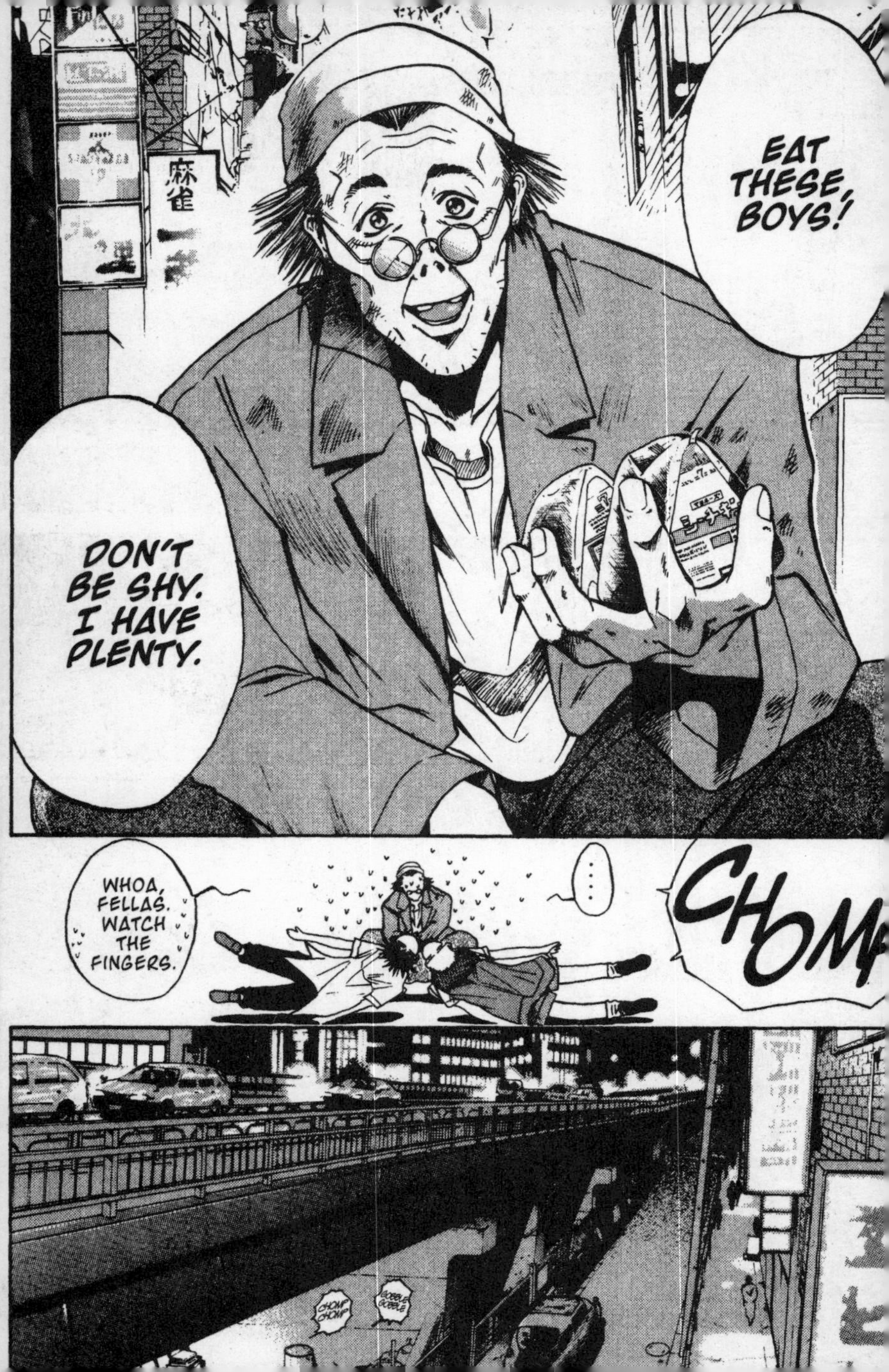
EAT THESE, BOYS!
DON'T BE SHY. I HAVE PLENTY.
CHOMP
...
WHOA, FELLAS. WATCH THE FINGERS.
GOBBLE GOBBLE
CHOMP CHOMP

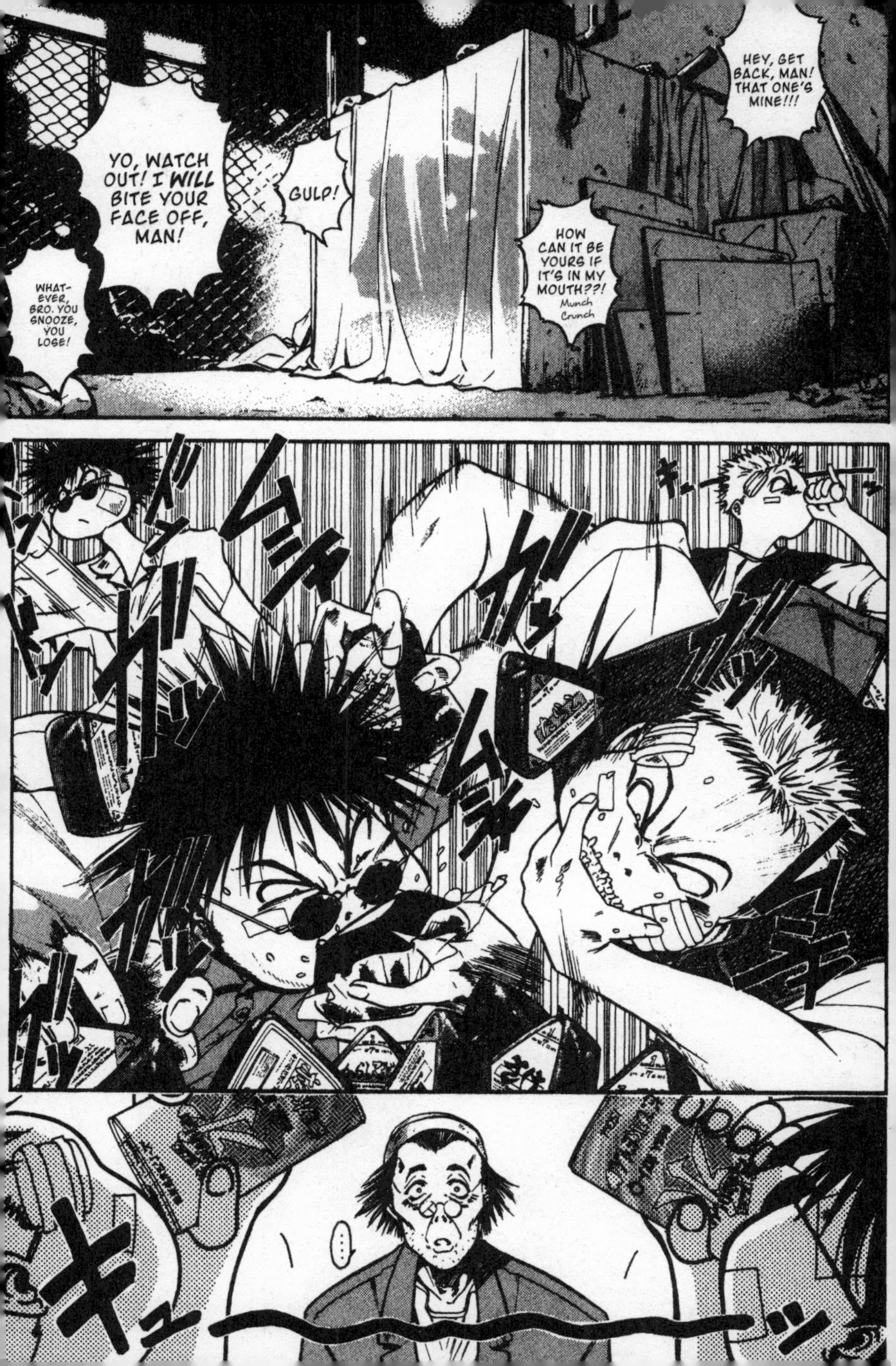
HEY, GET BACK, MAN! THAT ONE'S MINE!!!
HOW CAN IT BE YOURS IF IT'S IN MY MOUTH??!
Munch Crunch
GULP!
YO, WATCH OUT! I WILL BITE YOUR FACE OFF, MAN!
WHAT-EVER, BRO. YOU SNOOZE, YOU LOSE!
...

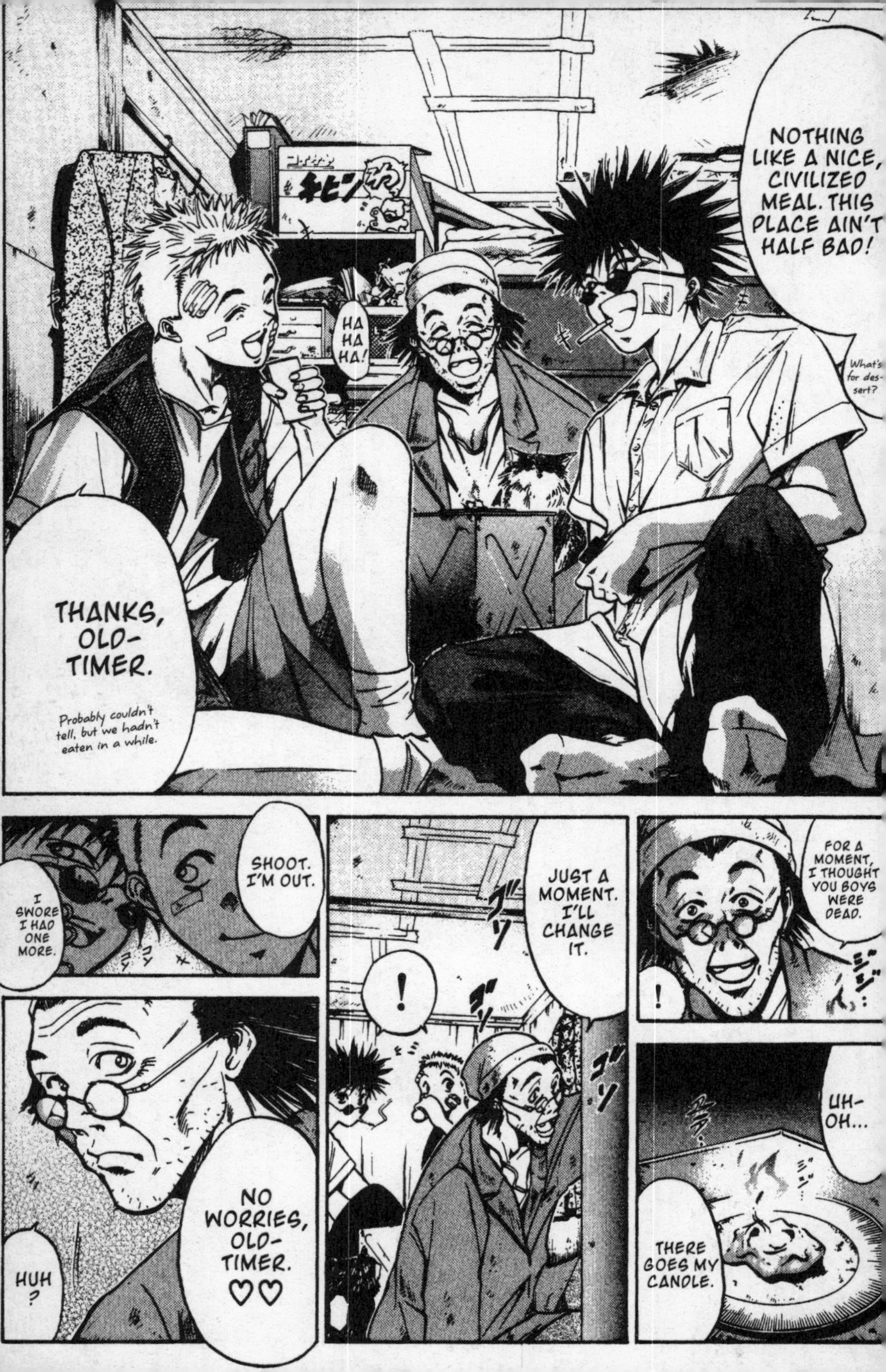
NOTHING LIKE A NICE, CIVILIZED MEAL. THIS PLACE AIN'T HALF BAD!
What's for dessert?
HA HA HA HA!
THANKS, OLD-TIMER.
Probably couldn't tell, but we hadn't eaten in a while.
FOR A MOMENT, I THOUGHT YOU BOYS WERE DEAD.
!
UH-OH...
THERE GOES MY CANDLE.
JUST A MOMENT. I'LL CHANGE IT.
!
SHOOT. I'M OUT.
I SWORE I HAD ONE MORE.
HUH?
NO WORRIES, OLD-TIMER. ♡♡

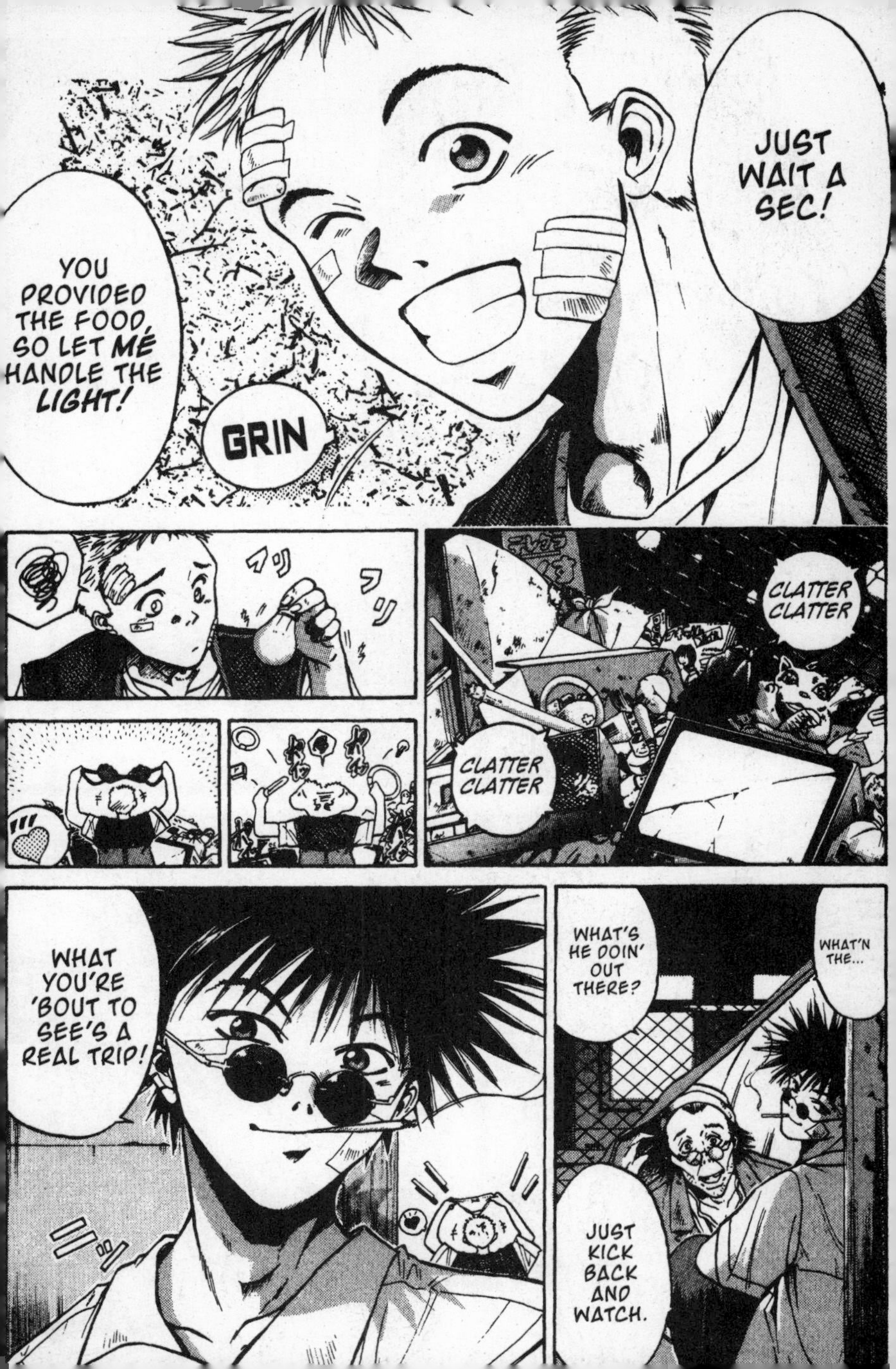
JUST WAIT A SEC!
YOU PROVIDED THE FOOD, SO LET ME HANDLE THE LIGHT!
GRIN
CLATTER CLATTER
CLATTER CLATTER
WHAT'N THE...
WHAT'S HE DOIN' OUT THERE?
JUST KICK BACK AND WATCH.
WHAT YOU'RE 'BOUT TO SEE'S A REAL TRIP!

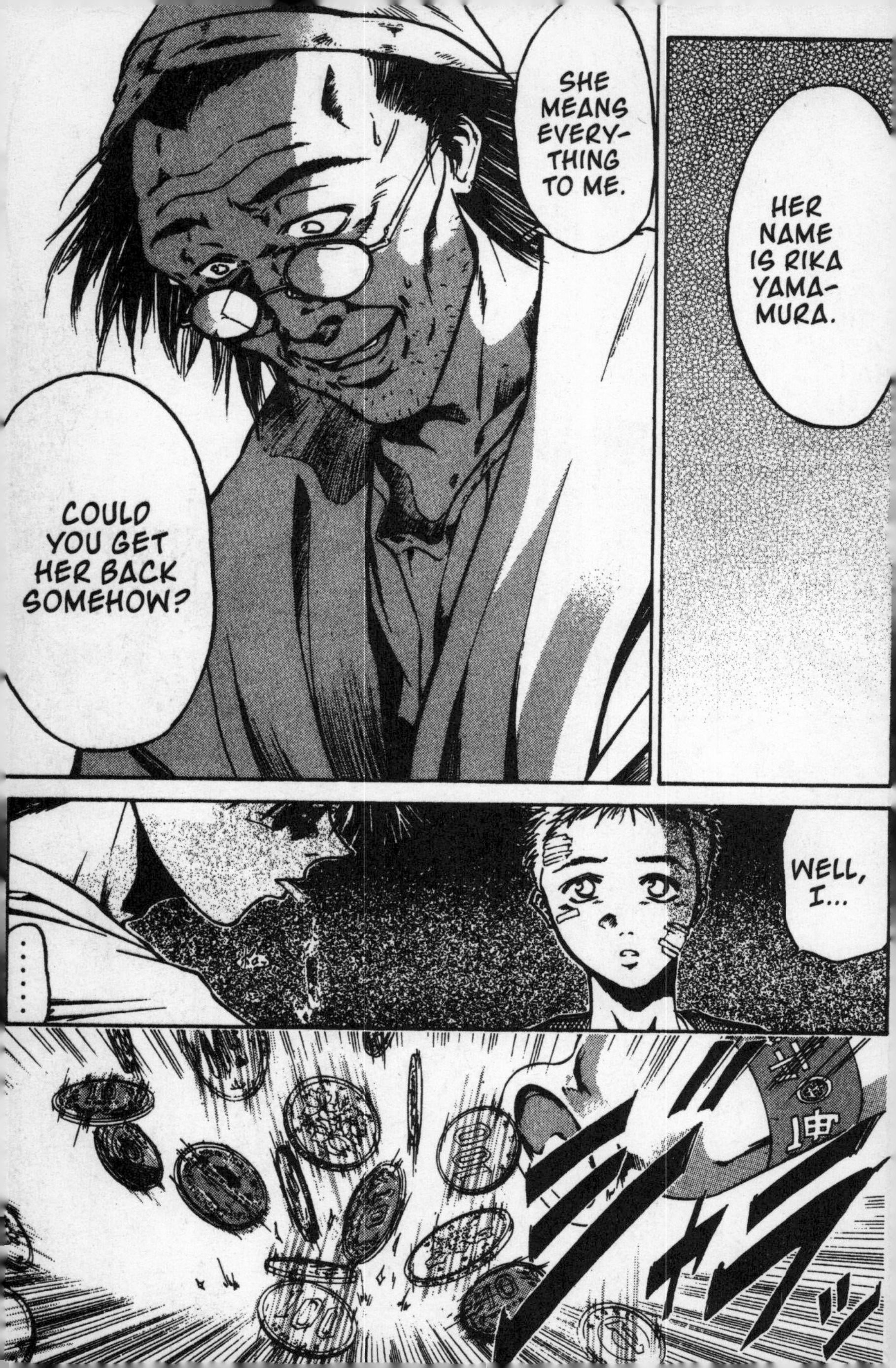
HER NAME IS RIKA YAMAMURA.
SHE MEANS EVERYTHING TO ME.
COULD YOU GET HER BACK SOMEHOW?
WELL, I...
......

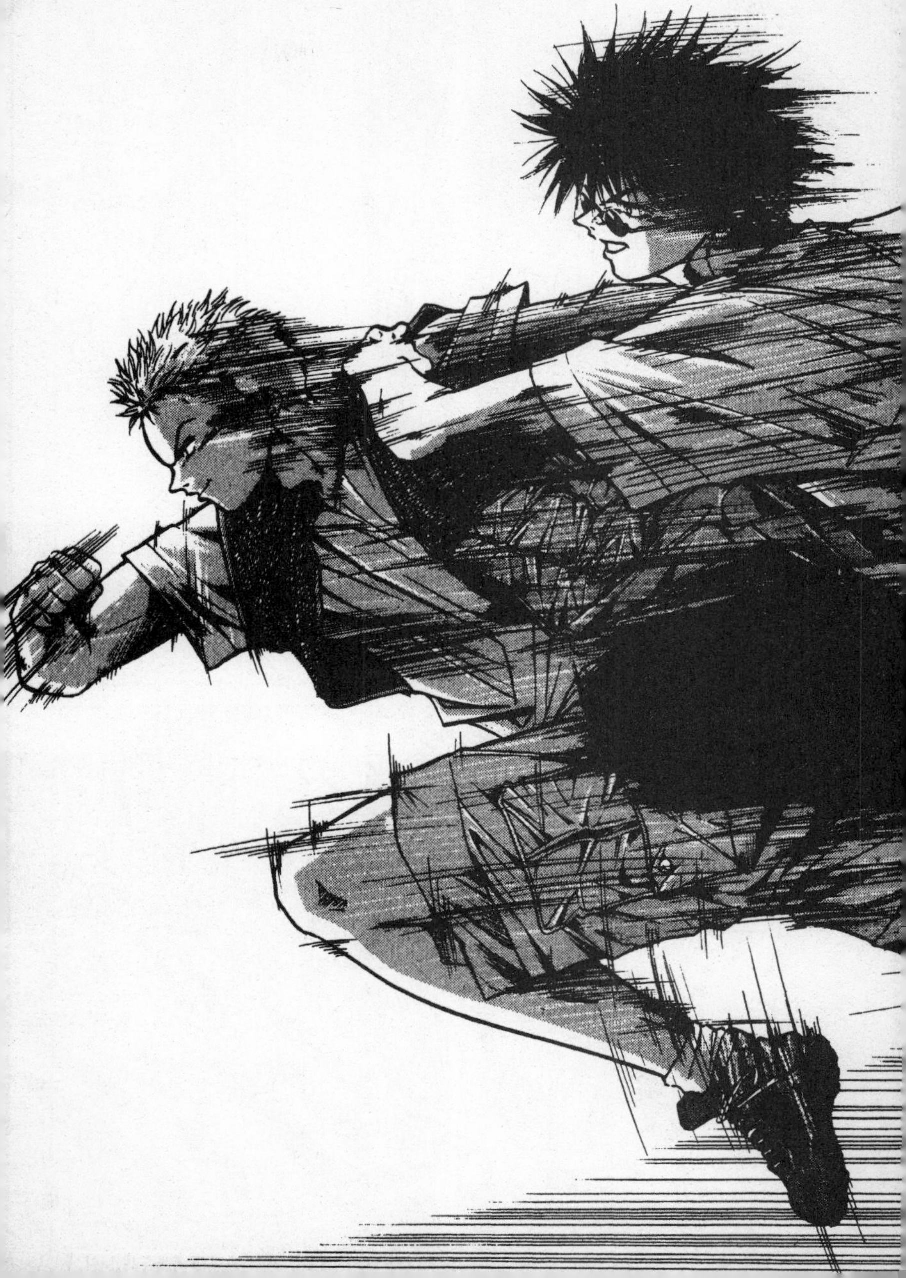

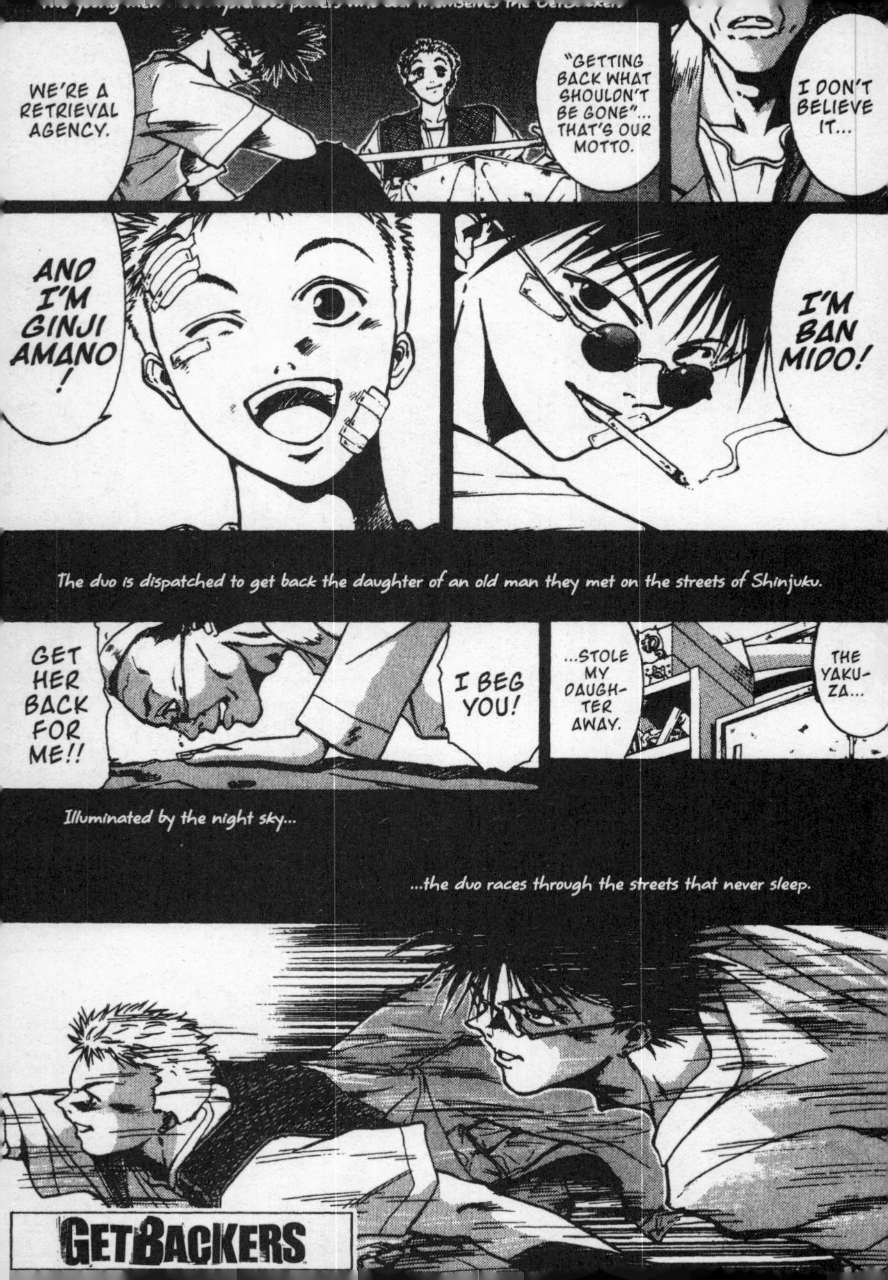
I DON'T BELIEVE IT...
"GETTING BACK WHAT SHOULDN'T BE GONE"... THAT'S OUR MOTTO.
WE'RE A RETRIEVAL AGENCY.
I'M BAN MIDO!
AND I'M GINJI AMANO!
The duo is dispatched to get back the daughter of an old man they met on the streets of Shinjuku.
THE YAKUZA...
...STOLE MY DAUGHTER AWAY.
I BEG YOU!
GET HER BACK FOR ME!!
Illuminated by the night sky...
...the duo races through the streets that never sleep.
GETBACKERS

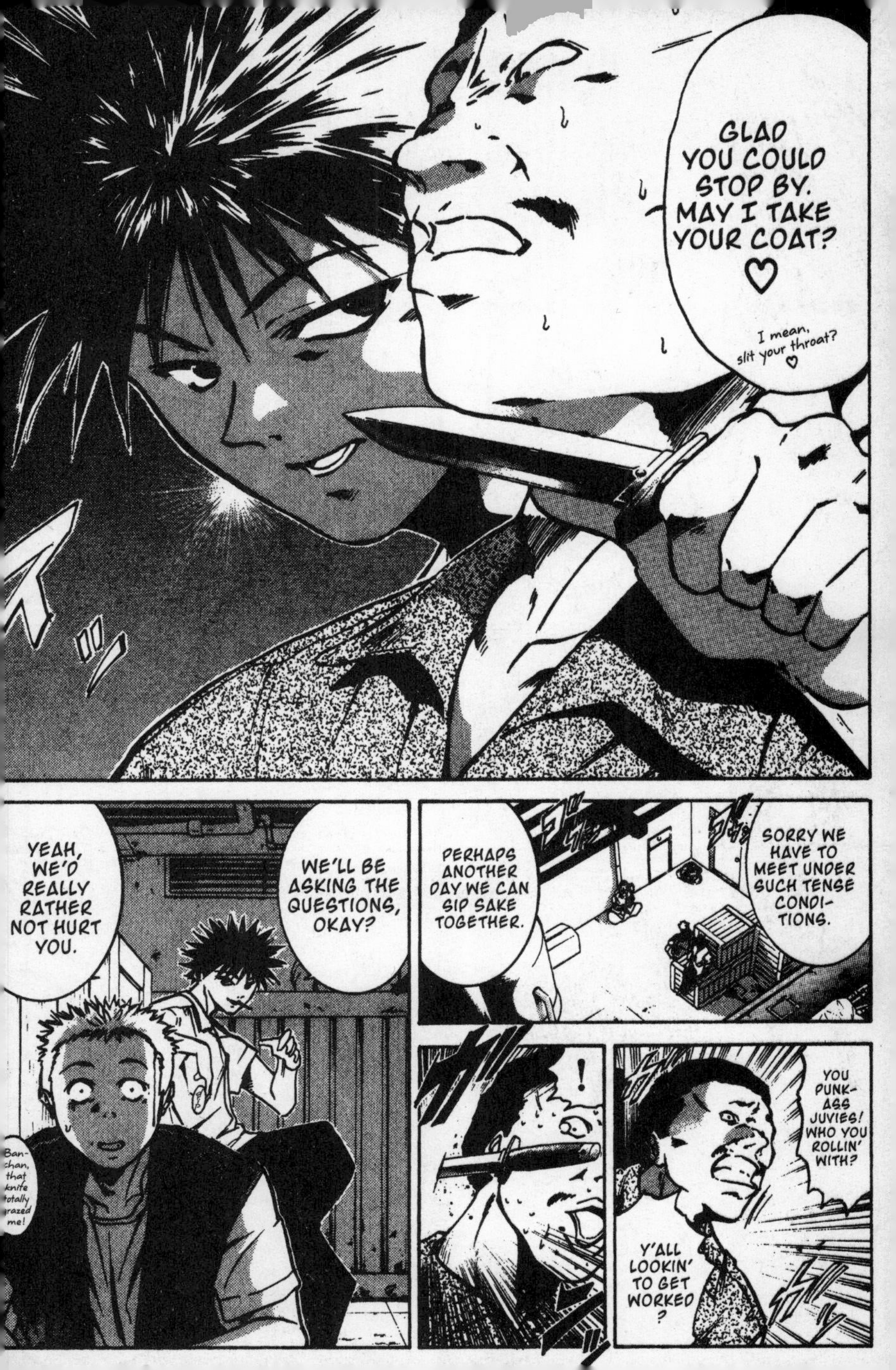
GLAD YOU COULD STOP BY. MAY I TAKE YOUR COAT? ♡
I mean, slit your throat? ♡
SORRY WE HAVE TO MEET UNDER SUCH TENSE CONDITIONS.
PERHAPS ANOTHER DAY WE CAN SIP SAKE TOGETHER.
WE'LL BE ASKING THE QUESTIONS, OKAY?
YEAH, WE'D REALLY RATHER NOT HURT YOU.
Ban-chan, that knife totally grazed me!
YOU PUNK-ASS JUVIES! WHO YOU ROLLIN' WITH?
Y'ALL LOOKIN' TO GET WORKED ?
!

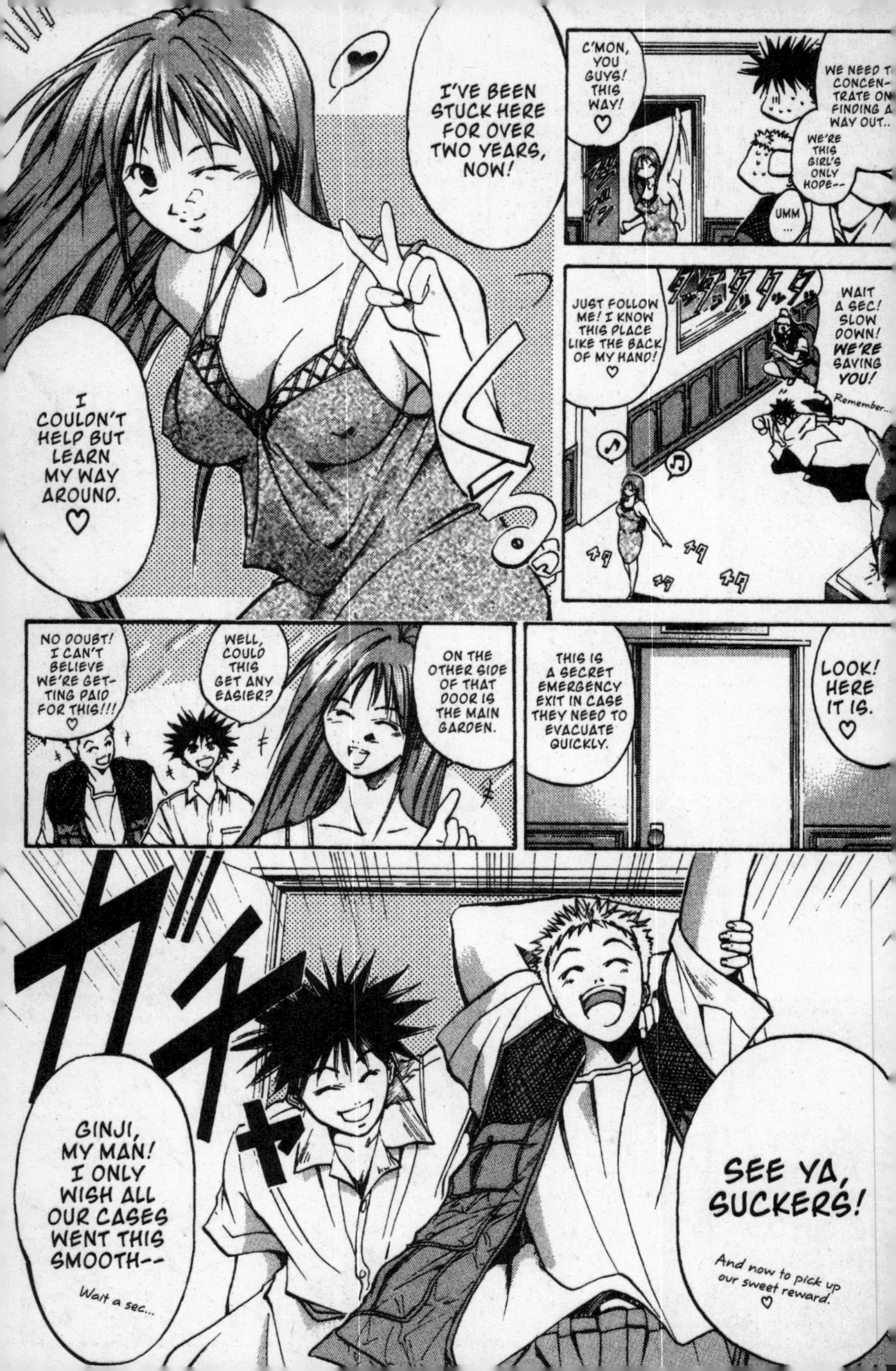
C'MON, YOU GUYS! THIS WAY! ♡
WE NEED TO CONCENTRATE ON FINDING A WAY OUT...
WE'RE THIS GIRL'S ONLY HOPE--
UMM ...
WAIT A SEC! SLOW DOWN! WE'RE SAVING YOU!
Remember...
JUST FOLLOW ME! I KNOW THIS PLACE LIKE THE BACK OF MY HAND! ♡
I'VE BEEN STUCK HERE FOR OVER TWO YEARS, NOW!
I COULDN'T HELP BUT LEARN MY WAY AROUND. ♡
LOOK! HERE IT IS. ♡
THIS IS A SECRET EMERGENCY EXIT IN CASE THEY NEED TO EVACUATE QUICKLY.
ON THE OTHER SIDE OF THAT DOOR IS THE MAIN GARDEN.
WELL, COULD THIS GET ANY EASIER?
NO DOUBT! I CAN'T BELIEVE WE'RE GETTING PAID FOR THIS!!! ♡
SEE YA, SUCKERS!
And now to pick up our sweet reward. ♡
GINJI, MY MAN! I ONLY WISH ALL OUR CASES WENT THIS SMOOTH--
Wait a sec...

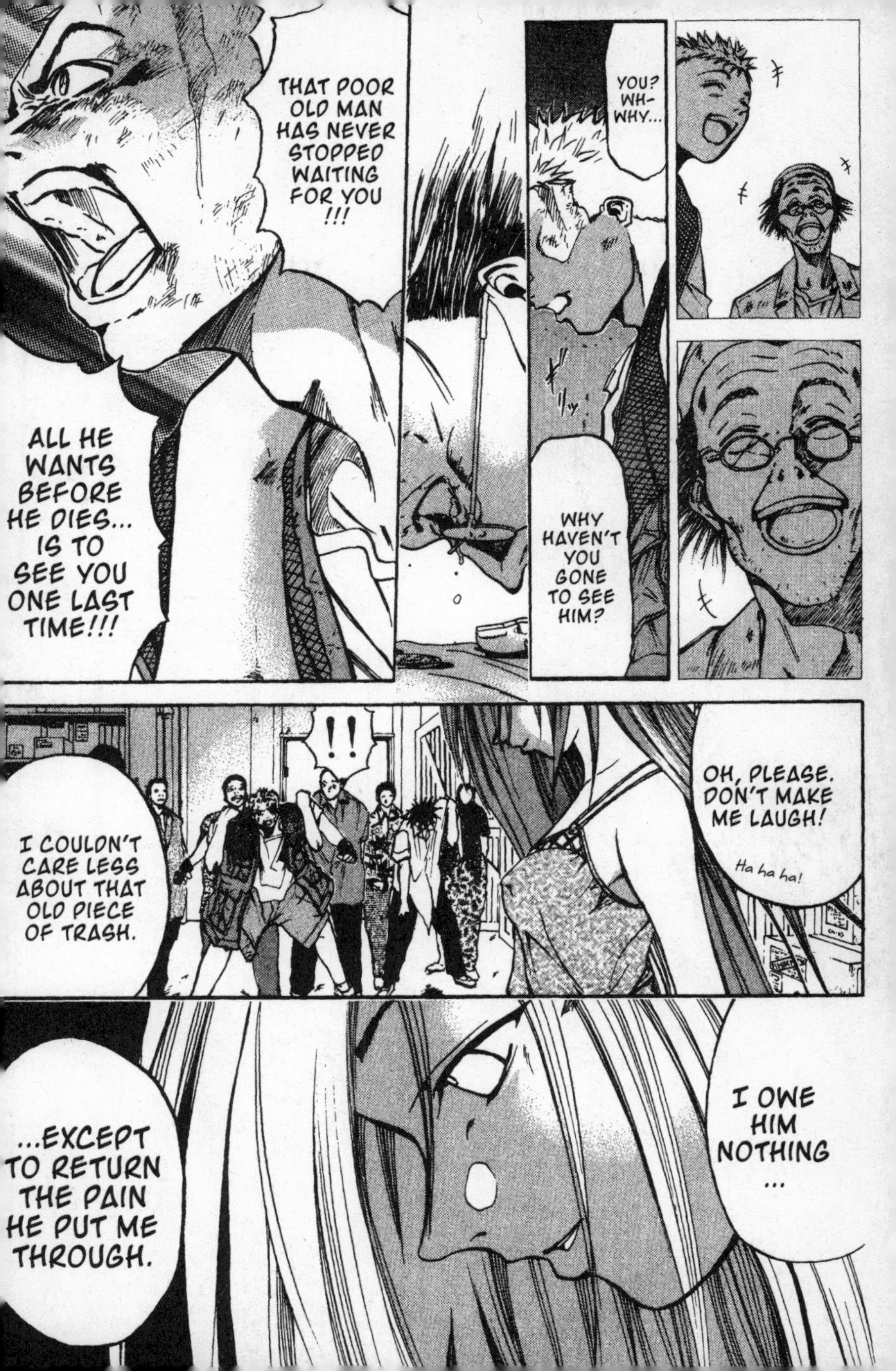
YOU? WH-WHY...
WHY HAVEN'T YOU GONE TO SEE HIM?
THAT POOR OLD MAN HAS NEVER STOPPED WAITING FOR YOU!!!
ALL HE WANTS BEFORE HE DIES... IS TO SEE YOU ONE LAST TIME!!!
OH, PLEASE. DON'T MAKE ME LAUGH!
Ha ha ha!
!!
I COULDN'T CARE LESS ABOUT THAT OLD PIECE OF TRASH.
I OWE HIM NOTHING...
...EXCEPT TO RETURN THE PAIN HE PUT ME THROUGH.

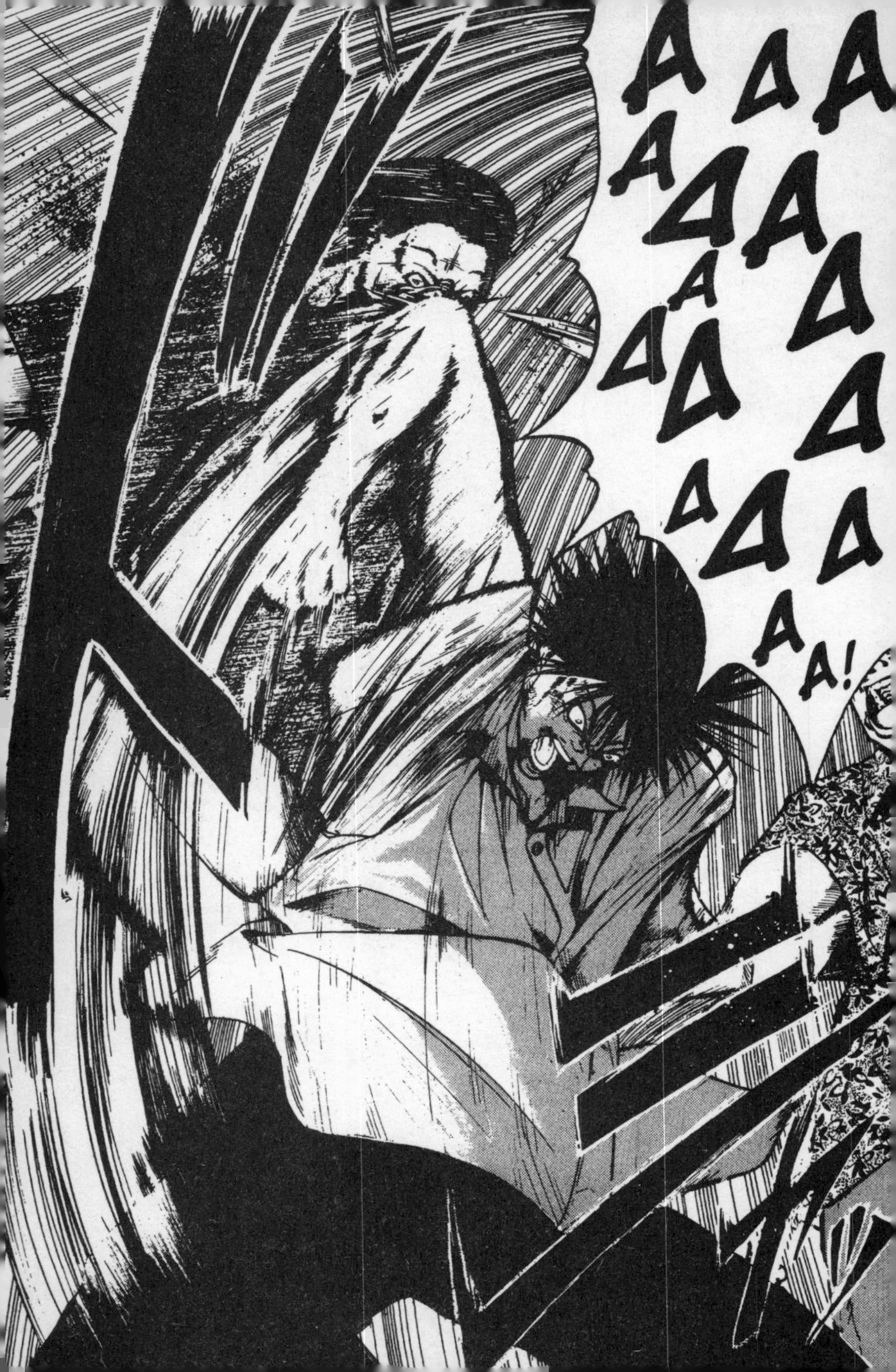
AAAAAAAAAAAAAAAAAAA!

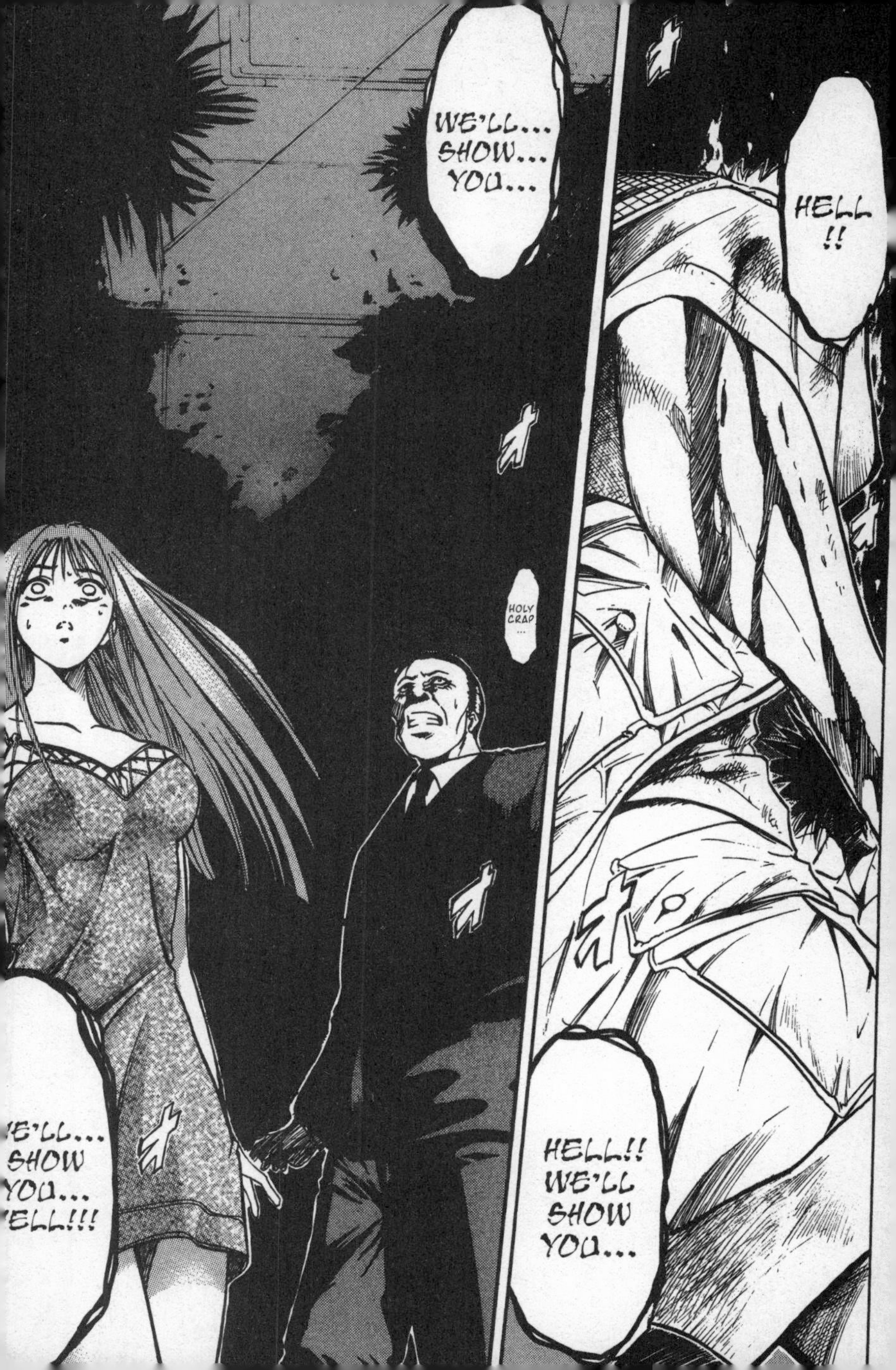
HELL !!
HELL!! WE'LL SHOW YOU...
WE'LL... SHOW... YOU...
HOLY CRAP...
E'LL... SHOW YOU... ELL!!!

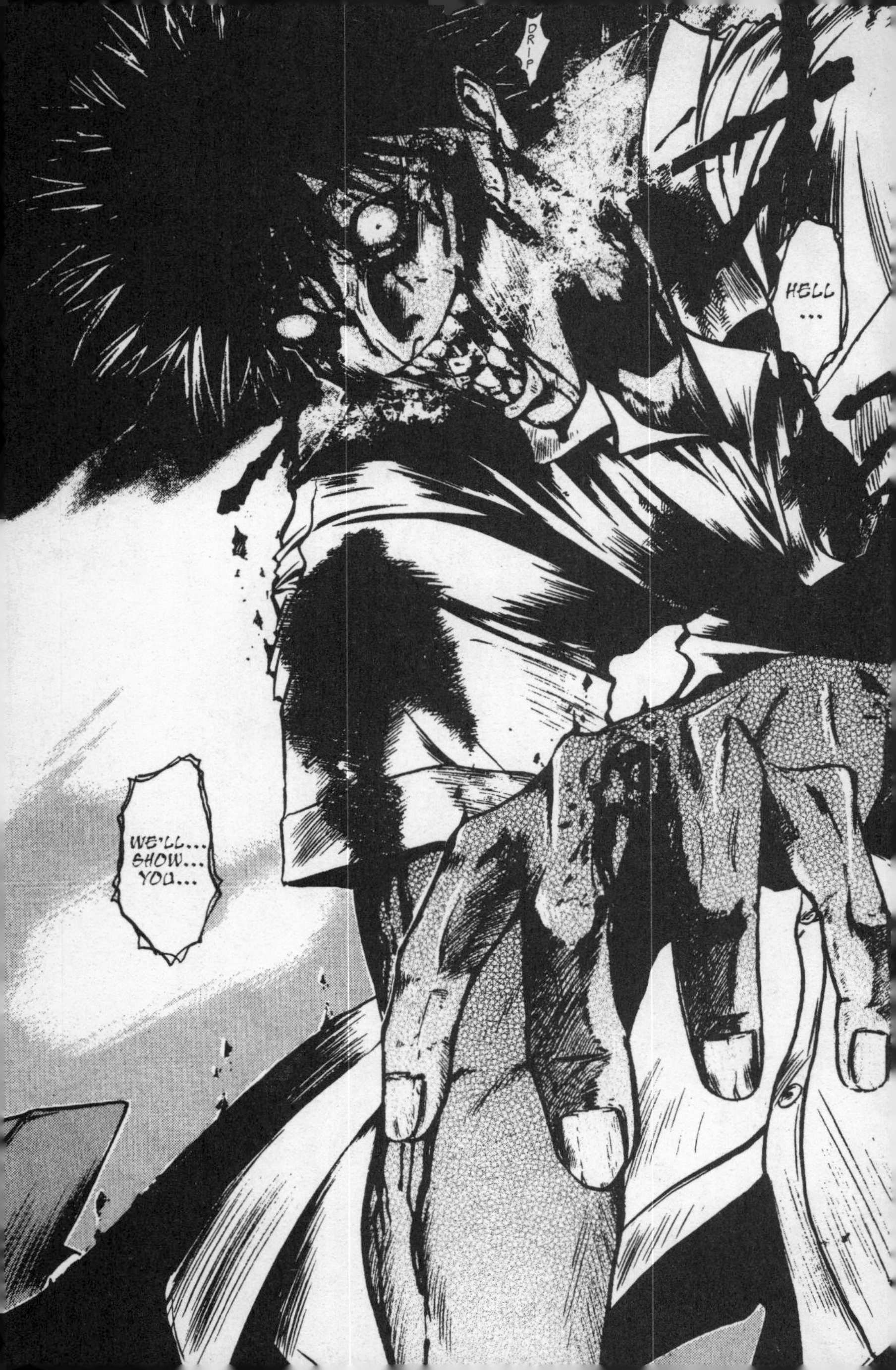
DRIP
HELL...
WE'LL... SHOW... YOU...

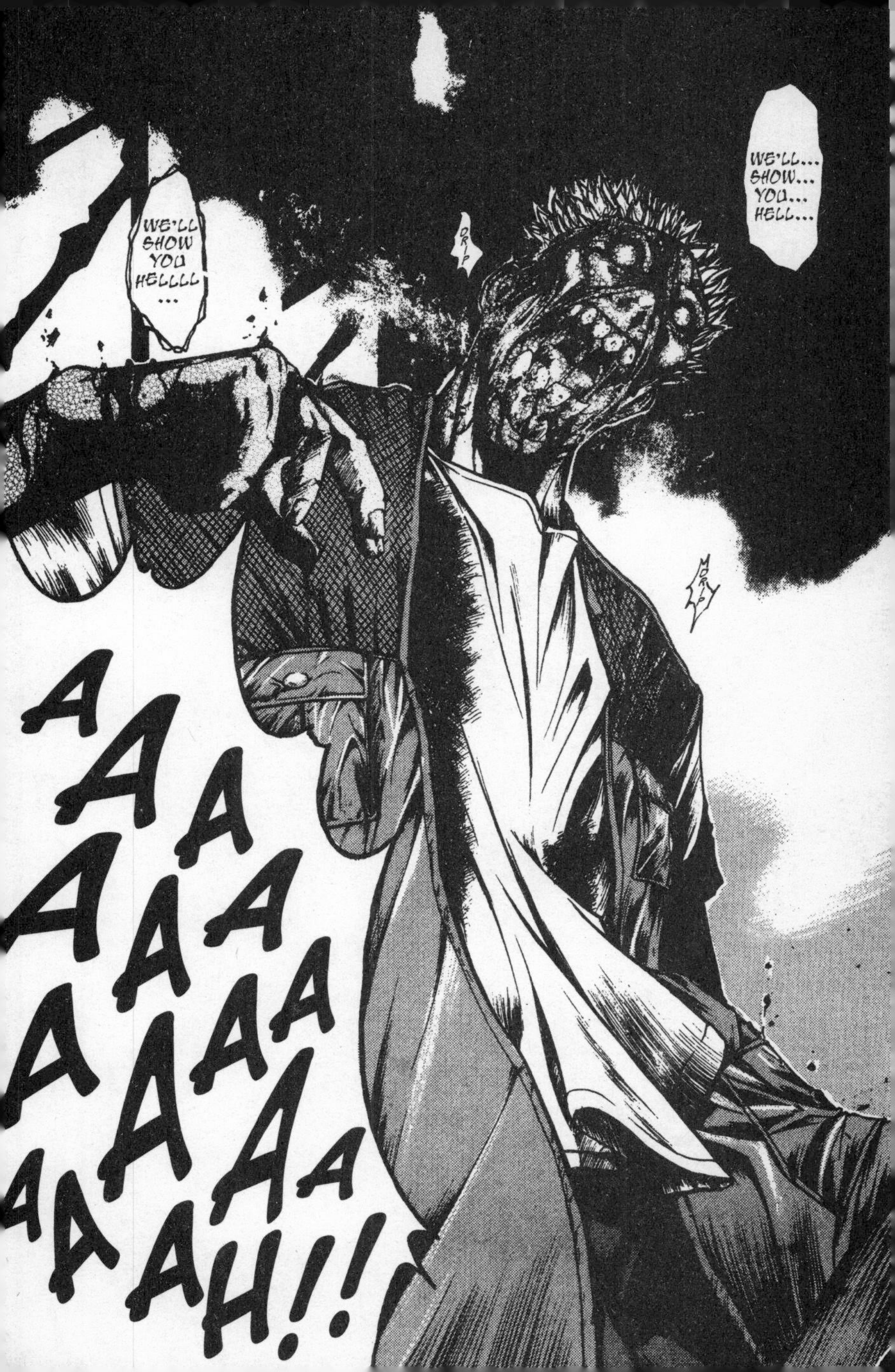
WE'LL... SHOW... YOU... HELL...
DRIP
DRIP
WE'LL SHOW YOU HELLLL ...
AAAAAAAAAAAAAAAAAAAAAH!!

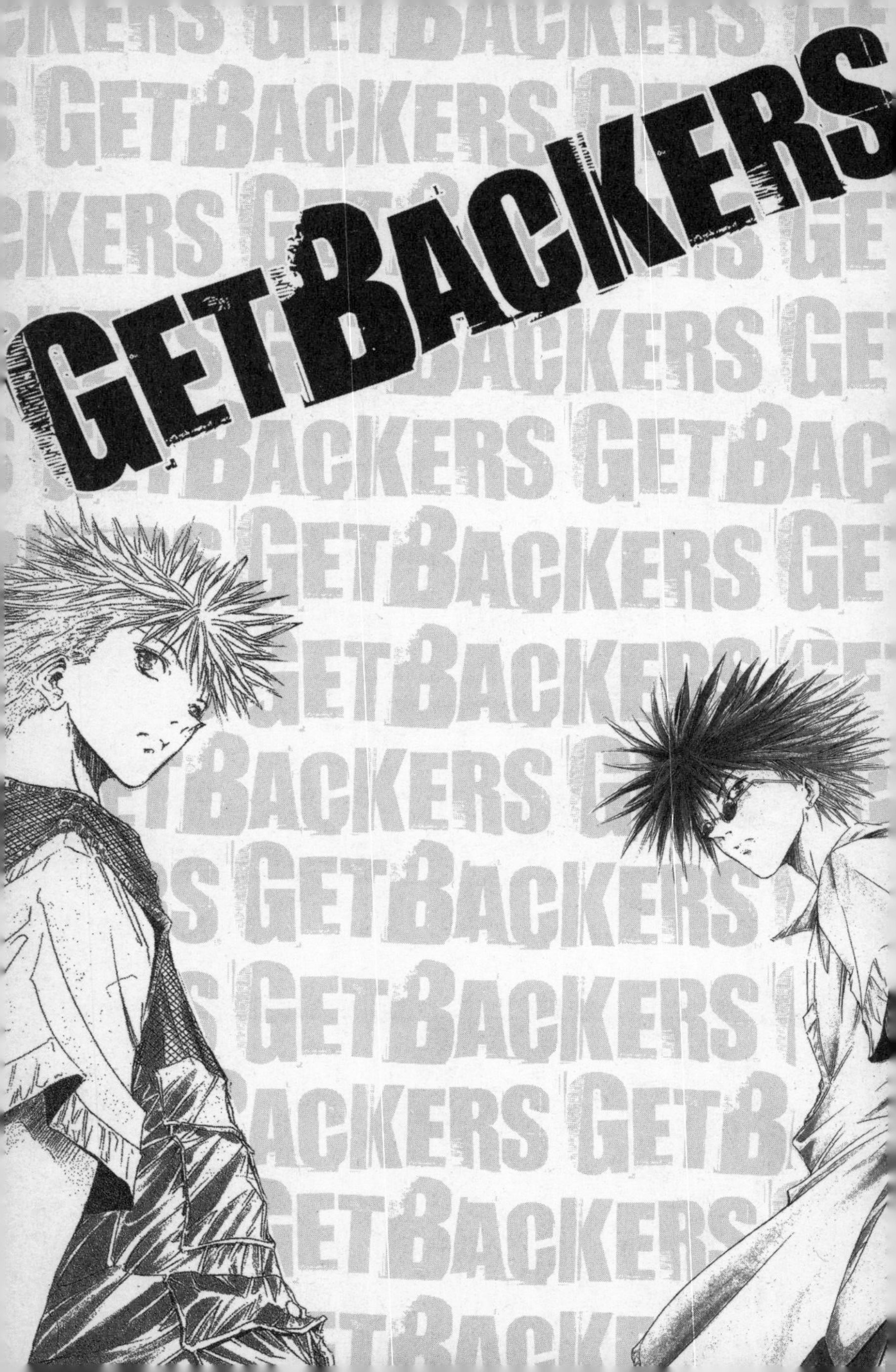
GETBACKERS

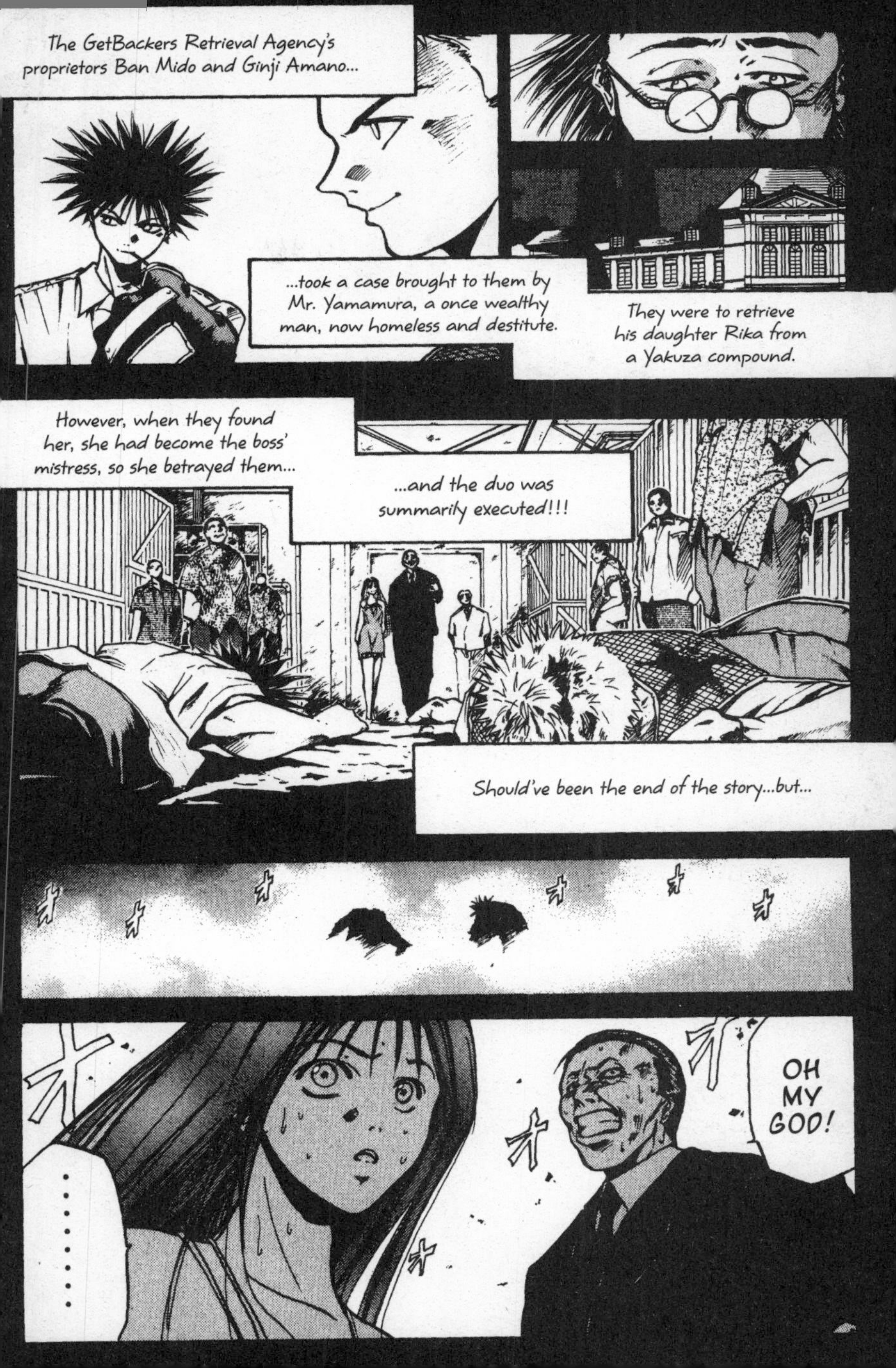

The GetBackers Retrieval Agency's proprietors Ban Mido and Ginji Amano...
...took a case brought to them by Mr. Yamamura, a once wealthy man, now homeless and destitute.
They were to retrieve his daughter Rika from a Yakuza compound.
However, when they found her, she had become the boss' mistress, so she betrayed them...
...and the duo was summarily executed!!!
Should've been the end of the story...but...
OH MY GOD!

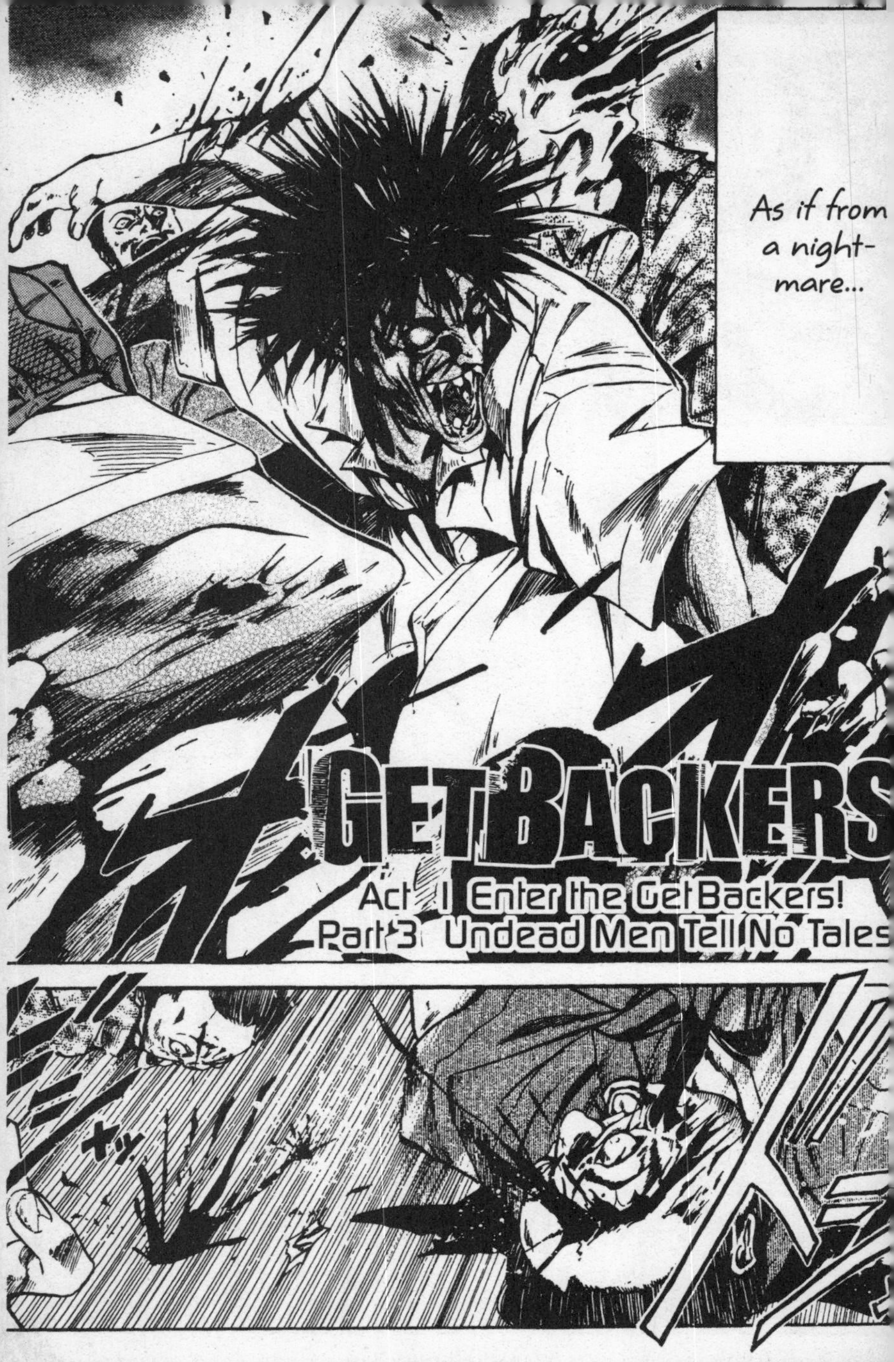
As if from a night-mare...
GET BACKERS
Act I Enter the Get Backers!
Part 3 Undead Men Tell No Tales

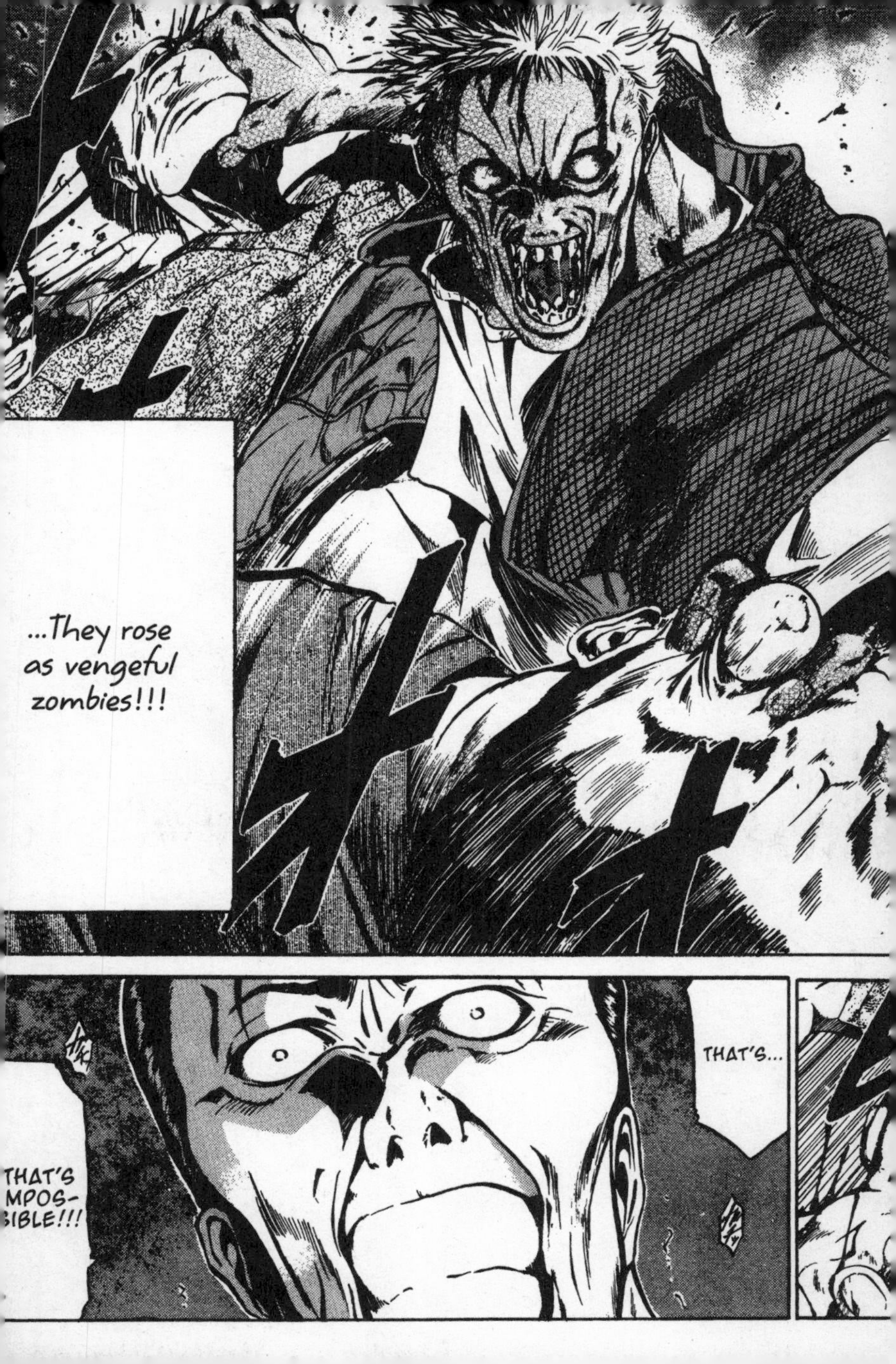
...They rose as vengeful zombies!!!
THAT'S...
THAT'S IMPOS-SIBLE!!!

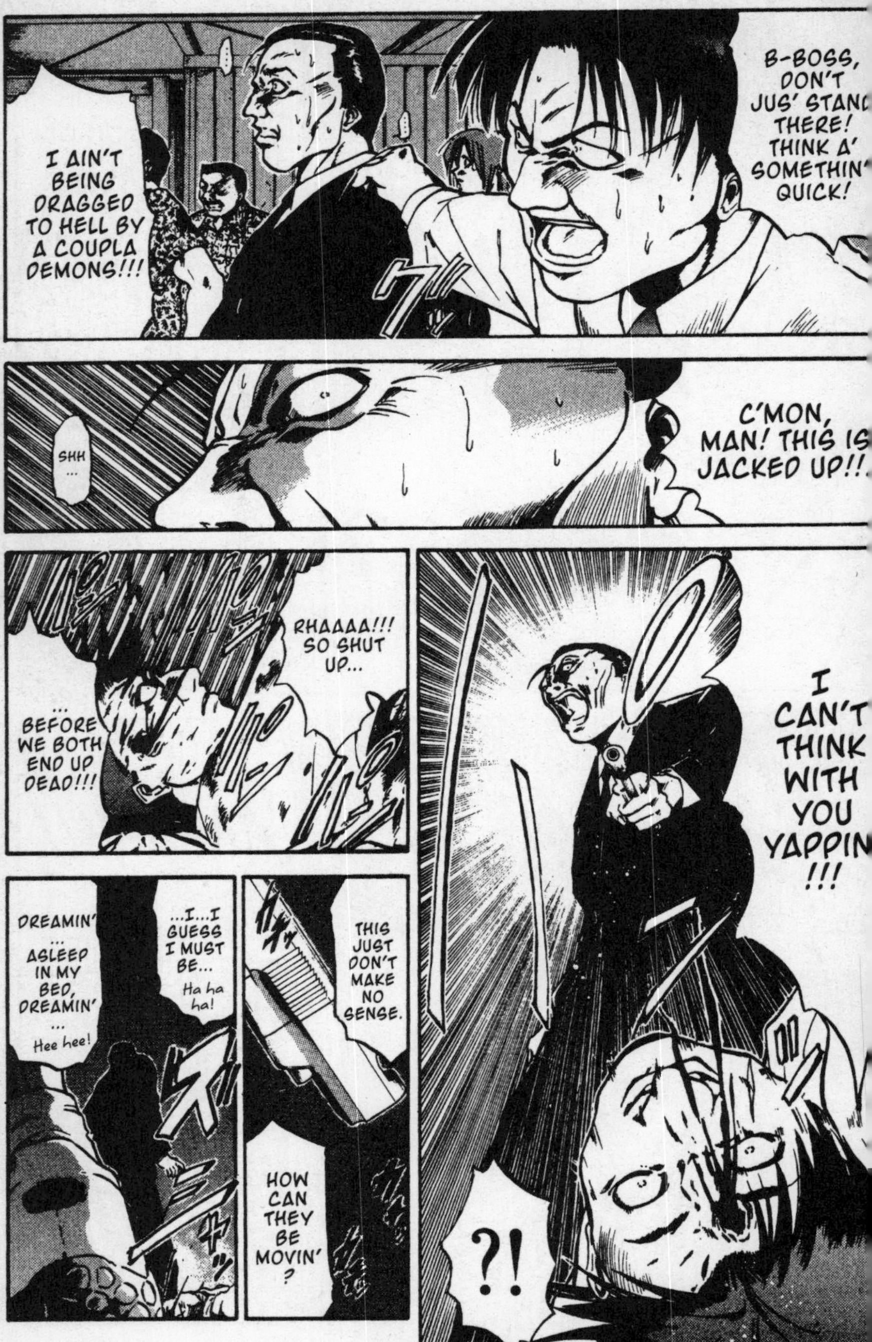
B-BOSS, DON'T JUS' STAND THERE! THINK A' SOMETHIN' QUICK!
...
...
I AIN'T BEING DRAGGED TO HELL BY A COUPLA DEMONS!!!
C'MON, MAN! THIS IS JACKED UP!!!
SHH ...
I CAN'T THINK WITH YOU YAPPIN !!!
?!
RHAAAA!!! SO SHUT UP...
... BEFORE WE BOTH END UP DEAD!!!
THIS JUST DON'T MAKE NO SENSE.
HOW CAN THEY BE MOVIN' ?
...I...I GUESS I MUST BE...
Ha ha ha!
DREAMIN' ... ASLEEP IN MY BED, DREAMIN' ...
Hee hee!

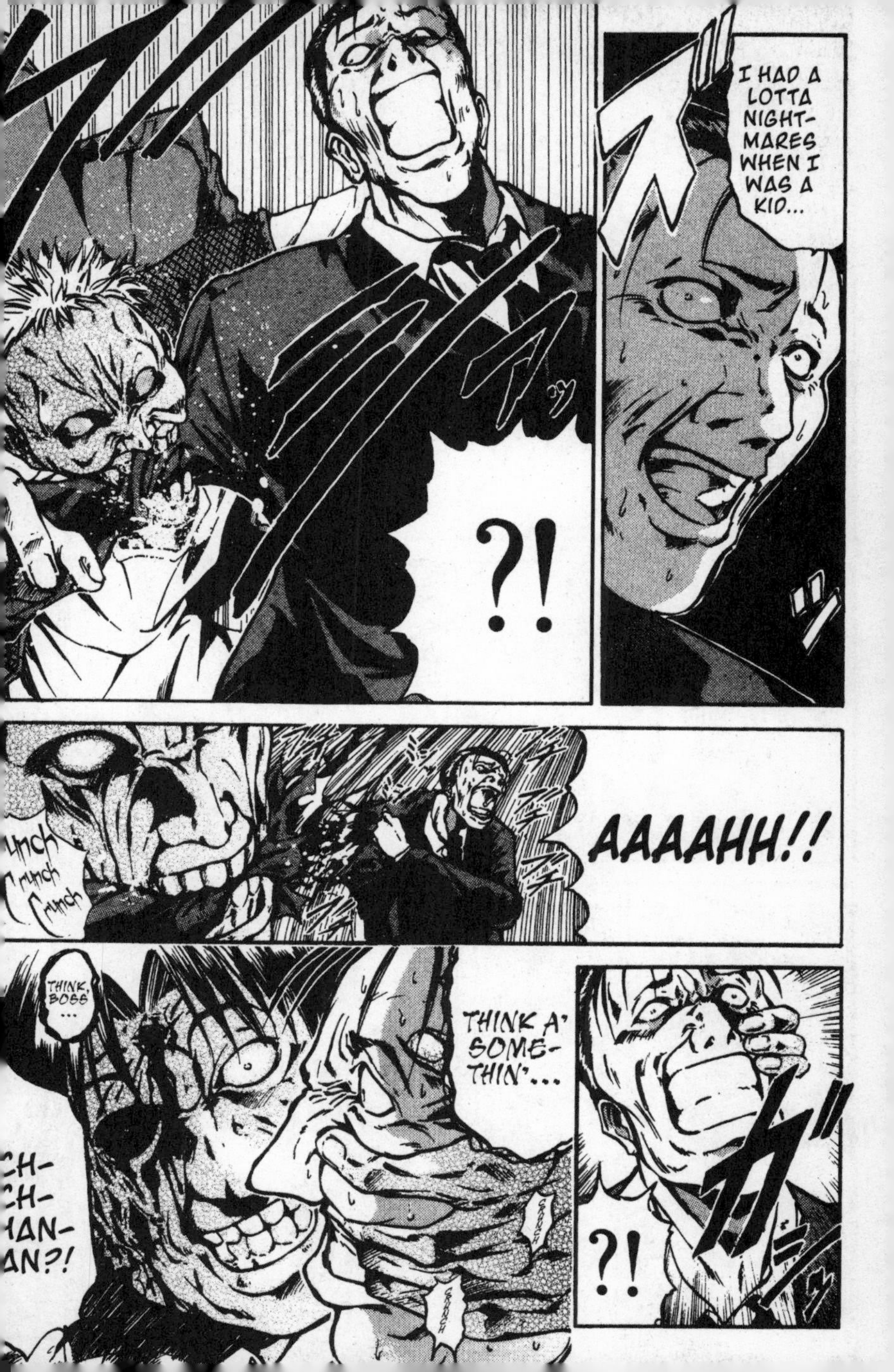
I HAD A LOTTA NIGHT-MARES WHEN I WAS A KID...
?!
AAAAHH!!
unch
runch
Crunch
?!
THINK A' SOME-THIN'...
THINK, BOSS ...
CH-CH-HAN-AN?!

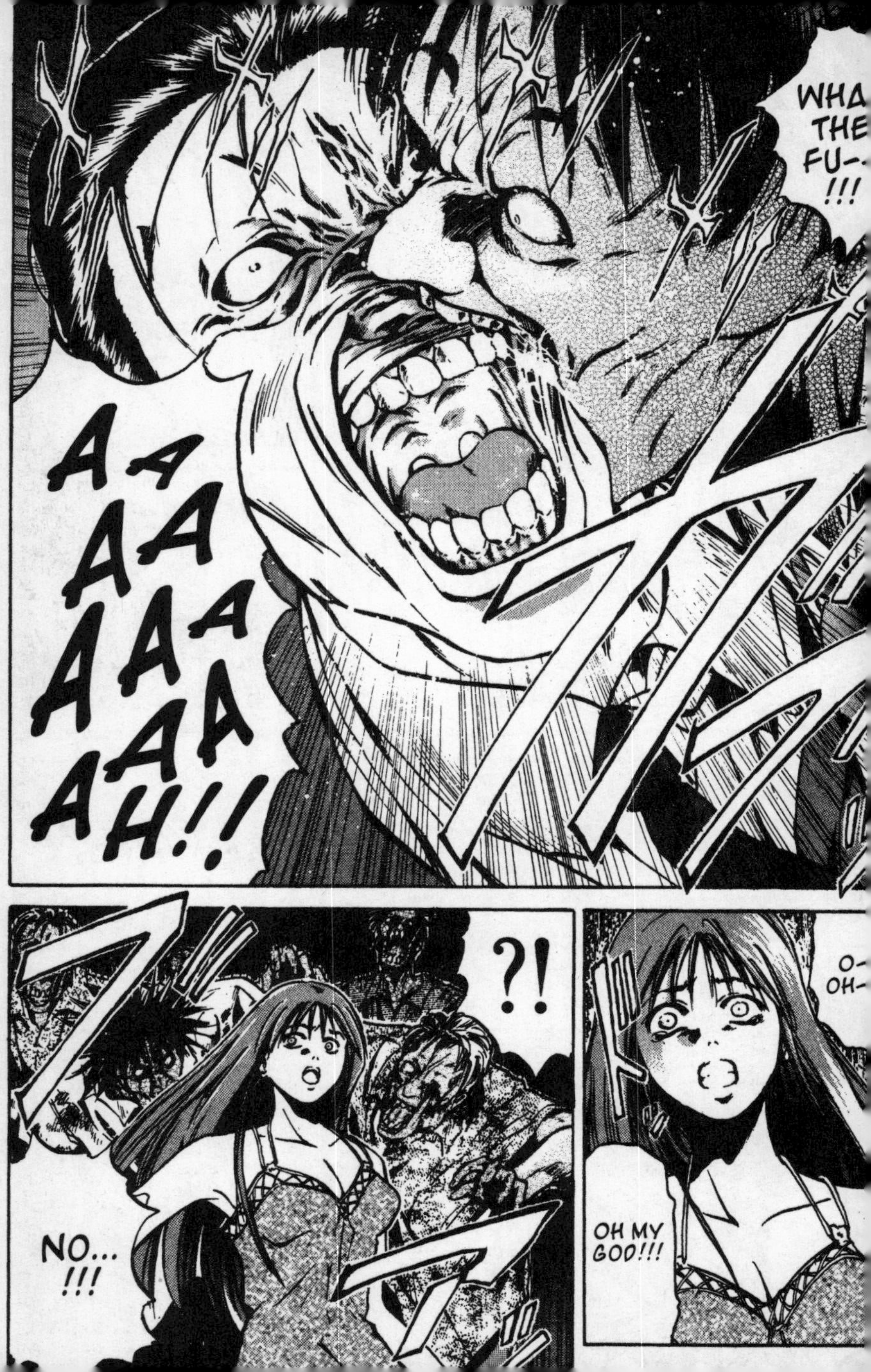
WHA THE FU-..!!!
AAAAAAAAAAAAH!!
O-OH-
OH MY GOD!!!
?!
NO...!!!

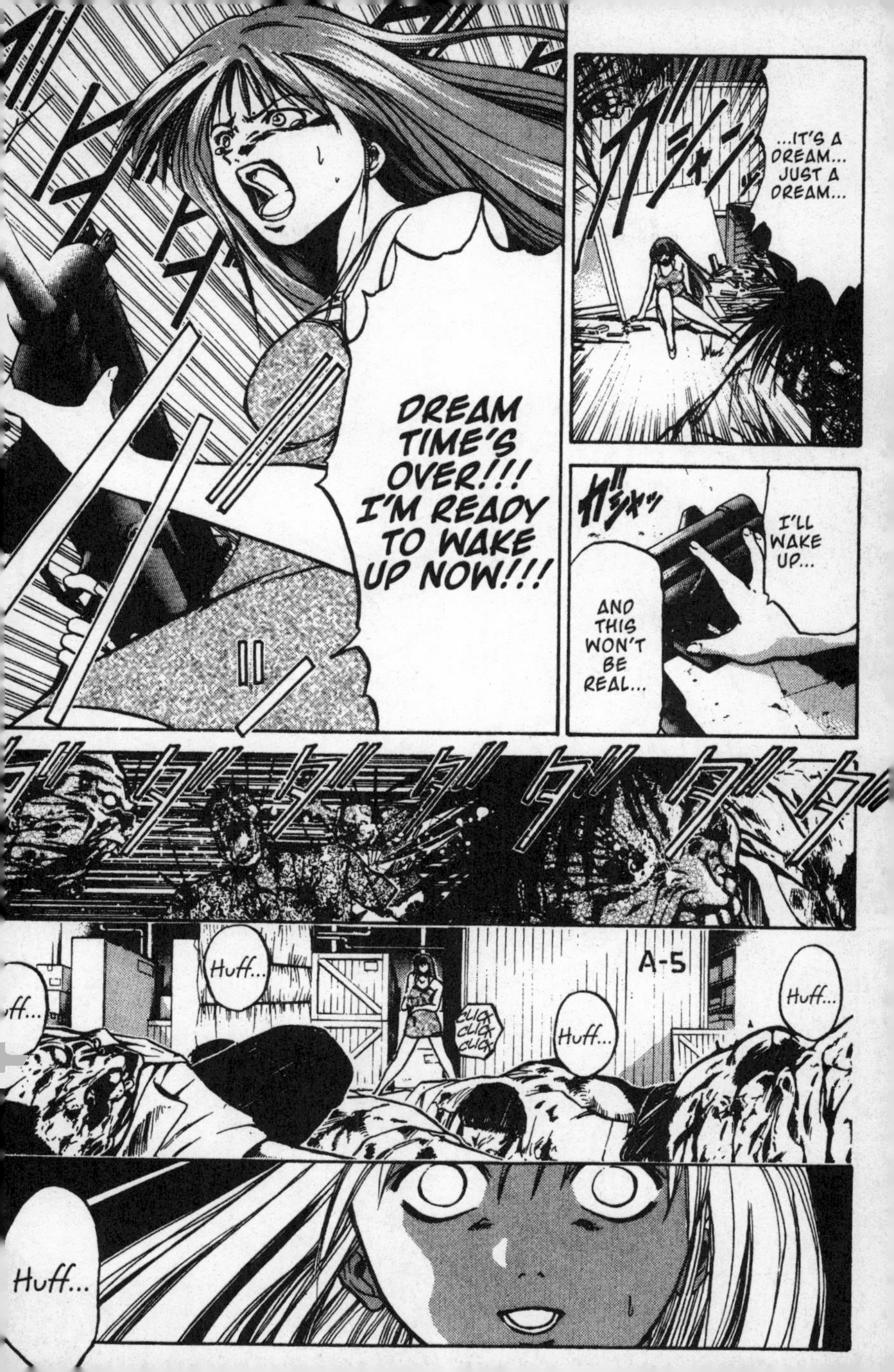
...IT'S A DREAM... JUST A DREAM...
I'LL WAKE UP...
AND THIS WON'T BE REAL...
DREAM TIME'S OVER!!! I'M READY TO WAKE UP NOW!!!
A-5
Huff...
Huff...
CLICK CLICK CLICK
Huff...
Huff...

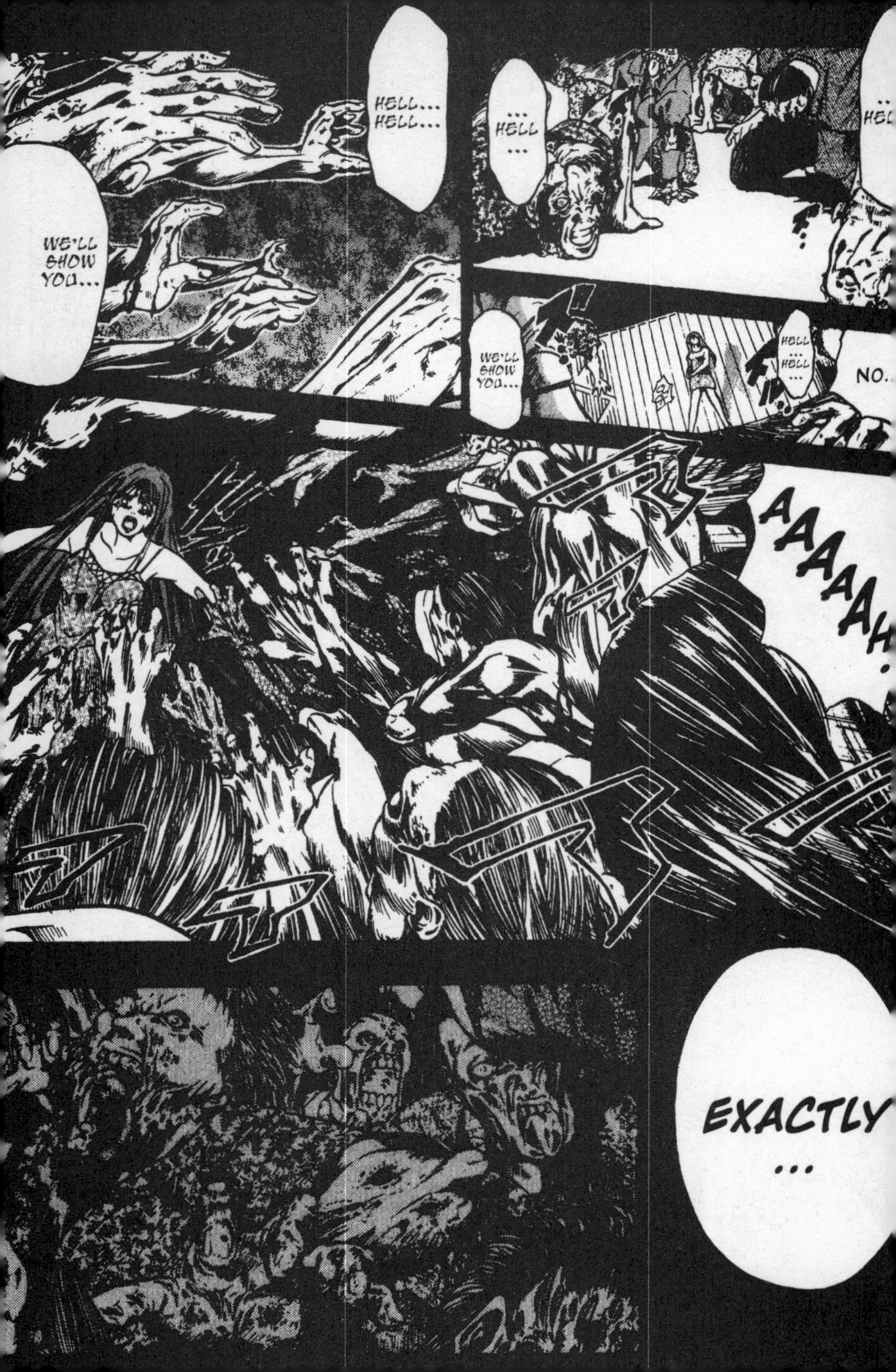
.. HEL
... HELL ...
NO...
HELL ... HELL ...
WE'LL SHOW YOU...
HELL... HELL...
WE'LL SHOW YOU...
AAAAAAH!
EXACTLY ...

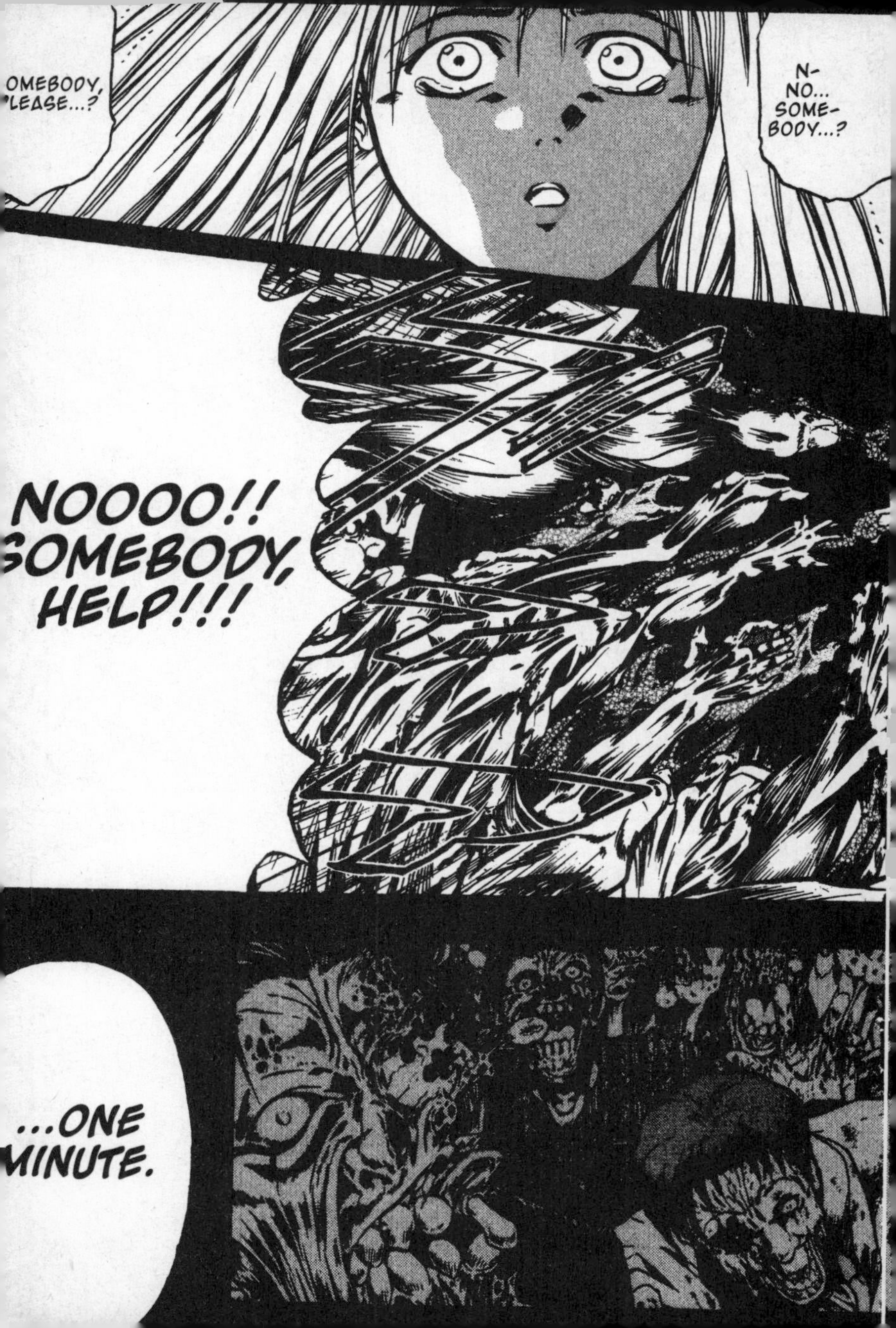
N- NO... SOME- BODY...?
OMEBODY, 'LEASE...?
NOOOO!! SOMEBODY, HELP!!!
...ONE MINUTE.

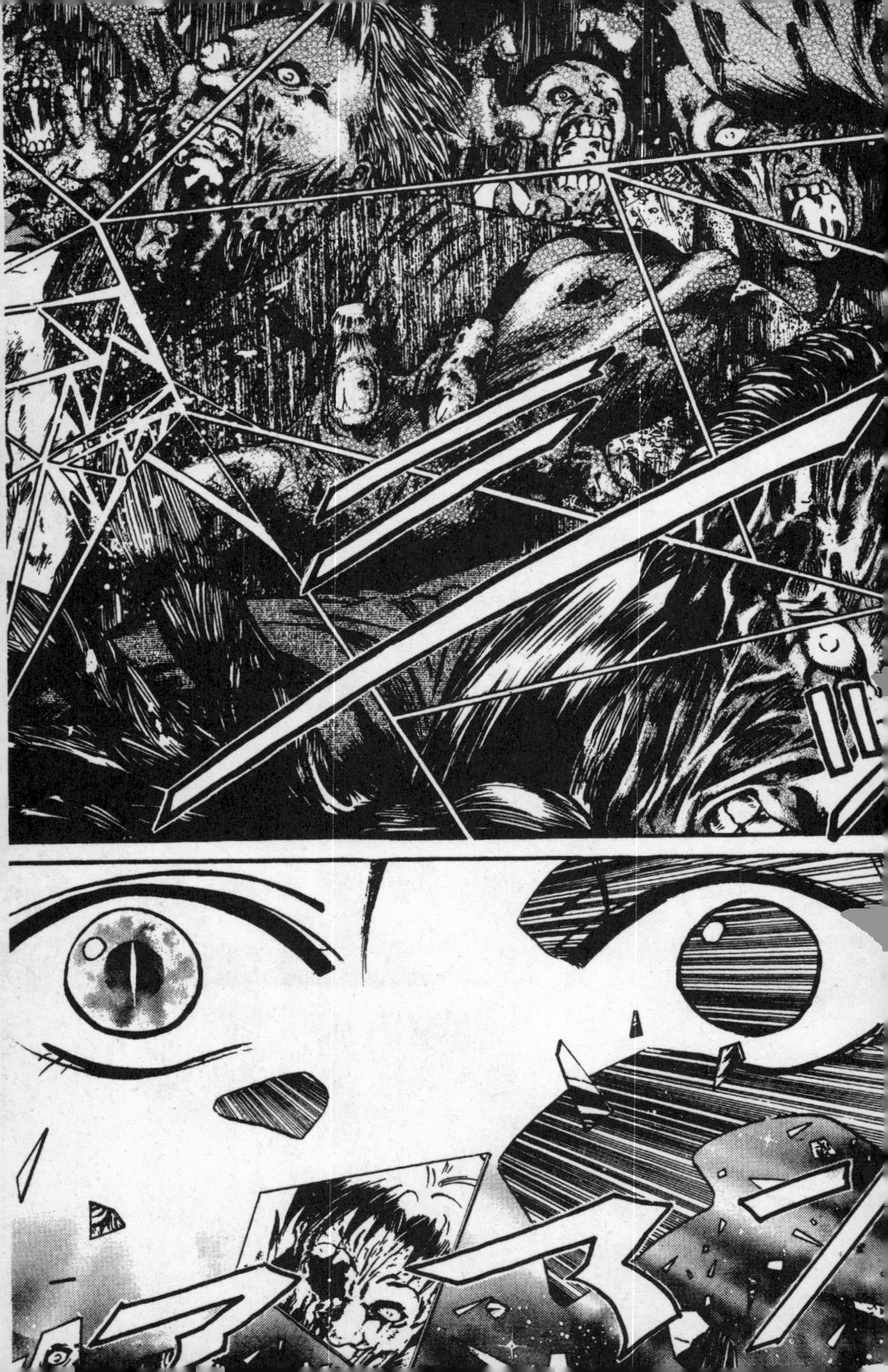

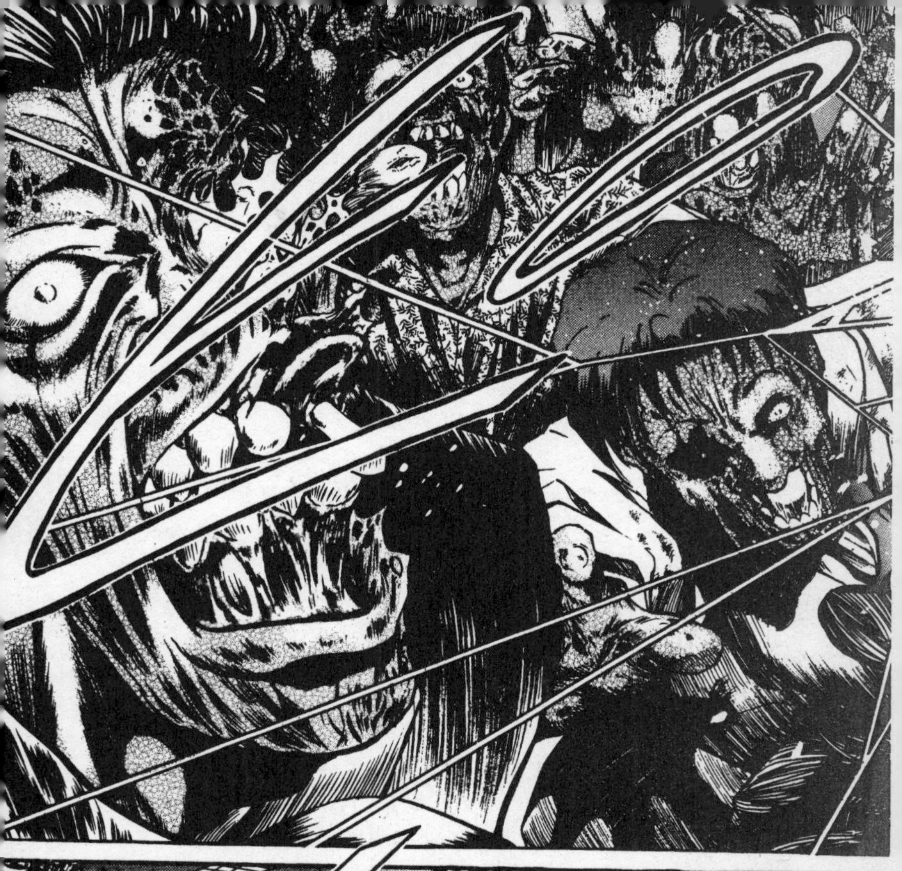
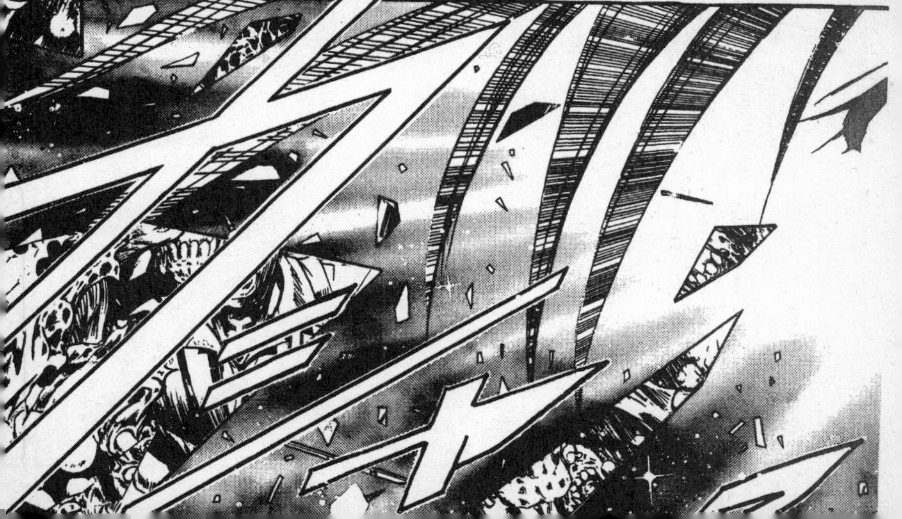

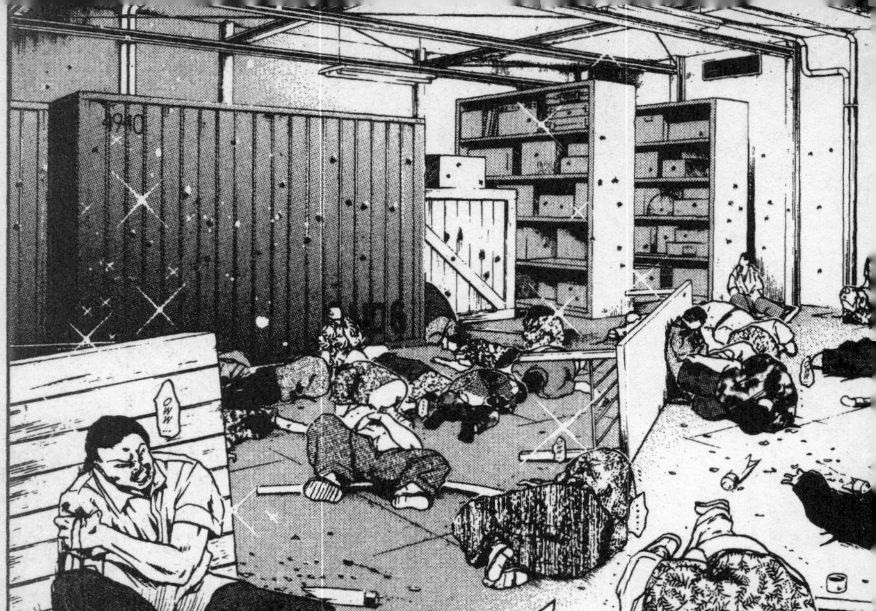
OWW...
OWW
?!

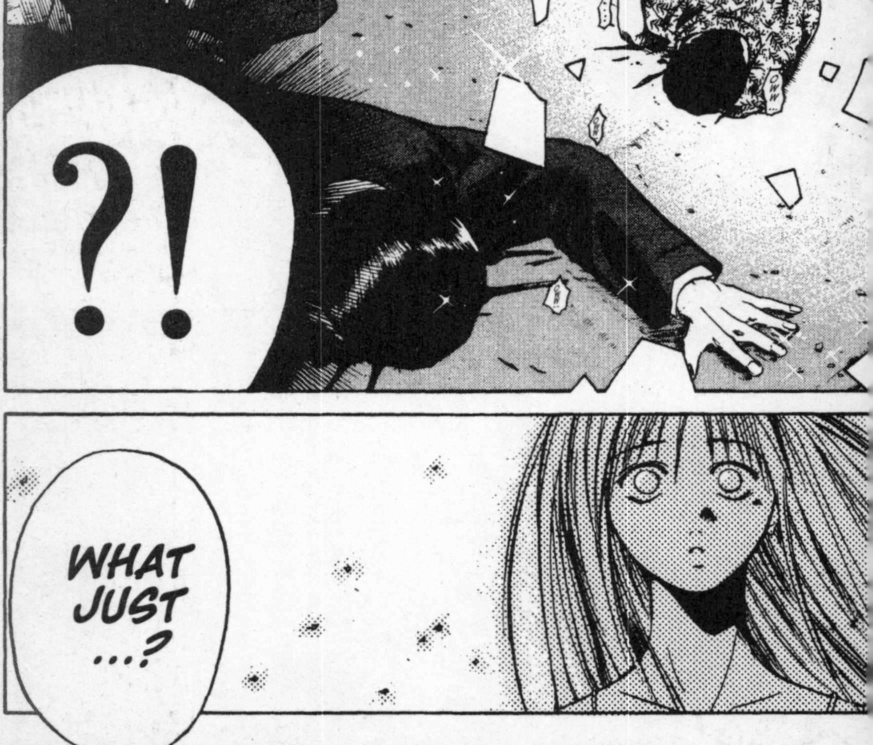
WHAT JUST ...?

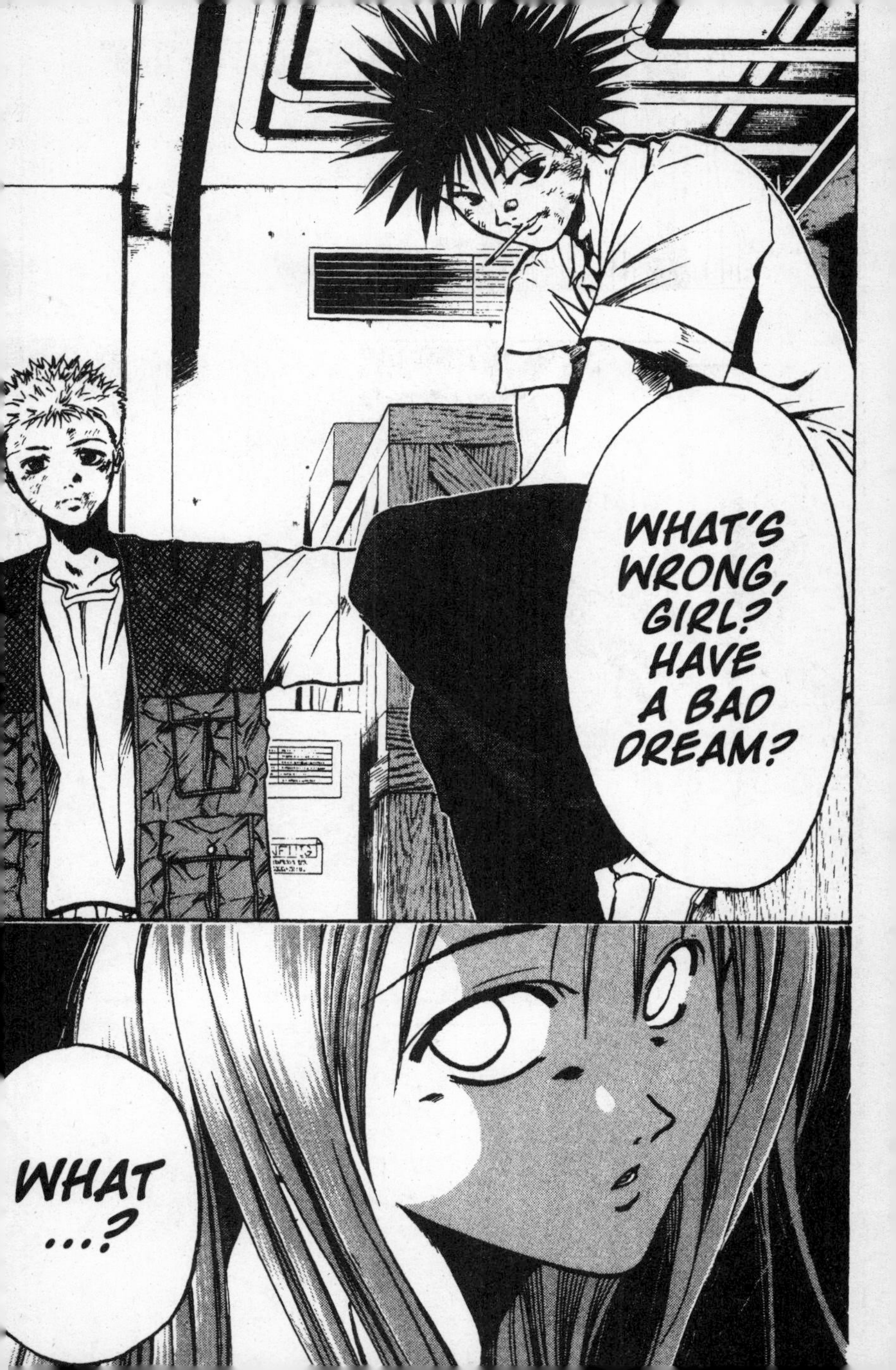
WHAT'S WRONG, GIRL? HAVE A BAD DREAM?
WHAT ...?

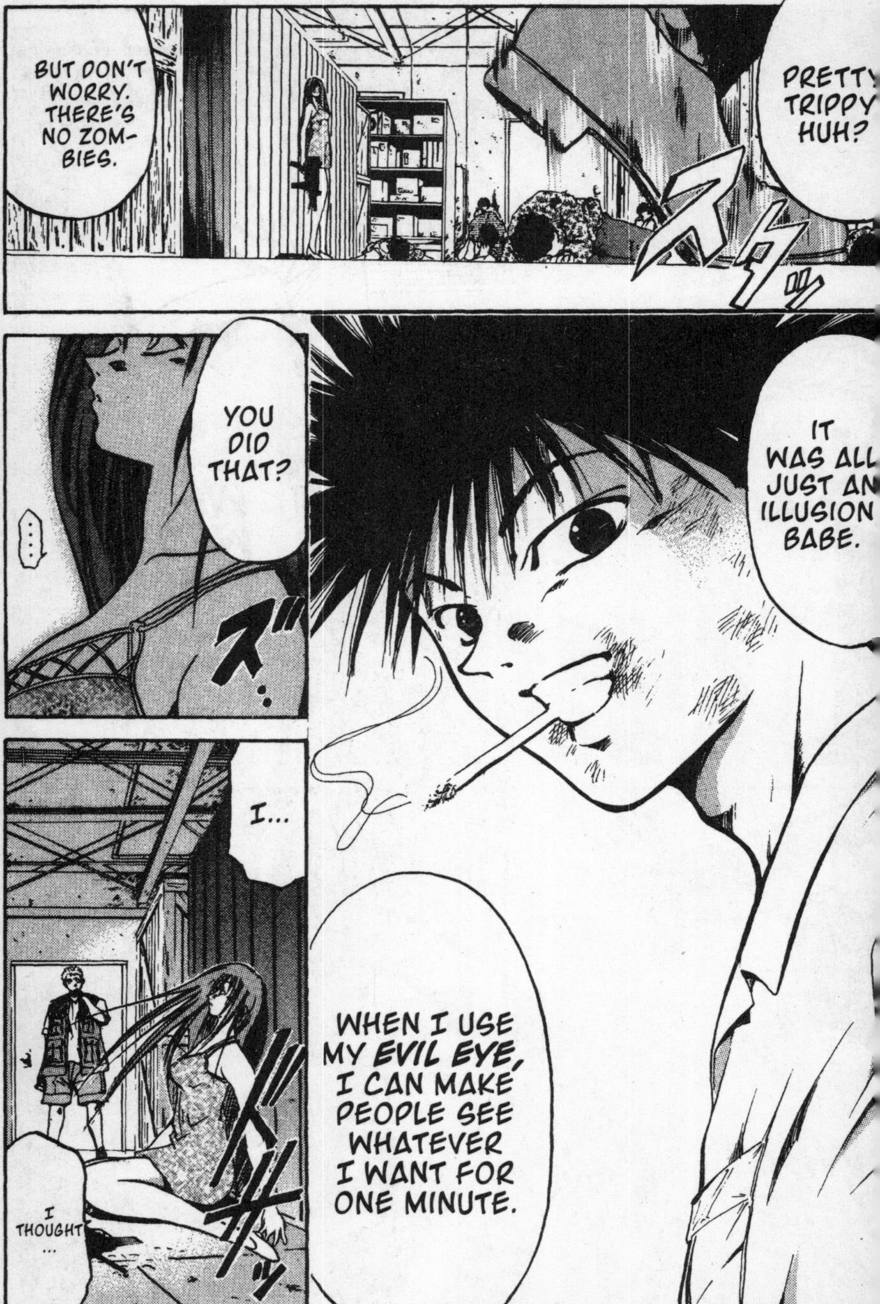
PRETTY TRIPPY HUH?
BUT DON'T WORRY. THERE'S NO ZOMBIES.
IT WAS ALL JUST AN ILLUSION BABE.
YOU DID THAT?
....
WHEN I USE MY *EVIL EYE*, I CAN MAKE PEOPLE SEE WHATEVER I WANT FOR ONE MINUTE.
I...
I THOUGHT ...

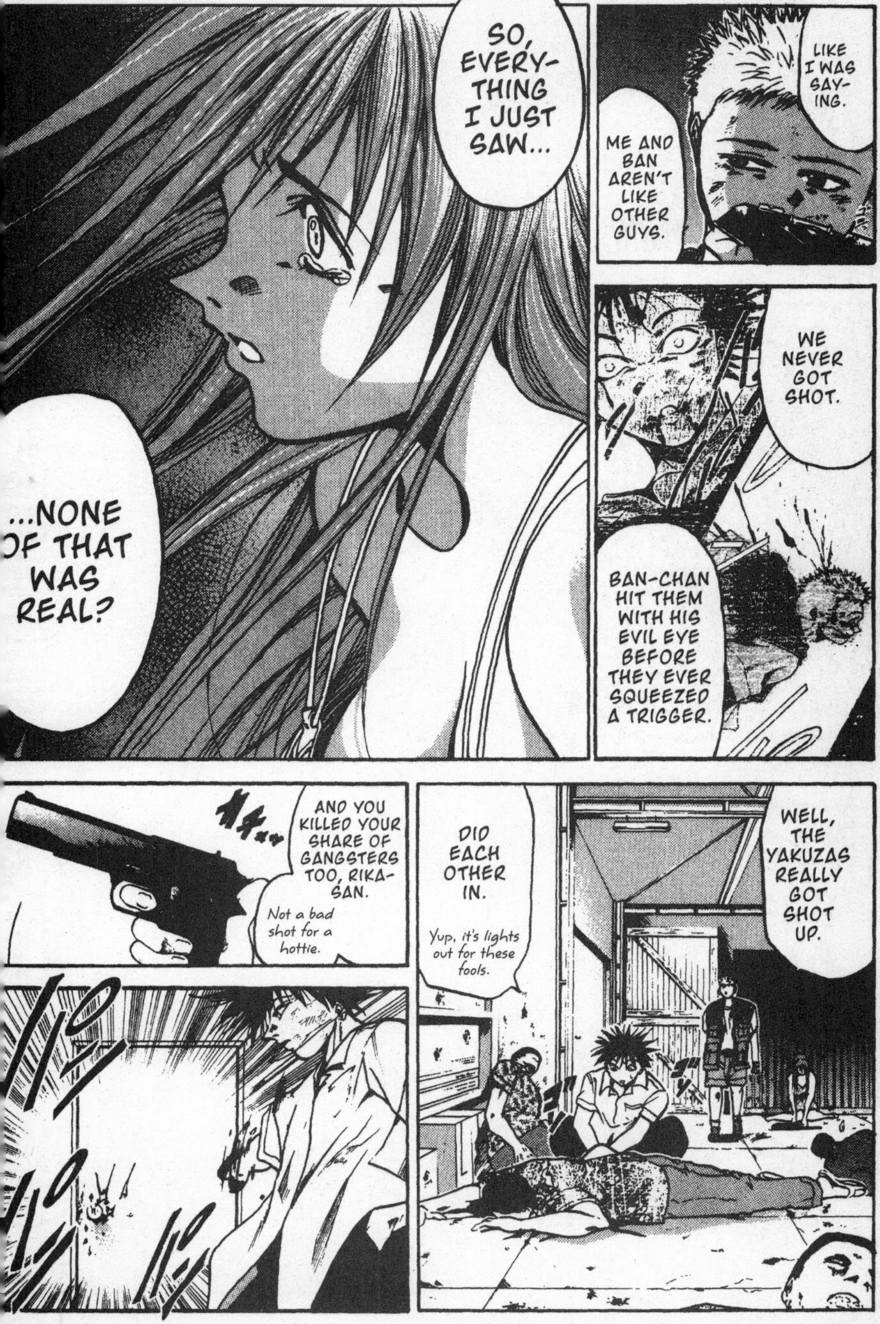
LIKE I WAS SAYING.
ME AND BAN AREN'T LIKE OTHER GUYS.
WE NEVER GOT SHOT.
BAN-CHAN HIT THEM WITH HIS EVIL EYE BEFORE THEY EVER SQUEEZED A TRIGGER.
SO, EVERYTHING I JUST SAW...
...NONE OF THAT WAS REAL?
WELL, THE YAKUZAS REALLY GOT SHOT UP.
DID EACH OTHER IN.
Yup, it's lights out for these fools.
AND YOU KILLED YOUR SHARE OF GANGSTERS TOO, RIKA-SAN.
Not a bad shot for a hottie.

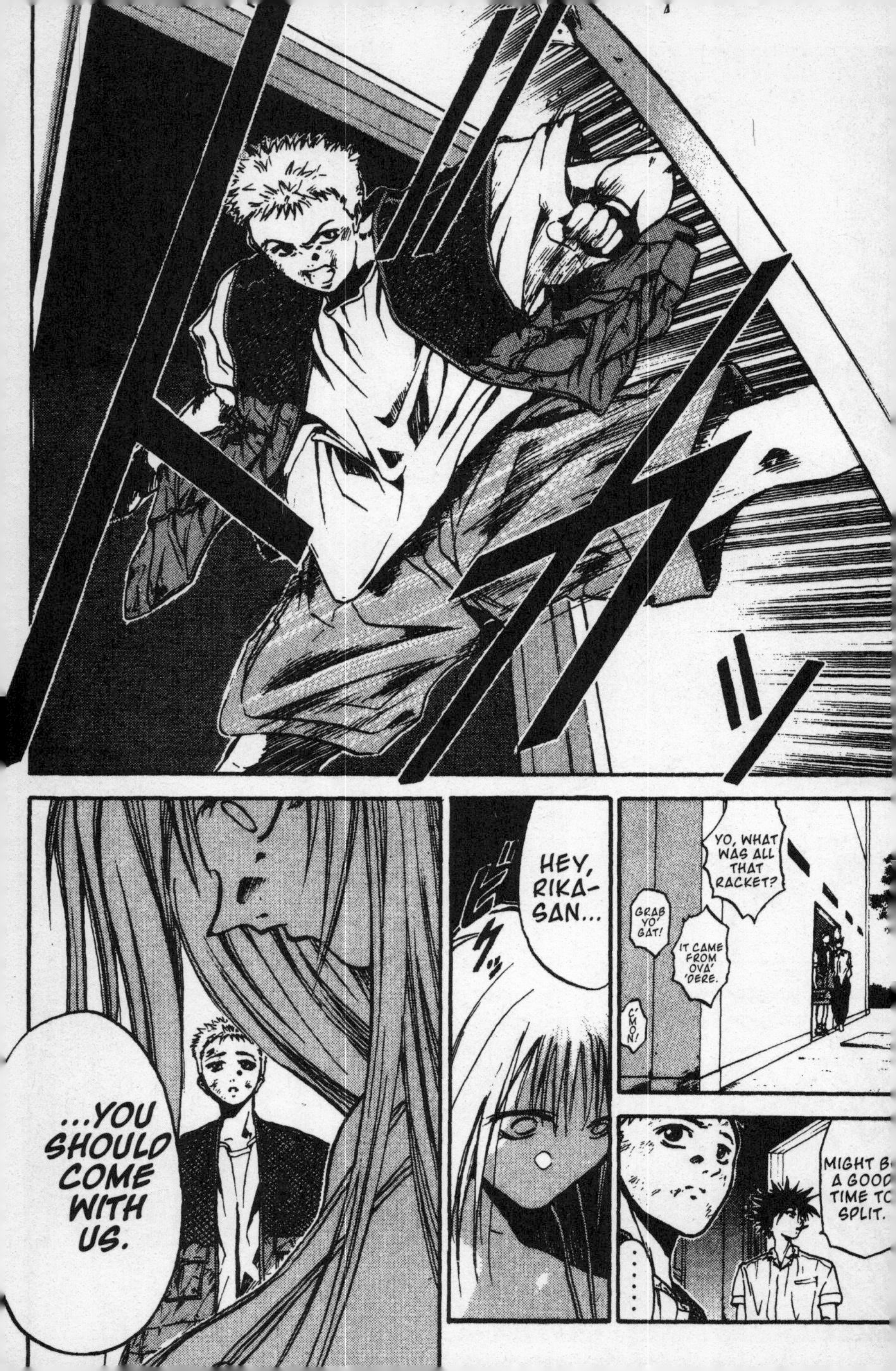
YO, WHAT WAS ALL THAT RACKET?
IT CAME FROM OVA' 'DERE.
GRAB YO' GAT!
C'MON!
MIGHT B A GOOD TIME TO SPLIT.
......
HEY, RIKA-SAN...
...YOU SHOULD COME WITH US.

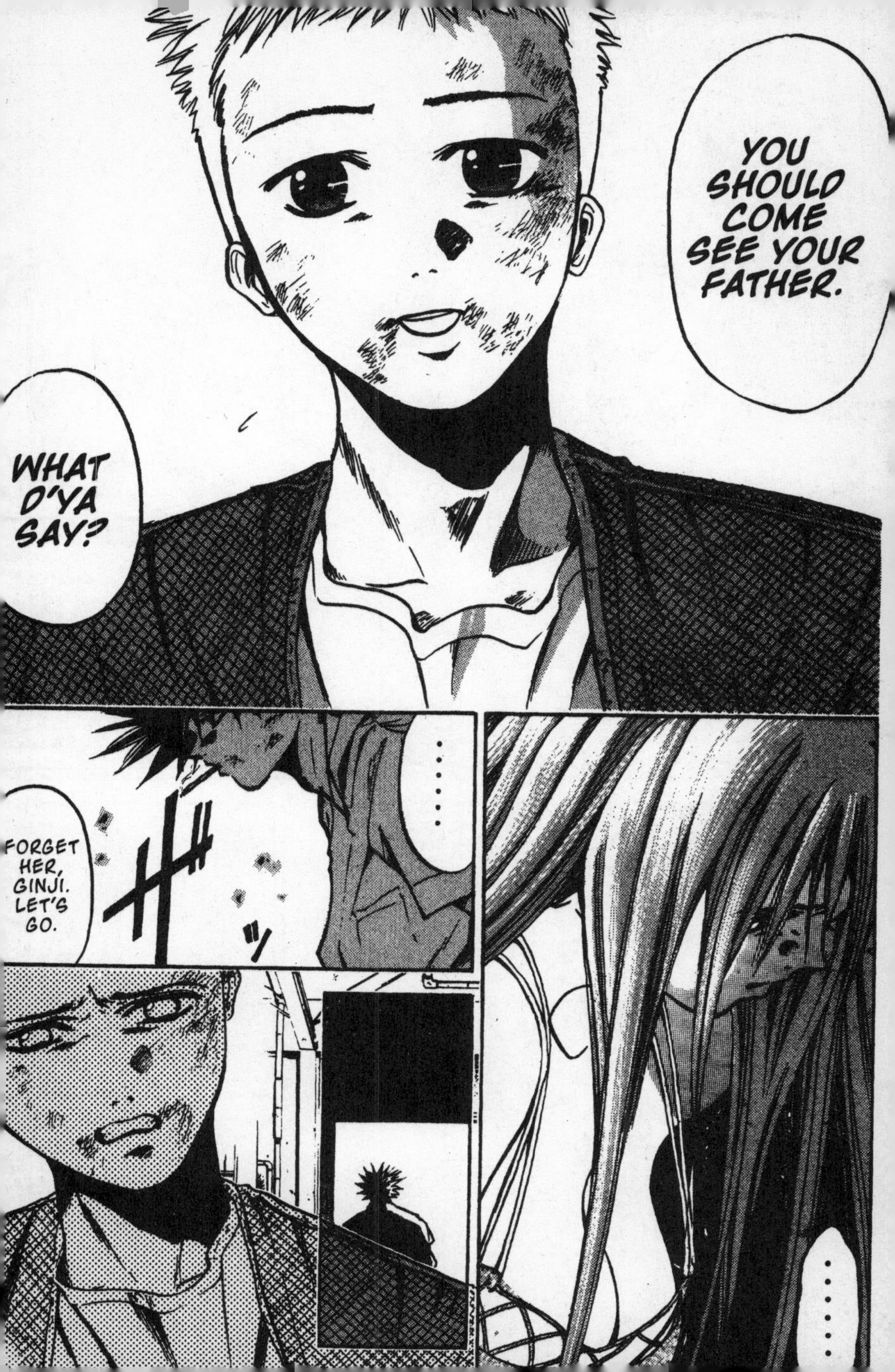
YOU SHOULD COME SEE YOUR FATHER.
WHAT D'YA SAY?
......
......
FORGET HER, GINJI. LET'S GO.

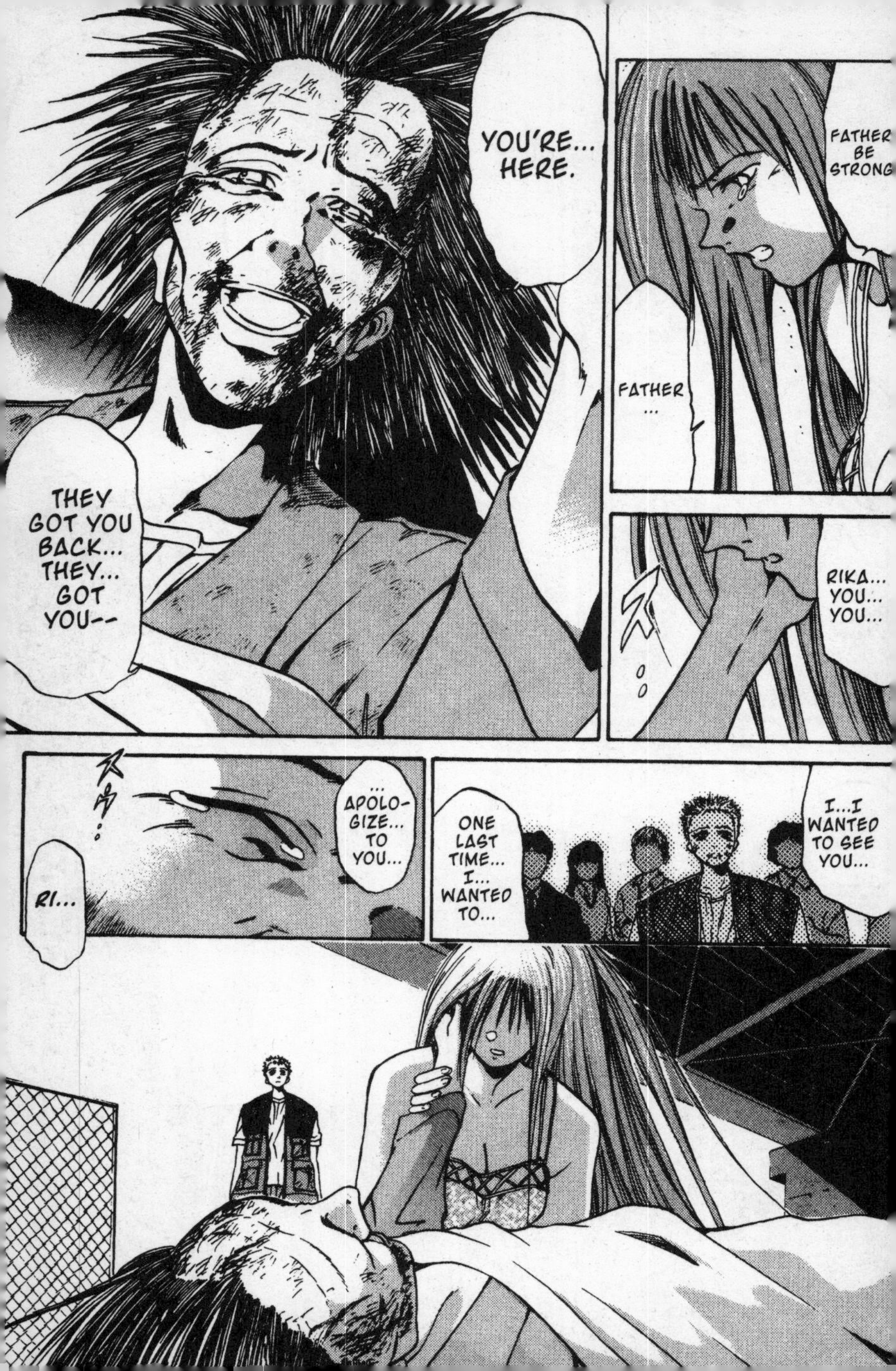
FATHER BE STRONG
FATHER ...
RIKA... YOU... YOU...
YOU'RE... HERE.
THEY GOT YOU BACK... THEY... GOT YOU--
I...I WANTED TO SEE YOU...
ONE LAST TIME... I... WANTED TO...
... APOLOGIZE... TO YOU...
RI...

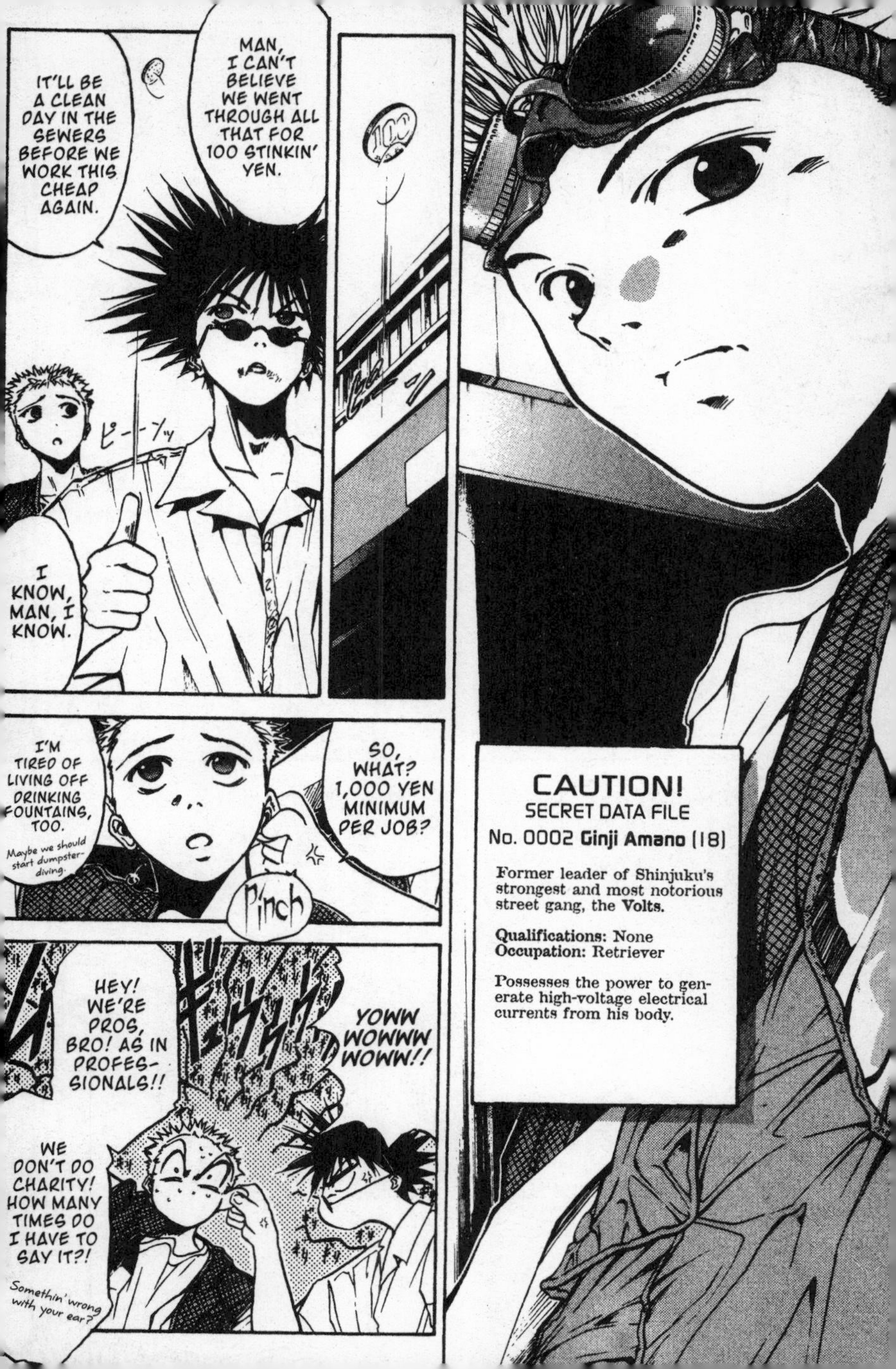
CAUTION!
SECRET DATA FILE
No. 0002 Ginji Amano (18)
Former leader of Shinjuku's strongest and most notorious street gang, the Volts.
Qualifications: None
Occupation: Retriever
Possesses the power to generate high-voltage electrical currents from his body.
MAN, I CAN'T BELIEVE WE WENT THROUGH ALL THAT FOR 100 STINKIN' YEN.
IT'LL BE A CLEAN DAY IN THE SEWERS BEFORE WE WORK THIS CHEAP AGAIN.
I KNOW, MAN, I KNOW.
SO, WHAT? 1,000 YEN MINIMUM PER JOB?
I'M TIRED OF LIVING OFF DRINKING FOUNTAINS, TOO.
Maybe we should start dumpster-diving.
Pinch
YOWW WOWWW WOWW!!
HEY! WE'RE PROS, BRO! AS IN PROFES-SIONALS!!
WE DON'T DO CHARITY! HOW MANY TIMES DO I HAVE TO SAY IT?!
Somethin' wrong with your ear?

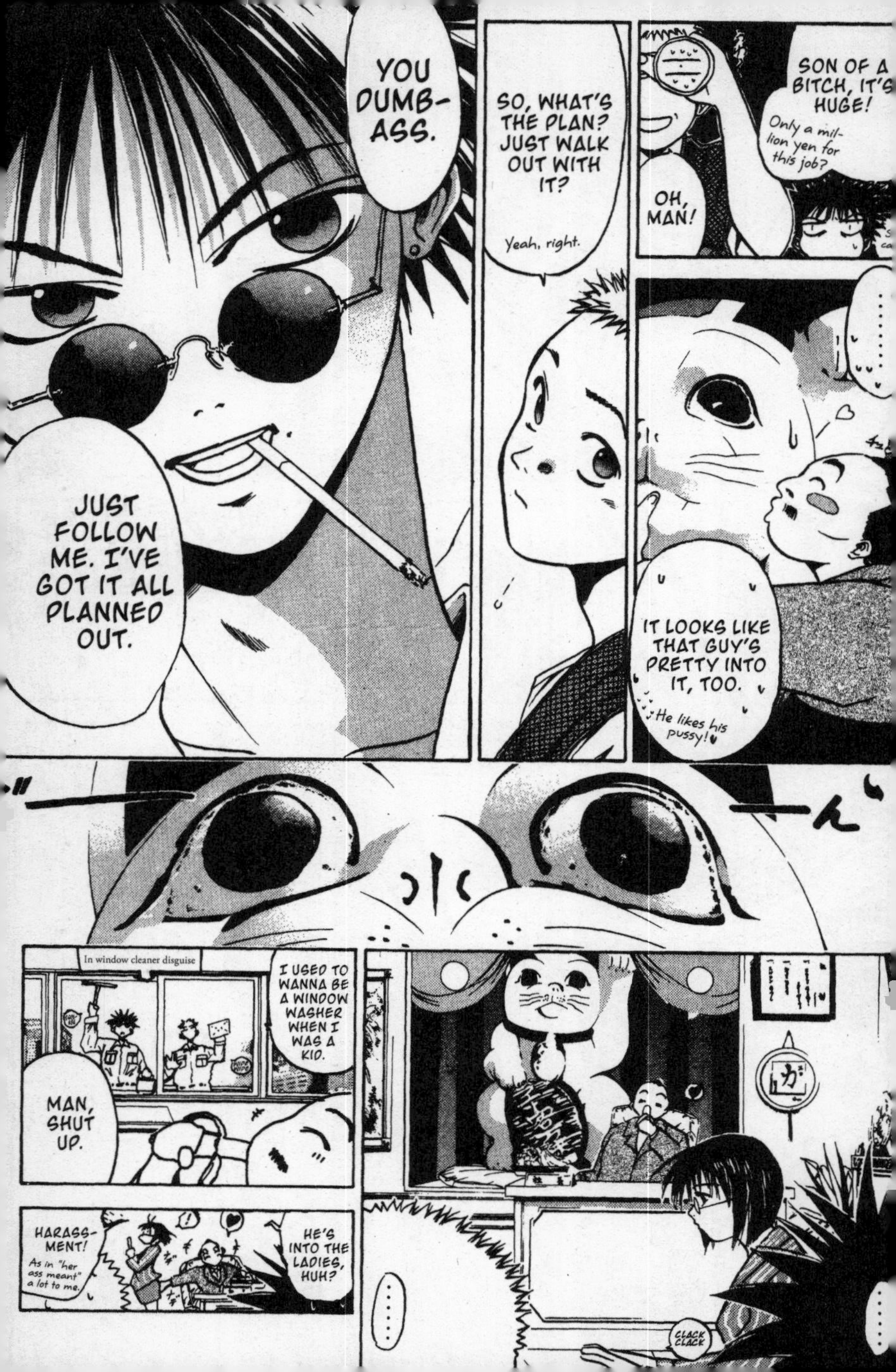
SON OF A BITCH, IT'S HUGE!
Only a million yen for this job?
OH, MAN!
....
IT LOOKS LIKE THAT GUY'S PRETTY INTO IT, TOO.
He likes his pussy!
SO, WHAT'S THE PLAN? JUST WALK OUT WITH IT?
Yeah, right.
YOU DUMB-ASS.
JUST FOLLOW ME. I'VE GOT IT ALL PLANNED OUT.
CLACK CLACK
......
In window cleaner disguise
I USED TO WANNA BE A WINDOW WASHER WHEN I WAS A KID.
MAN, SHUT UP.
HE'S INTO THE LADIES, HUH?
HARASSMENT!
As in "her ass meant" a lot to me.

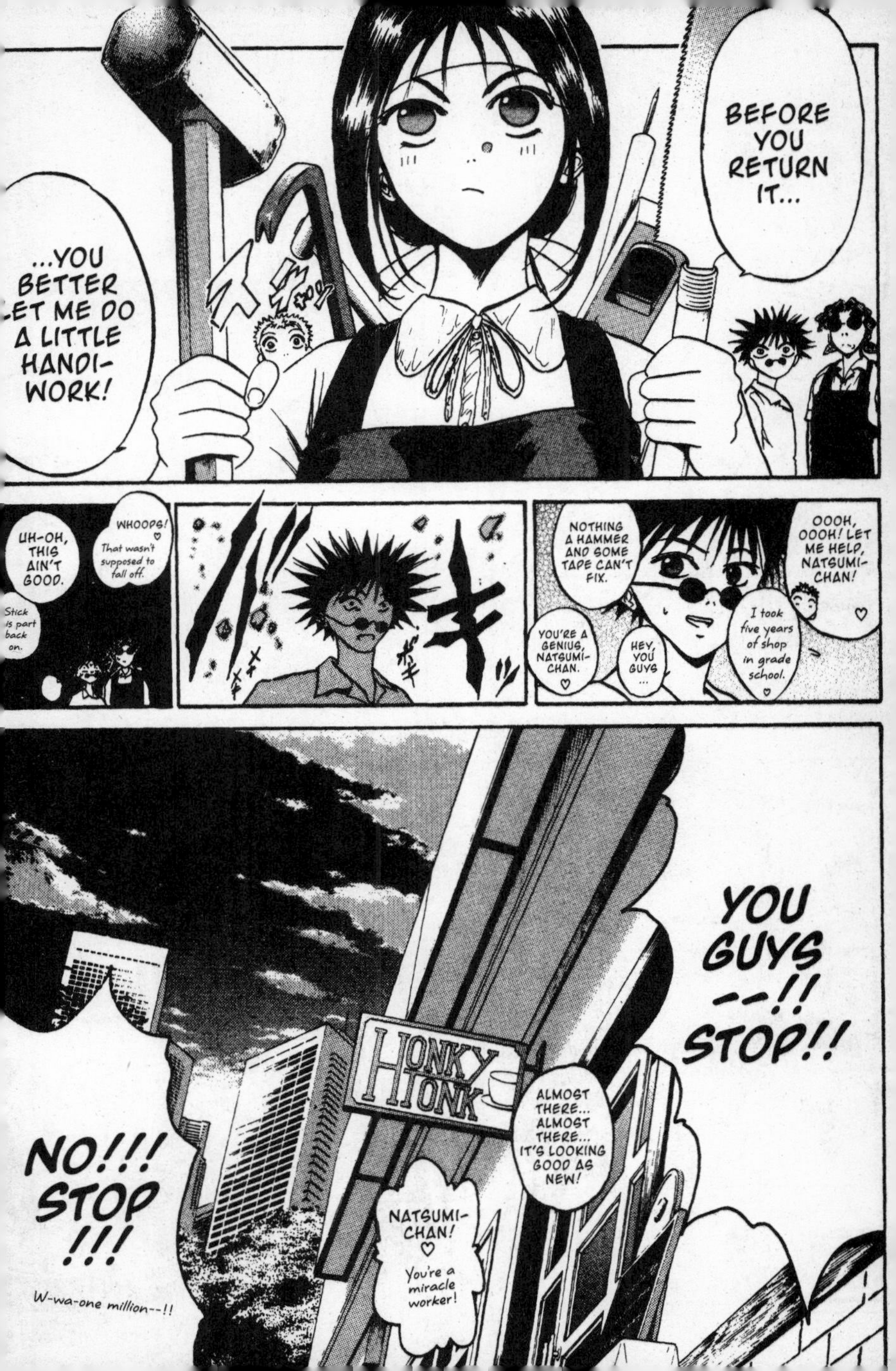

BEFORE YOU RETURN IT...
...YOU BETTER -ET ME DO A LITTLE HANDIWORK!
OOOH, OOOH! LET ME HELP, NATSUMI-CHAN! ♡
I took five years of shop in grade school. ♡
NOTHING A HAMMER AND SOME TAPE CAN'T FIX.
HEY, YOU GUYS ...
YOU'RE A GENIUS, NATSUMI-CHAN. ♡
WHOOPS! ♡ That wasn't supposed to fall off.
UH-OH, THIS AIN'T GOOD.
Stick is part back on.
YOU GUYS --!! STOP!!
HONKY TONK
ALMOST THERE... ALMOST THERE... IT'S LOOKING GOOD AS NEW!
NATSUMI-CHAN! ♡ You're a miracle worker!
NO!!! STOP!!!
W-wa-one million--!!

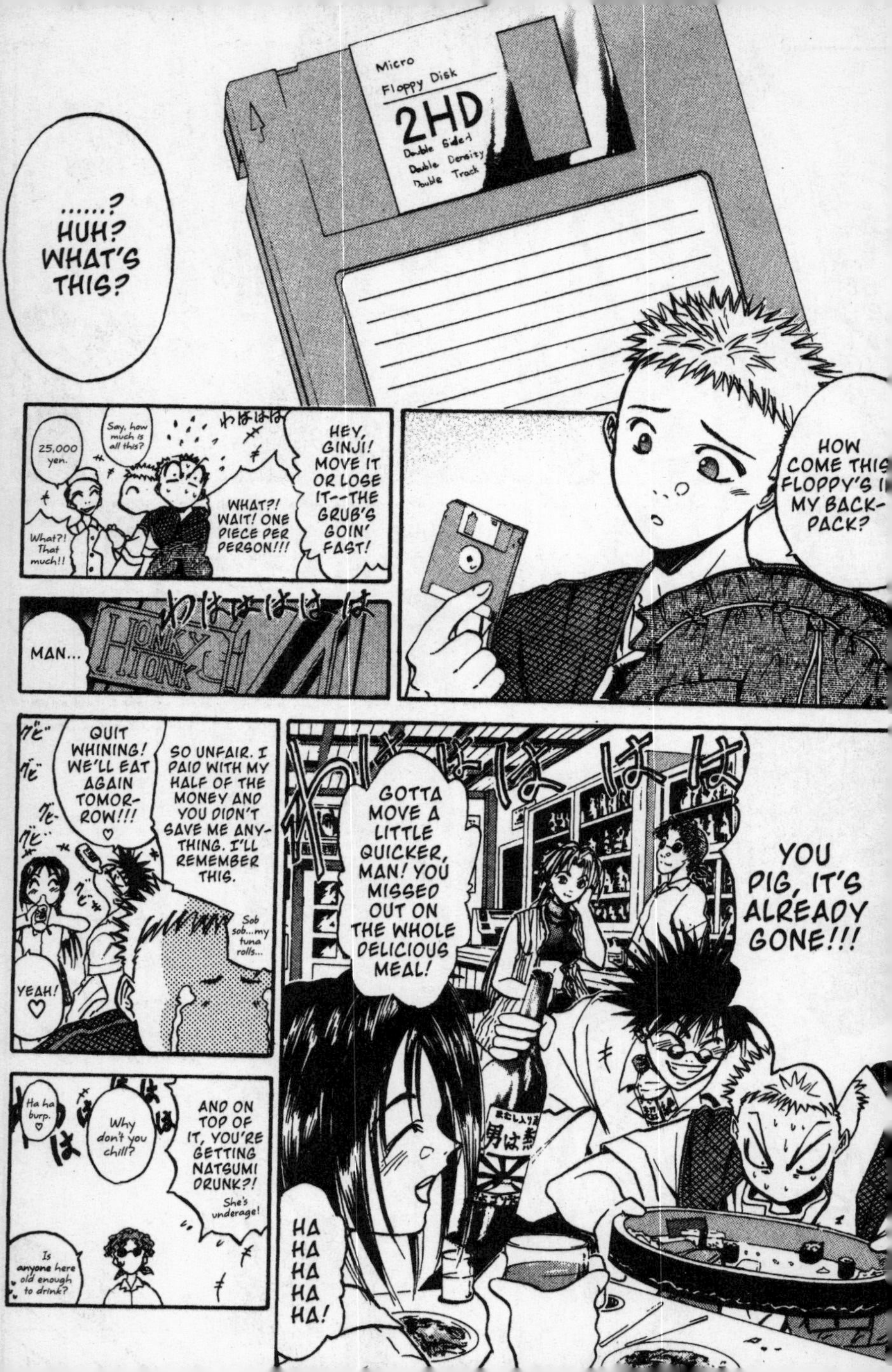

Micro Floppy Disk
2HD
Double Sided Double Density Double Track
......? HUH? WHAT'S THIS?
HOW COME THIS FLOPPY'S I MY BACK-PACK?
わははは
HEY, GINJI! MOVE IT OR LOSE IT--THE GRUB'S GOIN' FAST!
WHAT?! WAIT! ONE PIECE PER PERSON!!!
Say, how much is all this?
25,000 yen.
What?! That much!!
わはははは は
HONKY TONK
MAN...
YOU PIG, IT'S ALREADY GONE!!!
GOTTA MOVE A LITTLE QUICKER, MAN! YOU MISSED OUT ON THE WHOLE DELICIOUS MEAL!
HA HA HA HA HA!
SO UNFAIR. I PAID WITH MY HALF OF THE MONEY AND YOU DIDN'T SAVE ME ANYTHING. I'LL REMEMBER THIS.
QUIT WHINING! WE'LL EAT AGAIN TOMOR-ROW!!! ♡
グビ グビ グビ グビ
Sob sob...my tuna rolls...
YEAH! ♡
AND ON TOP OF IT, YOU'RE GETTING NATSUMI DRUNK?!
She's underage!
Why don't you chill?
Ha ha burp. ♡
Is anyone here old enough to drink?

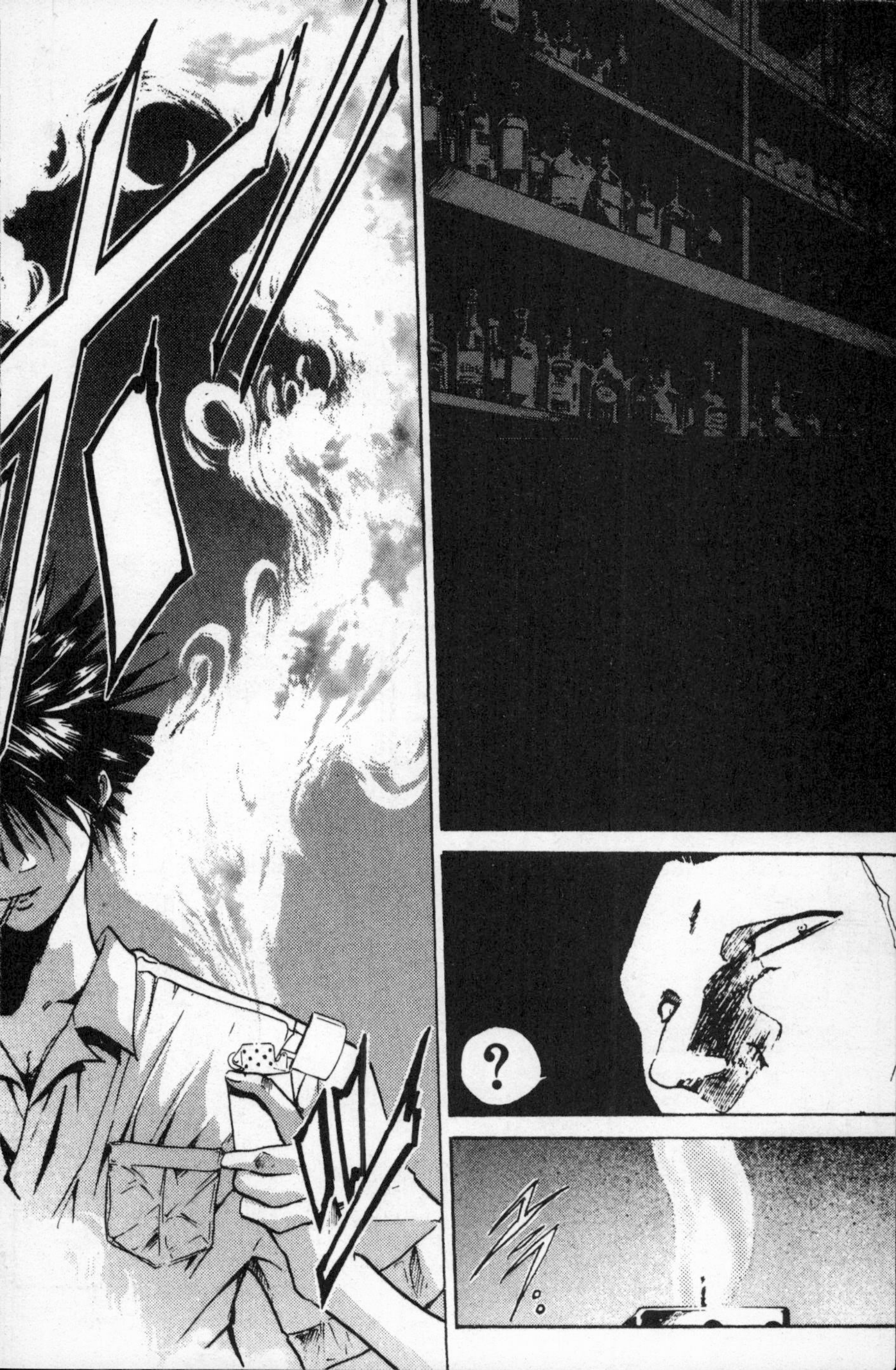
?

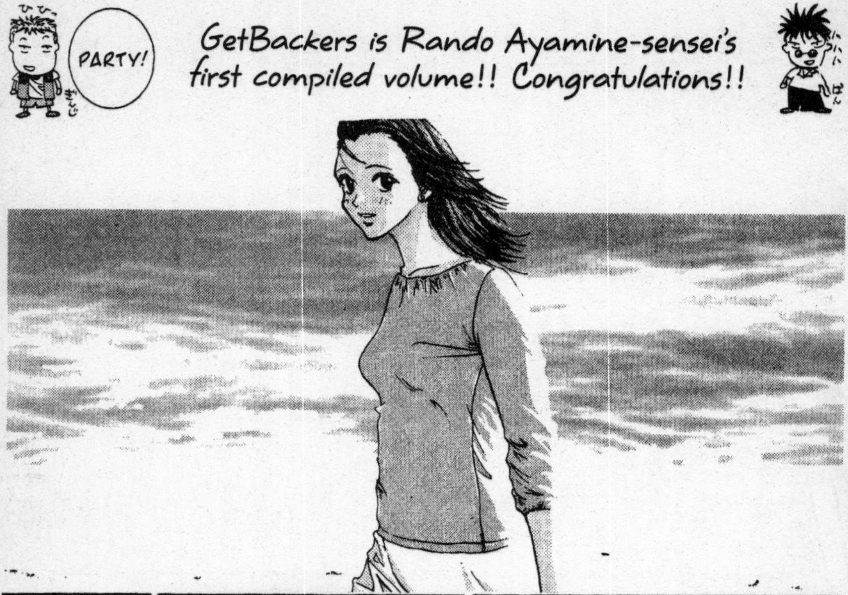
PARTY!
GetBackers is Rando Ayamine-sensei's first compiled volume!! Congratulations!!

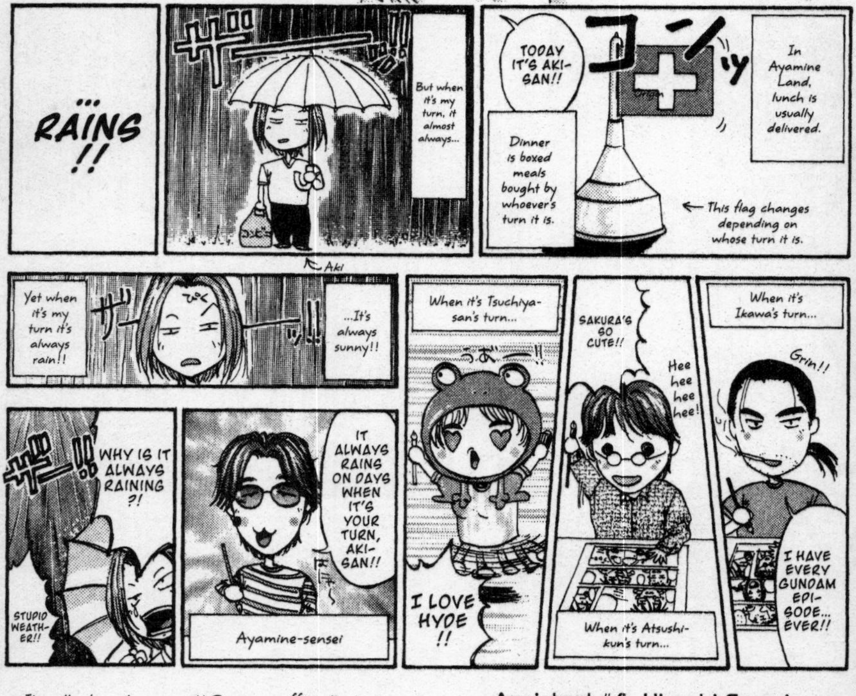
In Ayamine Land, lunch is usually delivered.
Dinner is boxed meals bought by whoever's turn it is.
TODAY IT'S AKI-SAN!!
← This flag changes depending on whose turn it is.
But when it's my turn, it almost always...
← Aki
...RAINS!!
When it's Ikawa's turn...
Grin!!
I HAVE EVERY GUNDAM EPI-SODE... EVER!!
SAKURA'S SO CUTE!!
Hee hee hee hee!
When it's Atsushi-kun's turn...
When it's Tsuchiya-san's turn...
I LOVE HYOE!!
...It's always sunny!!
Yet when it's my turn it's always rain!!
IT ALWAYS RAINS ON DAYS WHEN IT'S YOUR TURN, AKI-SAN!!
Ayamine-sensei
WHY IS IT ALWAYS RAINING?!
STUDIO WEATH-ER!!

It really does always rain!! Pisses me off!!! End.

Assistant #4 Hiroaki Enami

Introduction:

Blond, hip, pragmatic and cool, Ginji Amano has the power to generate electric currents with his body, like an electric eel. Dark-haired, hip, bespectacled and rambunctious, Ban Mido has the mystical, mysterious Evil Eye, the power to create illusions in the minds of his foe. Together, they are the GetBackers, the best retrieval team in the world. They can get back anything taken from their clients, and their success rate is...(almost)...100%! However, they have to scare up some clients soon or this spry detective duo will starve on the streets, homeless and without the money to pay for a single dinner date. Well, they can either get a paying client...or meet women that will pay for their meals. Perhaps getting the client will prove easier...

Table of Contents

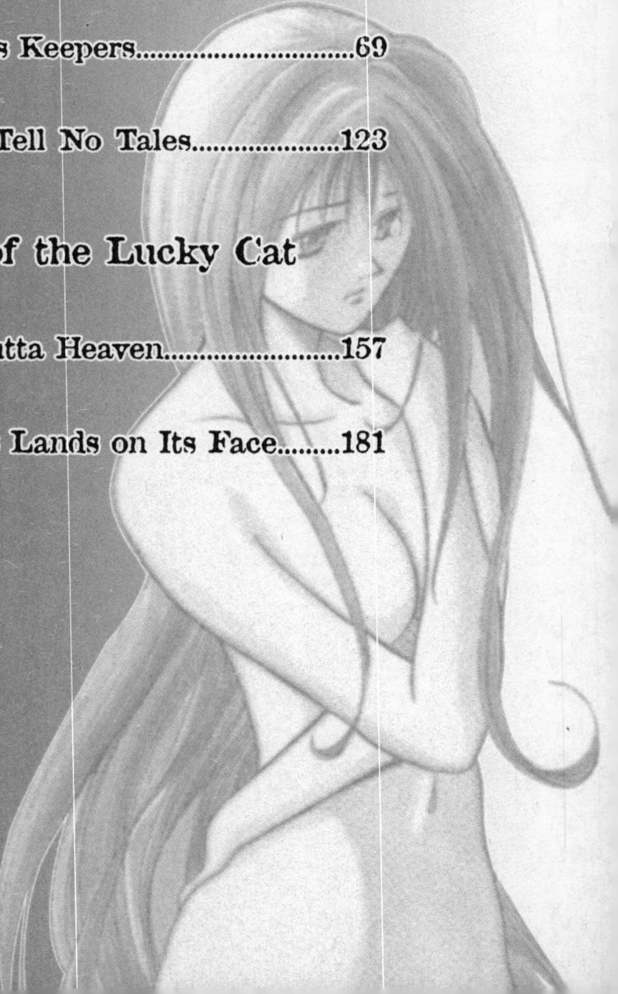

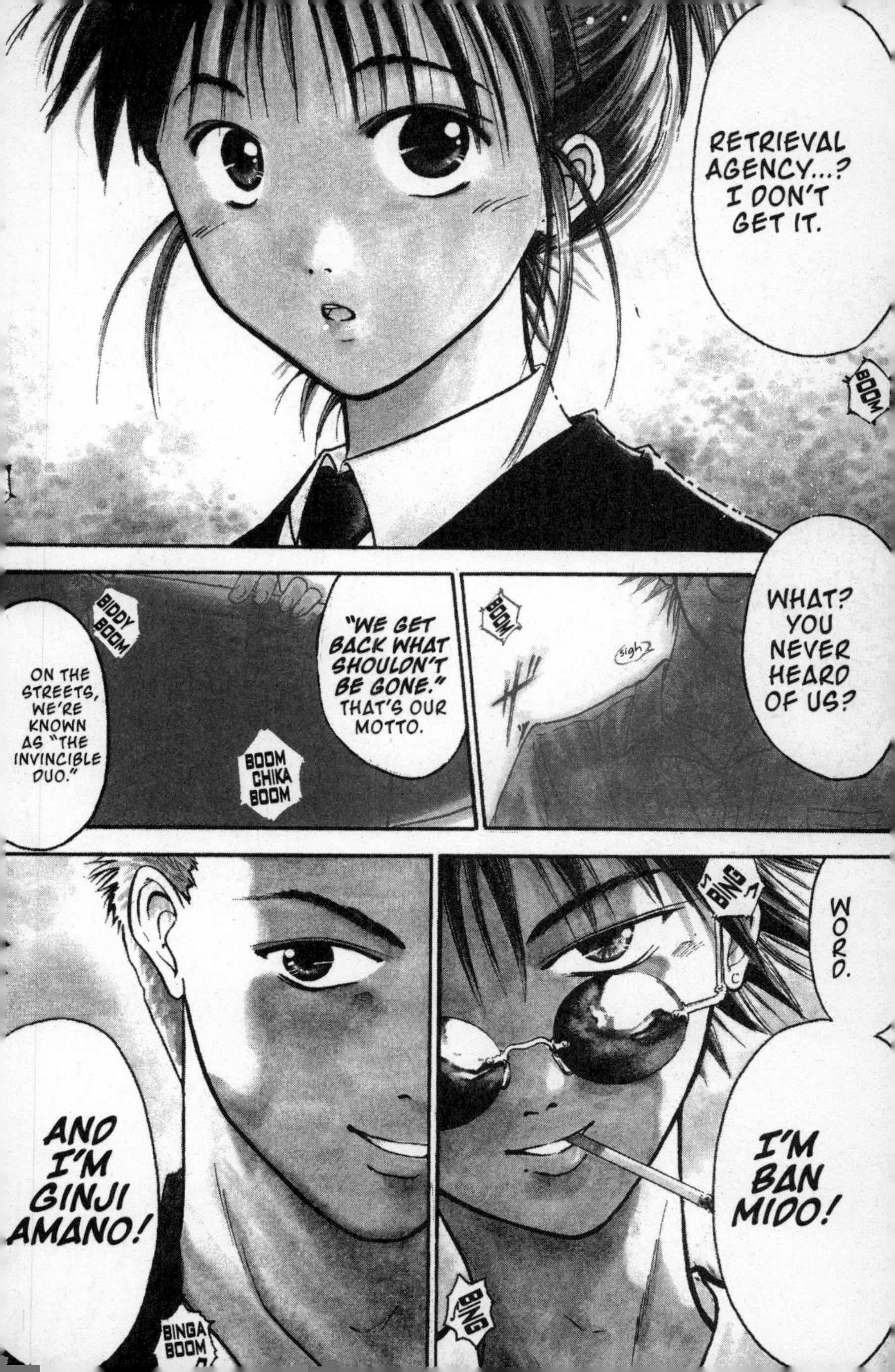
RETRIEVAL AGENCY...? I DON'T GET IT.
BOOM
WHAT? YOU NEVER HEARD OF US?
BOOM
sigh
"WE GET BACK WHAT SHOULDN'T BE GONE." THAT'S OUR MOTTO.
BIDDY BOOM
ON THE STREETS, WE'RE KNOWN AS "THE INVINCIBLE DUO."
BOOM CHIKA BOOM
BING
WORD.
I'M BAN MIDO!
BING
AND I'M GINJI AMANO!
BINGA BOOM

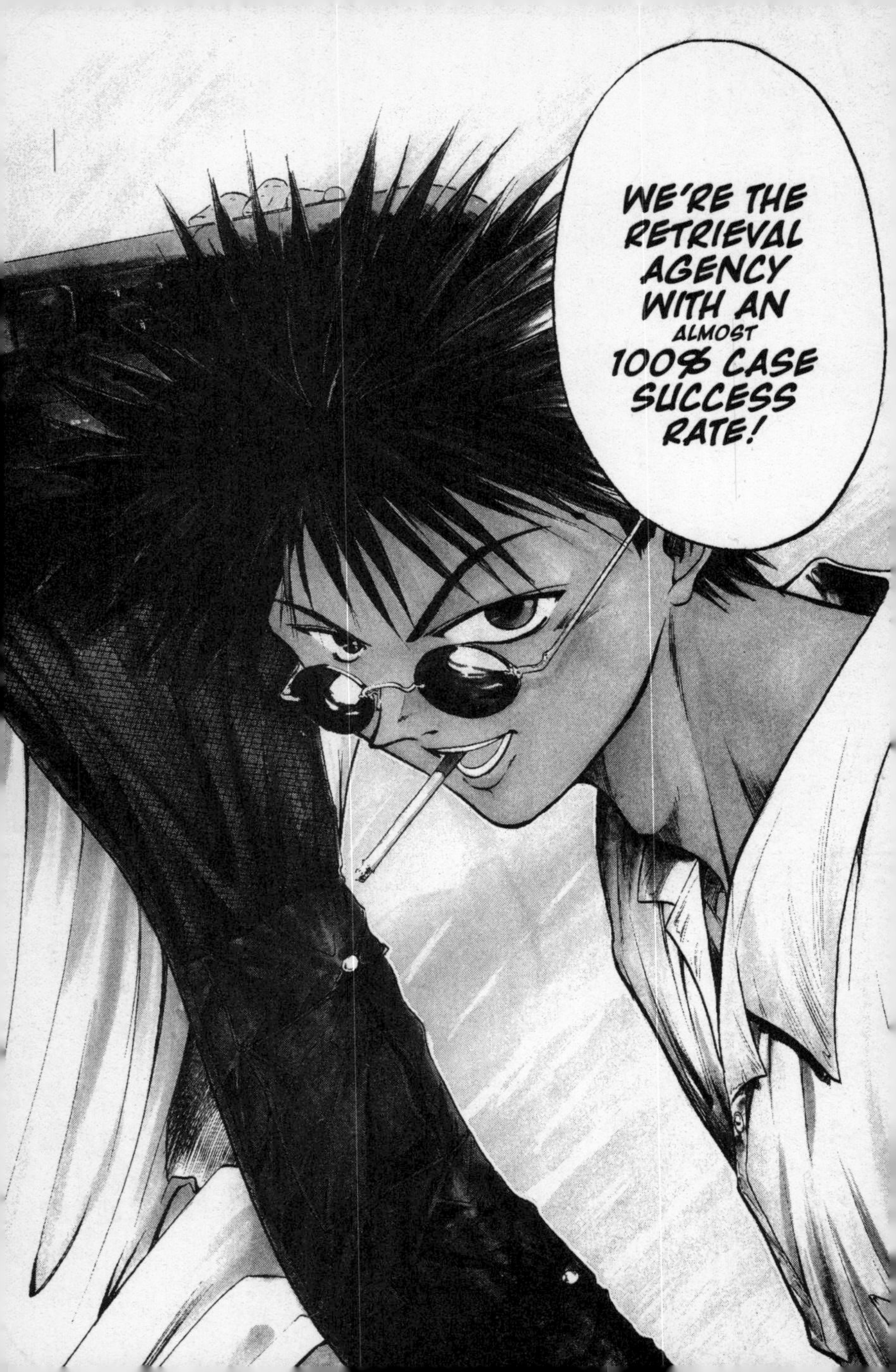
WE'RE THE RETRIEVAL AGENCY WITH AN ALMOST 100% CASE SUCCESS RATE!

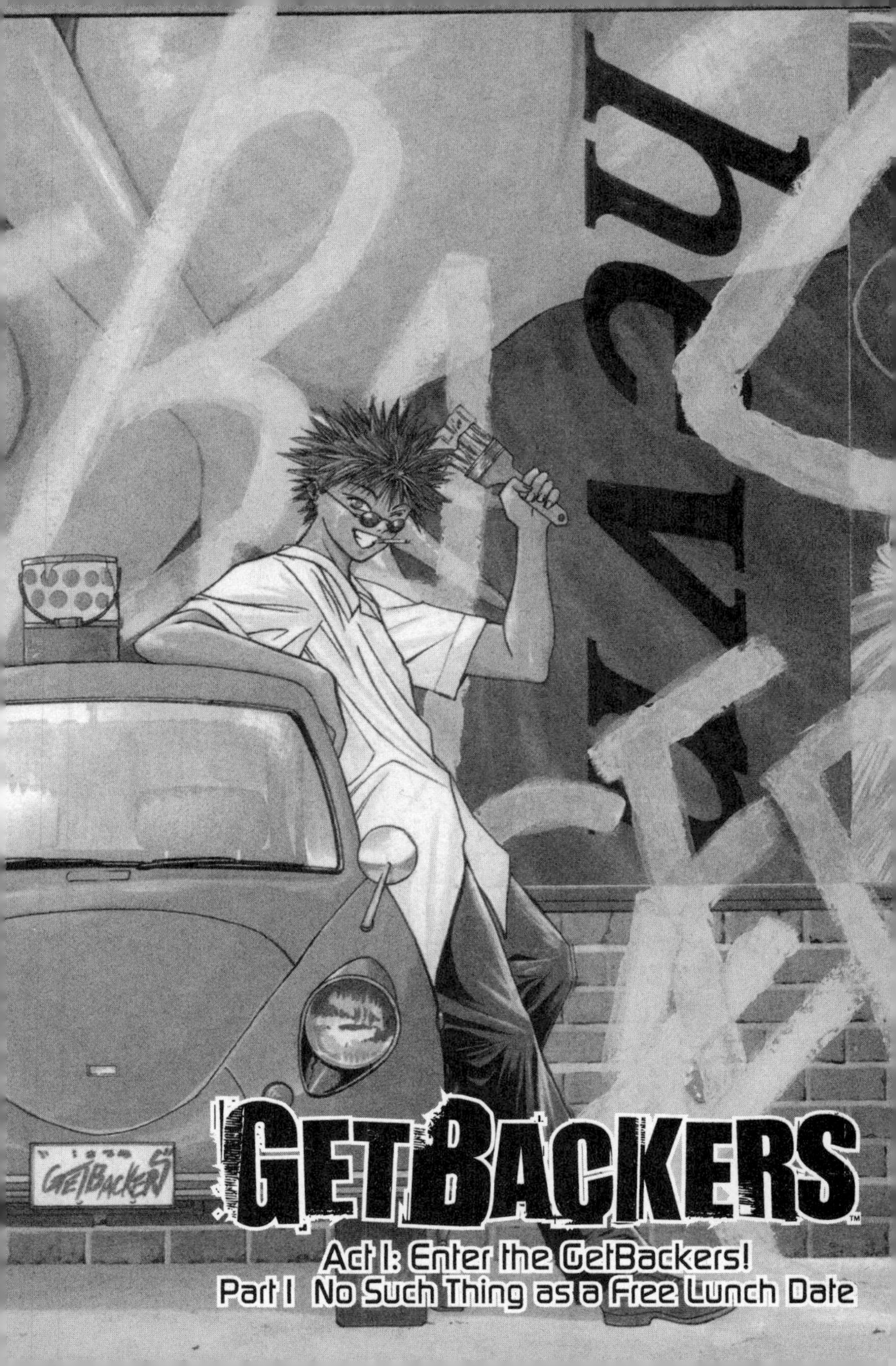
GETBACKERS
GETBACKERS™
Act I: Enter the GetBackers!
Part I No Such Thing as a Free Lunch Date

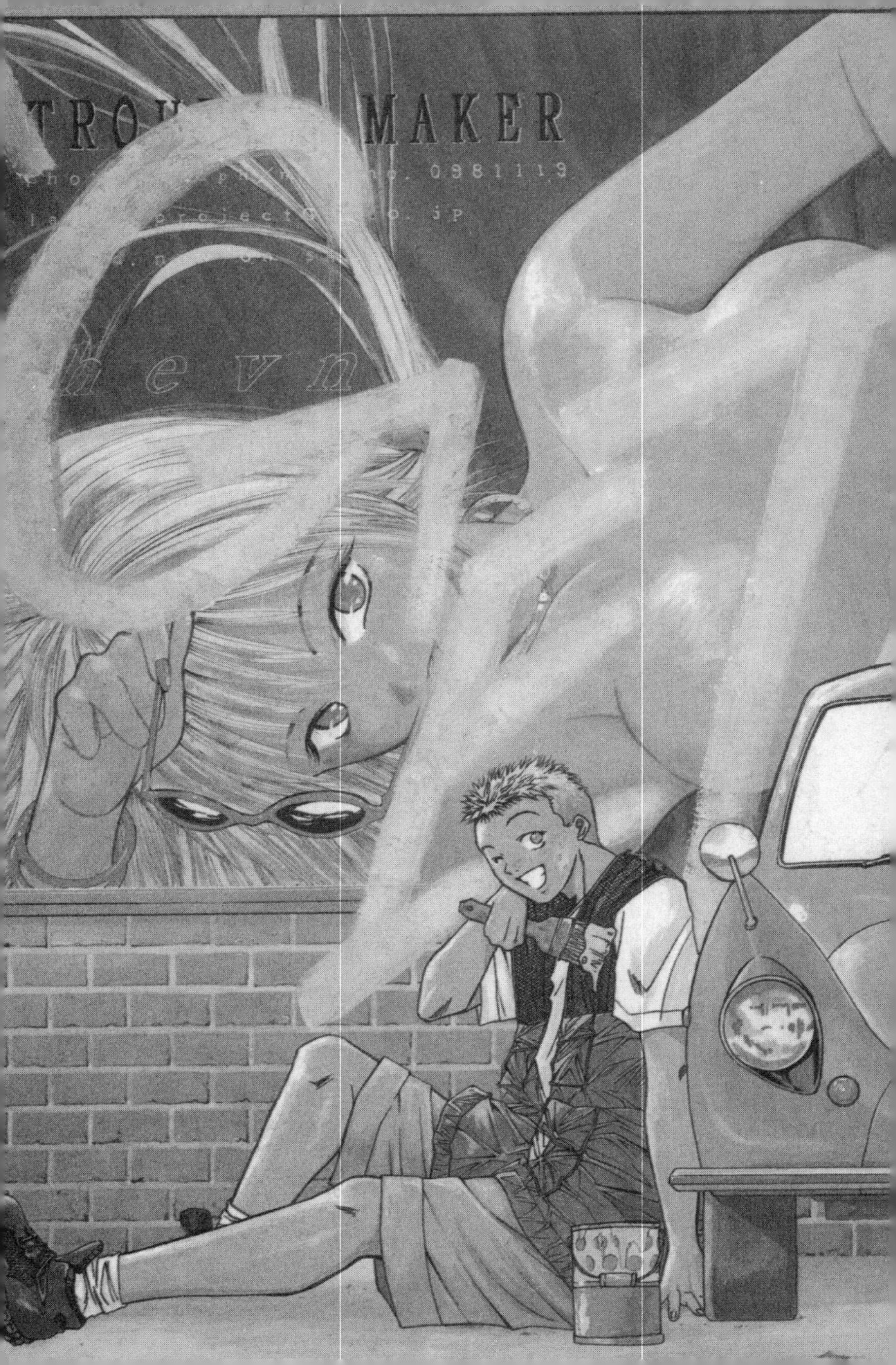
TROU
MAKER

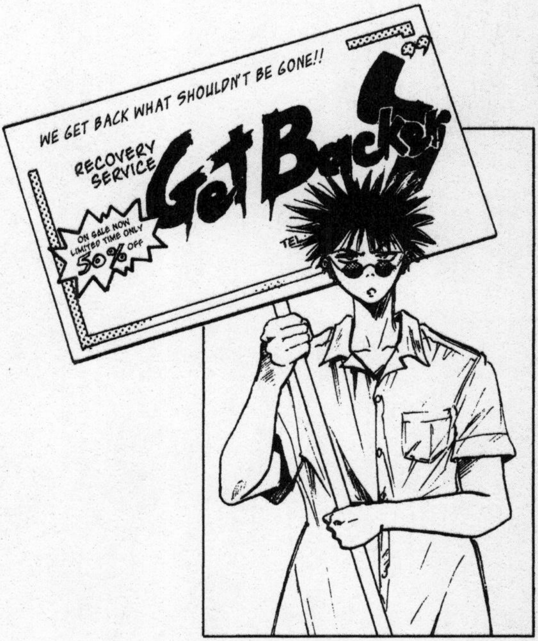
WE GET BACK WHAT SHOULDN'T BE GONE!!
RECOVERY SERVICE
GetBackers
ON SALE NOW LIMITED TIME ONLY 50% OFF
TEL

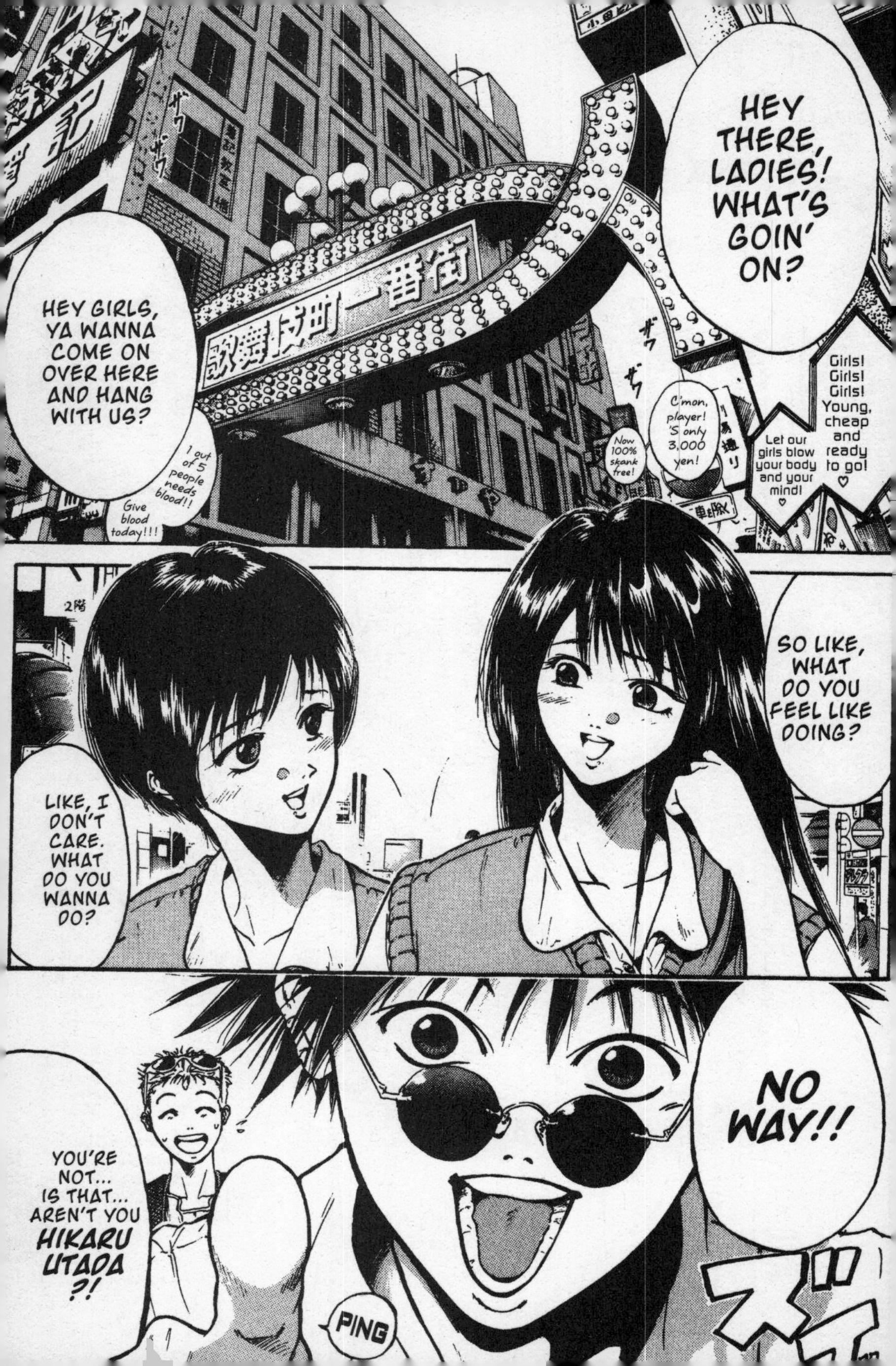
HEY THERE, LADIES! WHAT'S GOIN' ON?
Girls! Girls! Girls! Young, cheap and ready to go! ♡
Let our girls blow your body and your mind! ♡
C'mon, player! 'S only 3,000 yen!
Now 100% skank free!
歌舞伎町一番街
HEY GIRLS, YA WANNA COME ON OVER HERE AND HANG WITH US?
1 out of 5 people needs blood!!
Give blood today!!!
SO LIKE, WHAT DO YOU FEEL LIKE DOING?
LIKE, I DON'T CARE. WHAT DO YOU WANNA DO?
NO WAY!!
PING
YOU'RE NOT... IS THAT... AREN'T YOU HIKARU UTADA?!

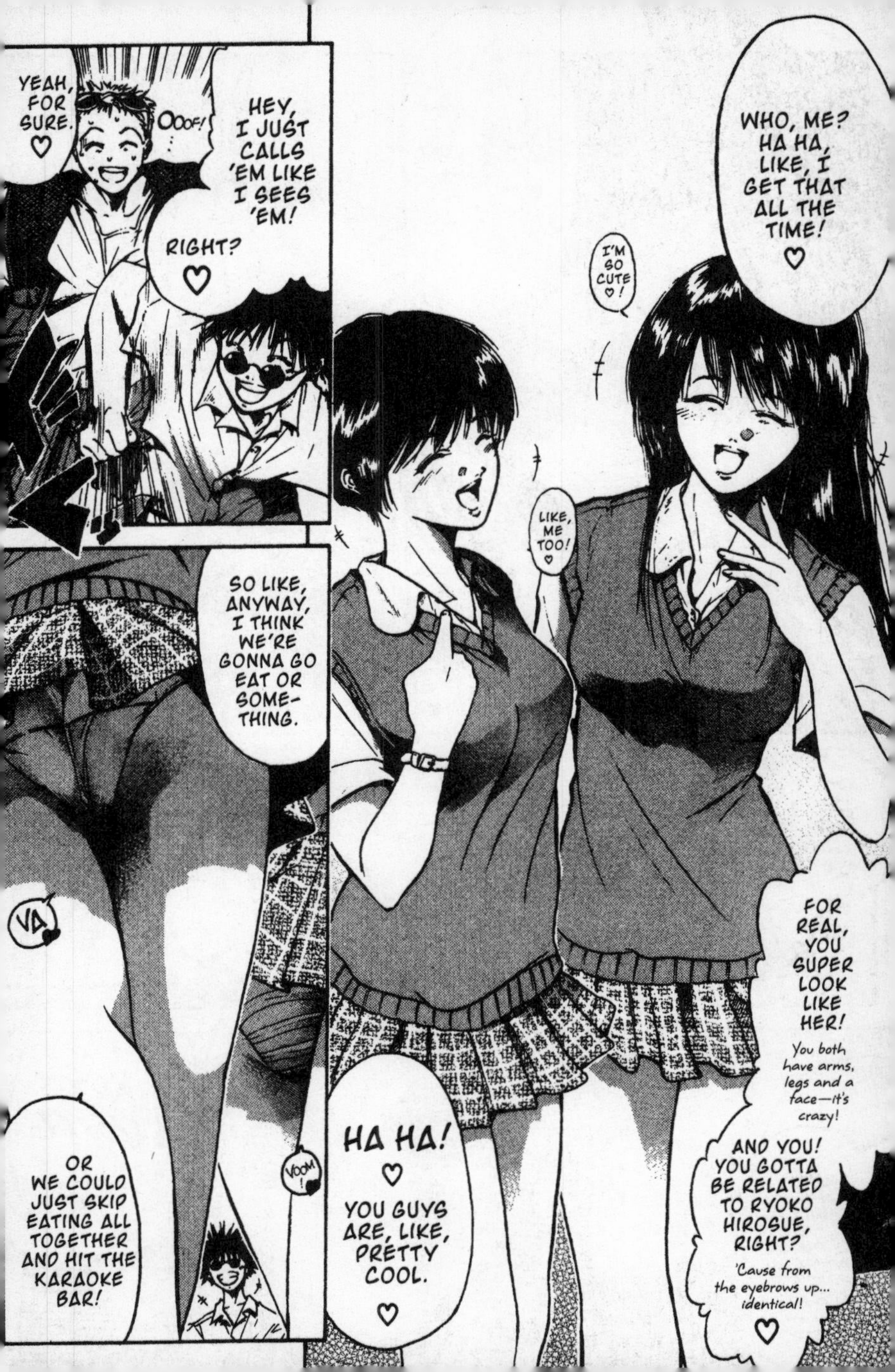
WHO, ME? HA HA, LIKE, I GET THAT ALL THE TIME! ♡
I'M SO CUTE ♡!
LIKE, ME TOO! ♡
FOR REAL, YOU SUPER LOOK LIKE HER!
You both have arms, legs and a face—it's crazy!
AND YOU! YOU GOTTA BE RELATED TO RYOKO HIROSUE, RIGHT?
'Cause from the eyebrows up... identical! ♡
HA HA! ♡ YOU GUYS ARE, LIKE, PRETTY COOL. ♡
HEY, I JUST CALLS 'EM LIKE I SEES 'EM!
OOOF!
YEAH, FOR SURE. ♡
RIGHT? ♡
SO LIKE, ANYWAY, I THINK WE'RE GONNA GO EAT OR SOME-THING.
VA
VOOM!
OR WE COULD JUST SKIP EATING ALL TOGETHER AND HIT THE KARAOKE BAR!

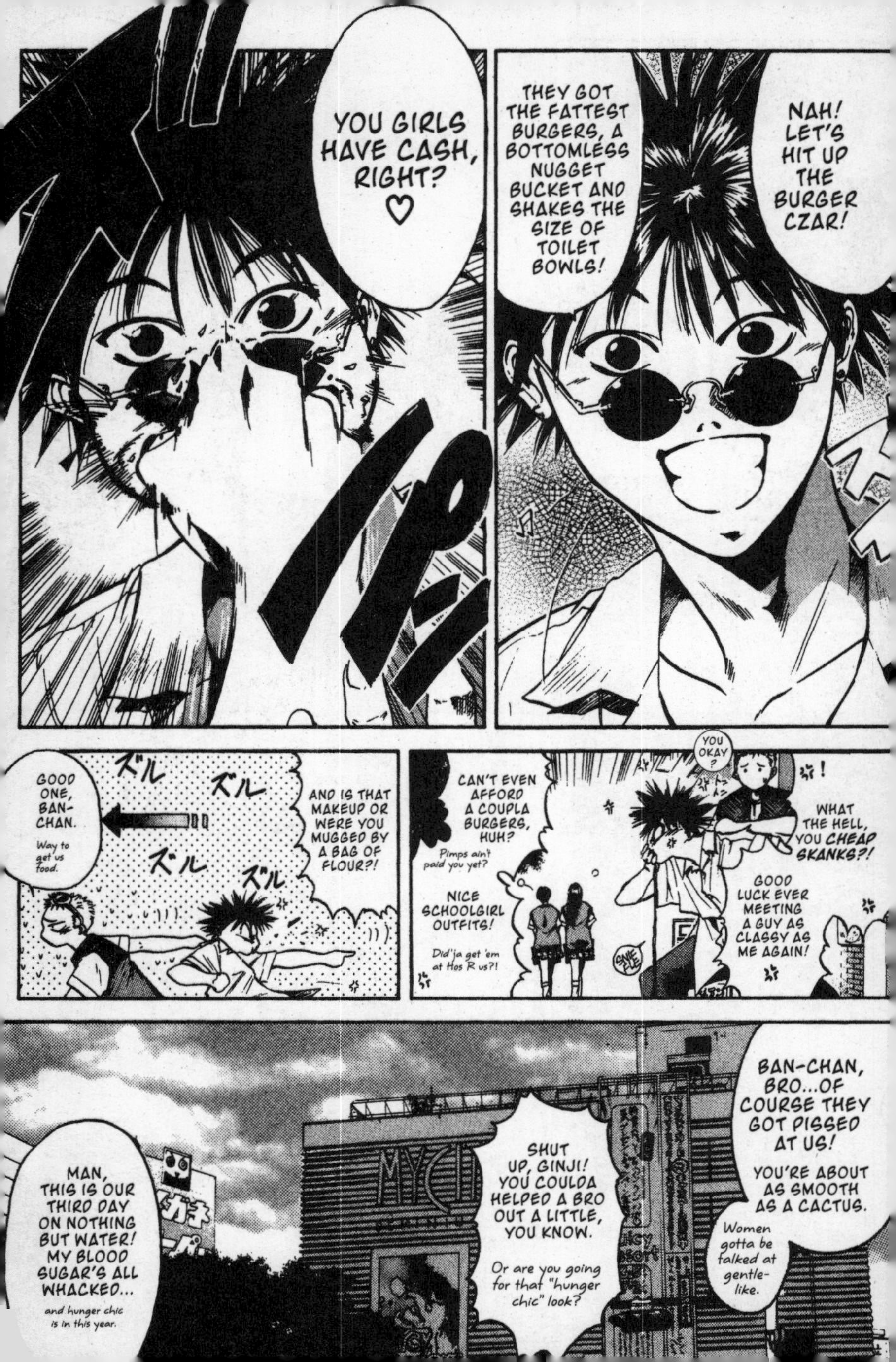
NAH! LET'S HIT UP THE BURGER CZAR!
THEY GOT THE FATTEST BURGERS, A BOTTOMLESS NUGGET BUCKET AND SHAKES THE SIZE OF TOILET BOWLS!
YOU GIRLS HAVE CASH, RIGHT? ♡
YOU OKAY?
WHAT THE HELL, YOU CHEAP SKANKS?!
GOOD LUCK EVER MEETING A GUY AS CLASSY AS ME AGAIN!
CAN'T EVEN AFFORD A COUPLA BURGERS, HUH?
Pimps ain't paid you yet?
NICE SCHOOLGIRL OUTFITS!
Did'ja get 'em at Hos R us?!
ズル
ズル
AND IS THAT MAKEUP OR WERE YOU MUGGED BY A BAG OF FLOUR?!
ズル
ズル
GOOD ONE, BAN-CHAN.
Way to get us food.
BAN-CHAN, BRO...OF COURSE THEY GOT PISSED AT US!
YOU'RE ABOUT AS SMOOTH AS A CACTUS.
Women gotta be talked at gentle-like.
SHUT UP, GINJI! YOU COULDA HELPED A BRO OUT A LITTLE, YOU KNOW.
Or are you going for that "hunger chic" look?
MAN, THIS IS OUR THIRD DAY ON NOTHING BUT WATER! MY BLOOD SUGAR'S ALL WHACKED...
and hunger chic is in this year.

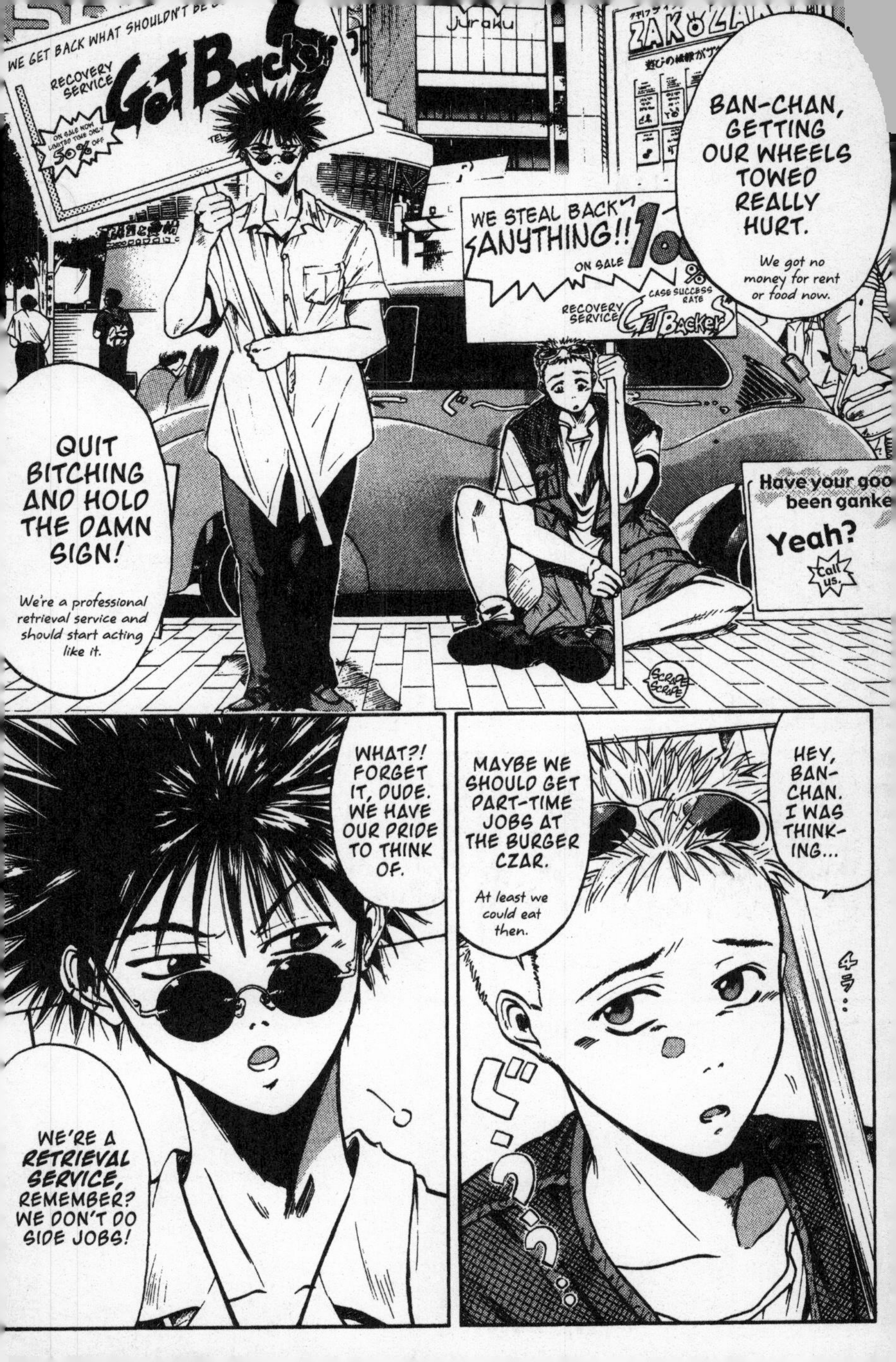
WE GET BACK WHAT SHOULDN'T BE
RECOVERY SERVICE
GetBackers
ON SALE NOW LIMITED TIME ONLY 50% OFF
juraku
BAN-CHAN, GETTING OUR WHEELS TOWED REALLY HURT.
We got no money for rent or food now.
WE STEAL BACK ANYTHING!!
ON SALE
CASE SUCCESS RATE
RECOVERY SERVICE
GetBackers
QUIT BITCHING AND HOLD THE DAMN SIGN!
We're a professional retrieval service and should start acting like it.
Yeah?
Call us.
SCRAPE SCRAPE
HEY, BAN-CHAN. I WAS THINKING...
MAYBE WE SHOULD GET PART-TIME JOBS AT THE BURGER CZAR.
At least we could eat then.
WHAT?! FORGET IT, DUDE. WE HAVE OUR PRIDE TO THINK OF.
WE'RE A RETRIEVAL SERVICE, REMEMBER? WE DON'T DO SIDE JOBS!

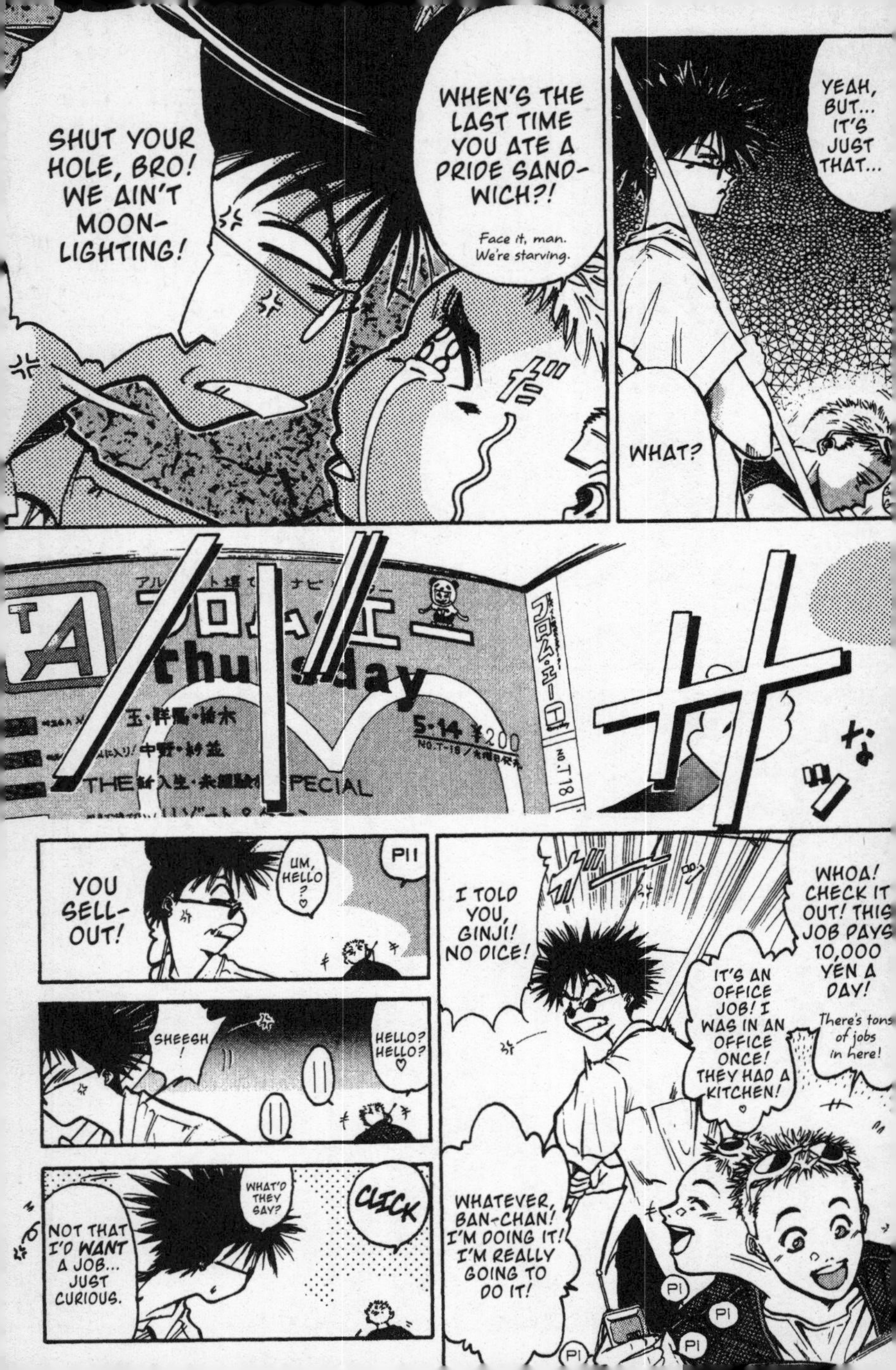
YEAH, BUT... IT'S JUST THAT...
WHAT?
WHEN'S THE LAST TIME YOU ATE A PRIDE SANDWICH?!
Face it, man. We're starving.
SHUT YOUR HOLE, BRO! WE AIN'T MOONLIGHTING!
thursday
5·14 ¥200
NO.T18
WHOA! CHECK IT OUT! THIS JOB PAYS 10,000 YEN A DAY!
There's tons of jobs in here!
IT'S AN OFFICE JOB! I WAS IN AN OFFICE ONCE! THEY HAD A KITCHEN!
I TOLD YOU, GINJI! NO DICE!
WHATEVER, BAN-CHAN! I'M DOING IT! I'M REALLY GOING TO DO IT!
PI
PI
PI
PI
PI!
UM, HELLO?
YOU SELL-OUT!
HELLO? HELLO?
SHEESH!
CLICK
WHAT'D THEY SAY?
NOT THAT I'D WANT A JOB... JUST CURIOUS.

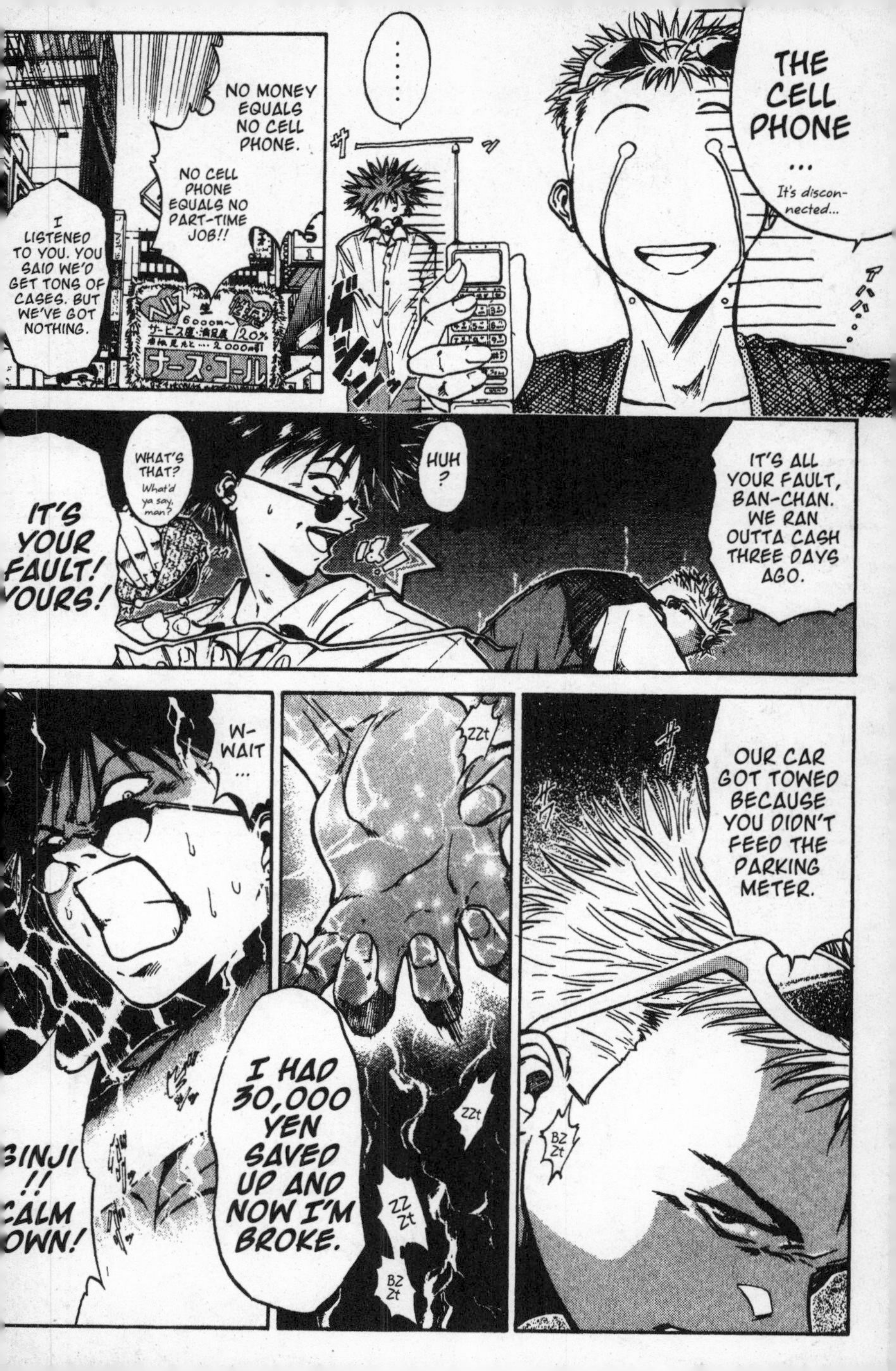
THE CELL PHONE ...
It's disconnected...
......
NO MONEY EQUALS NO CELL PHONE.
NO CELL PHONE EQUALS NO PART-TIME JOB!!
I LISTENED TO YOU. YOU SAID WE'D GET TONS OF CASES. BUT WE'VE GOT NOTHING.
ナース・コール
IT'S ALL YOUR FAULT, BAN-CHAN. WE RAN OUTTA CASH THREE DAYS AGO.
HUH ?
WHAT'S THAT? What'd ya say, man?
IT'S YOUR FAULT! YOURS!
OUR CAR GOT TOWED BECAUSE YOU DIDN'T FEED THE PARKING METER.
BZ Zt
ZZt
I HAD 30,000 YEN SAVED UP AND NOW I'M BROKE.
ZZt
ZZ Zt
BZ Zt
W-WAIT ...
GINJI !! CALM DOWN!

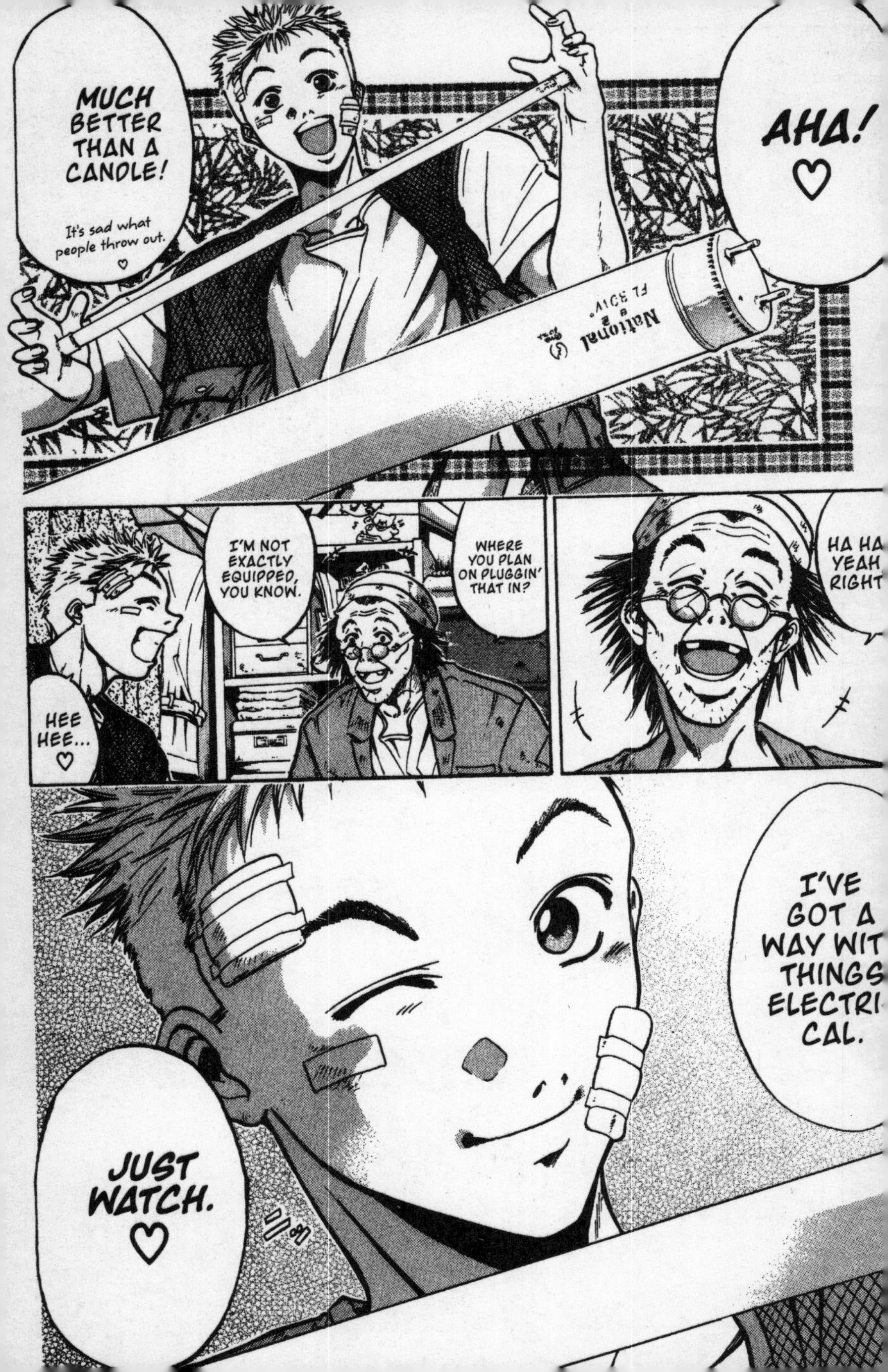
AHA! ♡
MUCH BETTER THAN A CANDLE!
It's sad what people throw out. ♡
HA HA YEAH RIGHT
WHERE YOU PLAN ON PLUGGIN' THAT IN?
I'M NOT EXACTLY EQUIPPED, YOU KNOW.
HEE HEE... ♡
I'VE GOT A WAY WIT THINGS ELECTRI-CAL.
JUST WATCH. ♡

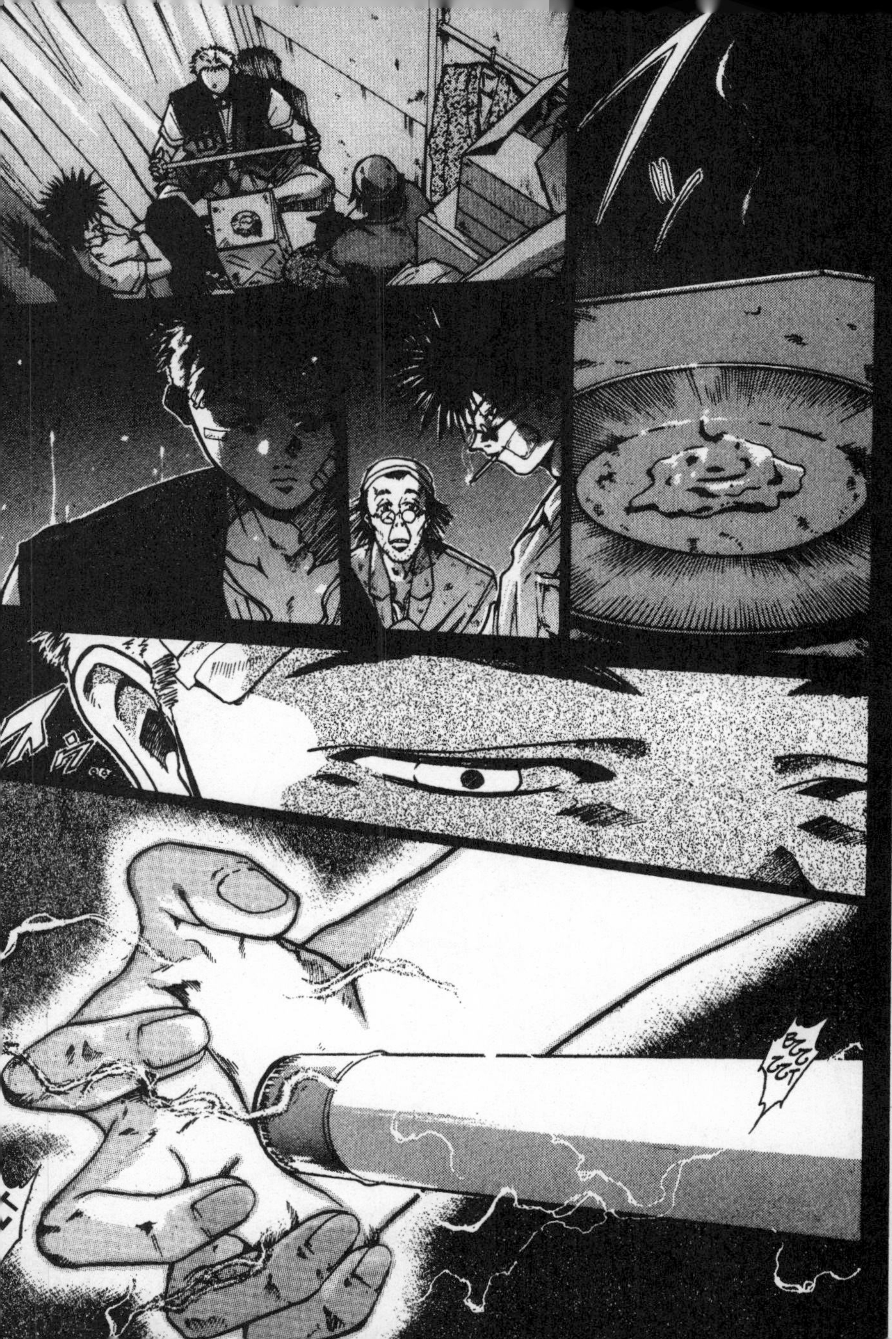
BZZZZZT

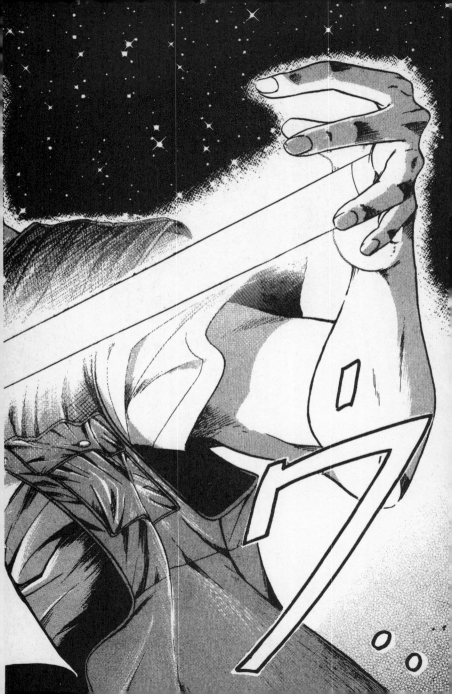

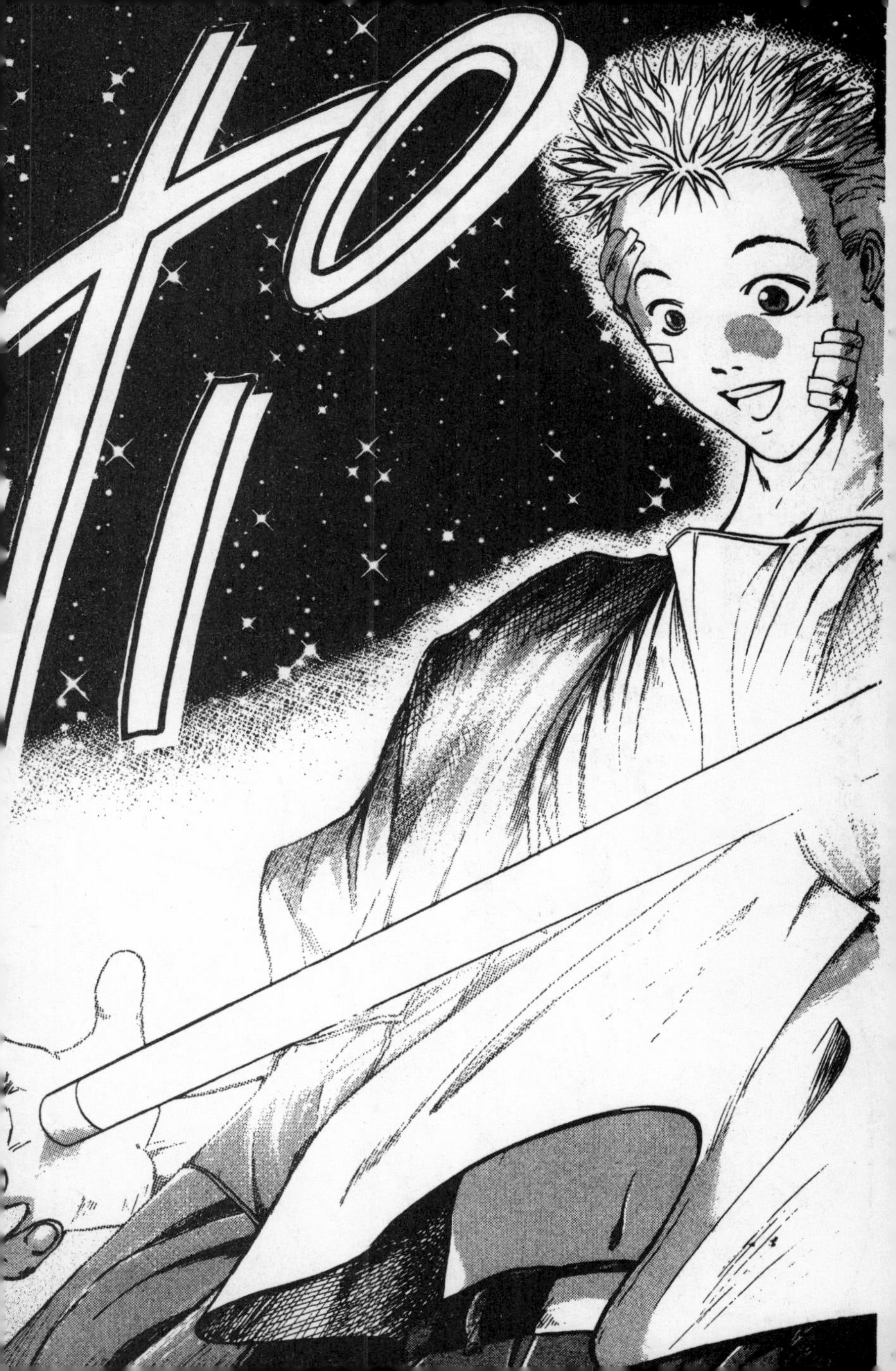
YO

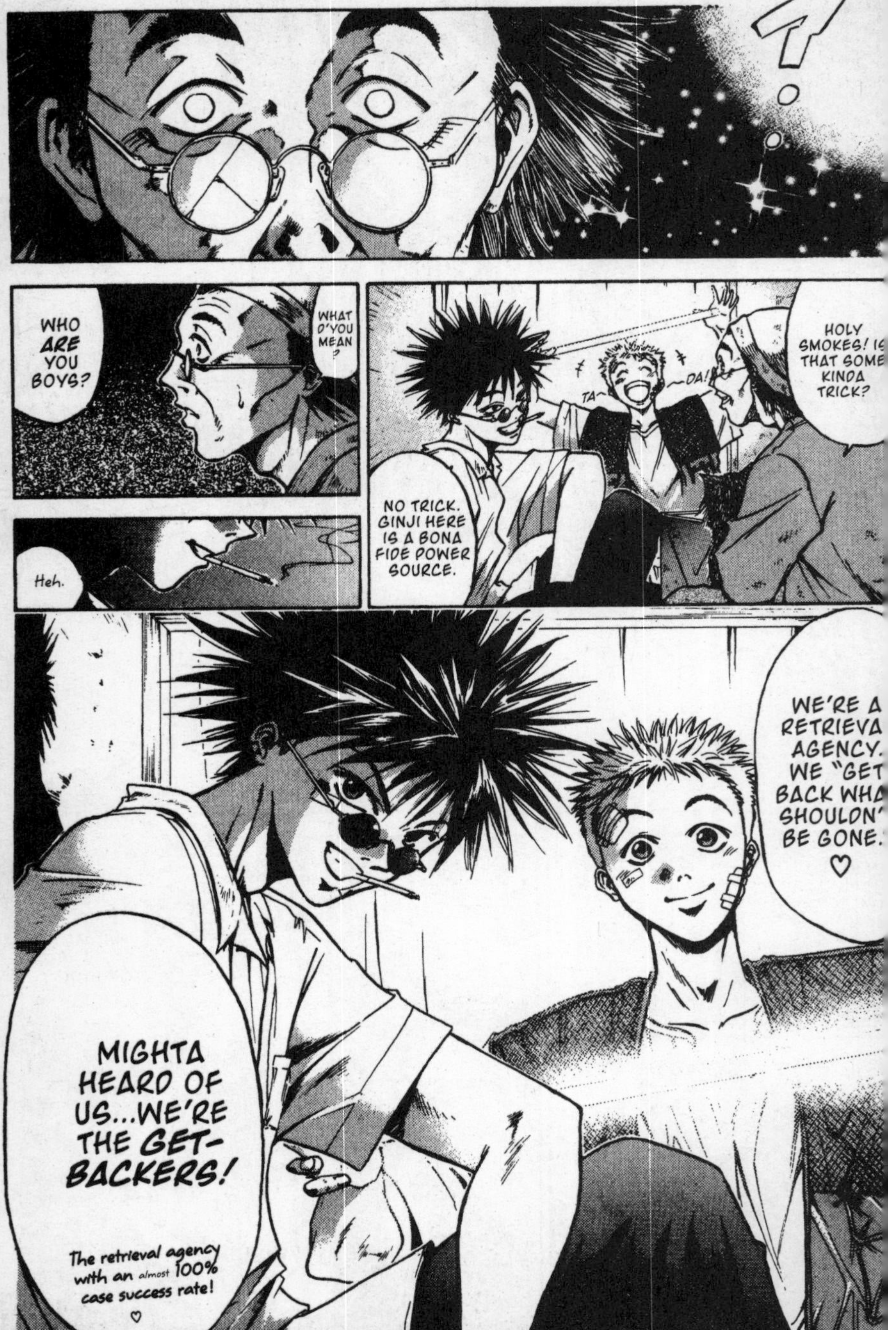

?
HOLY SMOKES! IS THAT SOME KINDA TRICK?
TA~
~DA!
NO TRICK. GINJI HERE IS A BONA FIDE POWER SOURCE.
WHO ARE YOU BOYS?
WHAT D'YOU MEAN?
Heh.
WE'RE A RETRIEVA AGENCY. WE "GET BACK WHA SHOULDN' BE GONE."
MIGHTA HEARD OF US...WE'RE THE GET-BACKERS!
The retrieval agency with an almost 100% case success rate!

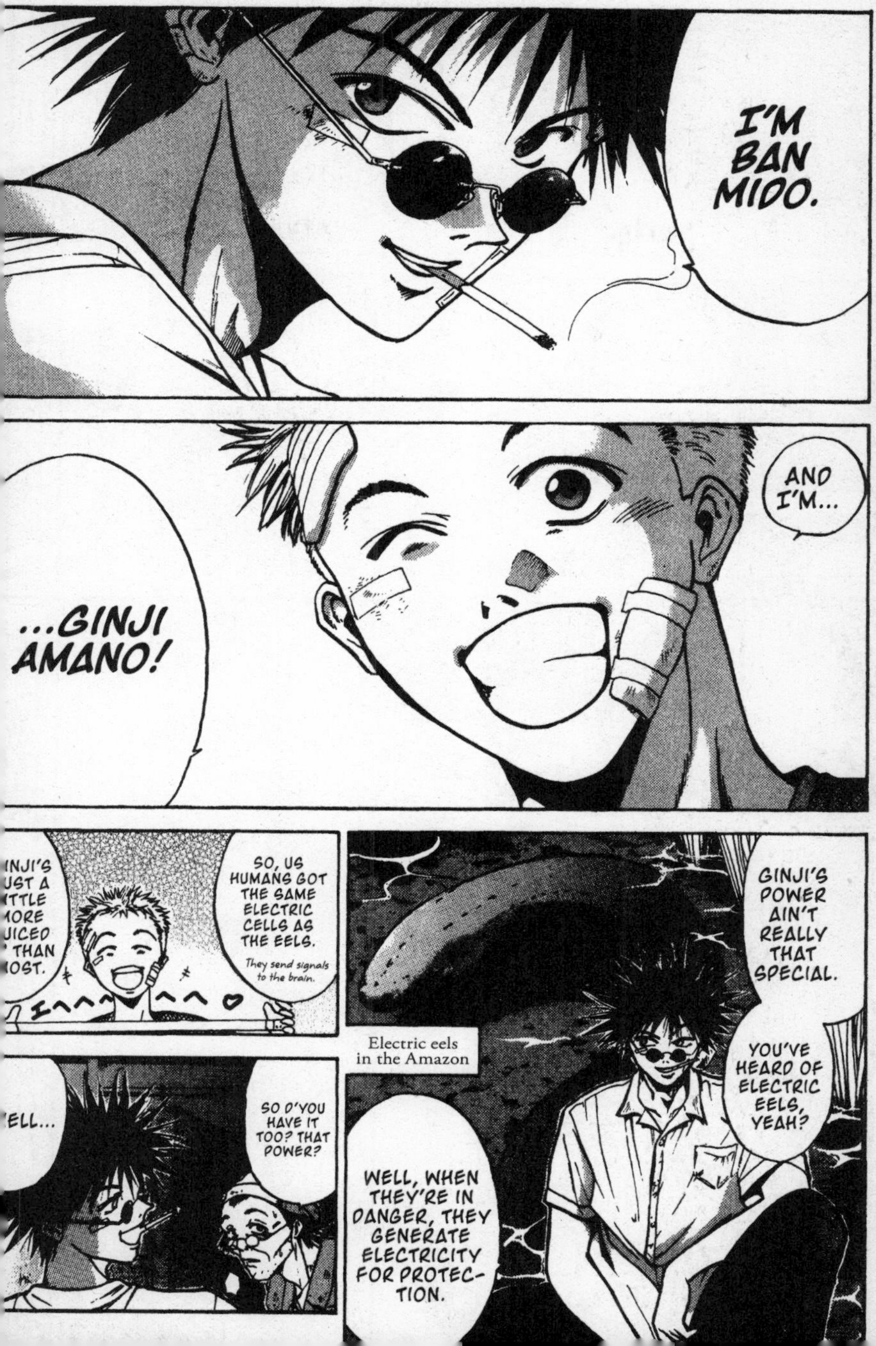
I'M BAN MIDO.
AND I'M...
...GINJI AMANO!
GINJI'S POWER AIN'T REALLY THAT SPECIAL.
YOU'VE HEARD OF ELECTRIC EELS, YEAH?
WELL, WHEN THEY'RE IN DANGER, THEY GENERATE ELECTRICITY FOR PROTECTION.
Electric eels in the Amazon
SO, US HUMANS GOT THE SAME ELECTRIC CELLS AS THE EELS.
They send signals to the brain.
INJI'S UST A ITTLE MORE UICED THAN OST.
I^^^ ^^
SO D'YOU HAVE IT TOO? THAT POWER?
ELL...

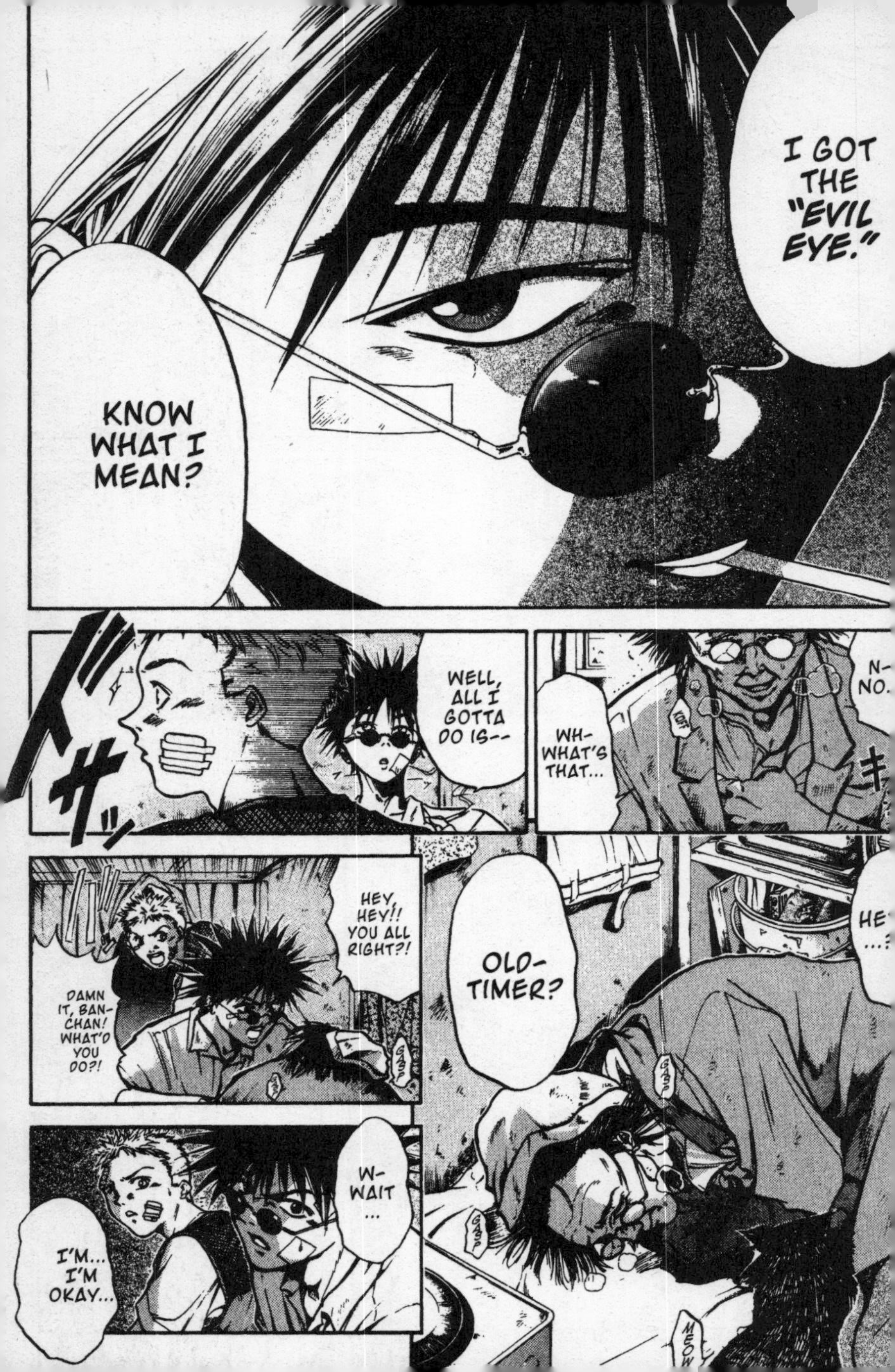
I GOT THE "EVIL EYE."
KNOW WHAT I MEAN?
N- NO.
WH- WHAT'S THAT...
WELL, ALL I GOTTA DO IS--
HE ...?
OLD-TIMER?
GASP
GASP
MEOW
HEY, HEY!! YOU ALL RIGHT?!
DAMN IT, BAN-CHAN! WHAT'D YOU DO?!
GASP
W- WAIT ...
I'M... I'M OKAY...

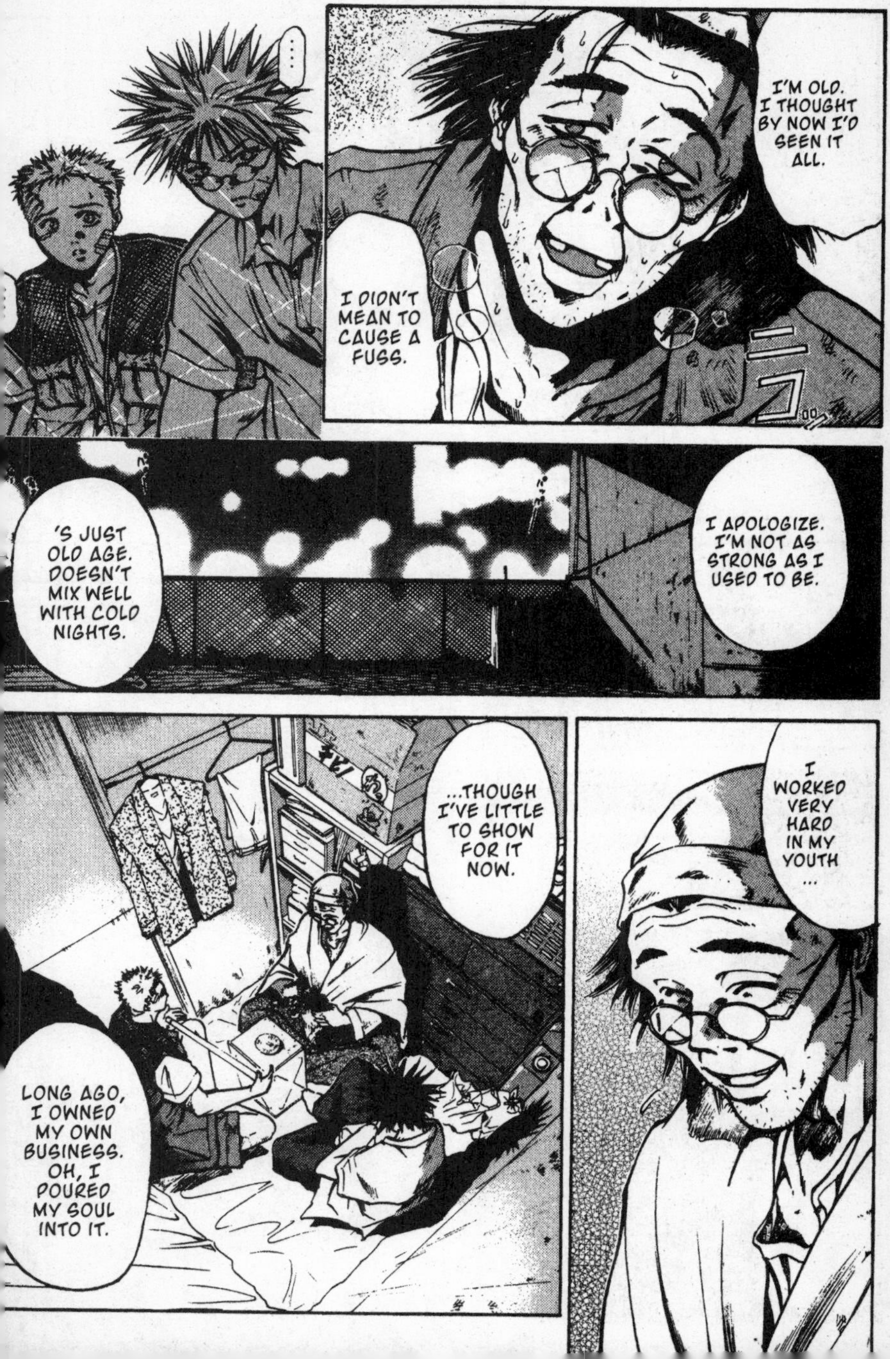
I'M OLD. I THOUGHT BY NOW I'D SEEN IT ALL.
I DIDN'T MEAN TO CAUSE A FUSS.
...
I APOLOGIZE. I'M NOT AS STRONG AS I USED TO BE.
'S JUST OLD AGE. DOESN'T MIX WELL WITH COLD NIGHTS.
I WORKED VERY HARD IN MY YOUTH ...
...THOUGH I'VE LITTLE TO SHOW FOR IT NOW.
LONG AGO, I OWNED MY OWN BUSINESS. OH, I POURED MY SOUL INTO IT.

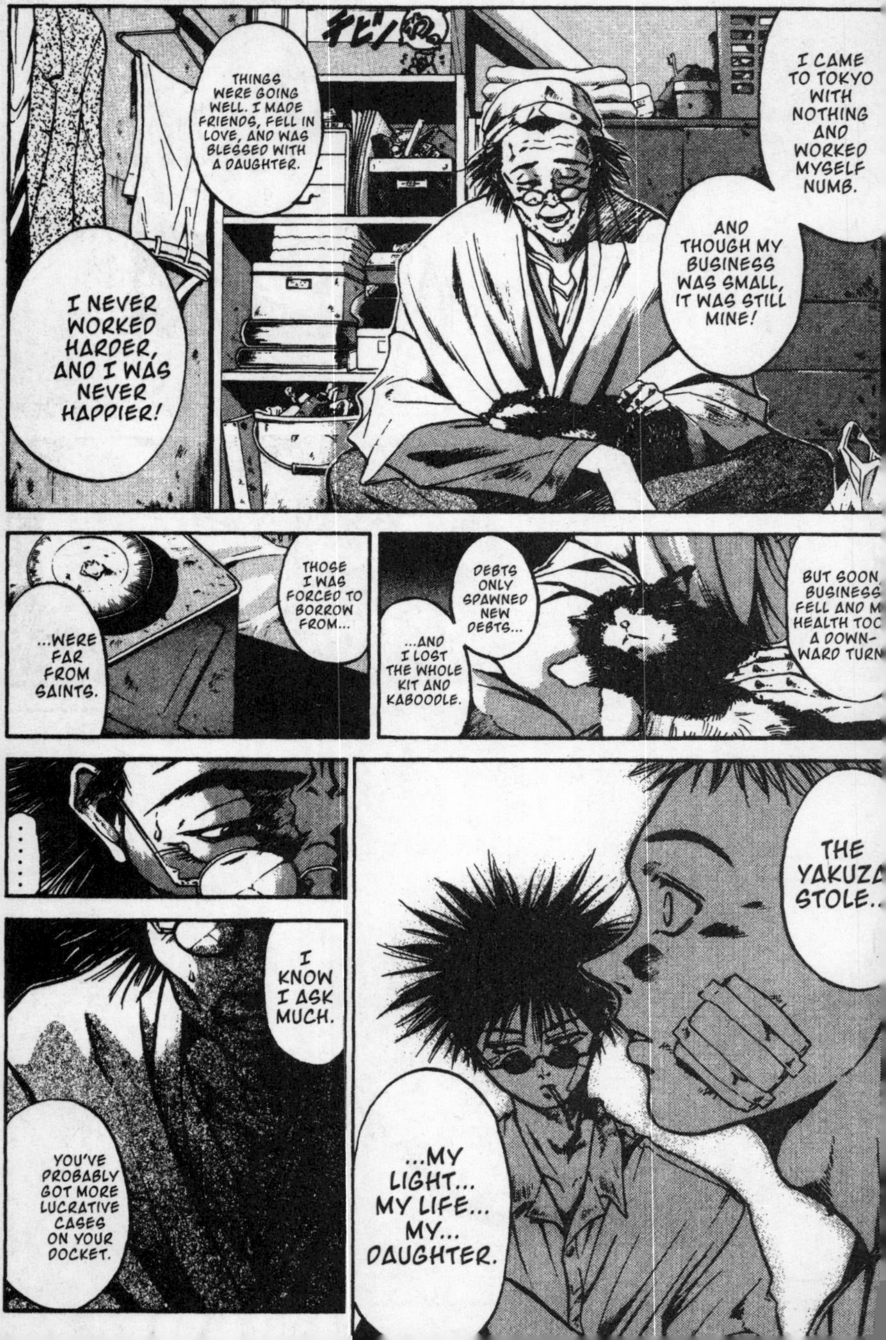
I CAME TO TOKYO WITH NOTHING AND WORKED MYSELF NUMB.
AND THOUGH MY BUSINESS WAS SMALL, IT WAS STILL MINE!
THINGS WERE GOING WELL. I MADE FRIENDS, FELL IN LOVE, AND WAS BLESSED WITH A DAUGHTER.
I NEVER WORKED HARDER, AND I WAS NEVER HAPPIER!
BUT SOON, BUSINESS FELL AND M HEALTH TOC A DOWN-WARD TURN
DEBTS ONLY SPAWNED NEW DEBTS...
...AND I LOST THE WHOLE KIT AND KABOODLE.
THOSE I WAS FORCED TO BORROW FROM...
...WERE FAR FROM SAINTS.
THE YAKUZA STOLE...
...MY LIGHT... MY LIFE... MY... DAUGHTER.
......
I KNOW I ASK MUCH.
YOU'VE PROBABLY GOT MORE LUCRATIVE CASES ON YOUR DOCKET.

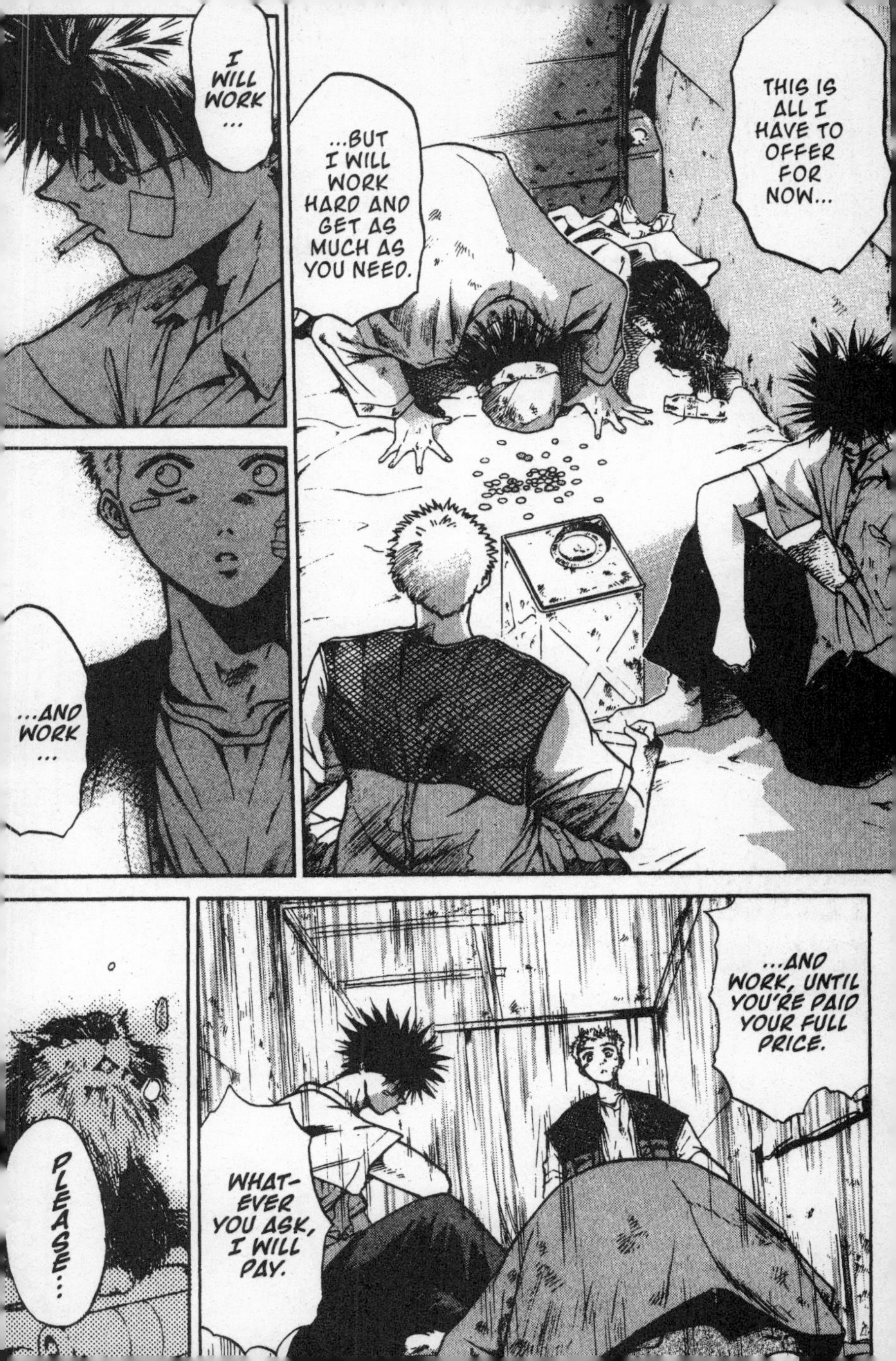
THIS IS ALL I HAVE TO OFFER FOR NOW...
...BUT I WILL WORK HARD AND GET AS MUCH AS YOU NEED.
I WILL WORK...
...AND WORK...
...AND WORK, UNTIL YOU'RE PAID YOUR FULL PRICE.
WHAT-EVER YOU ASK, I WILL PAY.
PLEASE...

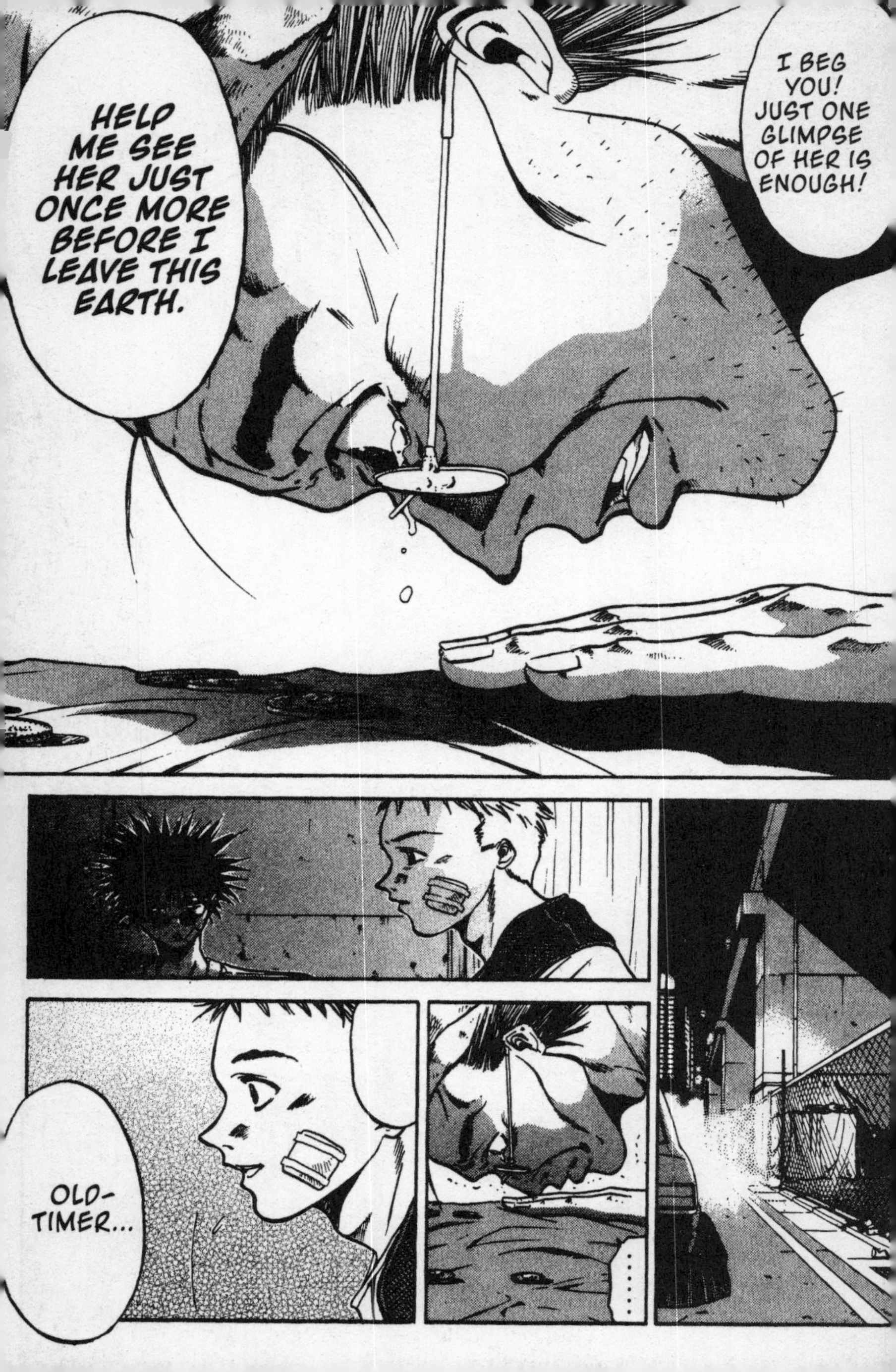
I BEG YOU! JUST ONE GLIMPSE OF HER IS ENOUGH!
HELP ME SEE HER JUST ONCE MORE BEFORE I LEAVE THIS EARTH.
......
OLD-TIMER...

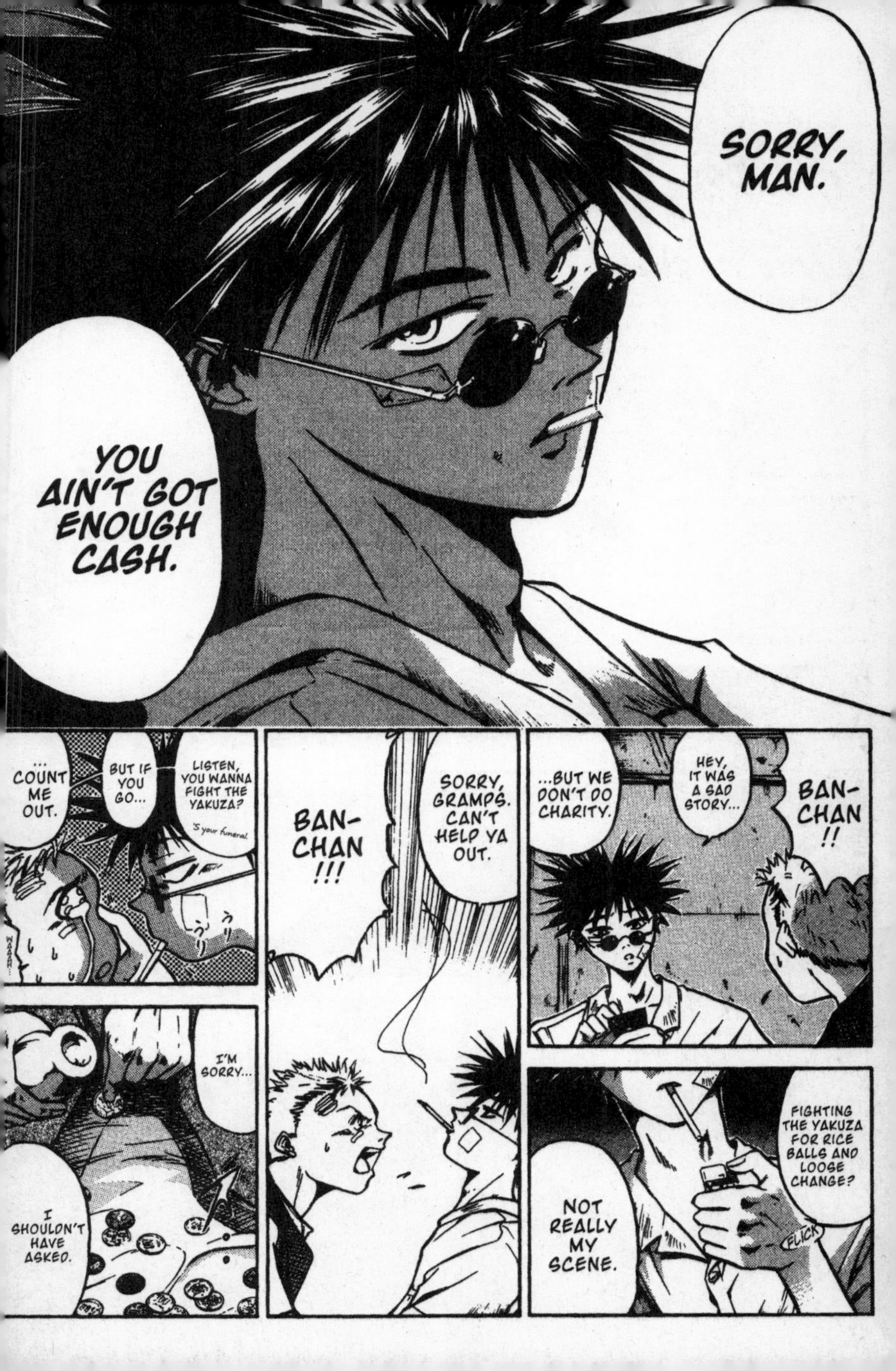
SORRY, MAN.
YOU AIN'T GOT ENOUGH CASH.
BAN-CHAN!!
HEY, IT WAS A SAD STORY...
...BUT WE DON'T DO CHARITY.
FIGHTING THE YAKUZA FOR RICE BALLS AND LOOSE CHANGE?
NOT REALLY MY SCENE.
FLICK
SORRY, GRAMPS. CAN'T HELP YA OUT.
BAN-CHAN!!!
LISTEN, YOU WANNA FIGHT THE YAKUZA?
'S your funeral.
BUT IF YOU GO...
...COUNT ME OUT.
WAAAH...
I'M SORRY...
I SHOULDN'T HAVE ASKED.

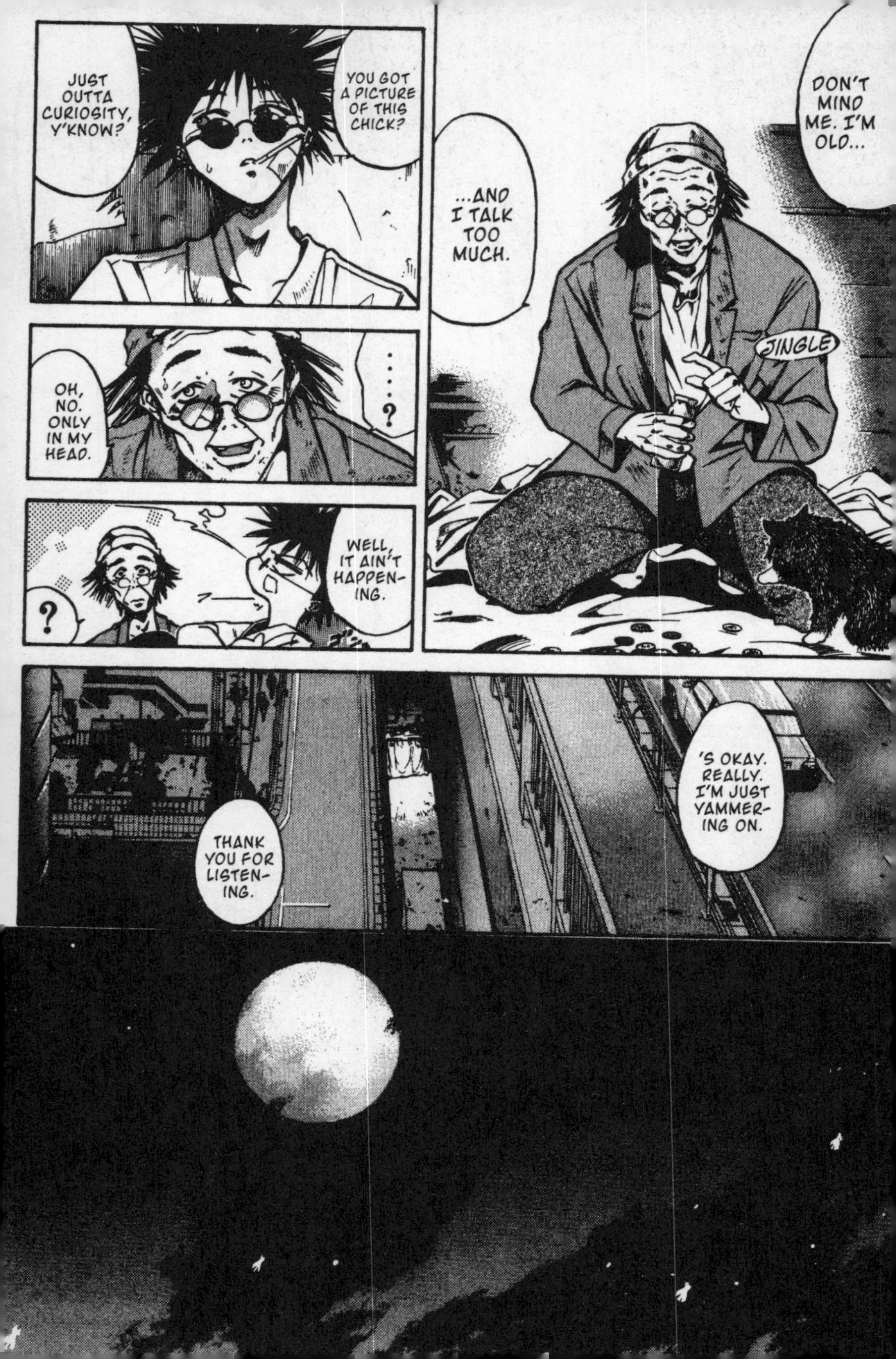
JUST OUTTA CURIOSITY, Y'KNOW?
YOU GOT A PICTURE OF THIS CHICK?
OH, NO. ONLY IN MY HEAD.
....?
?
WELL, IT AIN'T HAPPEN-ING.
DON'T MIND ME. I'M OLD...
...AND I TALK TOO MUCH.
JINGLE
THANK YOU FOR LISTEN-ING.
'S OKAY. REALLY. I'M JUST YAMMER-ING ON.

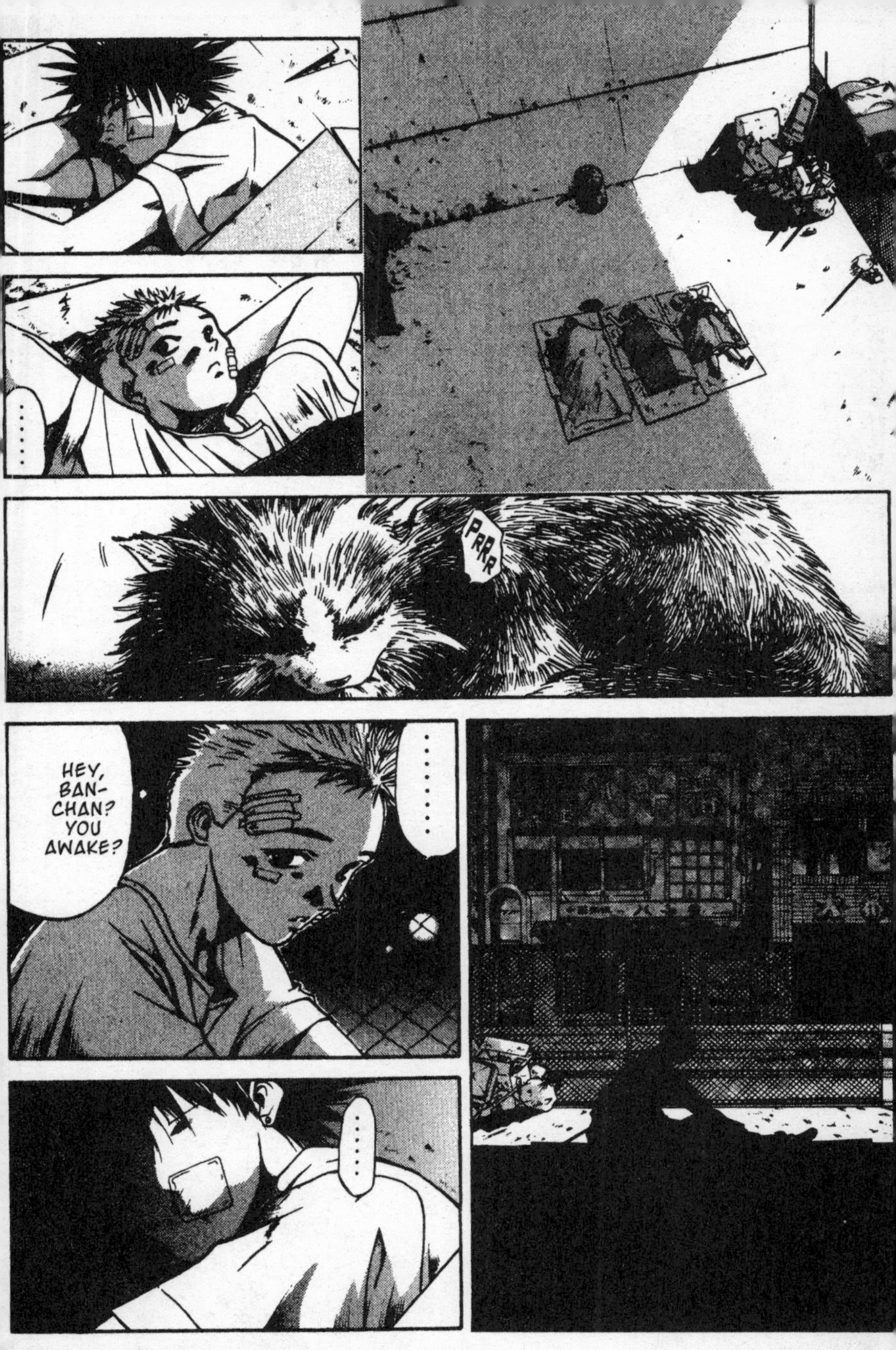
......
PRRR
......
HEY, BAN-CHAN? YOU AWAKE?
......

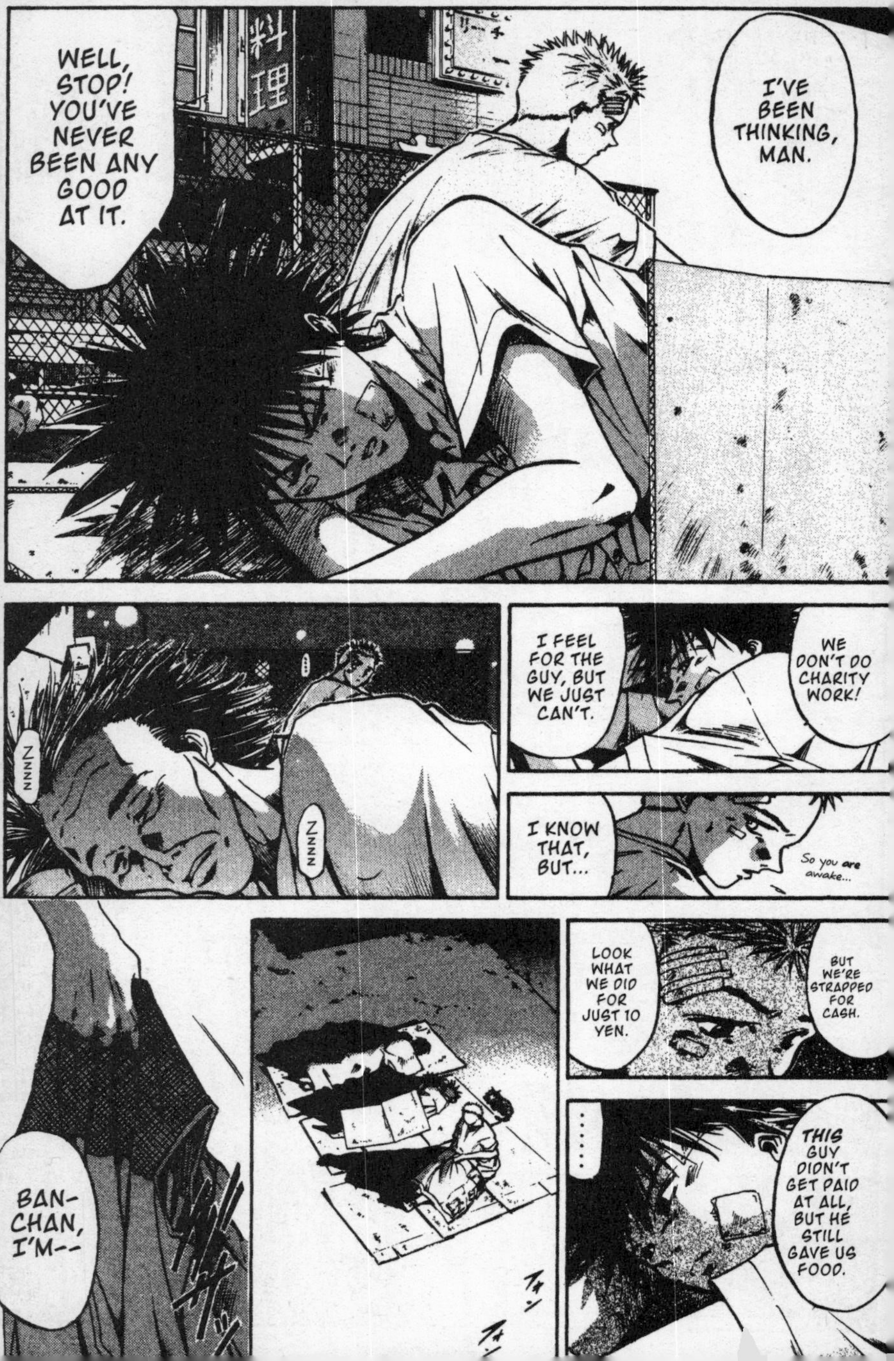
I'VE BEEN THINKING, MAN.
WELL, STOP! YOU'VE NEVER BEEN ANY GOOD AT IT.
料理
WE DON'T DO CHARITY WORK!
I FEEL FOR THE GUY, BUT WE JUST CAN'T.
I KNOW THAT, BUT...
So you are awake...
...
Zzzz
Zzzz
BUT WE'RE STRAPPED FOR CASH.
LOOK WHAT WE DID FOR JUST 10 YEN.
THIS GUY DIDN'T GET PAID AT ALL, BUT HE STILL GAVE US FOOD.
......
BAN-CHAN, I'M--

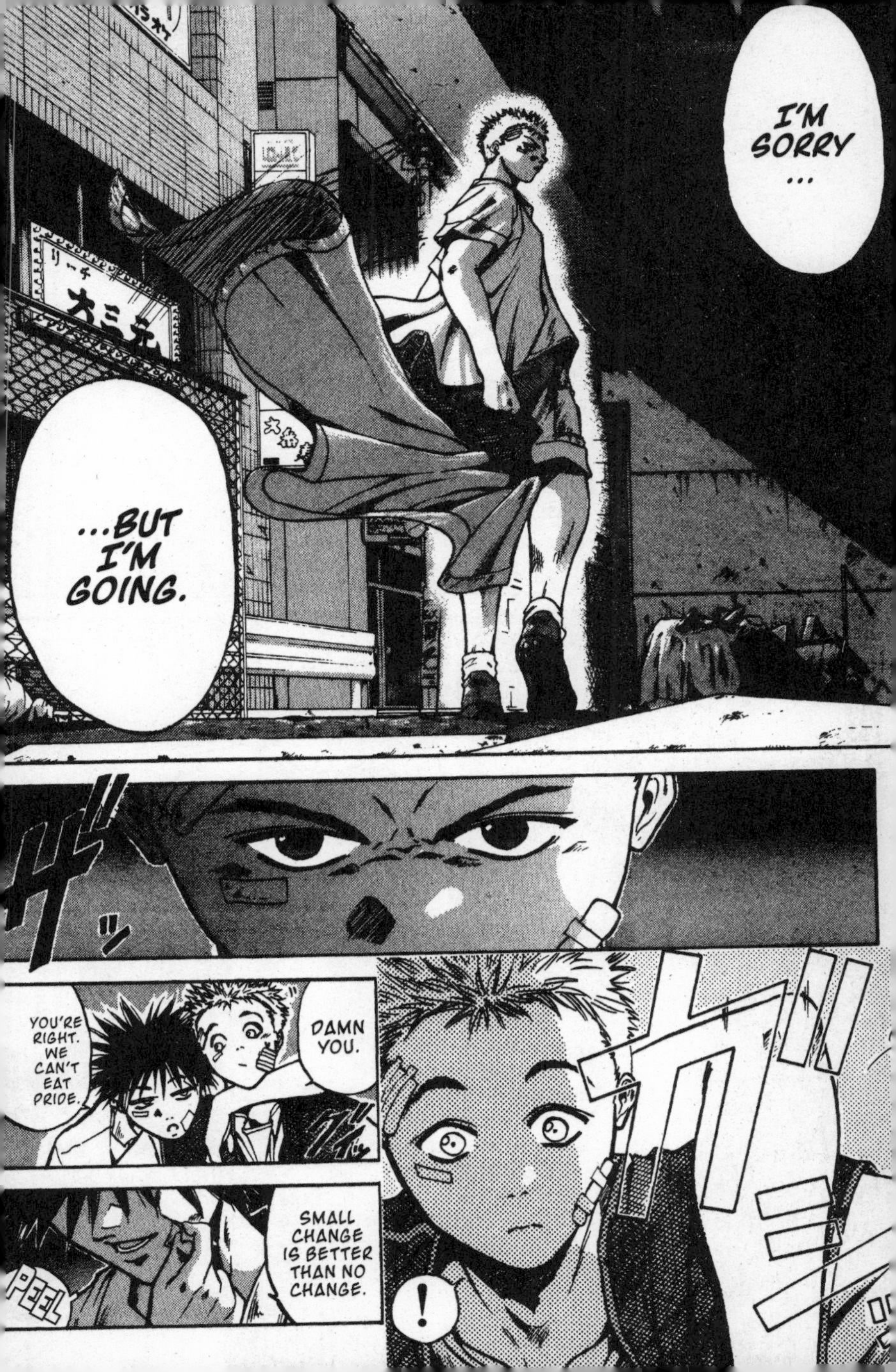

I'M SORRY ...
リーチ
大三元
...BUT I'M GOING.
!
DAMN YOU.
YOU'RE RIGHT. WE CAN'T EAT PRIDE.
SMALL CHANGE IS BETTER THAN NO CHANGE.
PEEL

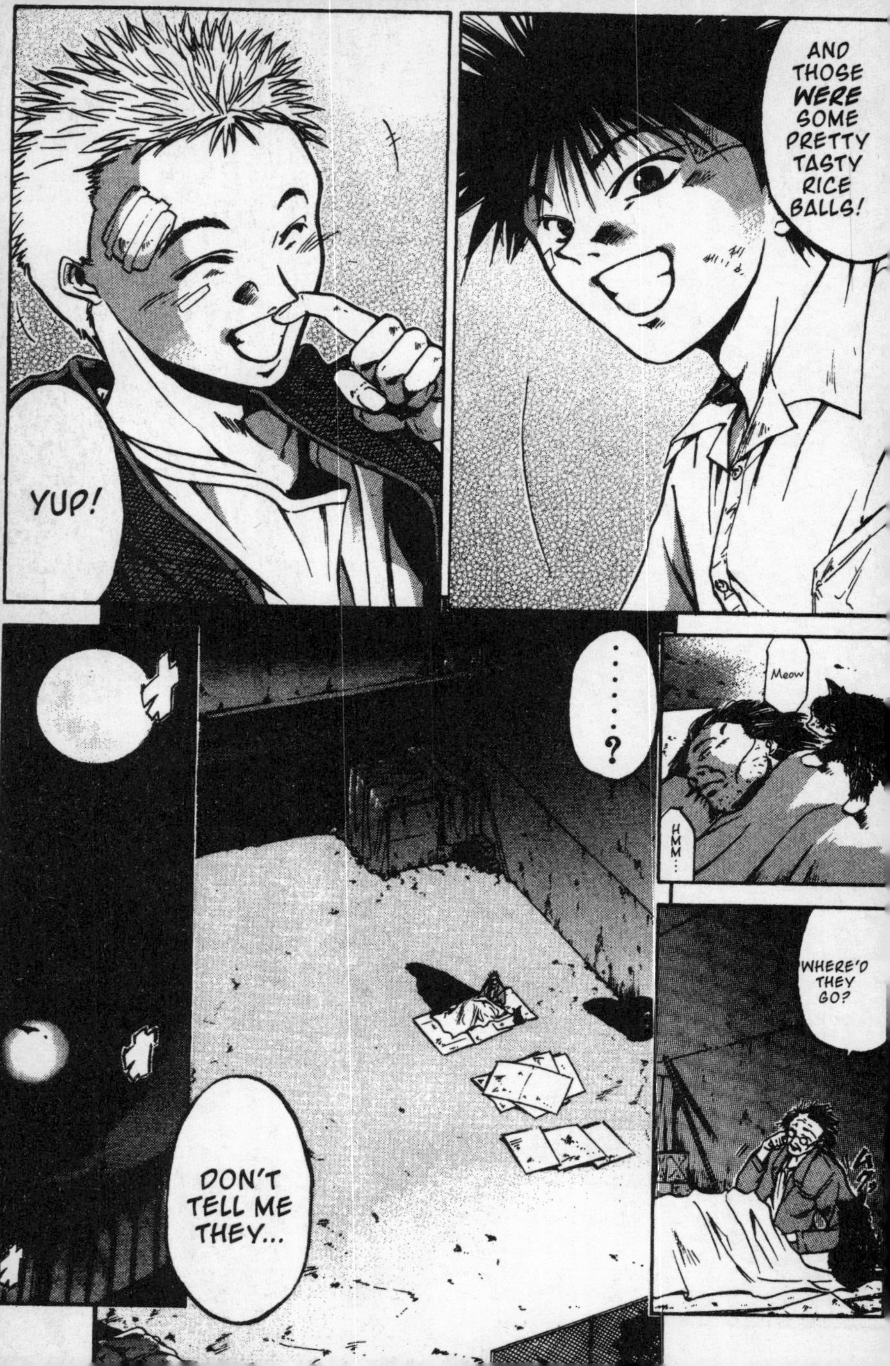
AND THOSE WERE SOME PRETTY TASTY RICE BALLS!
YUP!
Meow
HMM...
......?
WHERE'D THEY GO?
DON'T TELL ME THEY...

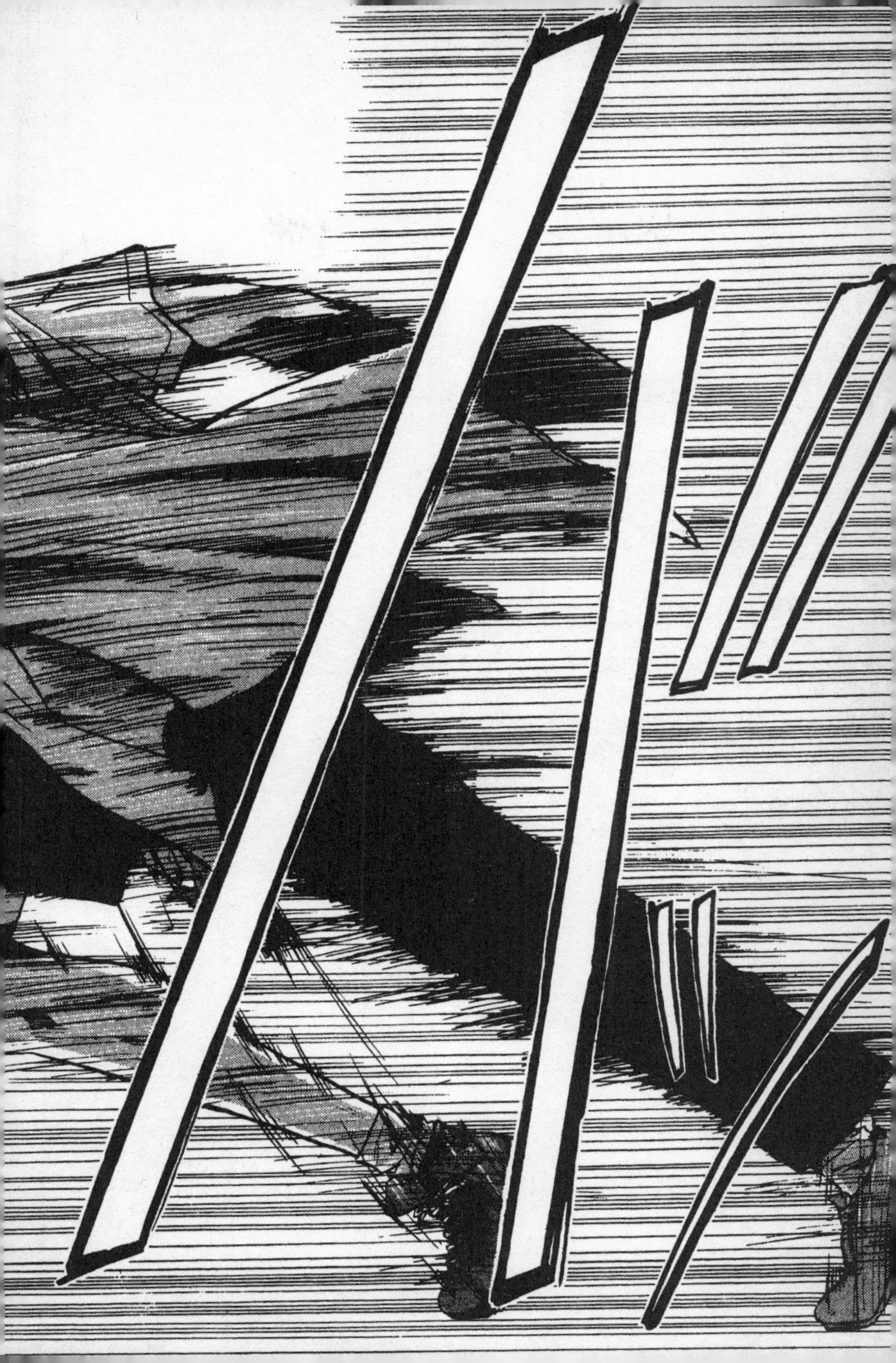

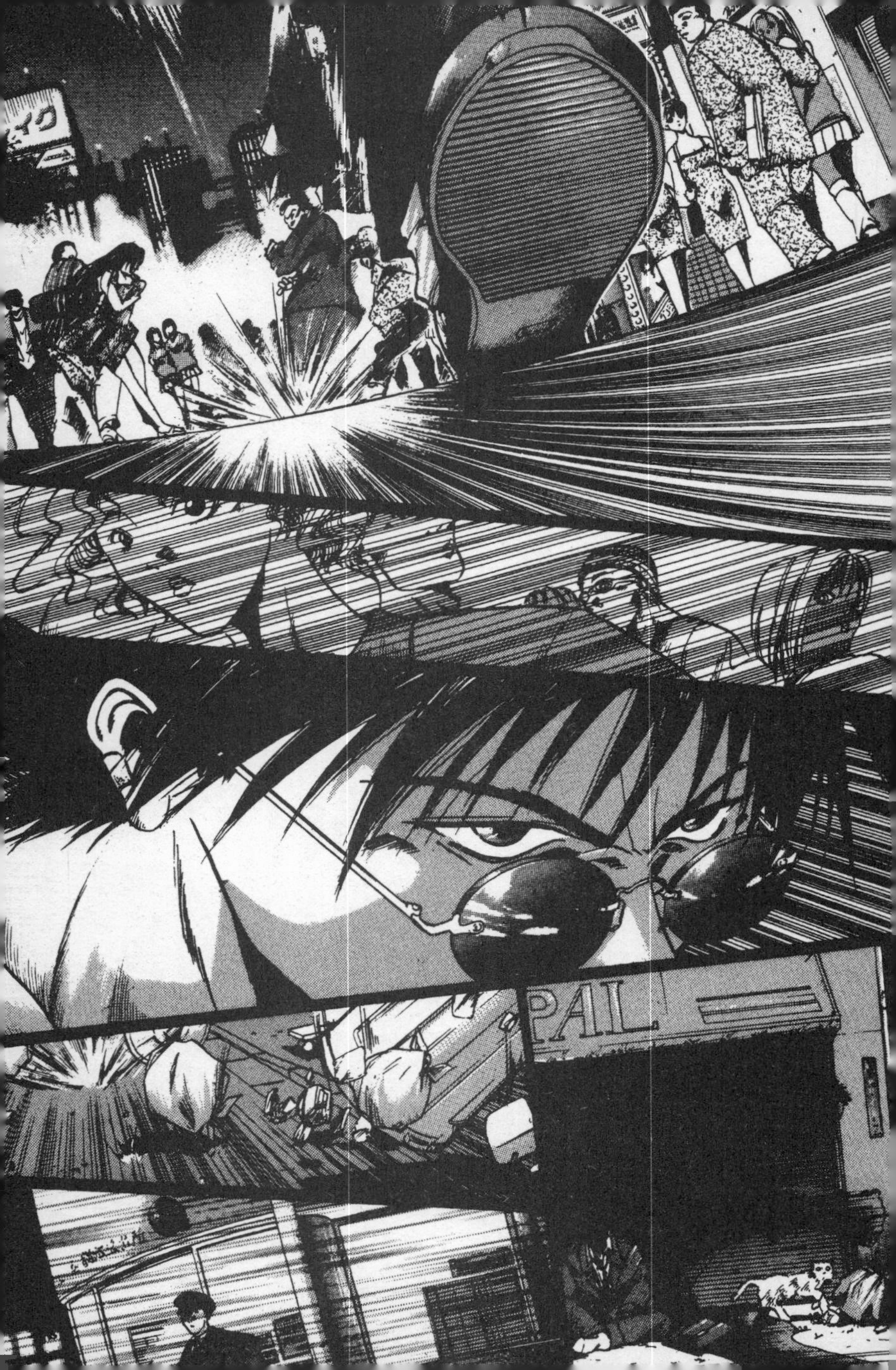
PAL

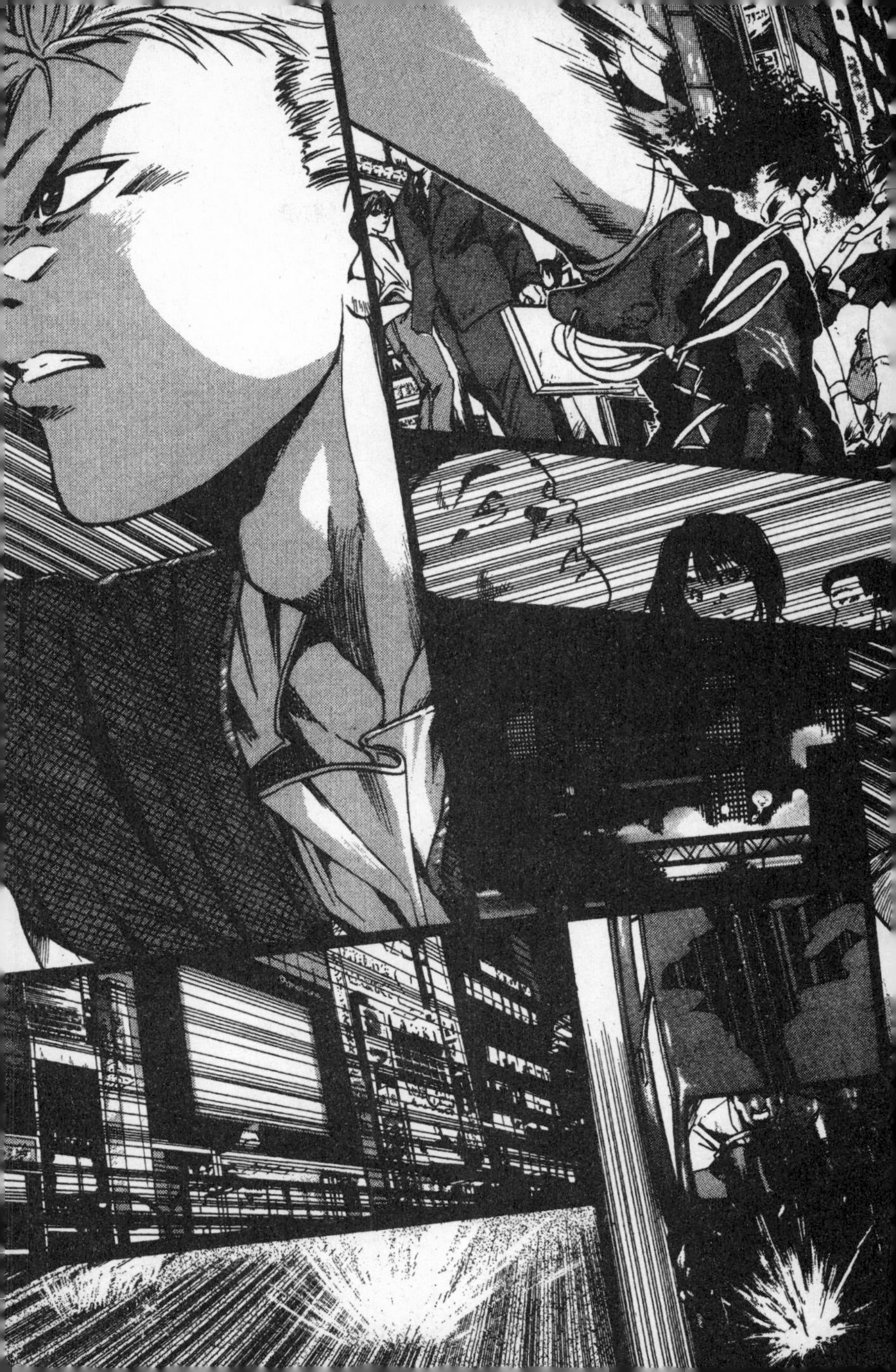

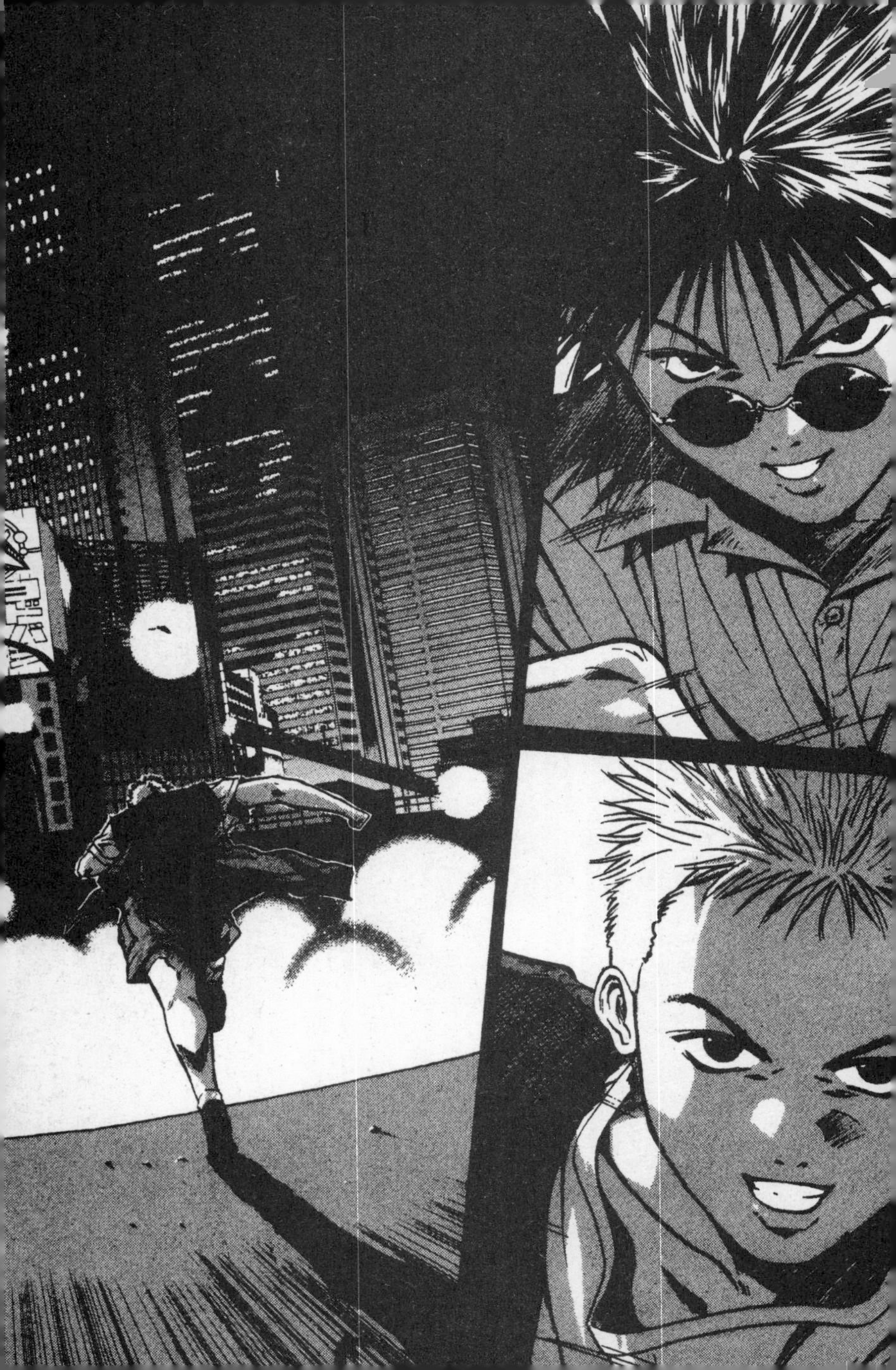

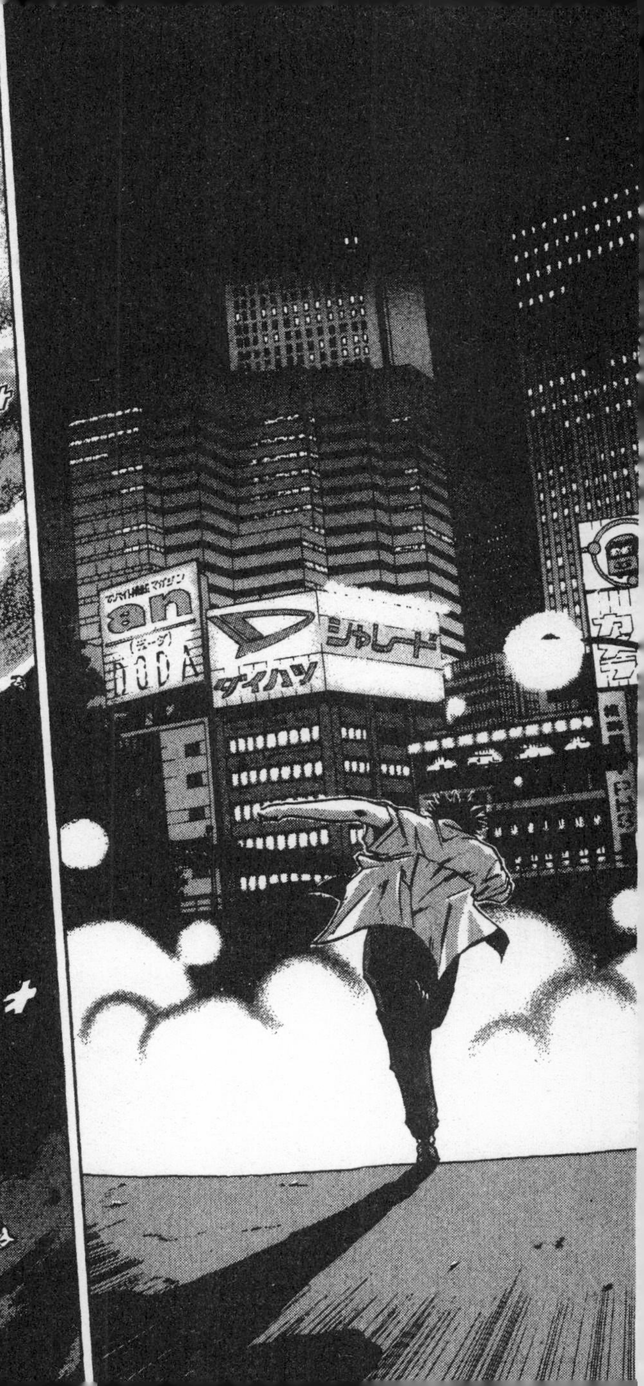
an
DODA
シャレード
ダイハツ
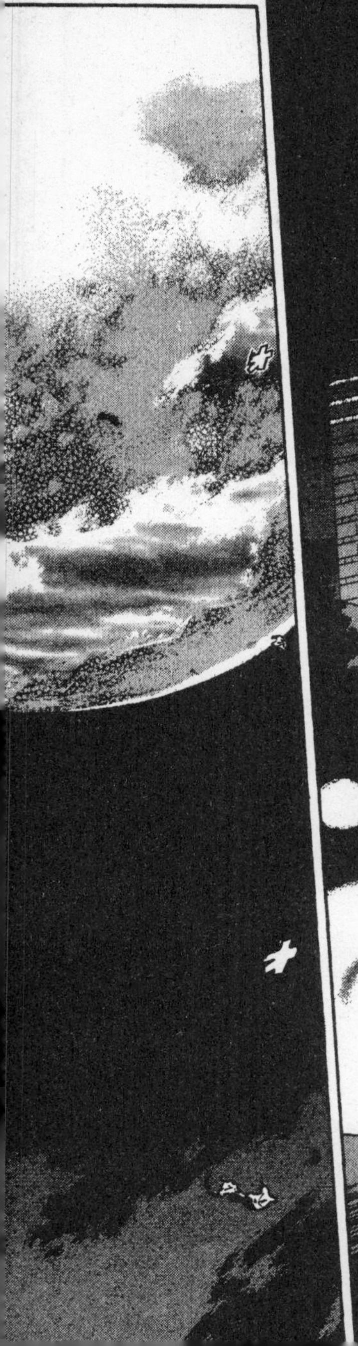

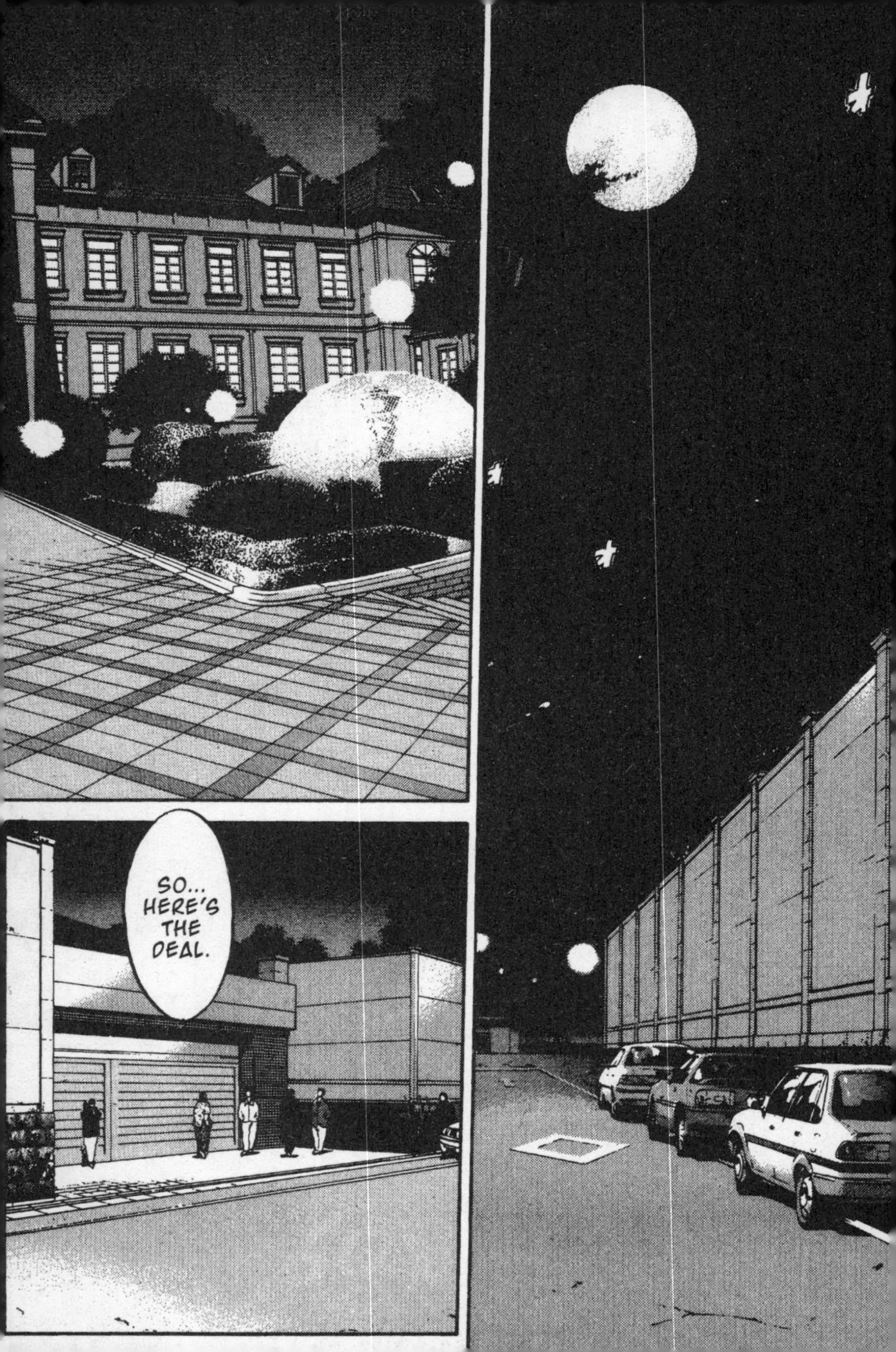
SO... HERE'S THE DEAL.

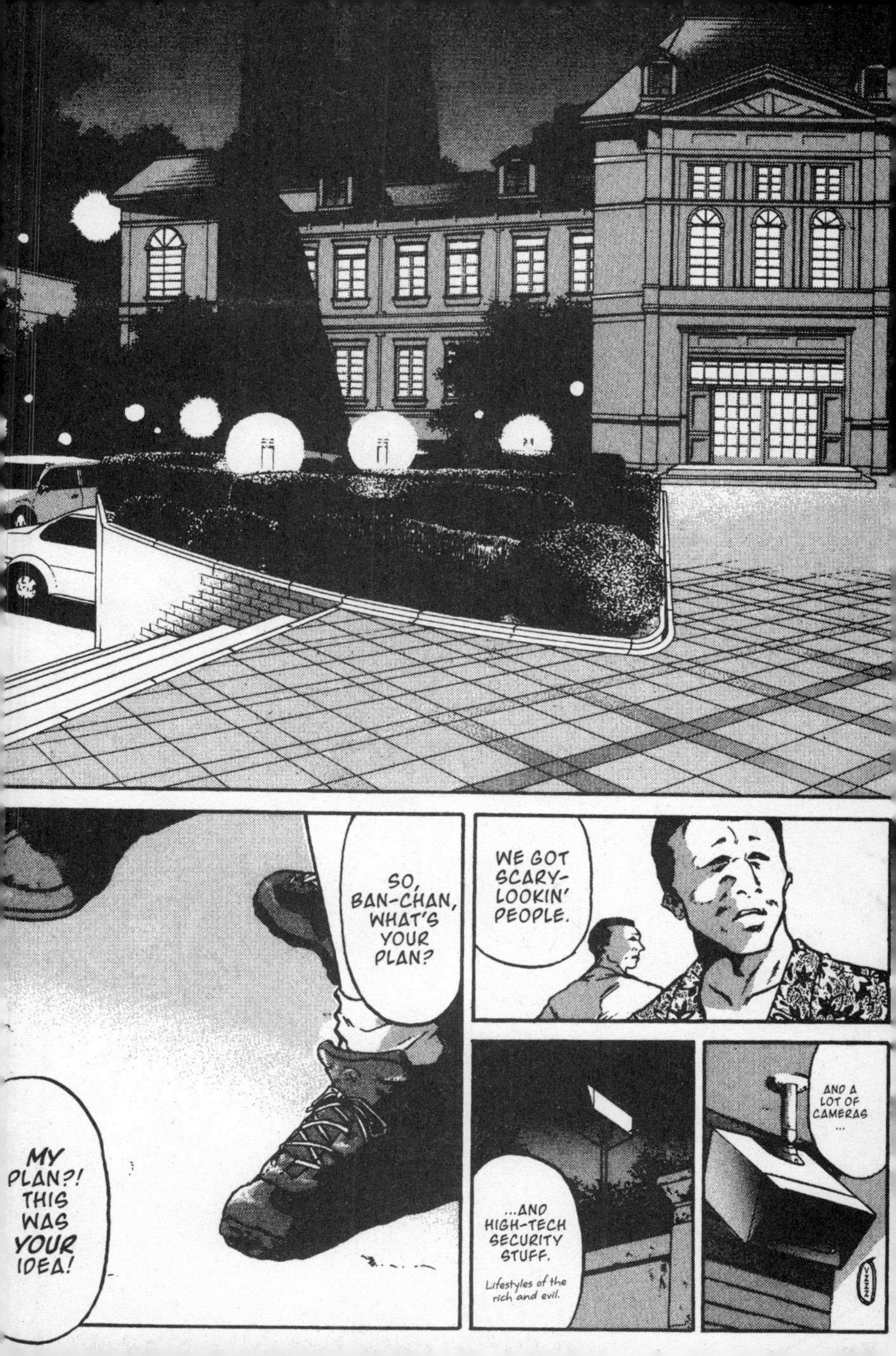
WE GOT SCARY-LOOKIN' PEOPLE.
AND A LOT OF CAMERAS ...
...AND HIGH-TECH SECURITY STUFF.
Lifestyles of the rich and evil.
SO, BAN-CHAN, WHAT'S YOUR PLAN?
MY PLAN?! THIS WAS YOUR IDEA!

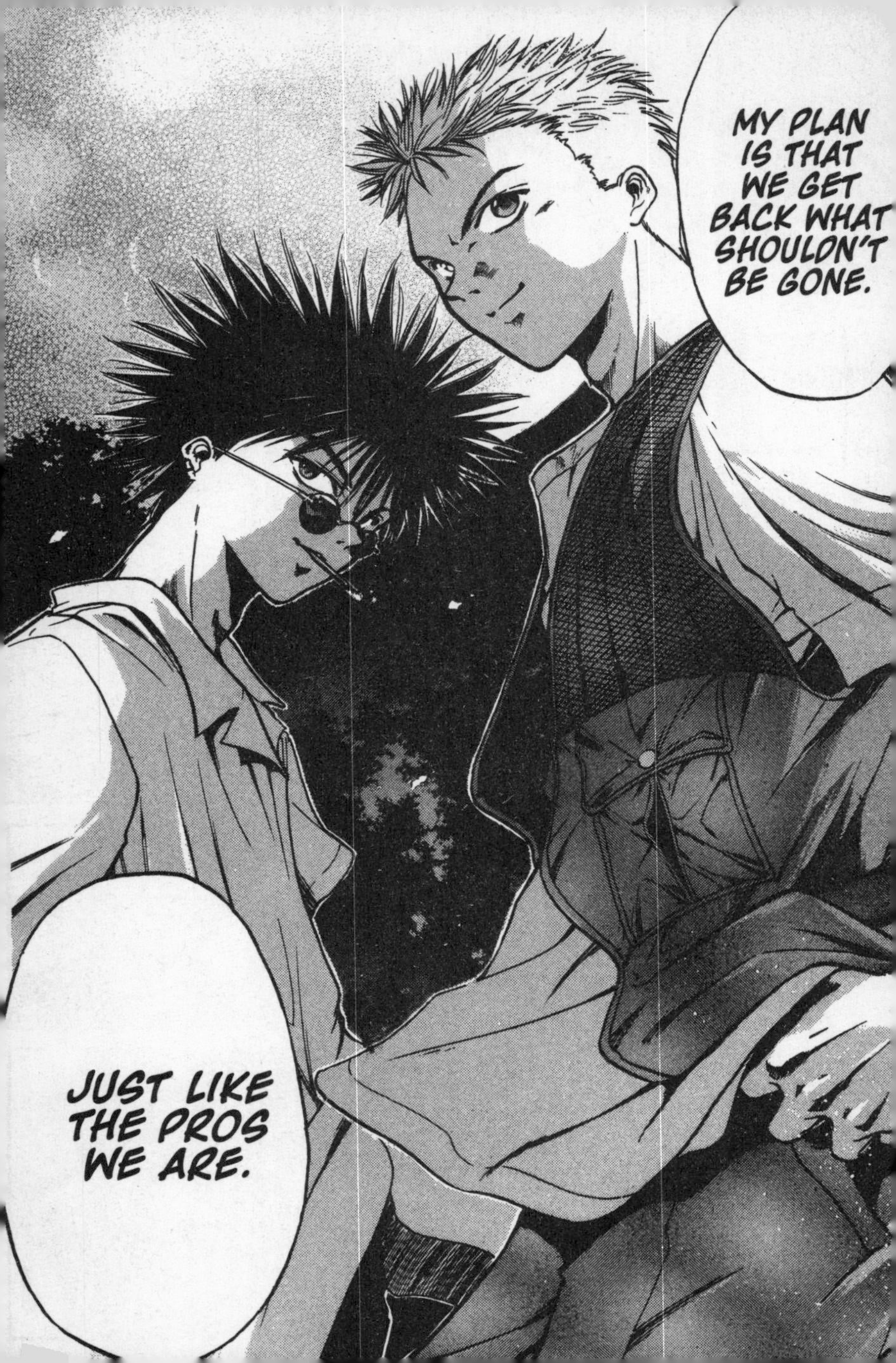
MY PLAN IS THAT WE GET BACK WHAT SHOULDN'T BE GONE.
JUST LIKE THE PROS WE ARE.

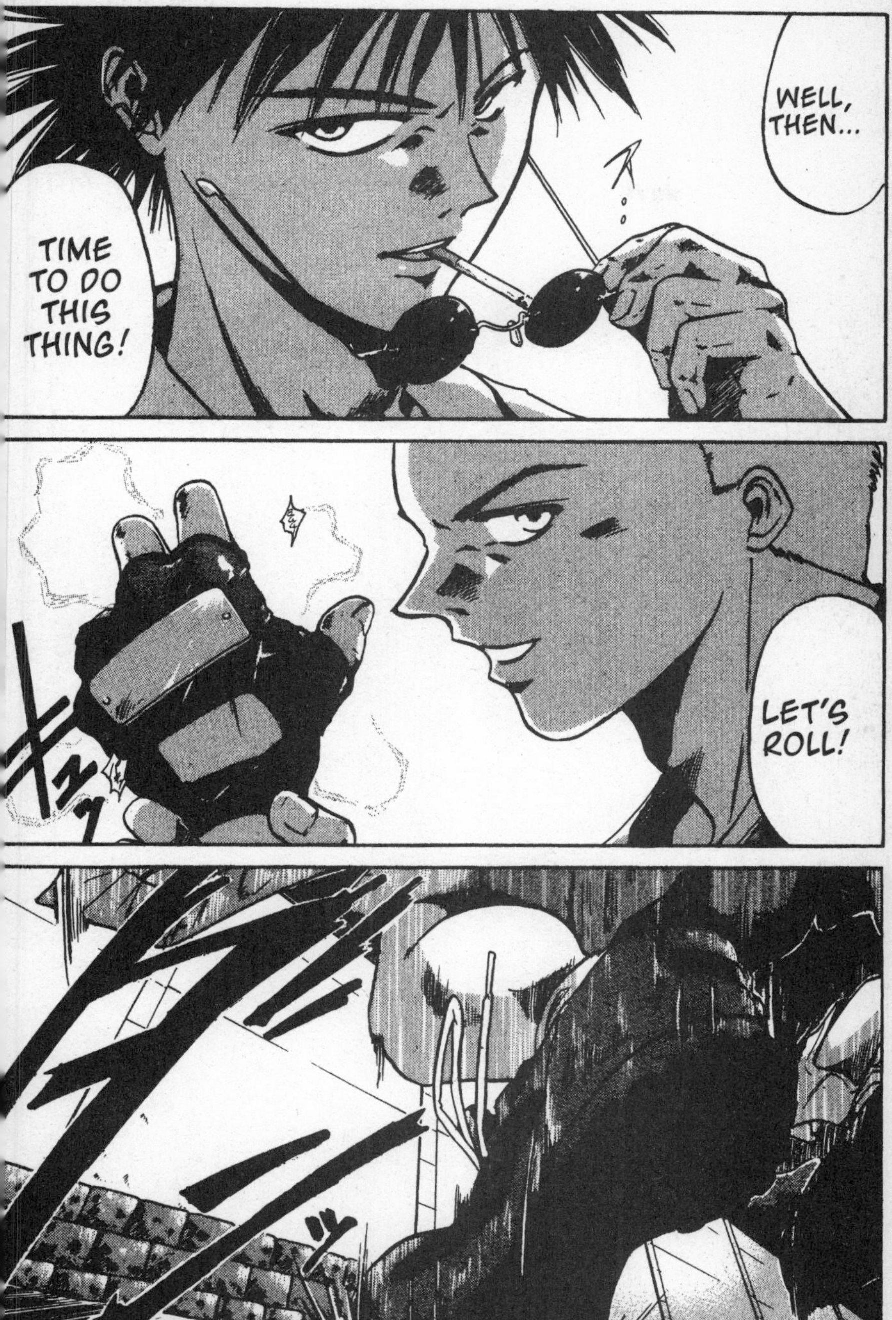
WELL, THEN...
TIME TO DO THIS THING!
LET'S ROLL!

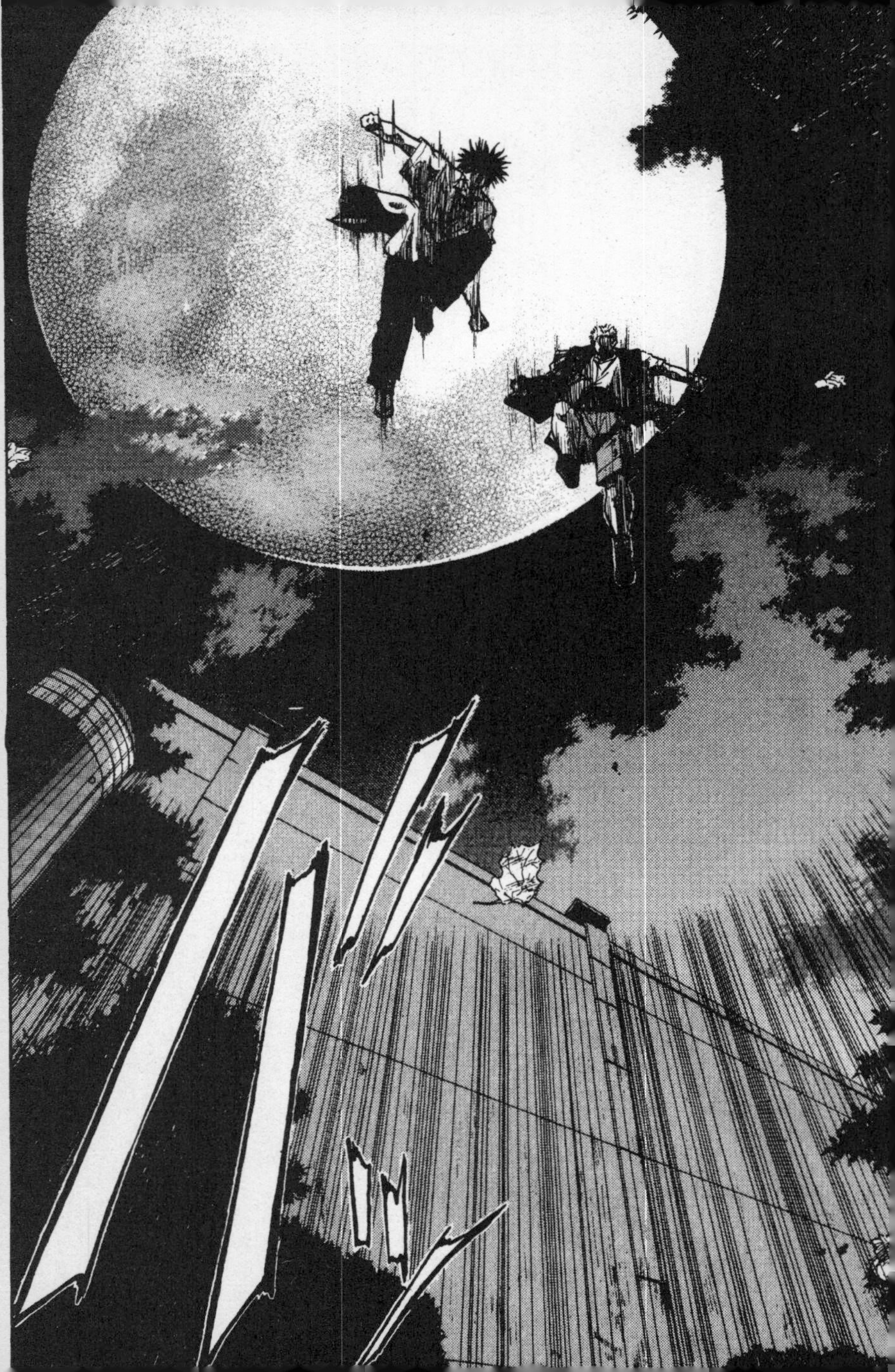

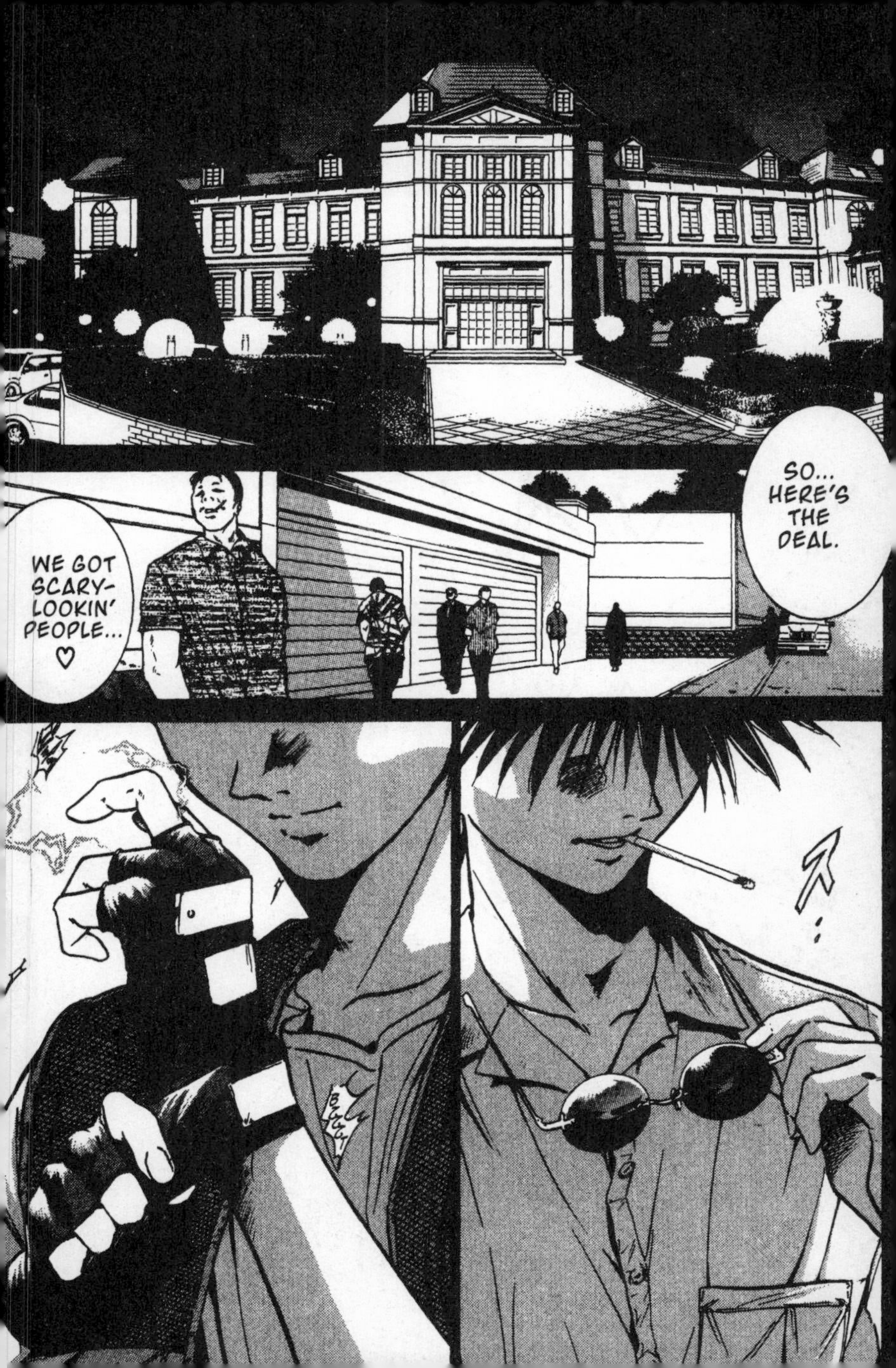
SO... HERE'S THE DEAL.
WE GOT SCARY-LOOKIN' PEOPLE... ♡

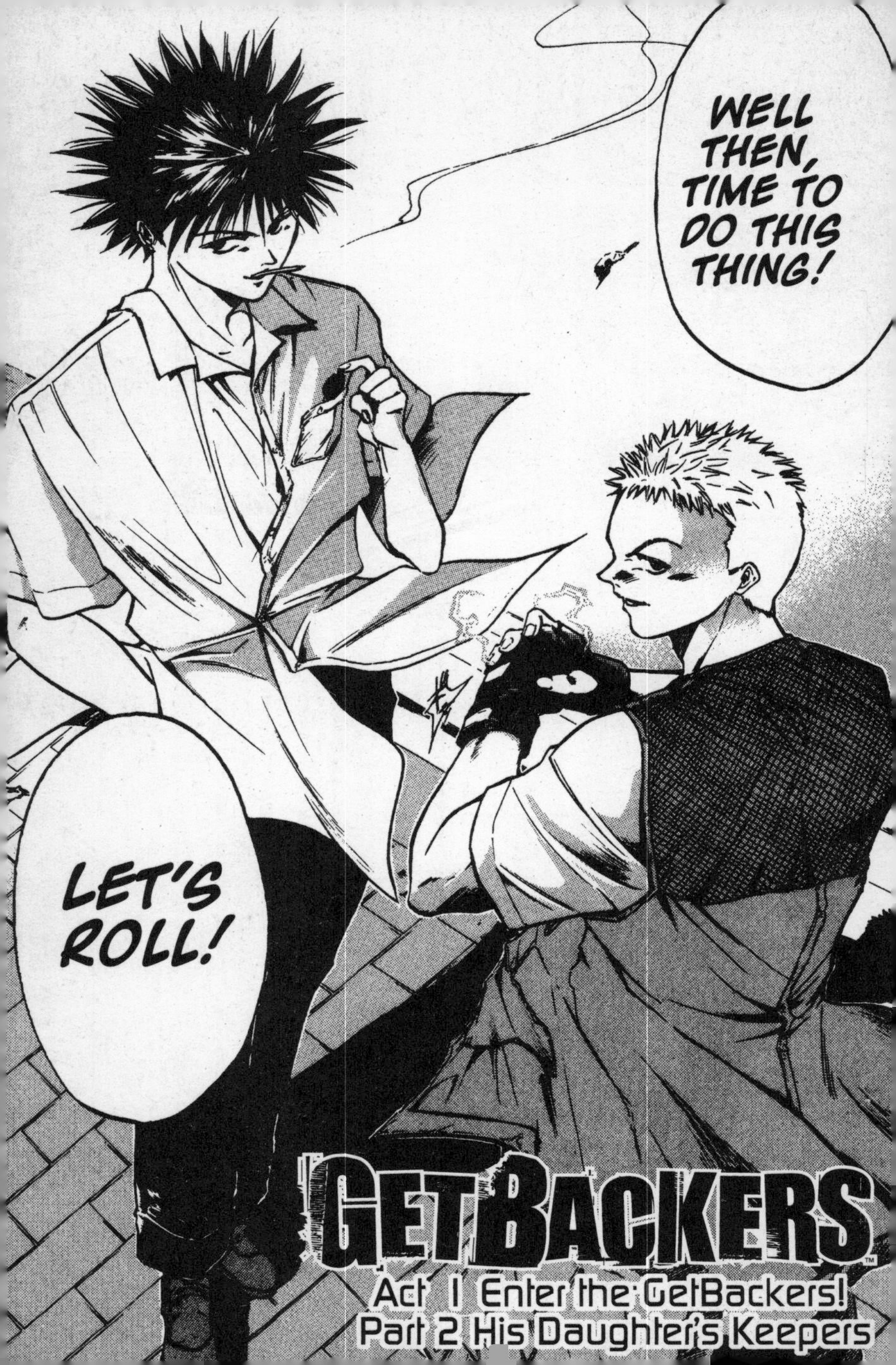
WELL THEN, TIME TO DO THIS THING!
LET'S ROLL!
GETBACKERS™
Act 1 Enter the GetBackers!
Part 2 His Daughter's Keepers

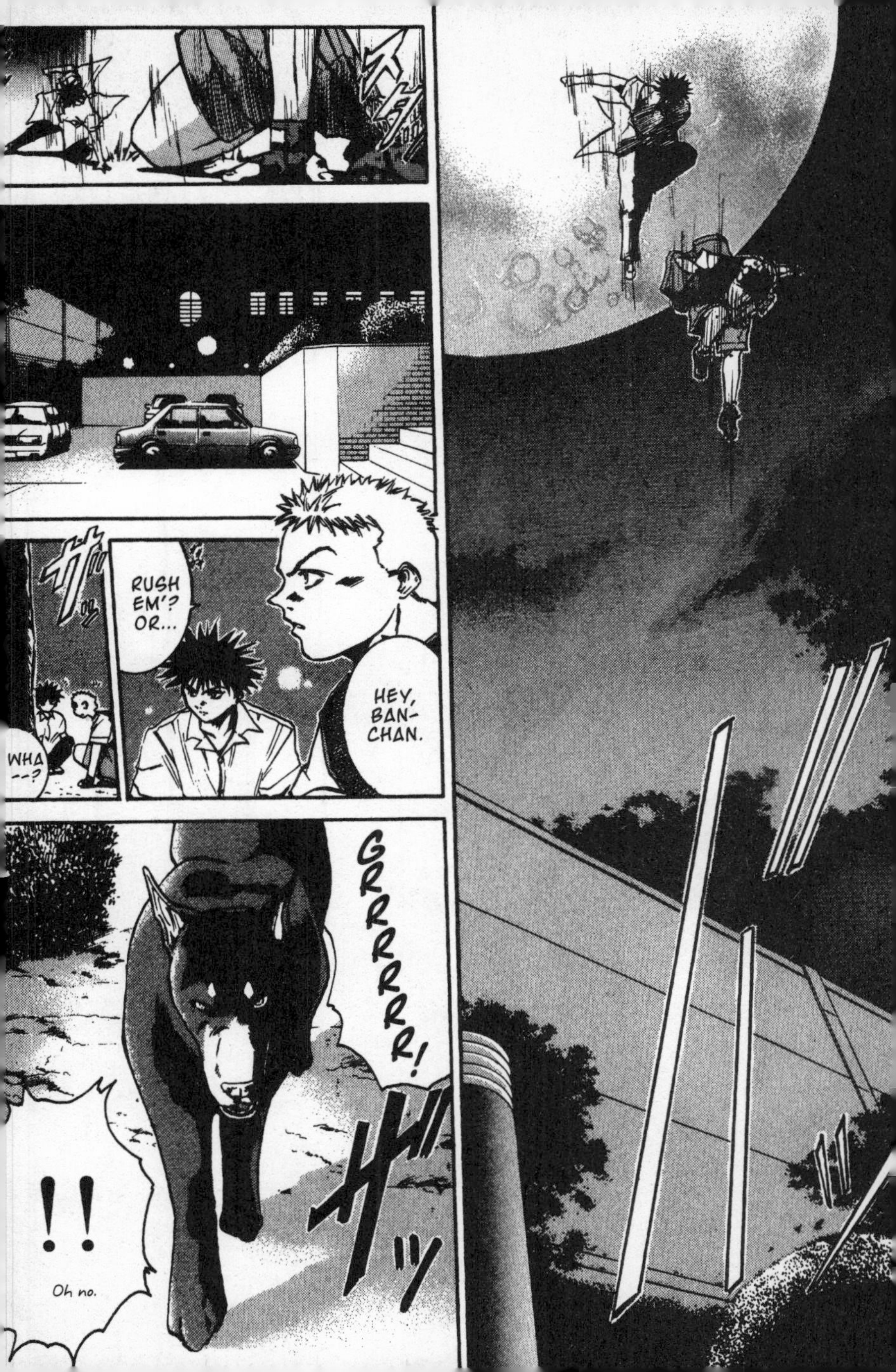
HEY, BAN-CHAN.
RUSH EM'? OR...
WHA--?
GRRRRRRR!
!!
Oh no.

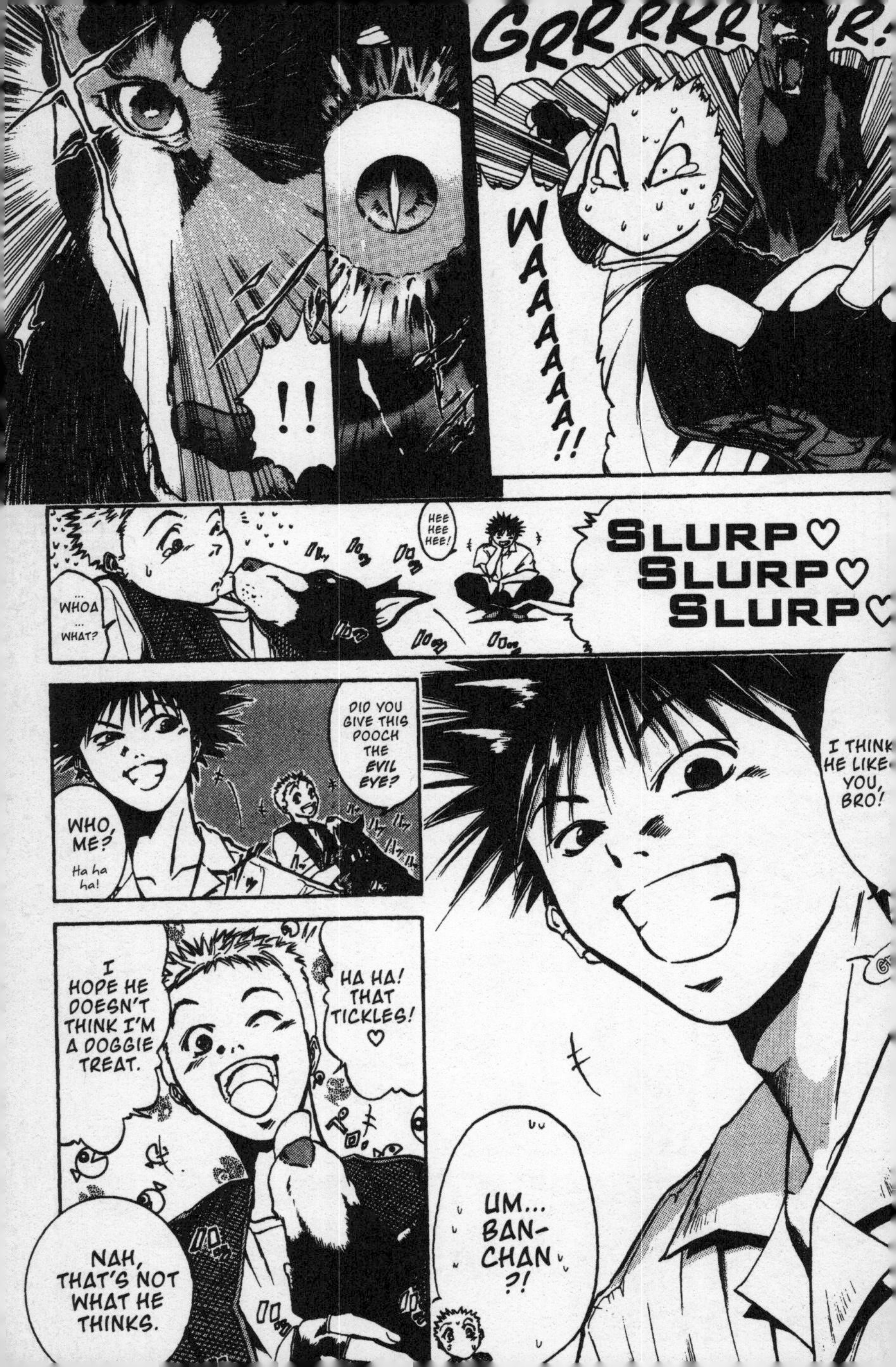
GRRRKKR R!
WAAAAAA!!
!!
SLURP♡ SLURP♡ SLURP♡
HEE HEE HEE!
...WHOA ... WHAT?
I THINK HE LIKE YOU, BRO!
UM... BAN-CHAN?!
DID YOU GIVE THIS POOCH THE EVIL EYE?
WHO, ME?
Ha ha ha!
HA HA! THAT TICKLES! ♡
I HOPE HE DOESN'T THINK I'M A DOGGIE TREAT.
NAH, THAT'S NOT WHAT HE THINKS.

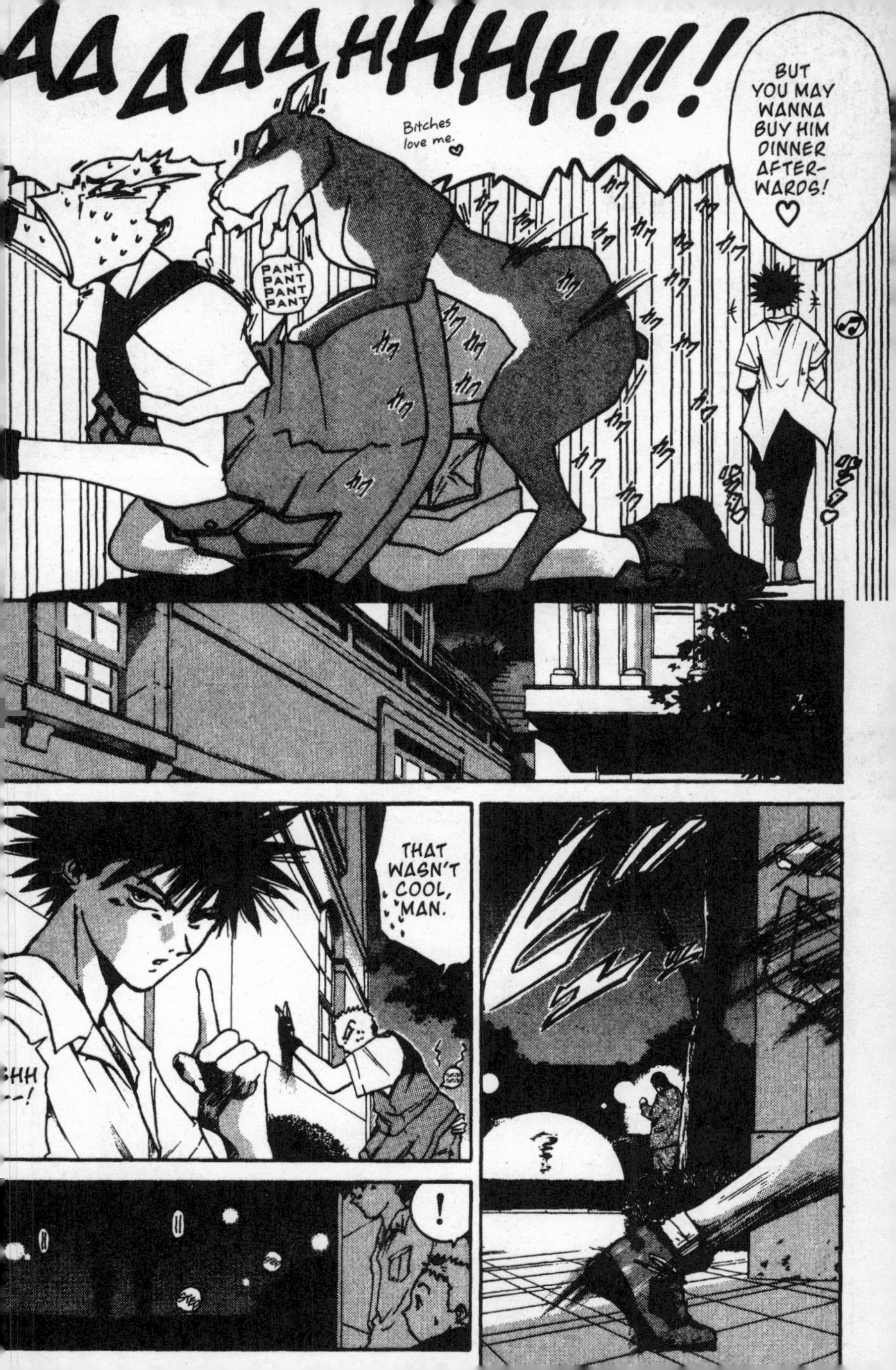
AAAAAHHHHH!!!
BUT YOU MAY WANNA BUY HIM DINNER AFTER-WARDS! ♡
Bitches love me. ♡
PANT PANT PANT PANT
THAT WASN'T COOL, MAN.
!

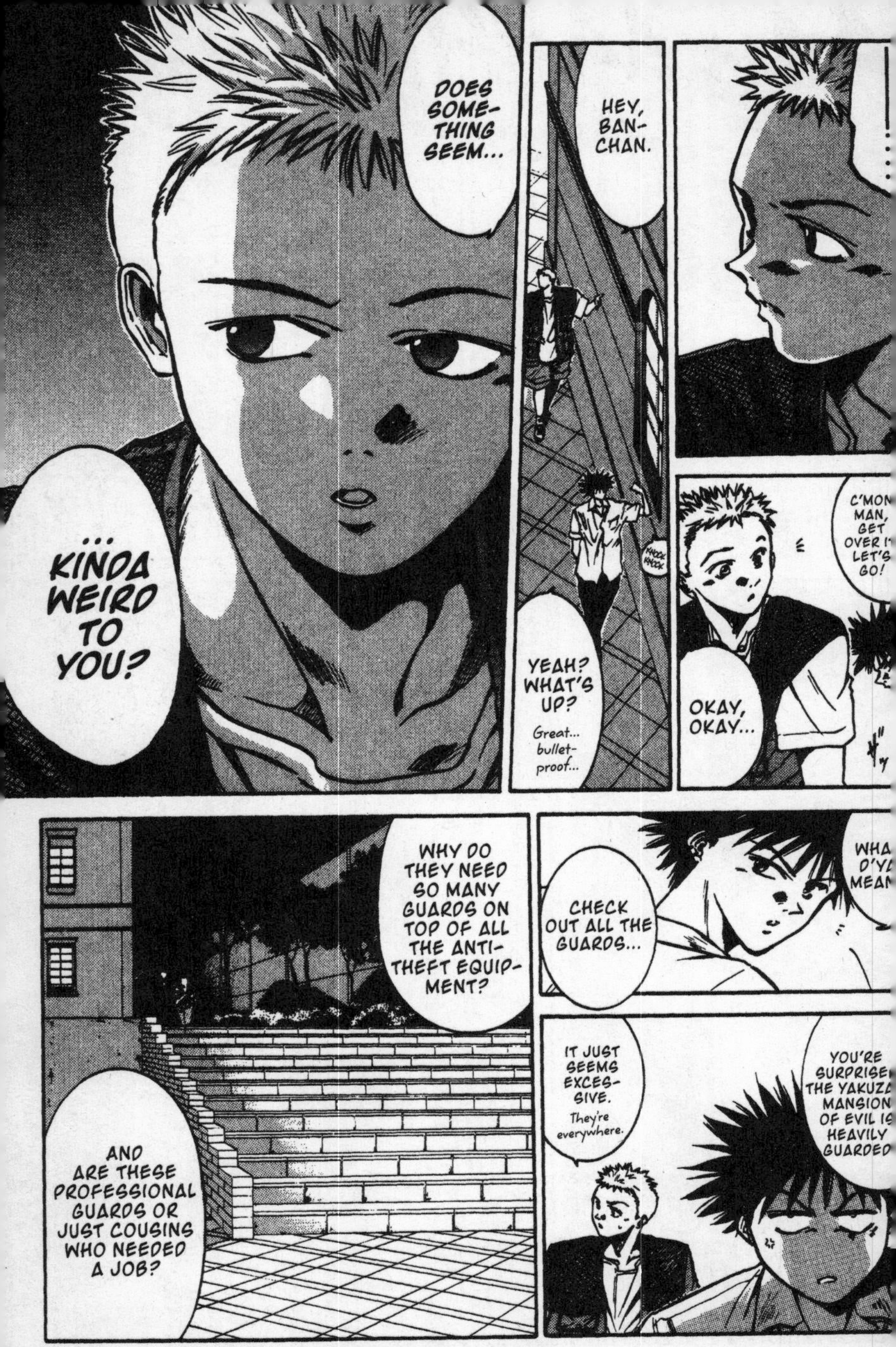
C'MON MAN, GET OVER I LET'S GO!
OKAY, OKAY...
HEY, BAN-CHAN.
KNOCK KNOCK
YEAH? WHAT'S UP?
Great... bullet-proof...
DOES SOME-THING SEEM...
...KINDA WEIRD TO YOU?
WHA D'Y MEAN
CHECK OUT ALL THE GUARDS...
YOU'RE SURPRISE THE YAKUZA MANSION OF EVIL IS HEAVILY GUARDED
IT JUST SEEMS EXCES-SIVE.
They're everywhere.
WHY DO THEY NEED SO MANY GUARDS ON TOP OF ALL THE ANTI-THEFT EQUIP-MENT?
AND ARE THESE PROFESSIONAL GUARDS OR JUST COUSINS WHO NEEDED A JOB?

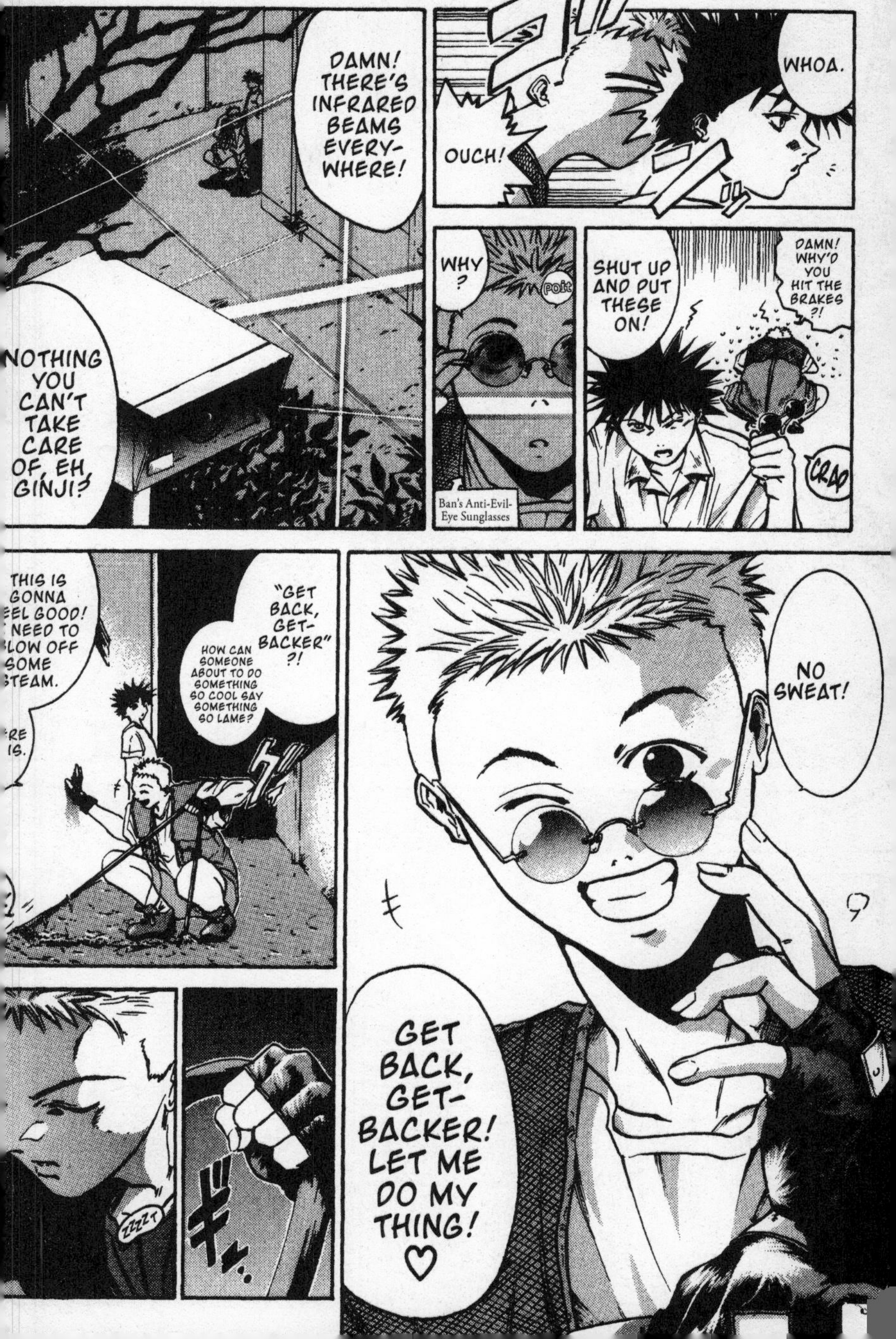
WHOA.
OUCH!
DAMN! WHY'D YOU HIT THE BRAKES?!
SHUT UP AND PUT THESE ON!
CRAP
WHY?
poit
Ban's Anti-Evil-Eye Sunglasses
DAMN! THERE'S INFRARED BEAMS EVERYWHERE!
NOTHING YOU CAN'T TAKE CARE OF, EH, GINJI?
NO SWEAT!
GET BACK, GET-BACKER! LET ME DO MY THING! ♡
"GET BACK, GET-BACKER"?!
HOW CAN SOMEONE ABOUT TO DO SOMETHING SO COOL SAY SOMETHING SO LAME?
THIS IS GONNA EEL GOOD! NEED TO LOW OFF SOME STEAM.
ZZZZT

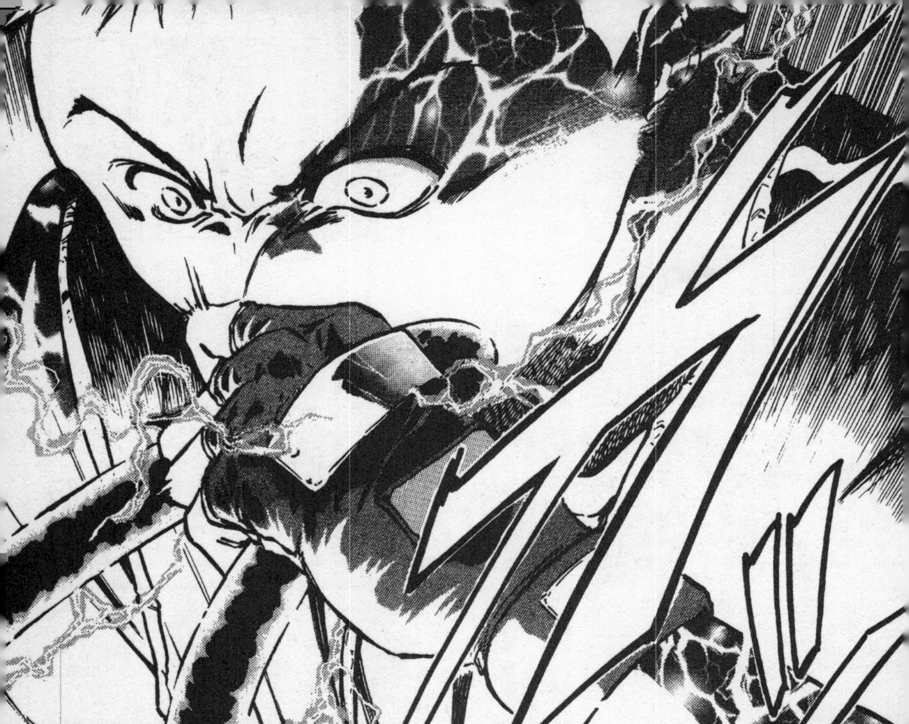
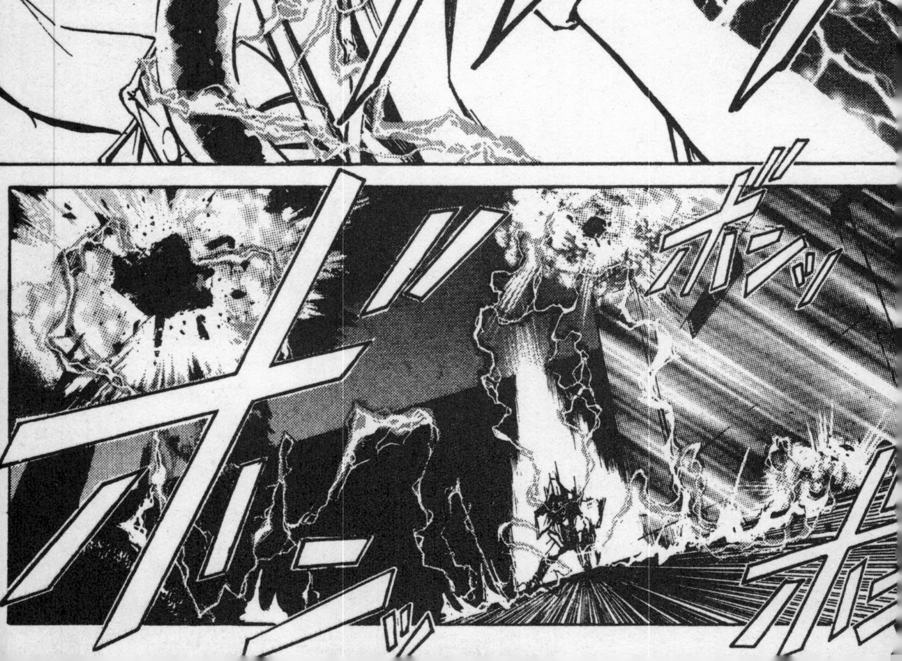

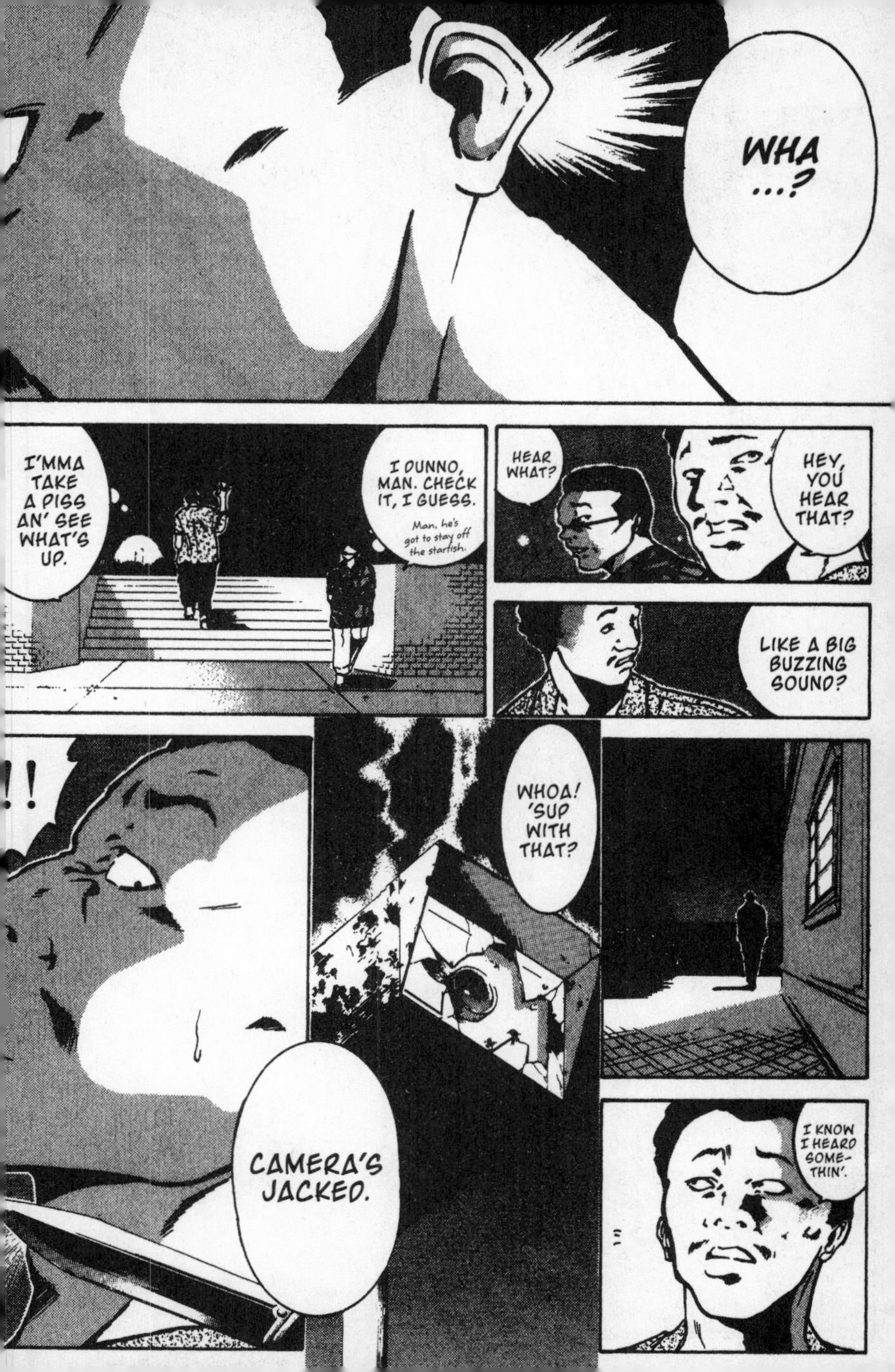
WHA ...?
HEY, YOU HEAR THAT?
HEAR WHAT?
LIKE A BIG BUZZING SOUND?
I DUNNO, MAN. CHECK IT, I GUESS.
Man, he's got to stay off the starfish.
I'MMA TAKE A PISS AN' SEE WHAT'S UP.
I KNOW I HEARD SOME-THIN'.
WHOA! 'SUP WITH THAT?
CAMERA'S JACKED.
!!

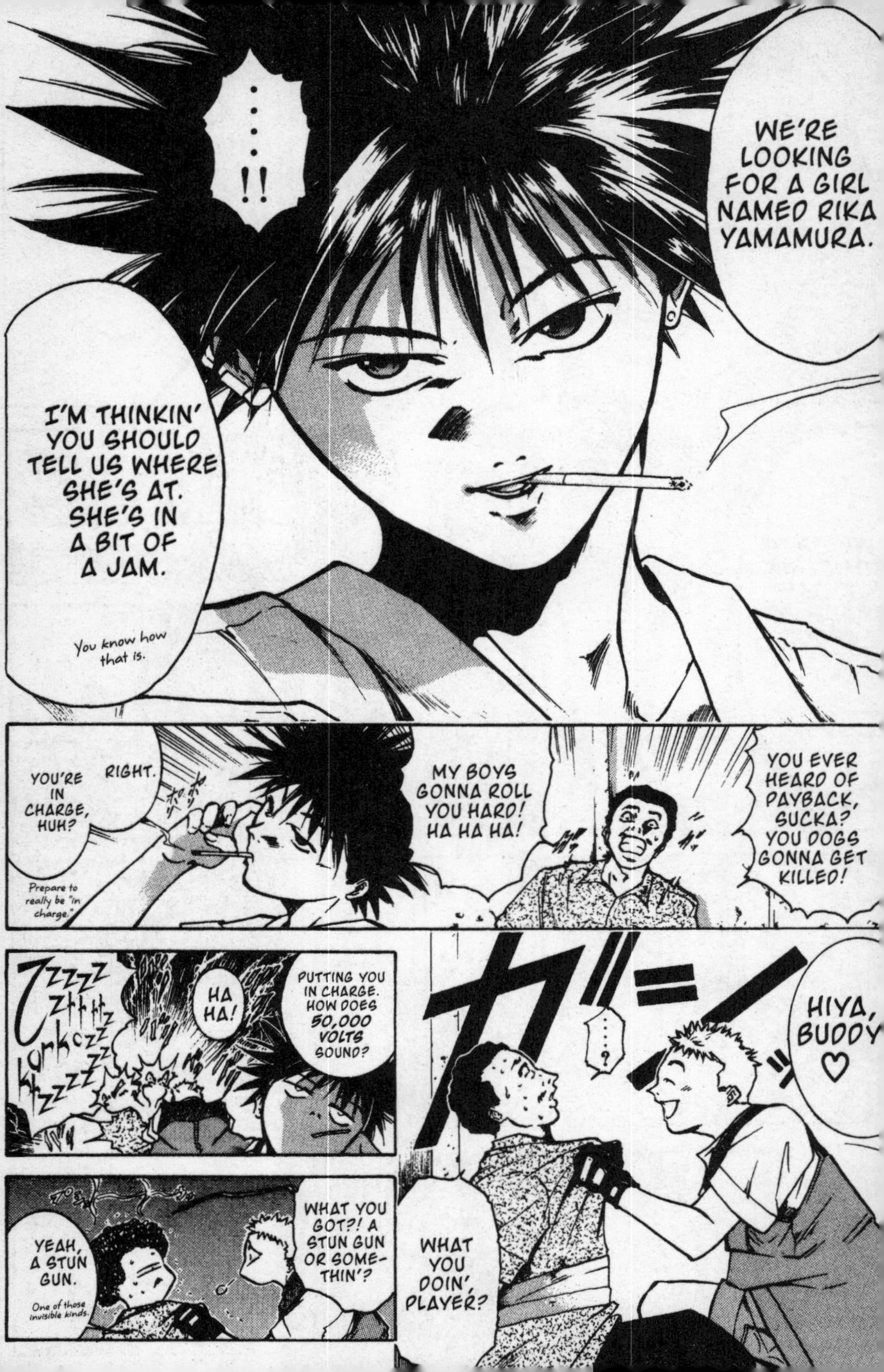
WE'RE LOOKING FOR A GIRL NAMED RIKA YAMAMURA.
...!!
I'M THINKIN' YOU SHOULD TELL US WHERE SHE'S AT. SHE'S IN A BIT OF A JAM.
You know how that is.
YOU EVER HEARD OF PAYBACK, SUCKA? YOU DOGS GONNA GET KILLED!
MY BOYS GONNA ROLL YOU HARD! HA HA HA!
RIGHT.
YOU'RE IN CHARGE, HUH?
Prepare to really be "in charge."
HIYA, BUDDY ♡
...?
WHAT YOU DOIN', PLAYER?
PUTTING YOU IN CHARGE. HOW DOES 50,000 VOLTS SOUND?
HA HA!
WHAT YOU GOT?! A STUN GUN OR SOMETHIN'?
YEAH, A STUN GUN.
One of those invisible kinds.

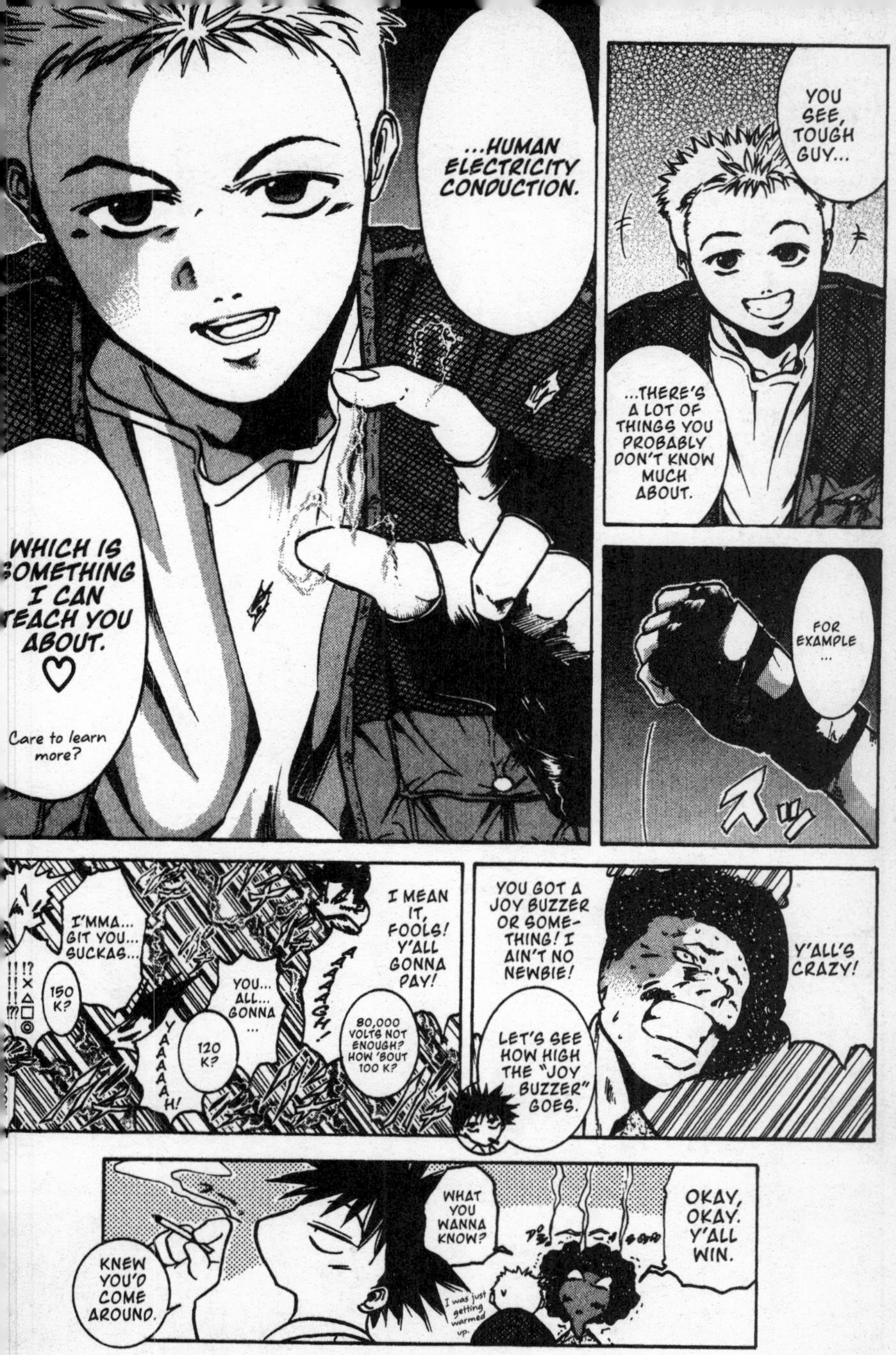
YOU SEE, TOUGH GUY...
...THERE'S A LOT OF THINGS YOU PROBABLY DON'T KNOW MUCH ABOUT.
FOR EXAMPLE ...
...HUMAN ELECTRICITY CONDUCTION.
WHICH IS SOMETHING I CAN TEACH YOU ABOUT. ♡
Care to learn more?
YOU GOT A JOY BUZZER OR SOME-THING! I AIN'T NO NEWBIE!
Y'ALL'S CRAZY!
LET'S SEE HOW HIGH THE "JOY BUZZER" GOES.
I MEAN IT, FOOLS! Y'ALL GONNA PAY!
80,000 VOLTS NOT ENOUGH? HOW 'BOUT 100 K?
AAAAGH!
YOU... ALL... GONNA ...
120 K?
YAAAAAH!
I'MMA... GIT YOU... SUCKAS...
150 K?
OKAY, OKAY. Y'ALL WIN.
WHAT YOU WANNA KNOW?
I was just getting warmed up.
KNEW YOU'D COME AROUND.

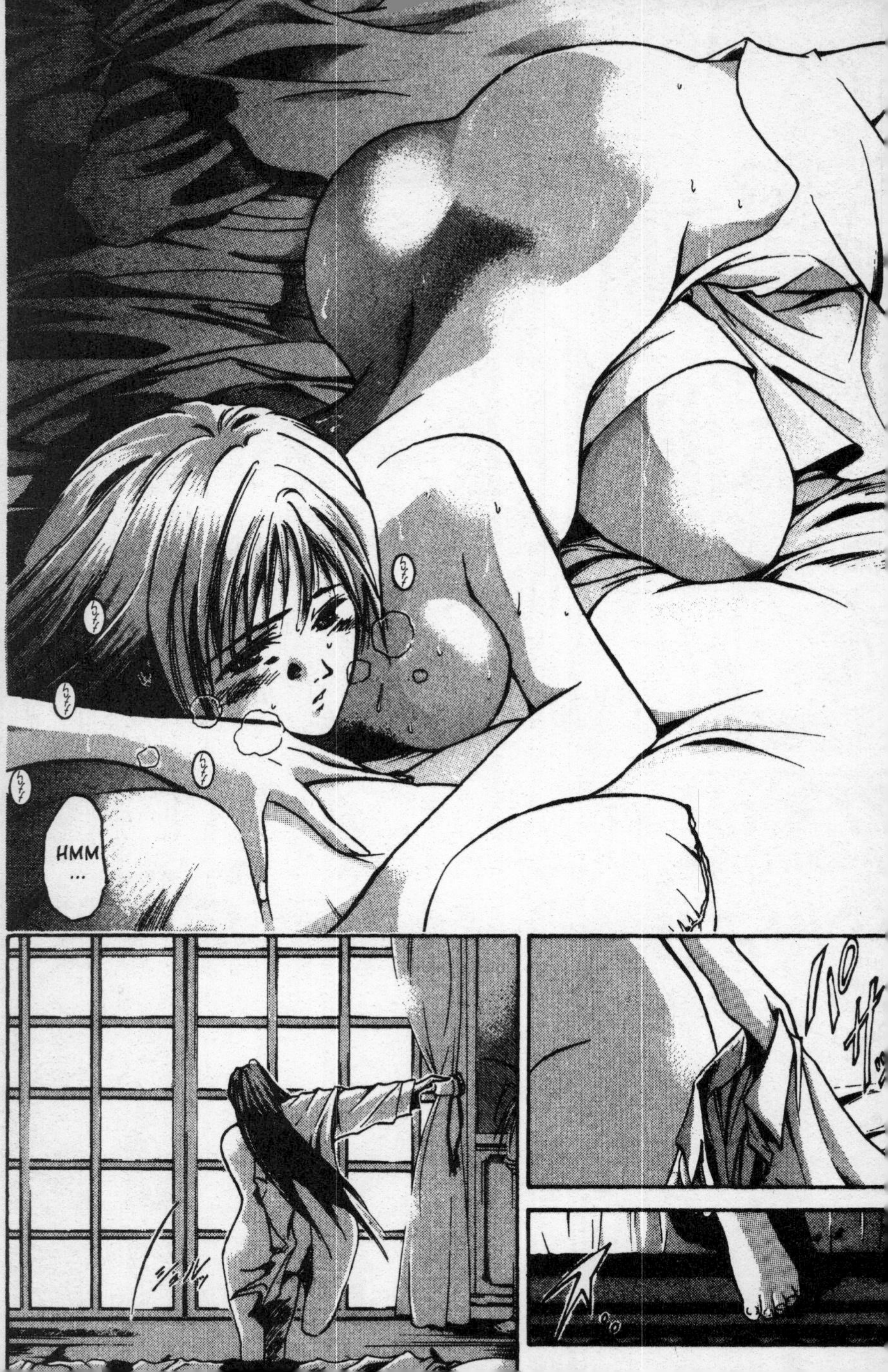
HMM
...

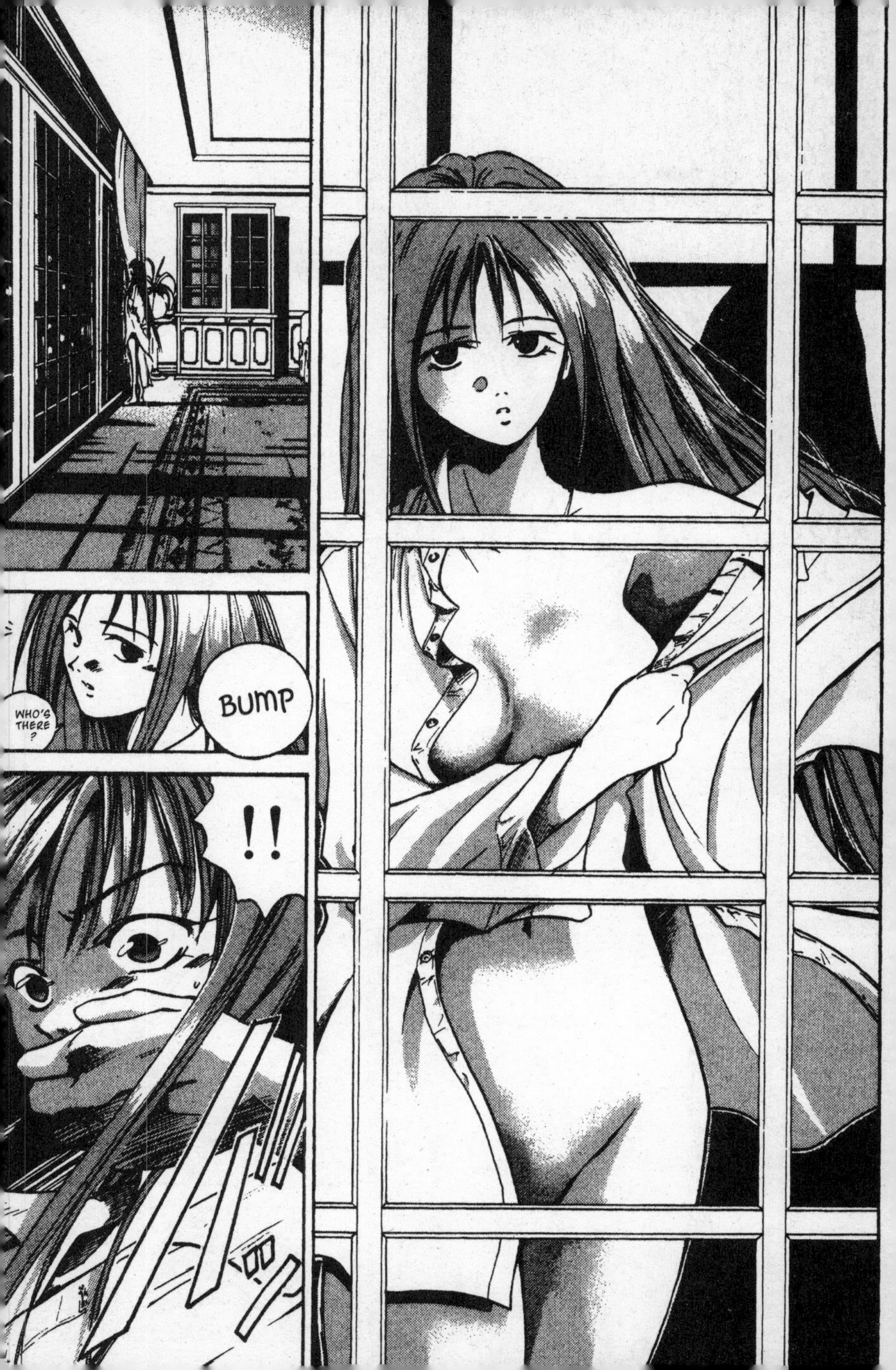
BUMP
WHO'S THERE ?
!!

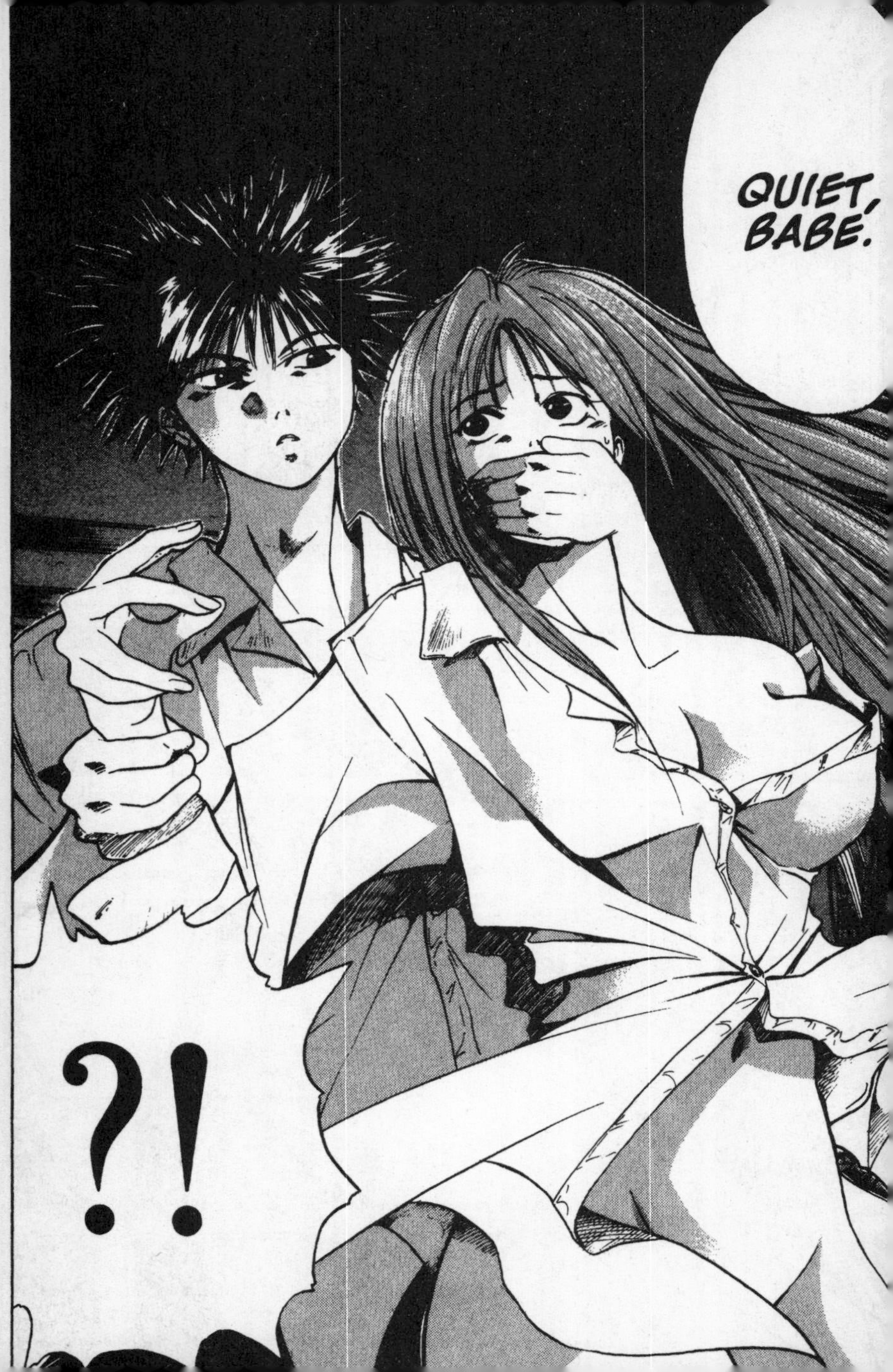
QUIET, BABE.
?!

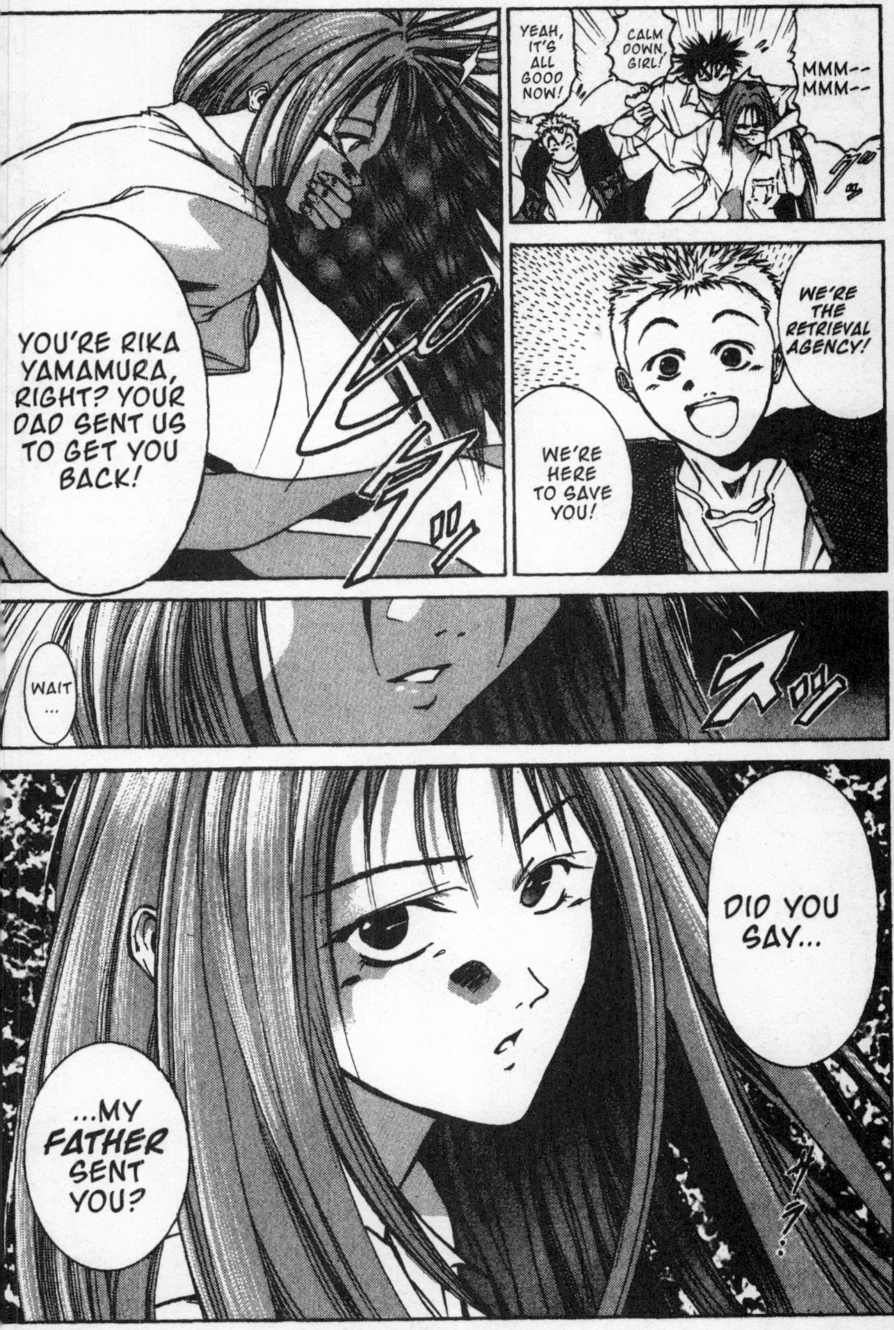

MMM-- MMM--
CALM DOWN, GIRL!
YEAH, IT'S ALL GOOD NOW!
YOU'RE RIKA YAMAMURA, RIGHT? YOUR DAD SENT US TO GET YOU BACK!
WE'RE THE RETRIEVAL AGENCY!
WE'RE HERE TO SAVE YOU!
WAIT ...
DID YOU SAY...
...MY FATHER SENT YOU?

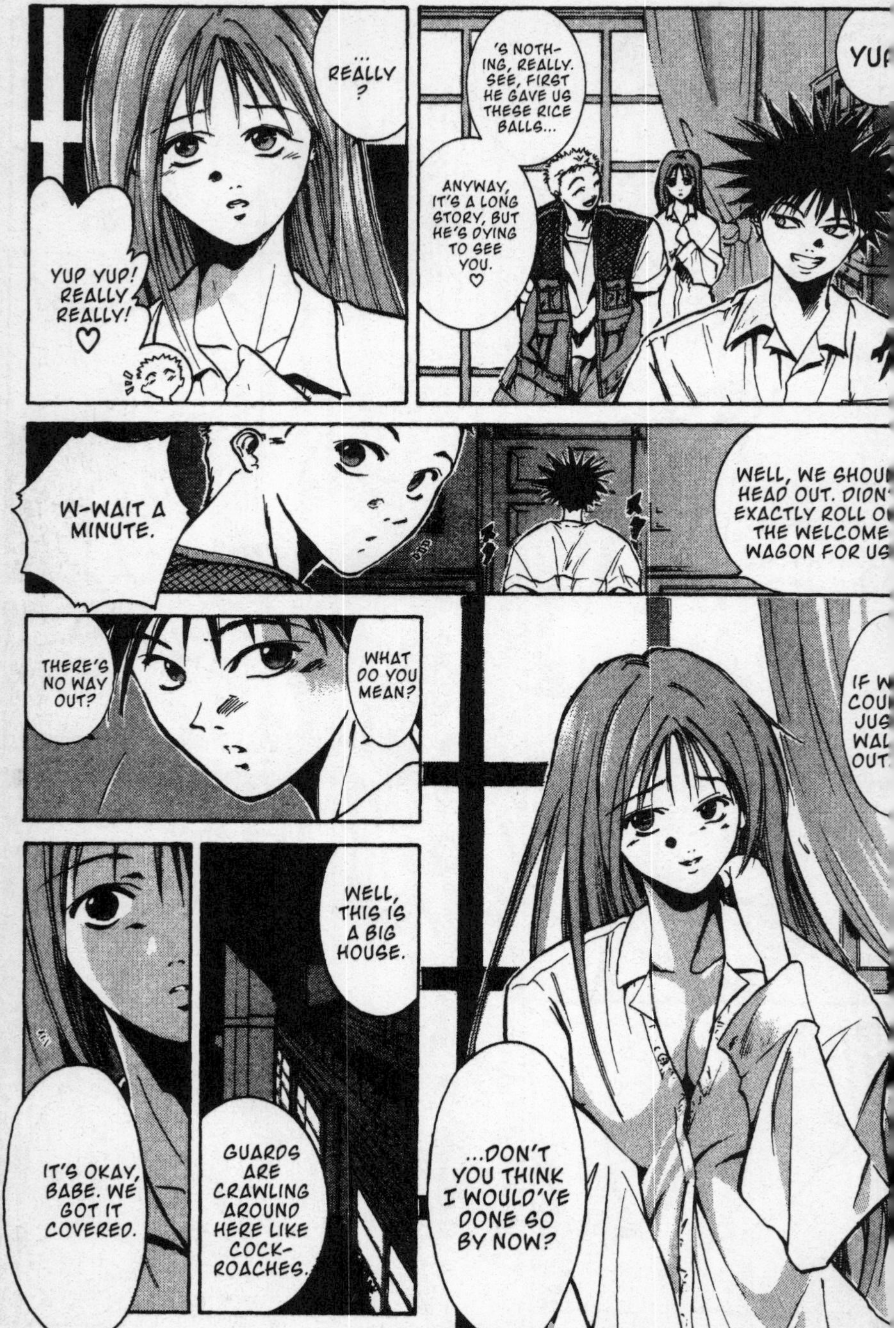
YUP
'S NOTHING, REALLY. SEE, FIRST HE GAVE US THESE RICE BALLS...
ANYWAY, IT'S A LONG STORY, BUT HE'S DYING TO SEE YOU. ♡
... REALLY ?
YUP YUP! REALLY REALLY! ♡
WELL, WE SHOU HEAD OUT. DIDN' EXACTLY ROLL O THE WELCOME WAGON FOR US
W-WAIT A MINUTE.
IF W COU JUS WAL OUT.
...DON'T YOU THINK I WOULD'VE DONE SO BY NOW?
WHAT DO YOU MEAN?
THERE'S NO WAY OUT?
WELL, THIS IS A BIG HOUSE.
GUARDS ARE CRAWLING AROUND HERE LIKE COCK-ROACHES.
IT'S OKAY, BABE. WE GOT IT COVERED.

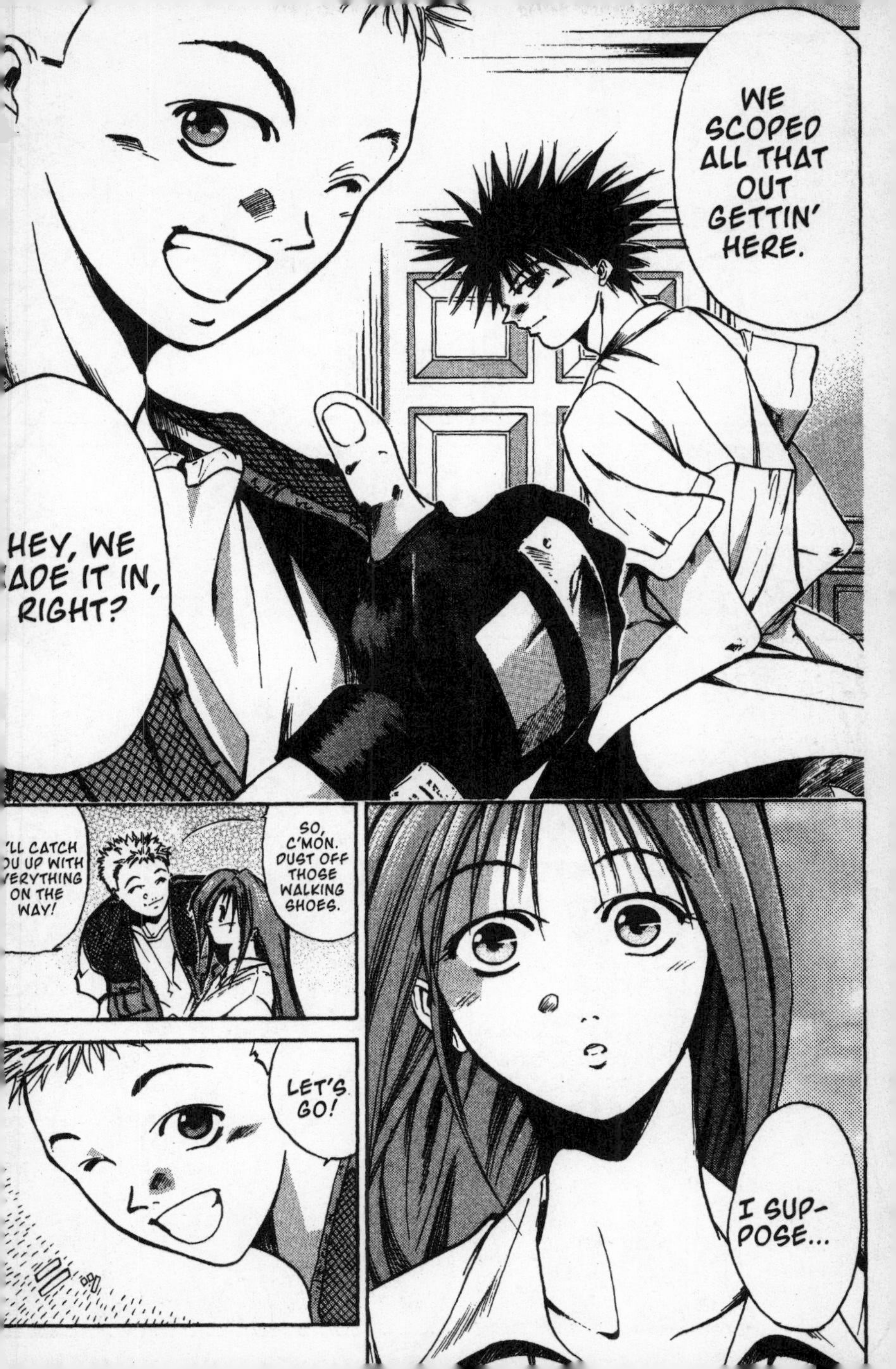
WE SCOPED ALL THAT OUT GETTIN' HERE.
HEY, WE ADE IT IN, RIGHT?
I SUP-POSE...
SO, C'MON. DUST OFF THOSE WALKING SHOES.
'LL CATCH OU UP WITH VERYTHING ON THE WAY!
LET'S GO!

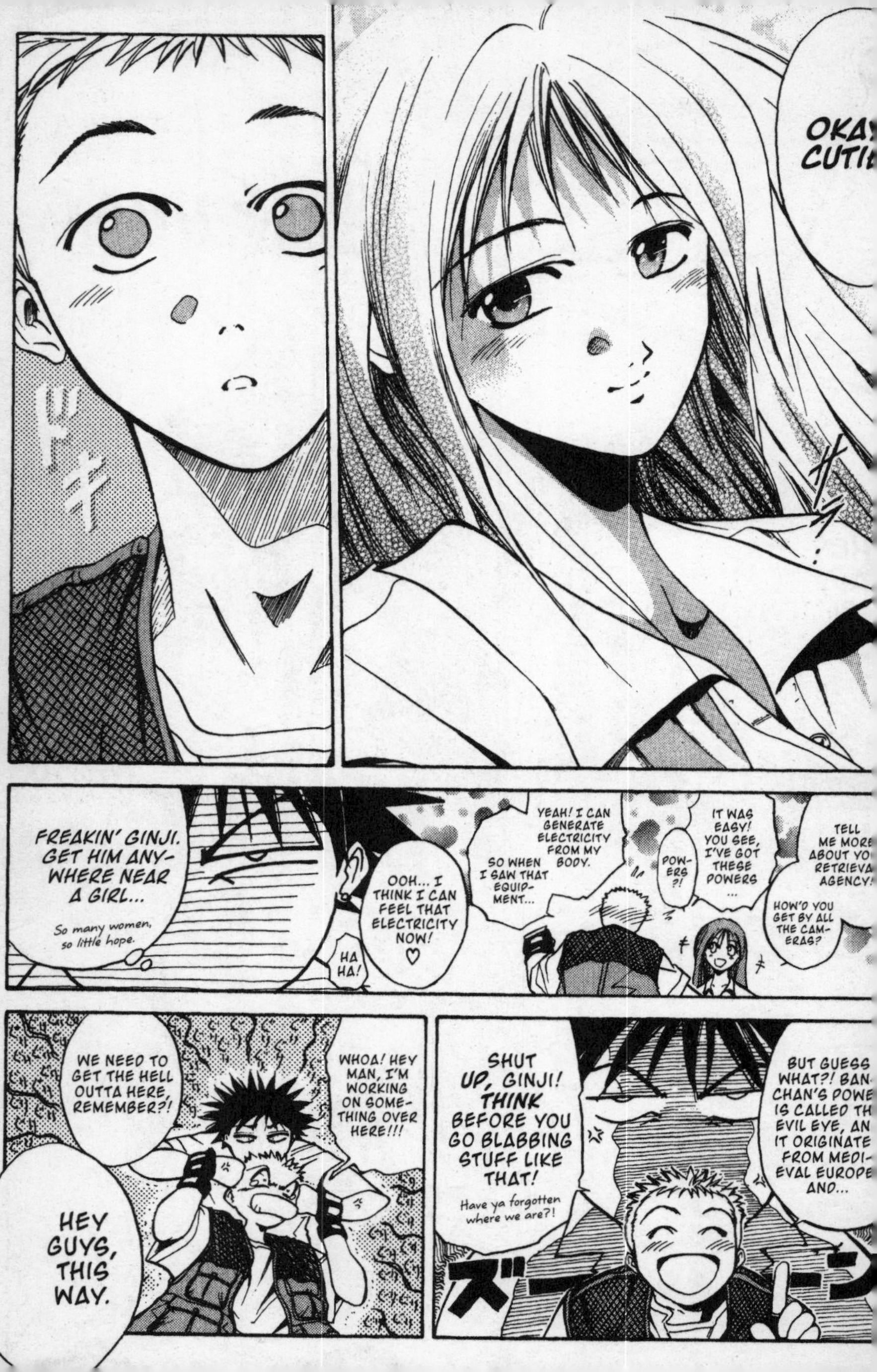
OKAY CUTIE
ドキ
TELL ME MORE ABOUT YO RETRIEVA AGENCY!
HOW'D YOU GET BY ALL THE CAMERAS?
IT WAS EASY! YOU SEE, I'VE GOT THESE POWERS...
POWERS?!
YEAH! I CAN GENERATE ELECTRICITY FROM MY BODY.
SO WHEN I SAW THAT EQUIPMENT...
OOH... I THINK I CAN FEEL THAT ELECTRICITY NOW! ♡
HA HA!
FREAKIN' GINJI. GET HIM ANYWHERE NEAR A GIRL...
So many women, so little hope.
BUT GUESS WHAT?! BAN-CHAN'S POWE IS CALLED TH EVIL EYE, AN IT ORIGINATE FROM MEDIEVAL EUROPE AND...
SHUT UP, GINJI! THINK BEFORE YOU GO BLABBING STUFF LIKE THAT!
Have ya forgotten where we are?!
ズーン
WHOA! HEY MAN, I'M WORKING ON SOMETHING OVER HERE!!!
WE NEED TO GET THE HELL OUTTA HERE, REMEMBER?!
HEY GUYS, THIS WAY.

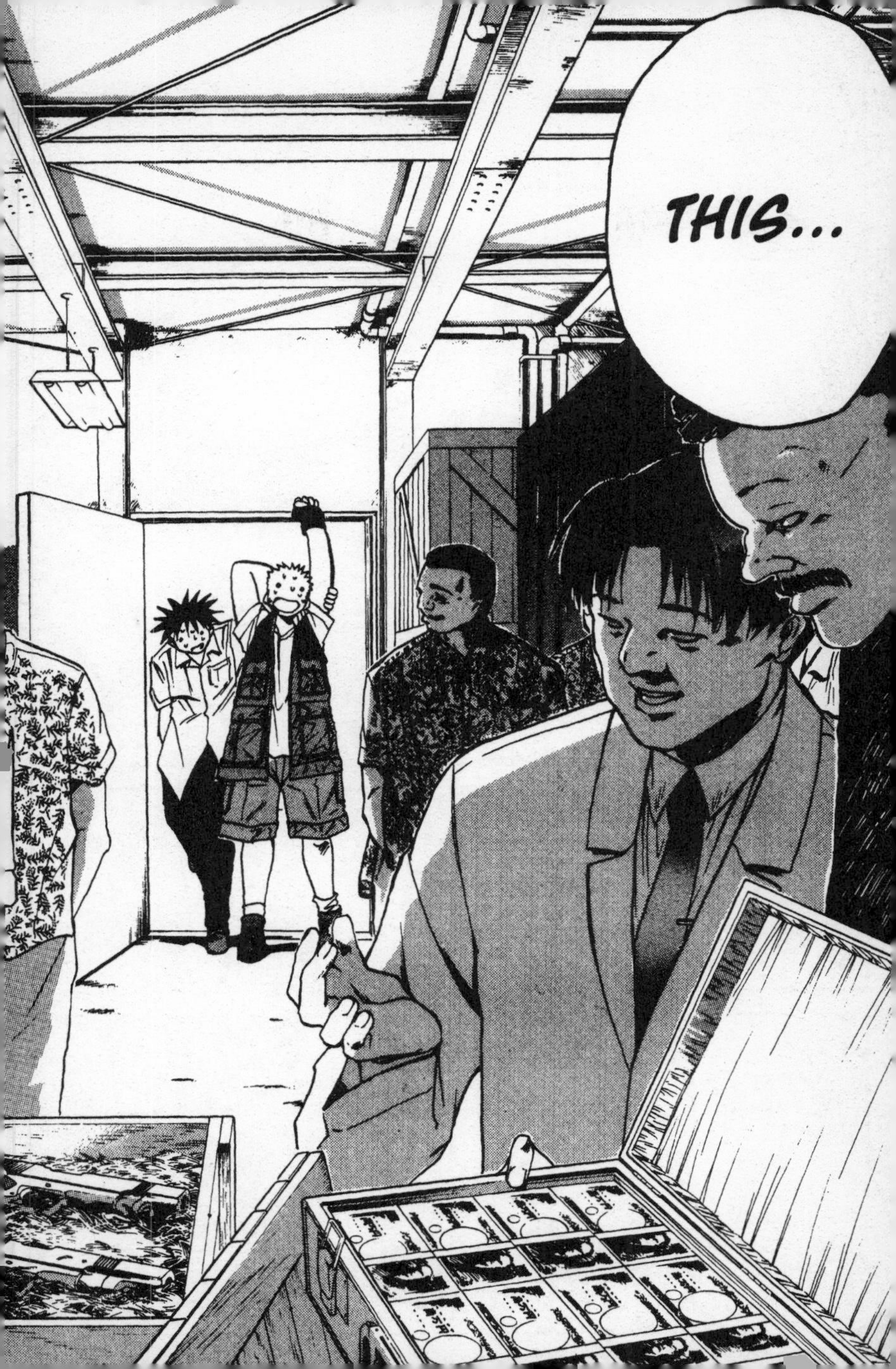
THIS...

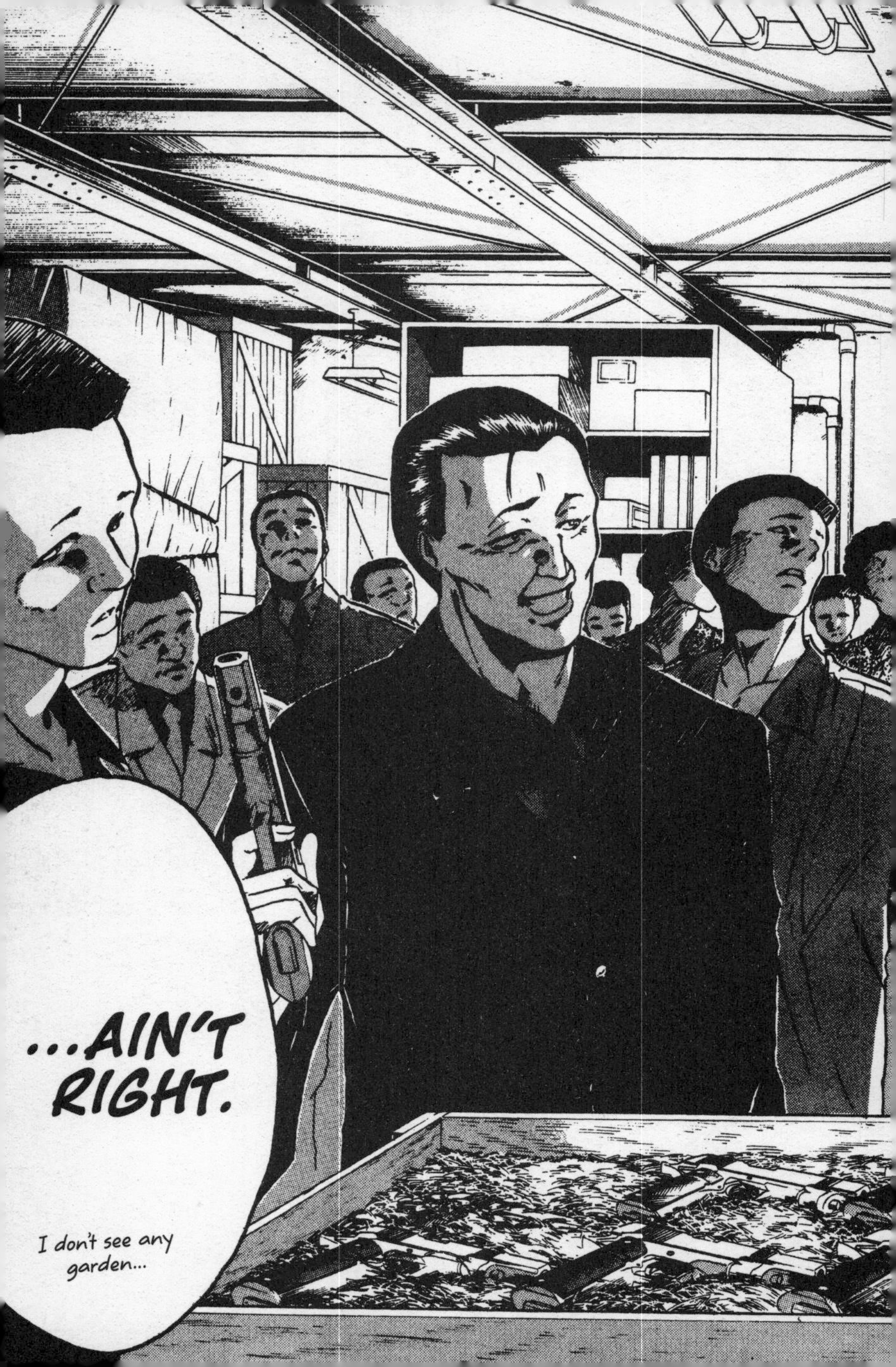
...AIN'T RIGHT.
I don't see any garden...

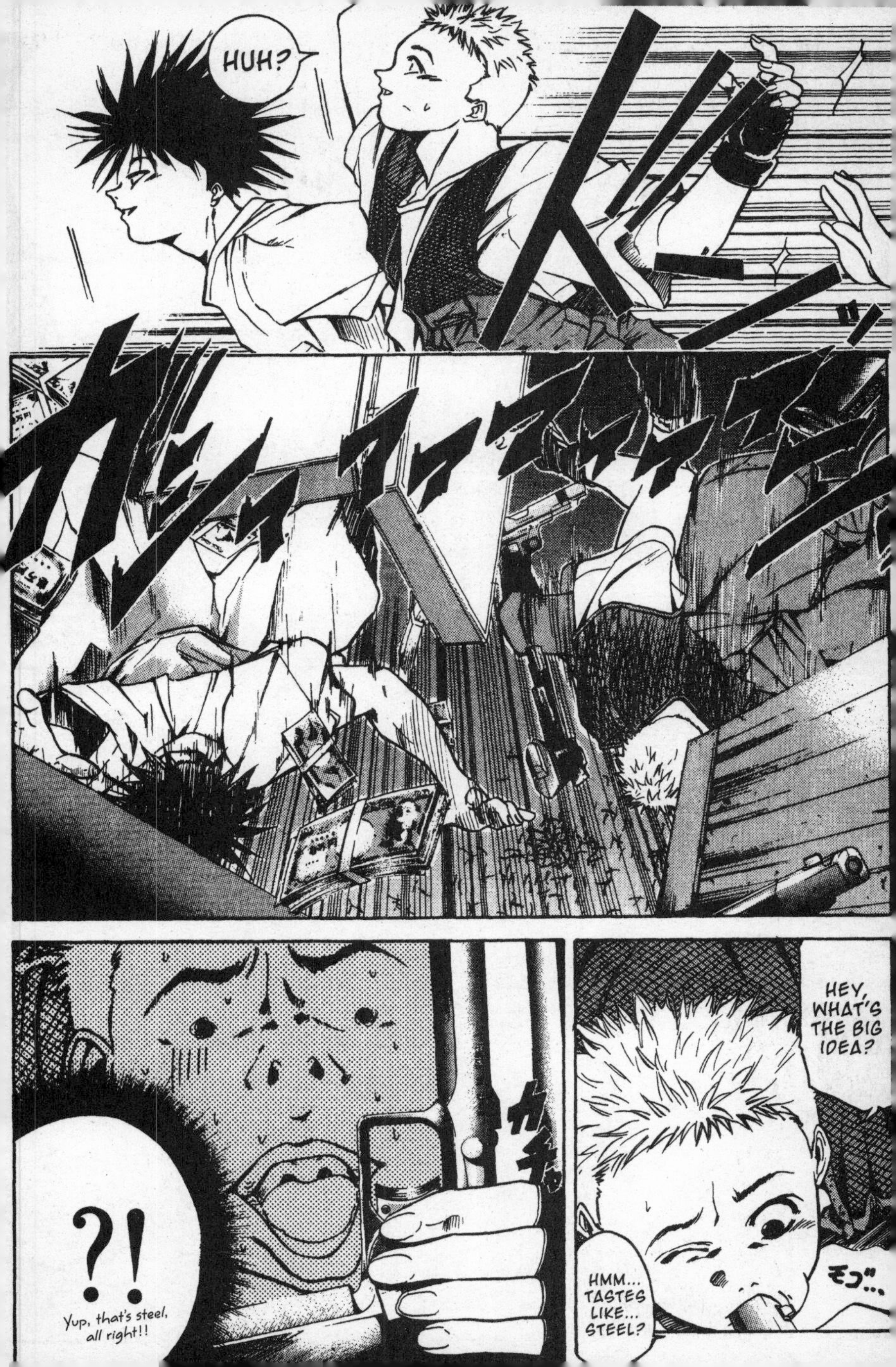
HUH?
HEY, WHAT'S THE BIG IDEA?
HMM... TASTES LIKE... STEEL?
モゴ…
?!
Yup, that's steel, all right!!

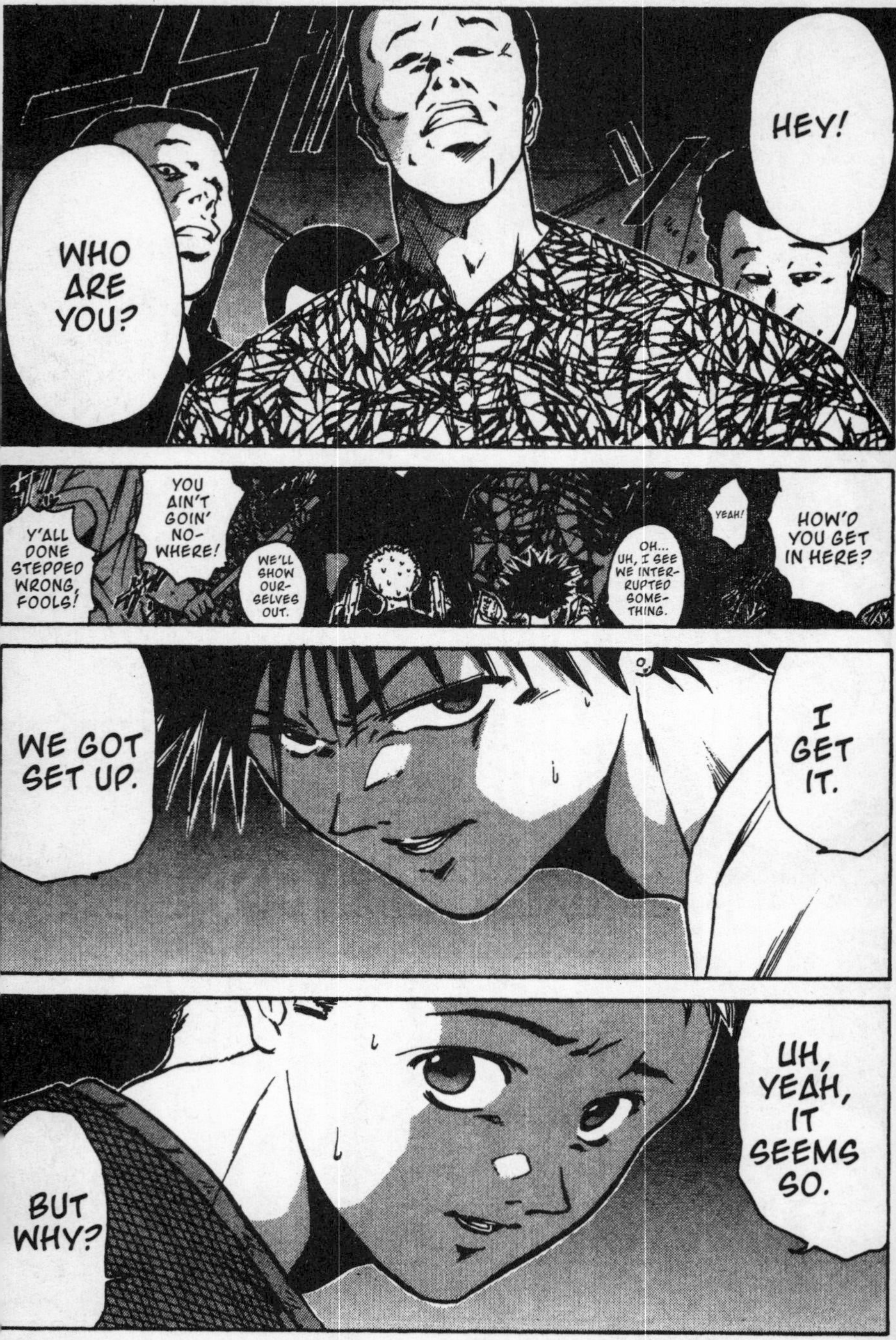
HEY!
WHO ARE YOU?
HOW'D YOU GET IN HERE?
YEAH!
OH... UH, I SEE WE INTERRUPTED SOMETHING.
WE'LL SHOW OURSELVES OUT.
YOU AIN'T GOIN' NOWHERE!
Y'ALL DONE STEPPED WRONG, FOOLS!
I GET IT.
WE GOT SET UP.
UH, YEAH, IT SEEMS SO.
BUT WHY?

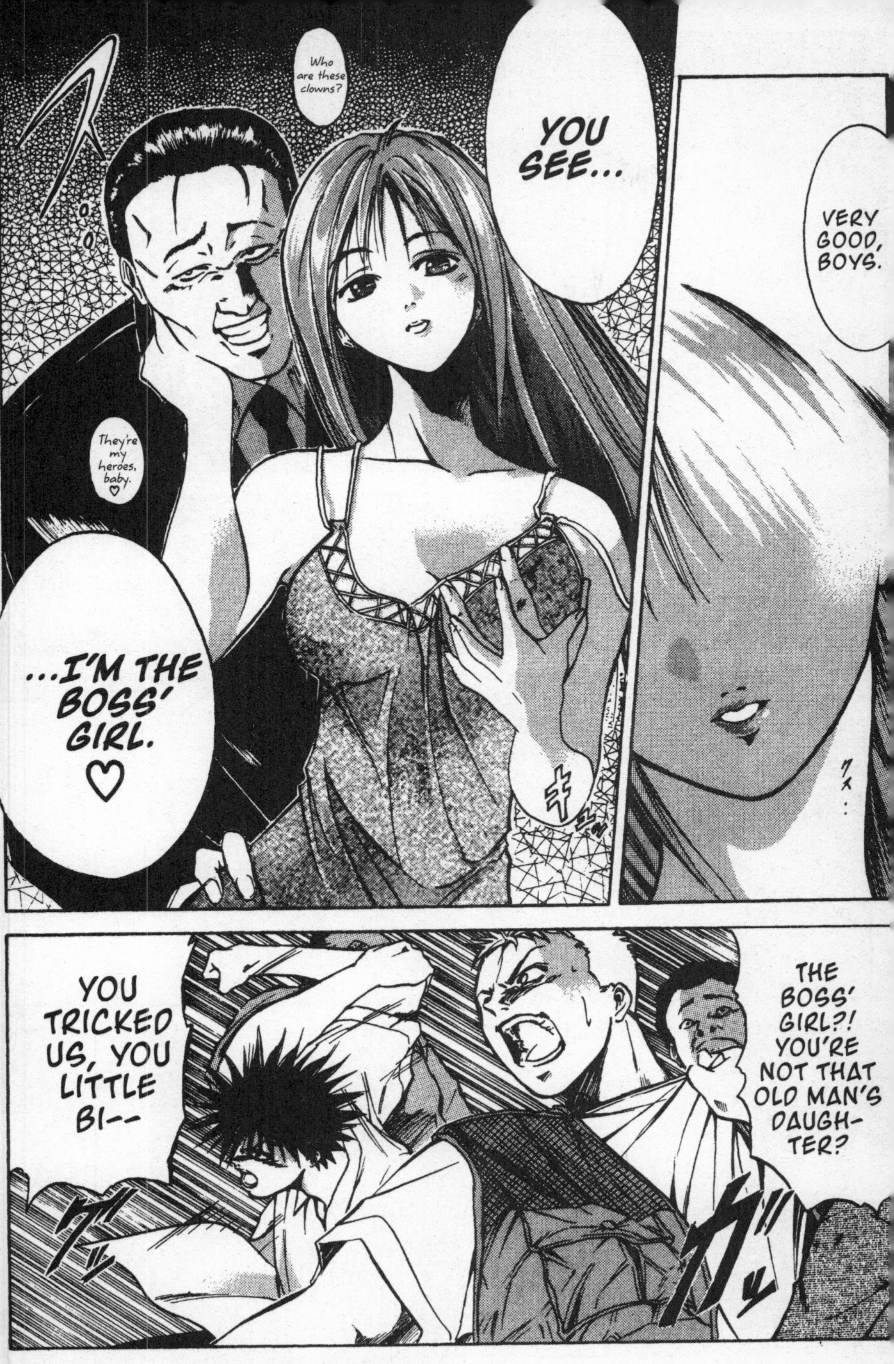
VERY GOOD, BOYS.
YOU SEE...
Who are these clowns?
They're my heroes, baby. ♡
...I'M THE BOSS' GIRL. ♡
THE BOSS' GIRL?! YOU'RE NOT THAT OLD MAN'S DAUGHTER?
YOU TRICKED US, YOU LITTLE BI--

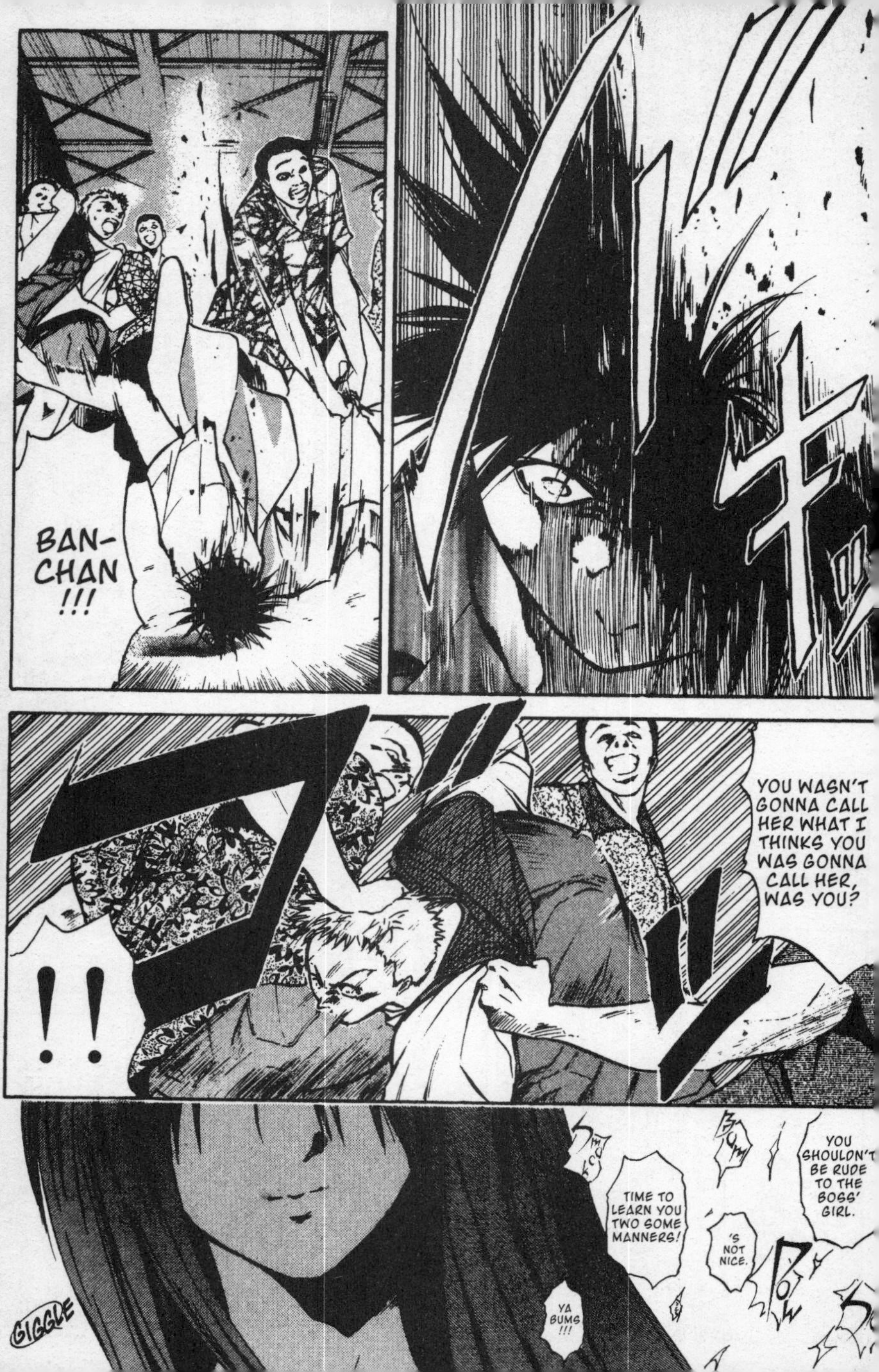
BAN-CHAN !!!
YOU WASN'T GONNA CALL HER WHAT I THINKS YOU WAS GONNA CALL HER, WAS YOU?
!!
YOU SHOULDN'T BE RUDE TO THE BOSS' GIRL.
'S NOT NICE.
TIME TO LEARN YOU TWO SOME MANNERS!
YA BUMS !!!
GIGGLE

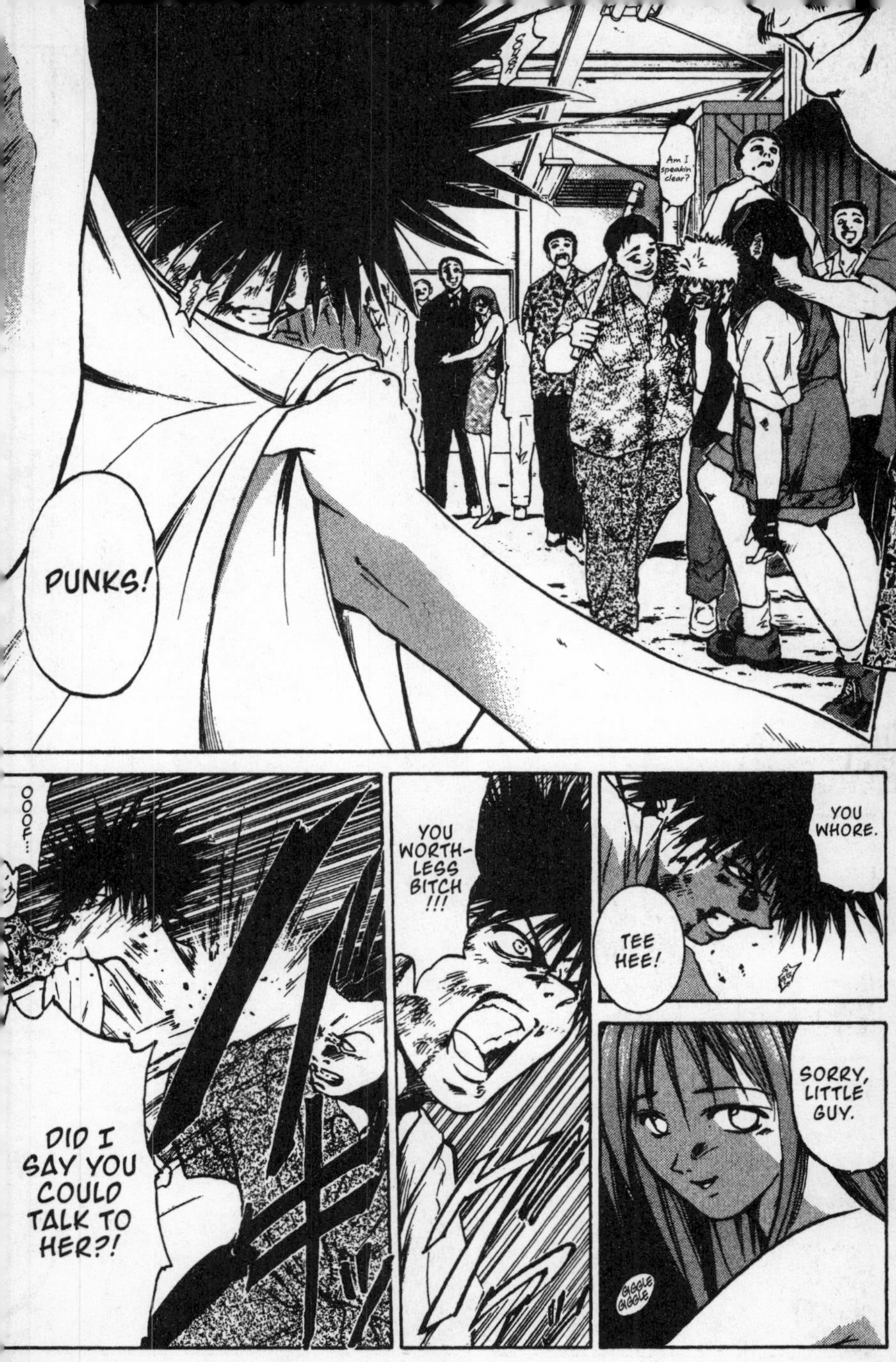
COUGH
Am I speakin' clear?
PUNKS!
YOU WHORE.
TEE HEE!
SORRY, LITTLE GUY.
GIGGLE GIGGLE
YOU WORTH-LESS BITCH!!!
OOOF...
DID I SAY YOU COULD TALK TO HER?!

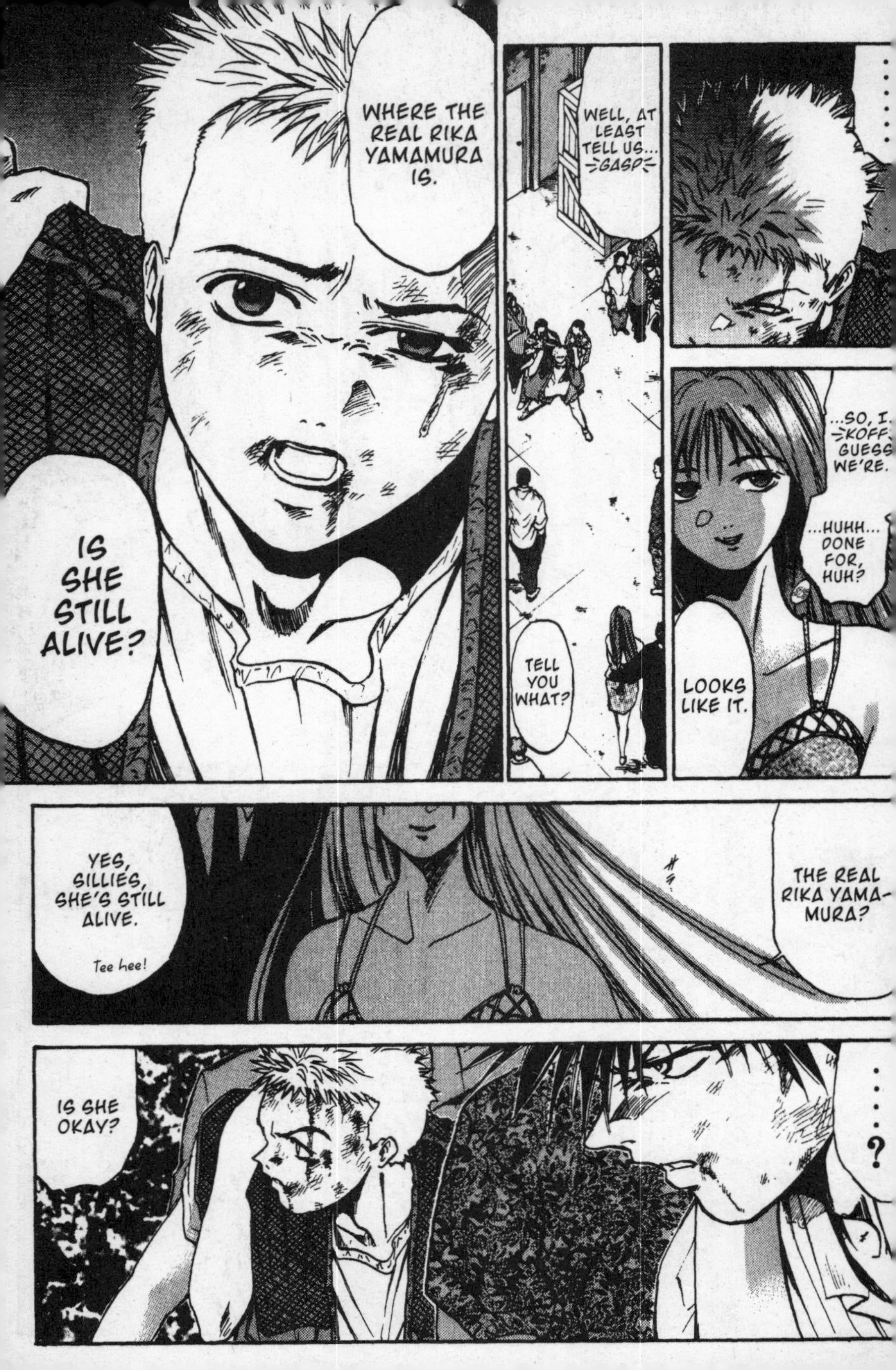
......
...SO, I. KOFF GUESS WE'RE.
...HUHH... DONE FOR, HUH?
LOOKS LIKE IT.
WELL, AT LEAST TELL US... GASP
TELL YOU WHAT?
WHERE THE REAL RIKA YAMAMURA IS.
IS SHE STILL ALIVE?
THE REAL RIKA YAMA-MURA?
YES, SILLIES, SHE'S STILL ALIVE.
Tee hee!
......?
IS SHE OKAY?

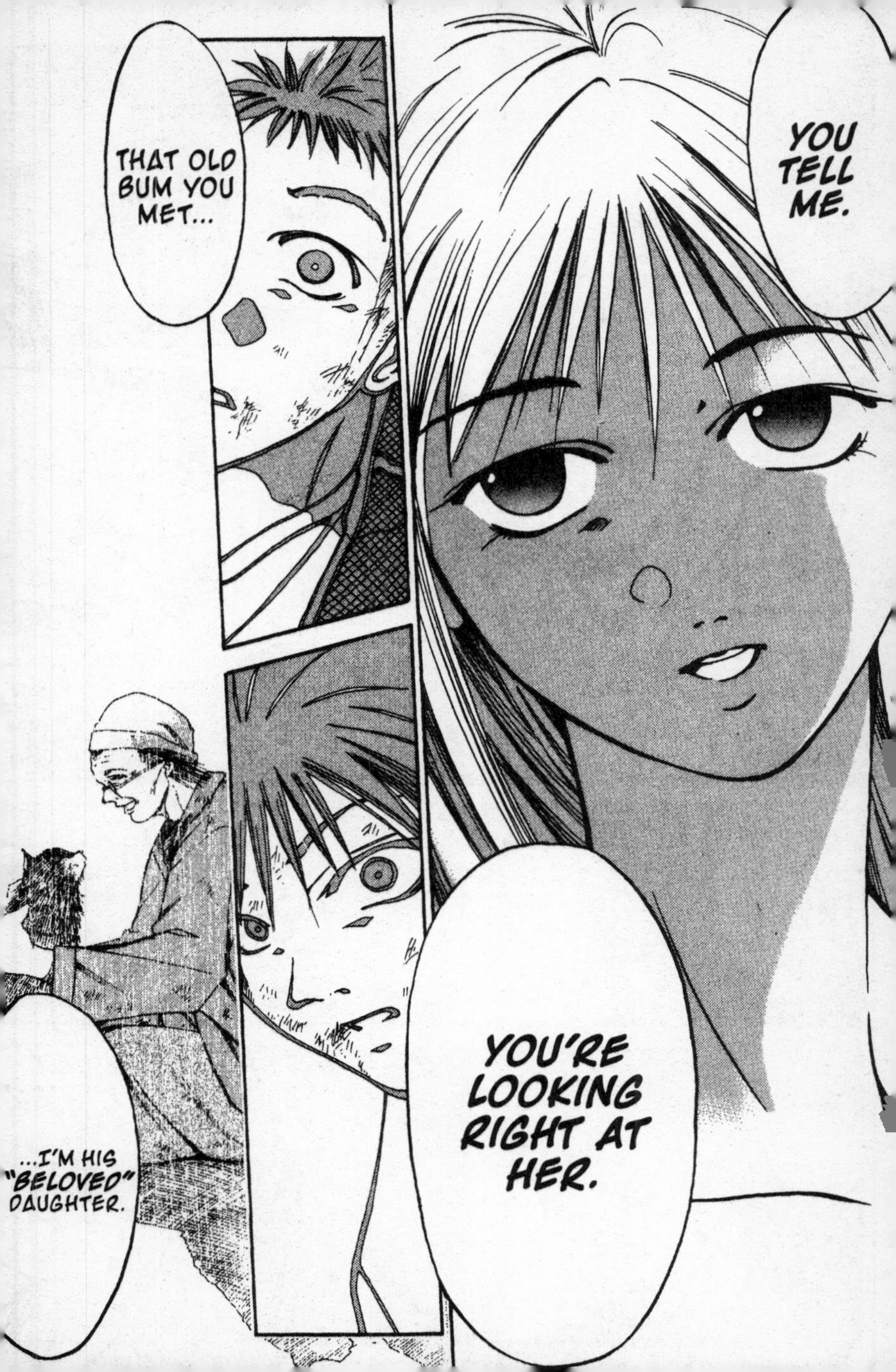
YOU TELL ME.
THAT OLD BUM YOU MET...
...I'M HIS "BELOVED" DAUGHTER.
YOU'RE LOOKING RIGHT AT HER.

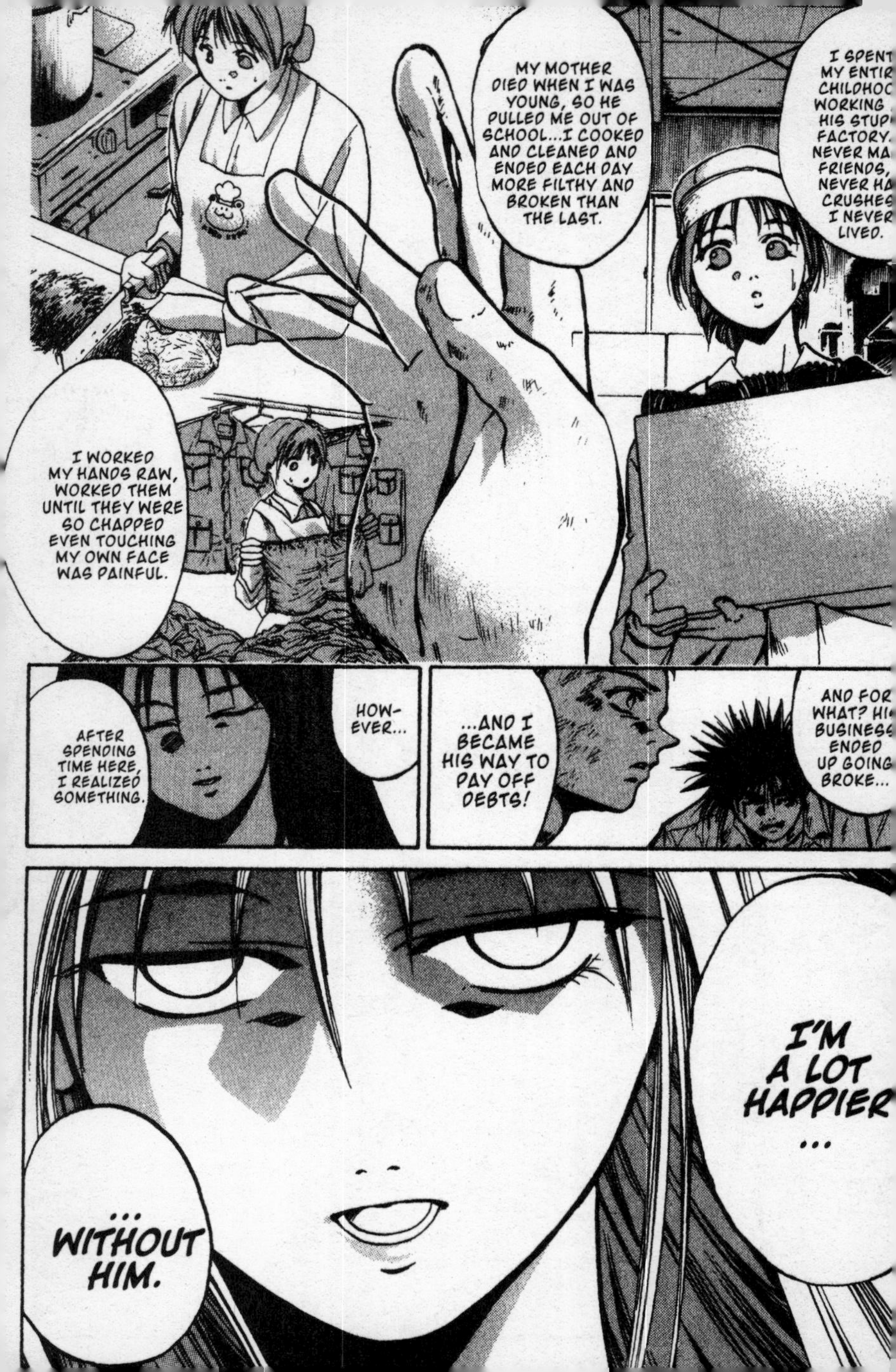
I SPENT MY ENTIR CHILDHOO WORKING HIS STUP FACTORY. NEVER MA FRIENDS, NEVER HA CRUSHES I NEVER LIVED.
MY MOTHER DIED WHEN I WAS YOUNG, SO HE PULLED ME OUT OF SCHOOL...I COOKED AND CLEANED AND ENDED EACH DAY MORE FILTHY AND BROKEN THAN THE LAST.
I WORKED MY HANDS RAW, WORKED THEM UNTIL THEY WERE SO CHAPPED EVEN TOUCHING MY OWN FACE WAS PAINFUL.
AND FOR WHAT? HI BUSINESS ENDED UP GOING BROKE...
...AND I BECAME HIS WAY TO PAY OFF DEBTS!
HOW-EVER...
AFTER SPENDING TIME HERE, I REALIZED SOMETHING.
I'M A LOT HAPPIER ...
... WITHOUT HIM.

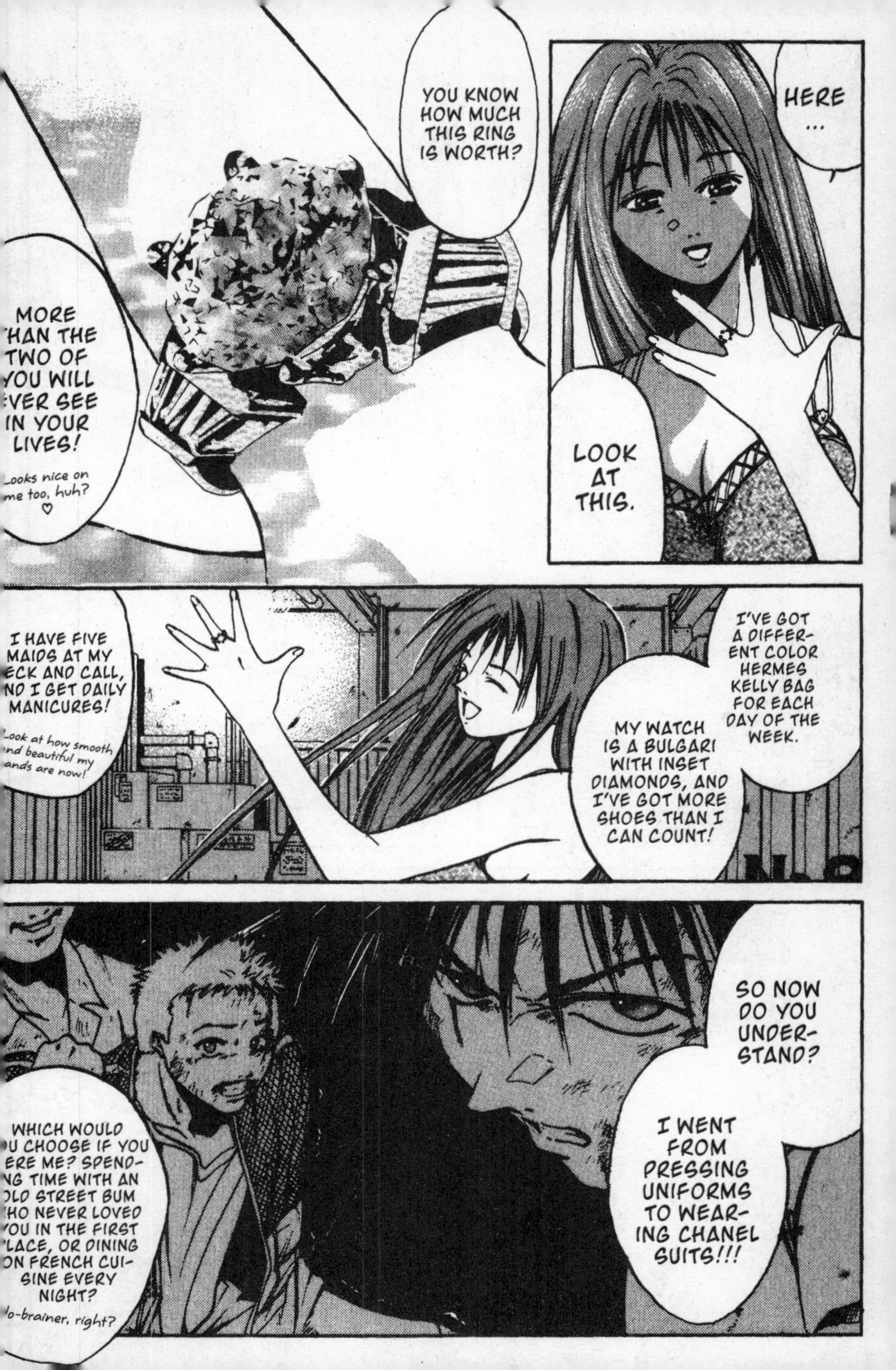
HERE ...
LOOK AT THIS.
YOU KNOW HOW MUCH THIS RING IS WORTH?
MORE HAN THE TWO OF OU WILL VER SEE IN YOUR LIVES!
ooks nice on me too, huh? ♡
I'VE GOT A DIFFERENT COLOR HERMES KELLY BAG FOR EACH DAY OF THE WEEK.
MY WATCH IS A BULGARI WITH INSET DIAMONDS, AND I'VE GOT MORE SHOES THAN I CAN COUNT!
I HAVE FIVE MAIDS AT MY ECK AND CALL, ND I GET DAILY MANICURES!
ook at how smooth nd beautiful my ands are now!
SO NOW DO YOU UNDERSTAND?
I WENT FROM PRESSING UNIFORMS TO WEARING CHANEL SUITS!!!
WHICH WOULD OU CHOOSE IF YOU ERE ME? SPENDING TIME WITH AN OLD STREET BUM HO NEVER LOVED OU IN THE FIRST LACE, OR DINING ON FRENCH CUISINE EVERY NIGHT?
o-brainer, right?

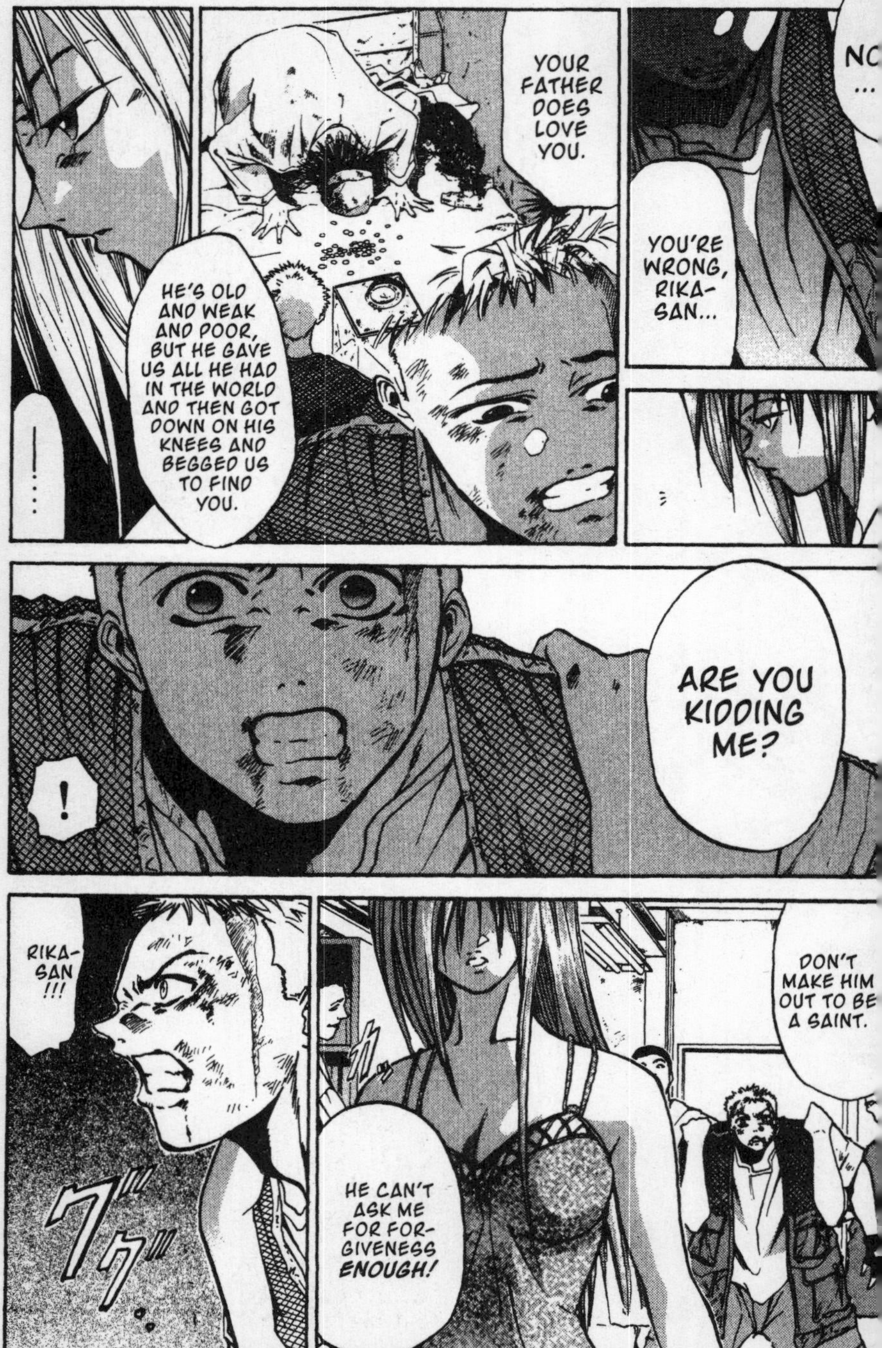
NO ...
YOU'RE WRONG, RIKA-SAN...
YOUR FATHER DOES LOVE YOU.
HE'S OLD AND WEAK AND POOR, BUT HE GAVE US ALL HE HAD IN THE WORLD AND THEN GOT DOWN ON HIS KNEES AND BEGGED US TO FIND YOU.
!....
ARE YOU KIDDING ME?
!
DON'T MAKE HIM OUT TO BE A SAINT.
HE CAN'T ASK ME FOR FOR-GIVENESS ENOUGH!
RIKA-SAN!!!

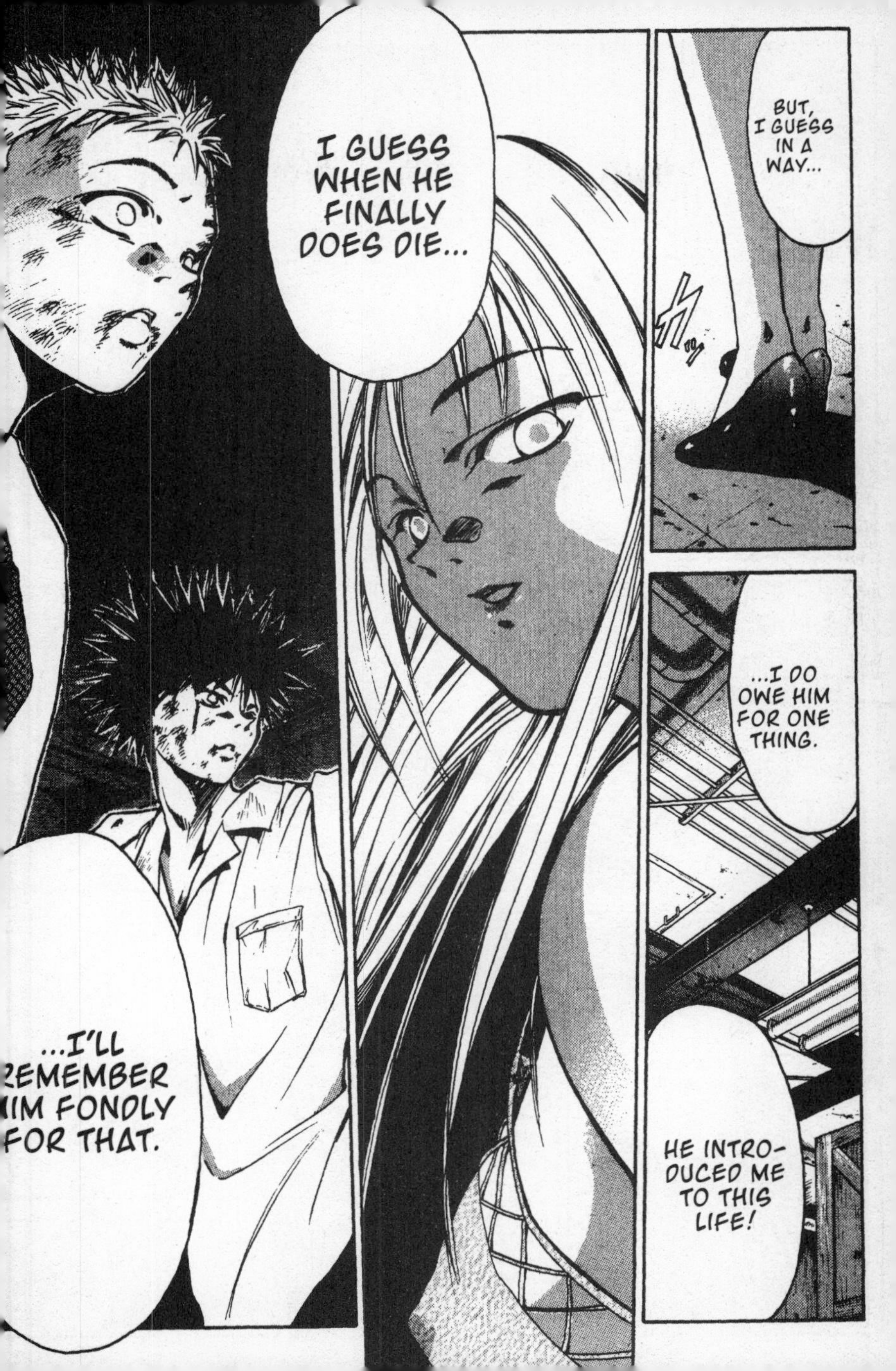
BUT, I GUESS IN A WAY...
...I DO OWE HIM FOR ONE THING.
HE INTRO-DUCED ME TO THIS LIFE!
I GUESS WHEN HE FINALLY DOES DIE...
...I'LL REMEMBER HIM FONDLY FOR THAT.

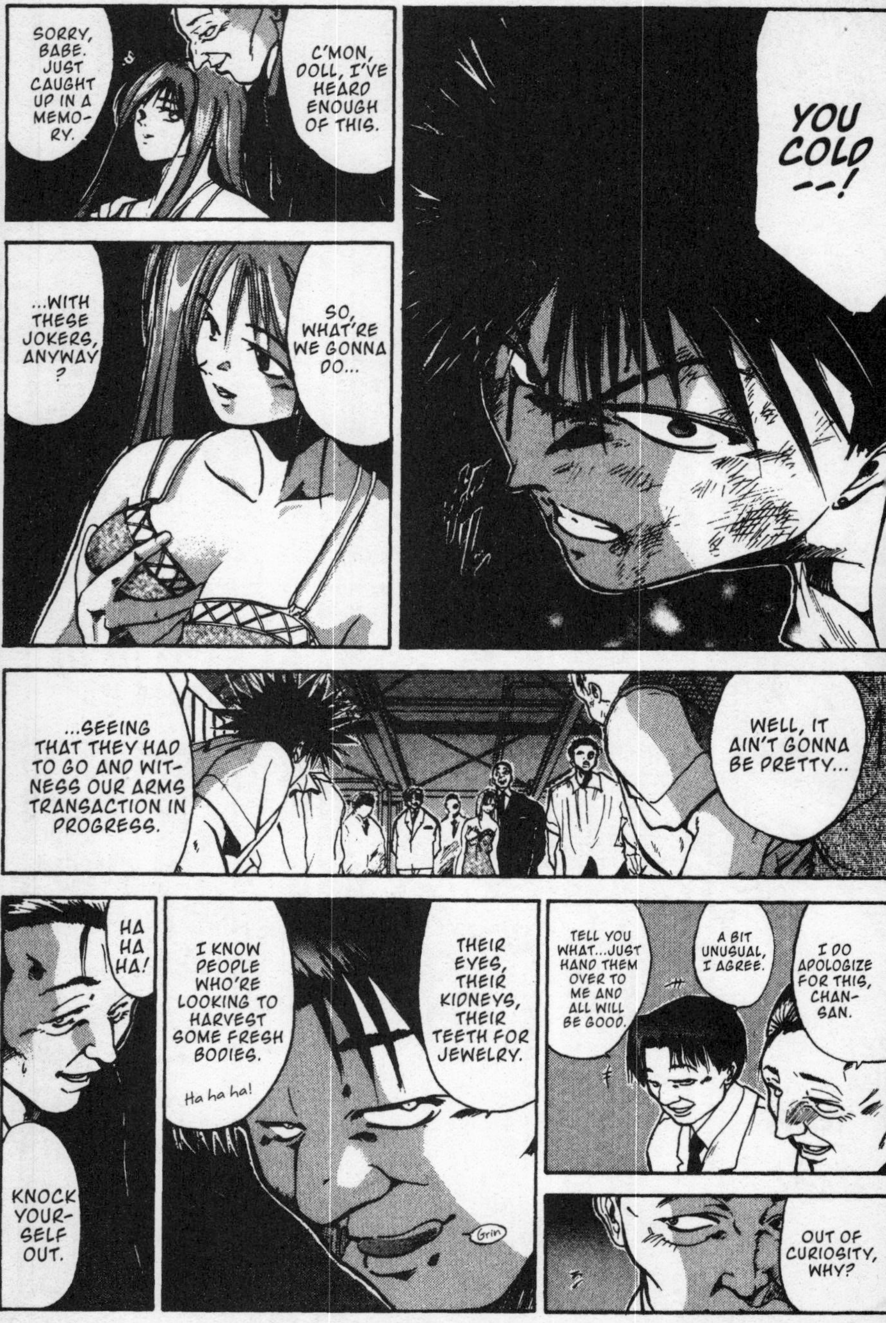
YOU COLD --!
C'MON, DOLL, I'VE HEARD ENOUGH OF THIS.
SORRY, BABE. JUST CAUGHT UP IN A MEMORY.
SO, WHAT'RE WE GONNA DO...
...WITH THESE JOKERS, ANYWAY?
WELL, IT AIN'T GONNA BE PRETTY...
...SEEING THAT THEY HAD TO GO AND WITNESS OUR ARMS TRANSACTION IN PROGRESS.
I DO APOLOGIZE FOR THIS, CHAN-SAN.
A BIT UNUSUAL, I AGREE.
TELL YOU WHAT...JUST HAND THEM OVER TO ME AND ALL WILL BE GOOD.
OUT OF CURIOSITY, WHY?
I KNOW PEOPLE WHO'RE LOOKING TO HARVEST SOME FRESH BODIES.
THEIR EYES, THEIR KIDNEYS, THEIR TEETH FOR JEWELRY.
Ha ha ha!
Grin
HA HA HA!
KNOCK YOURSELF OUT.

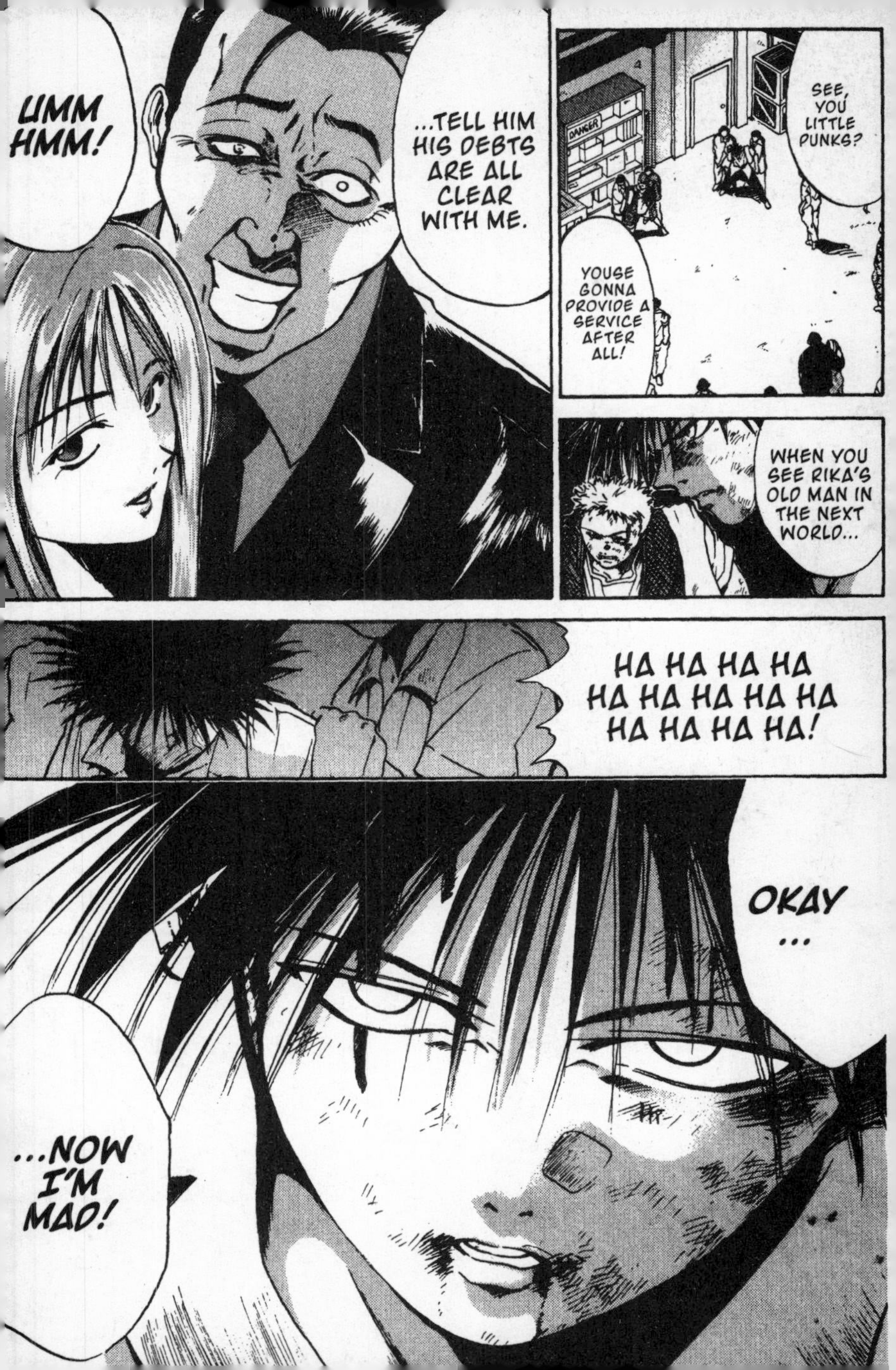
SEE, YOU LITTLE PUNKS?
YOUSE GONNA PROVIDE A SERVICE AFTER ALL!
WHEN YOU SEE RIKA'S OLD MAN IN THE NEXT WORLD...
...TELL HIM HIS DEBTS ARE ALL CLEAR WITH ME.
UMM HMM!
HA HA HA HA HA HA HA HA HA HA HA HA HA!
OKAY ...
...NOW I'M MAD!

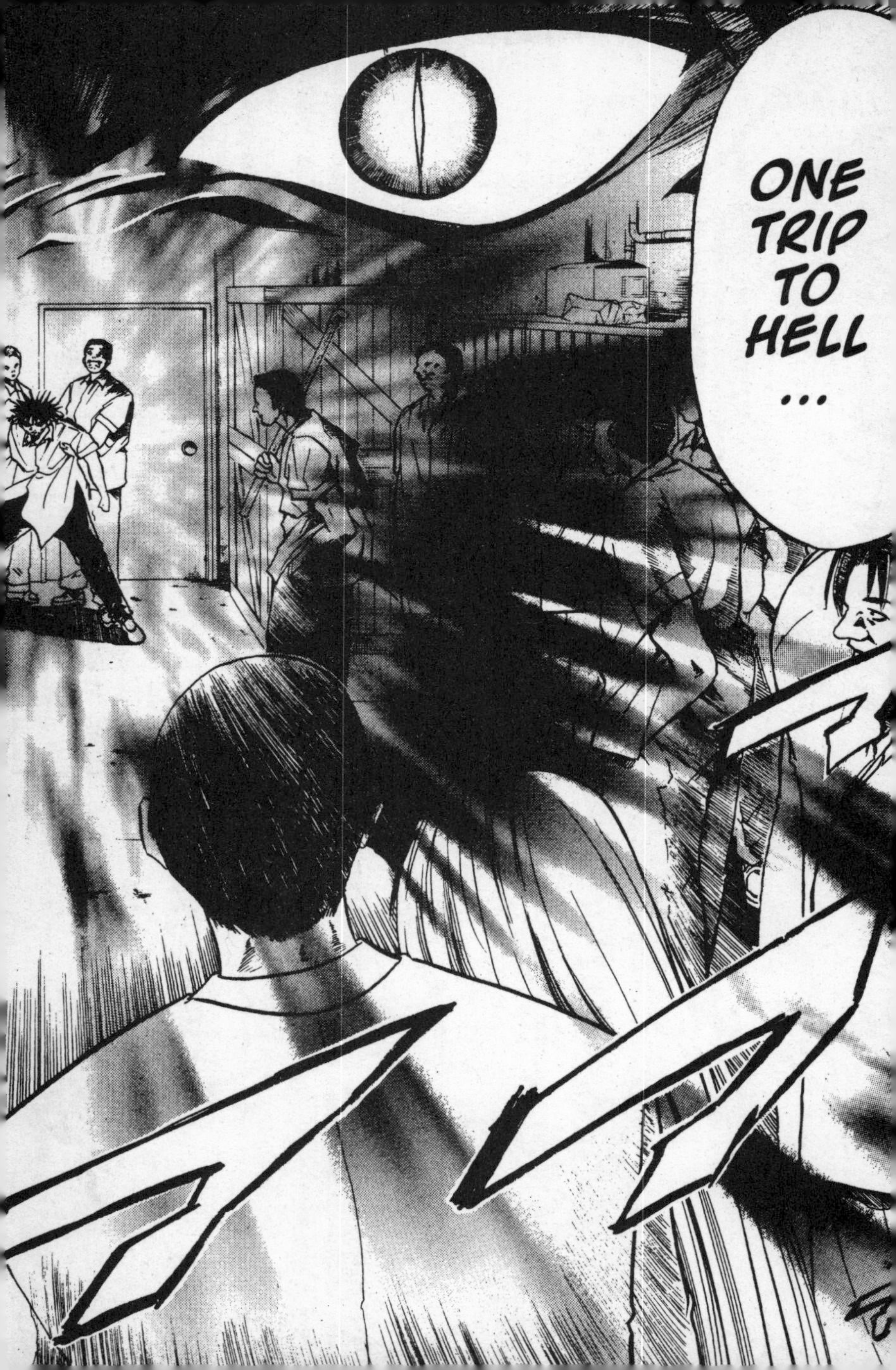
ONE TRIP TO HELL ...

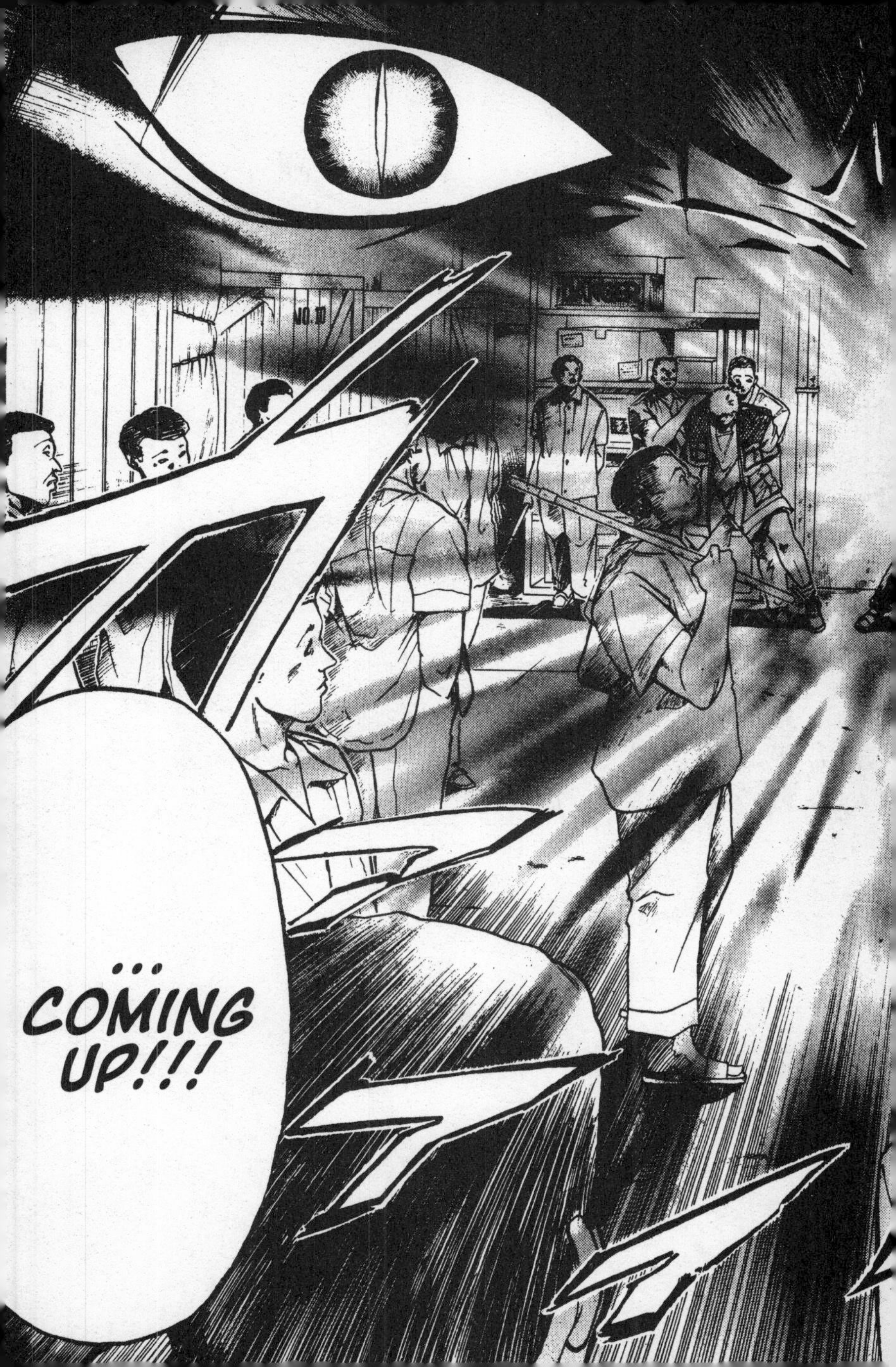
...COMING UP!!!
DANGER
NO.10

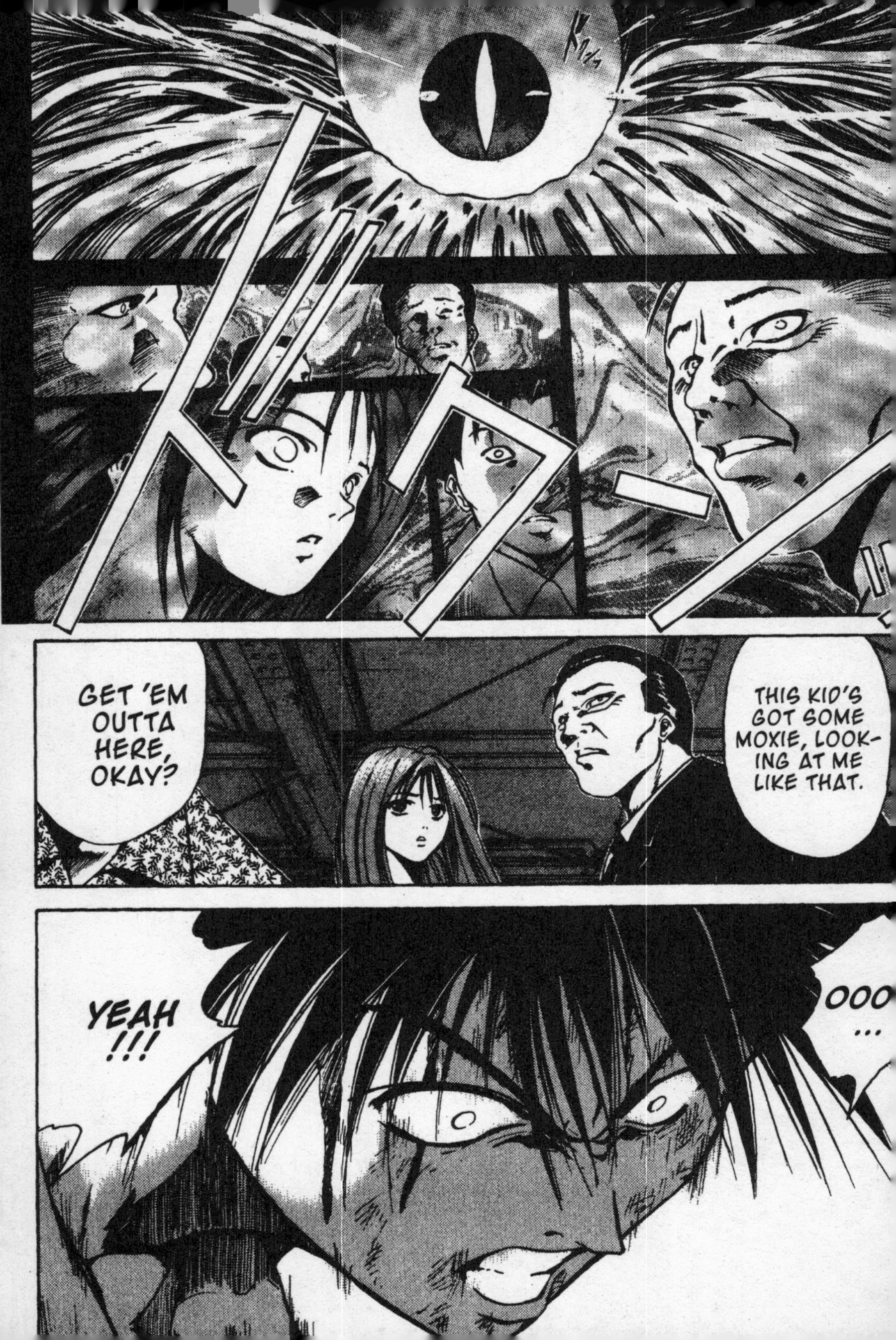
THIS KID'S GOT SOME MOXIE, LOOKING AT ME LIKE THAT.
GET 'EM OUTTA HERE, OKAY?
OOO ...
YEAH !!!

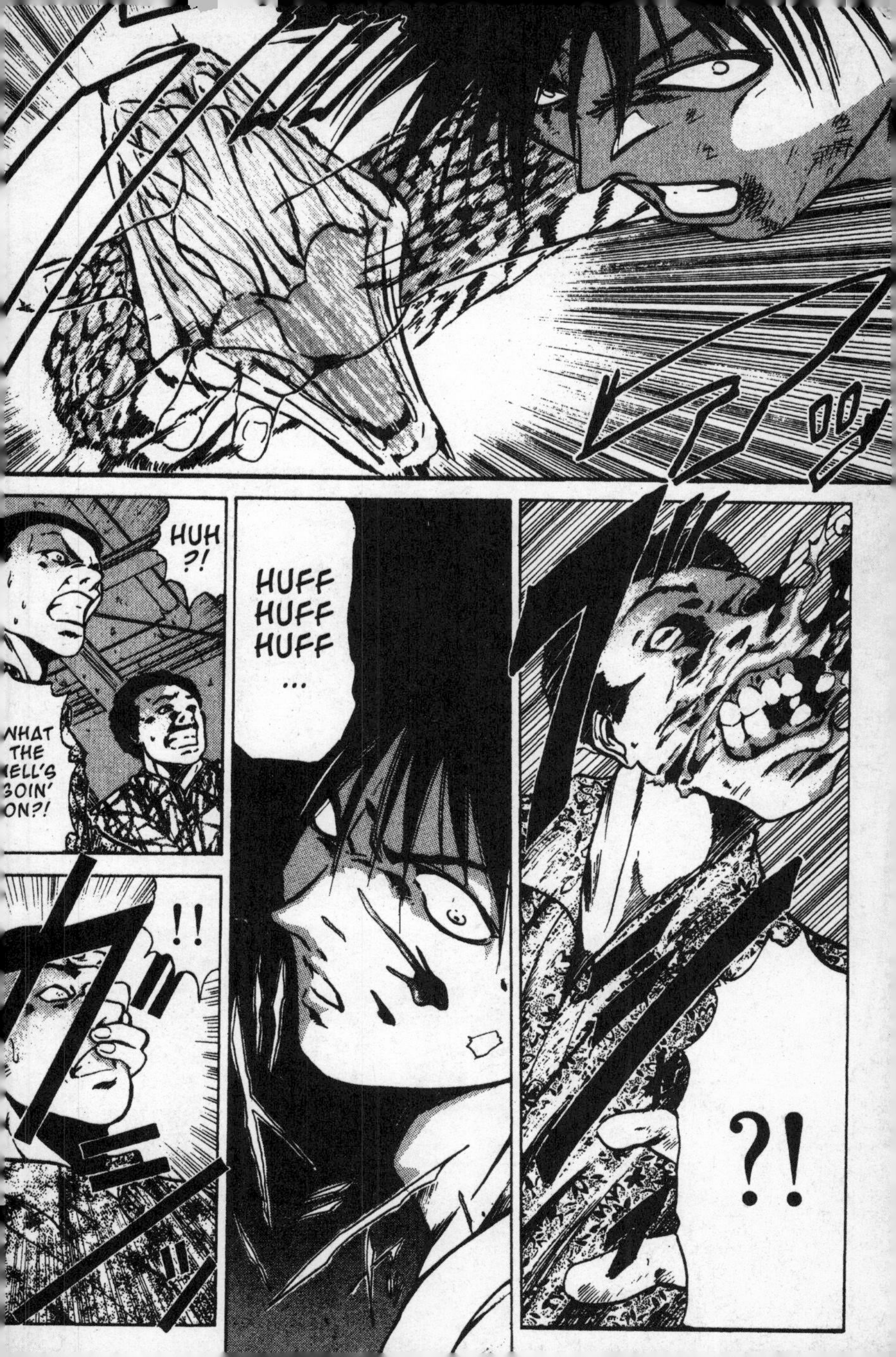
HUFF HUFF HUFF ...
HUH ?!
WHAT THE HELL'S GOIN' ON?!
!!
?!

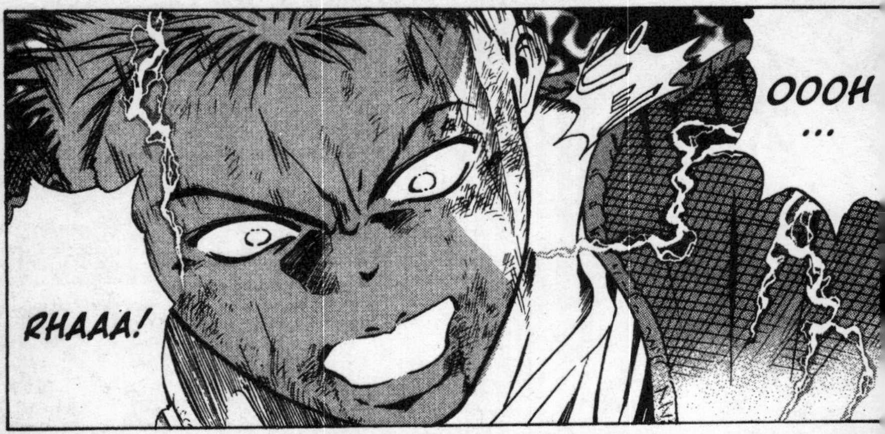
OOOH ...
RHAAA!

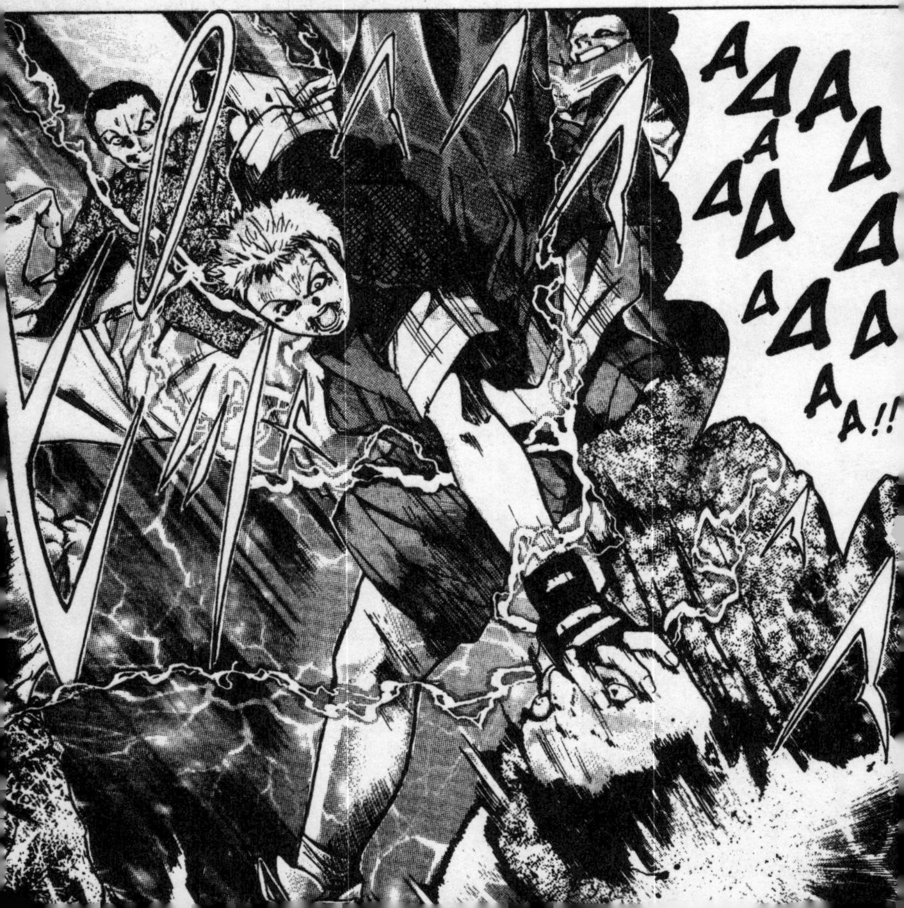
AAAAAAAAAAAAAAAA!!

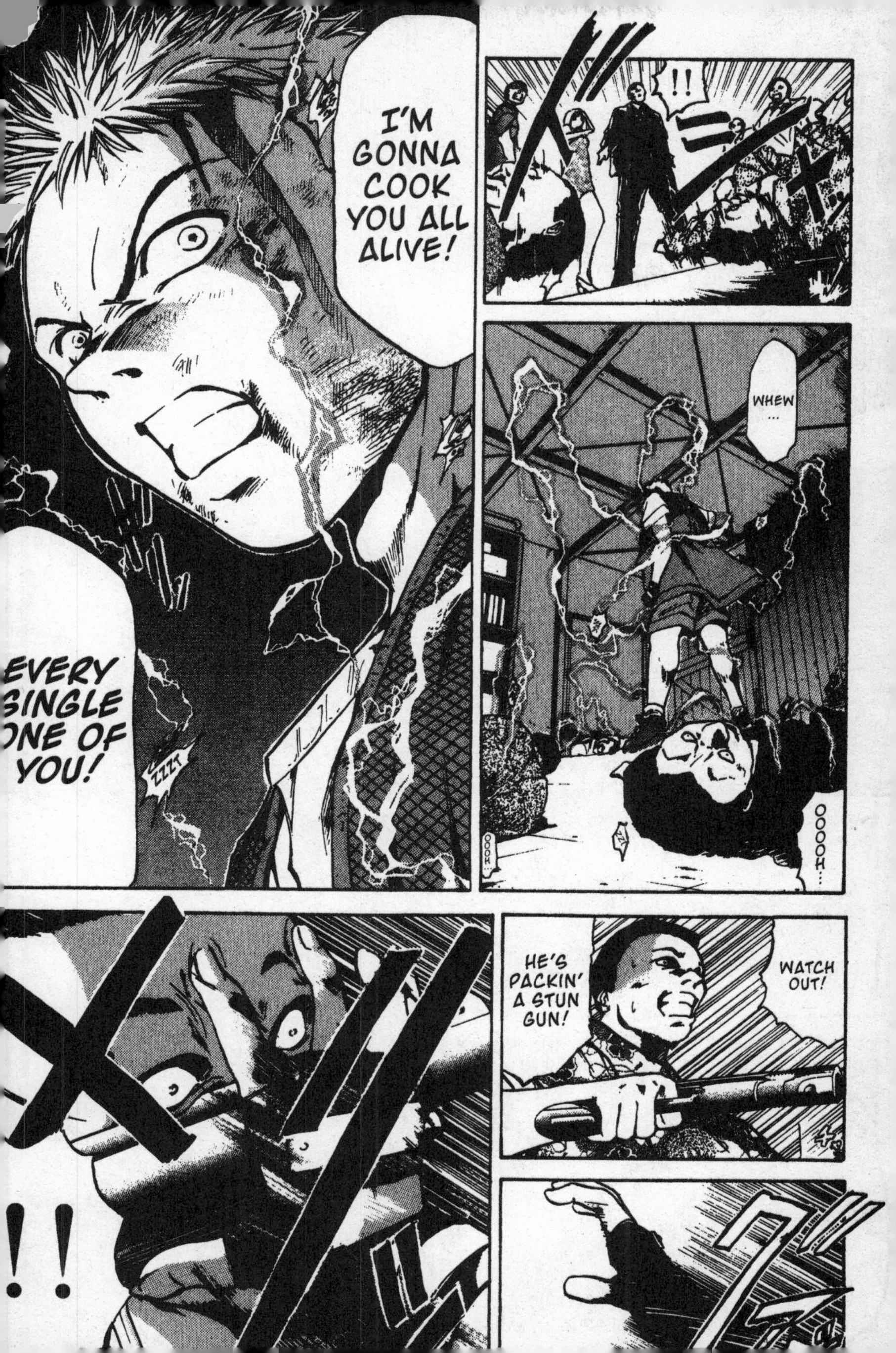
!!
WHEW...
OOOOH...
OOOH...
I'M GONNA COOK YOU ALL ALIVE!
EVERY SINGLE ONE OF YOU!
ZZZT
WATCH OUT!
HE'S PACKIN' A STUN GUN!
!!

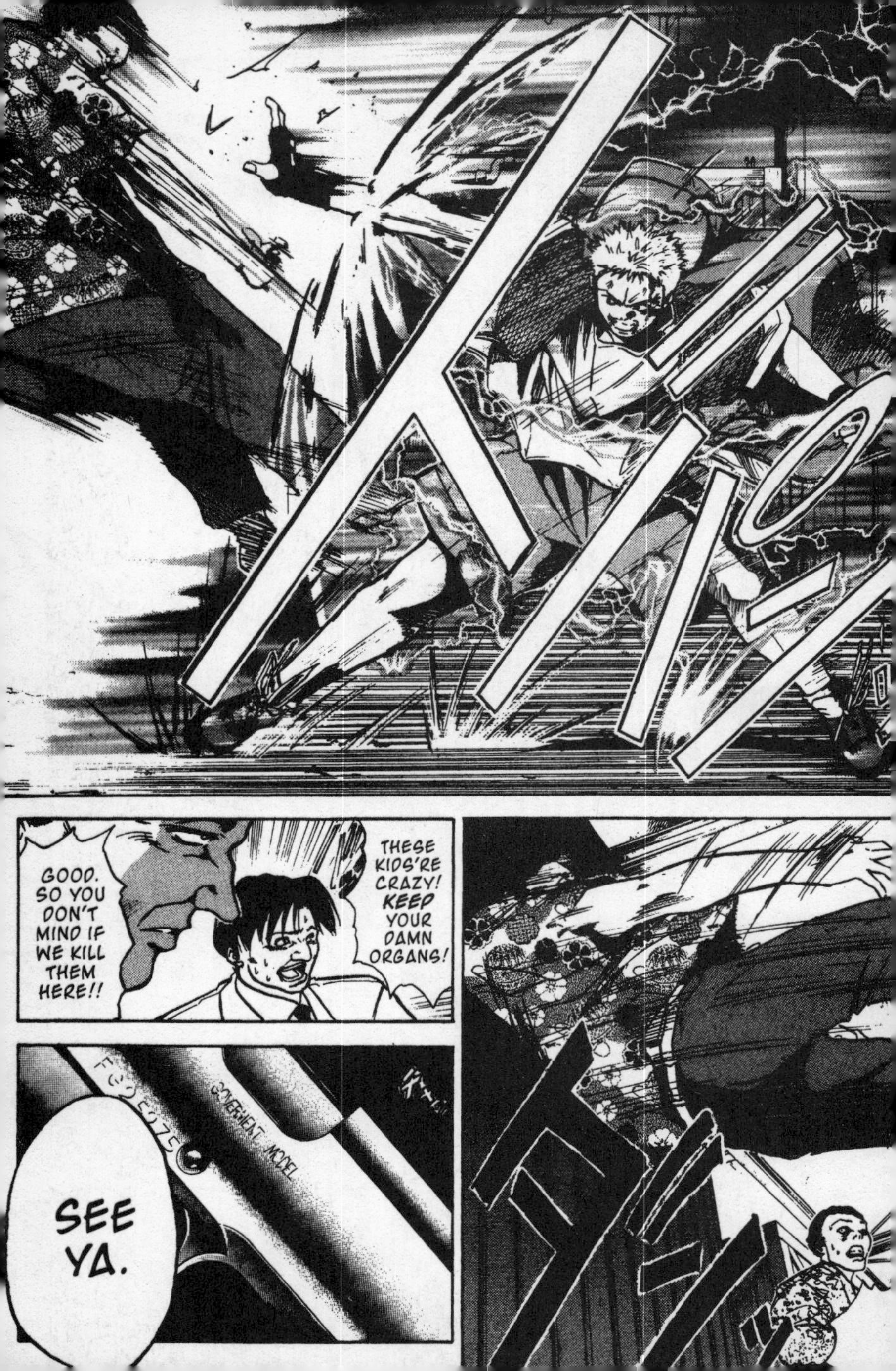
THESE KIDS'RE CRAZY! KEEP YOUR DAMN ORGANS!
GOOD. SO YOU DON'T MIND IF WE KILL THEM HERE!!
OVERHEAT MODEL
SEE YA.

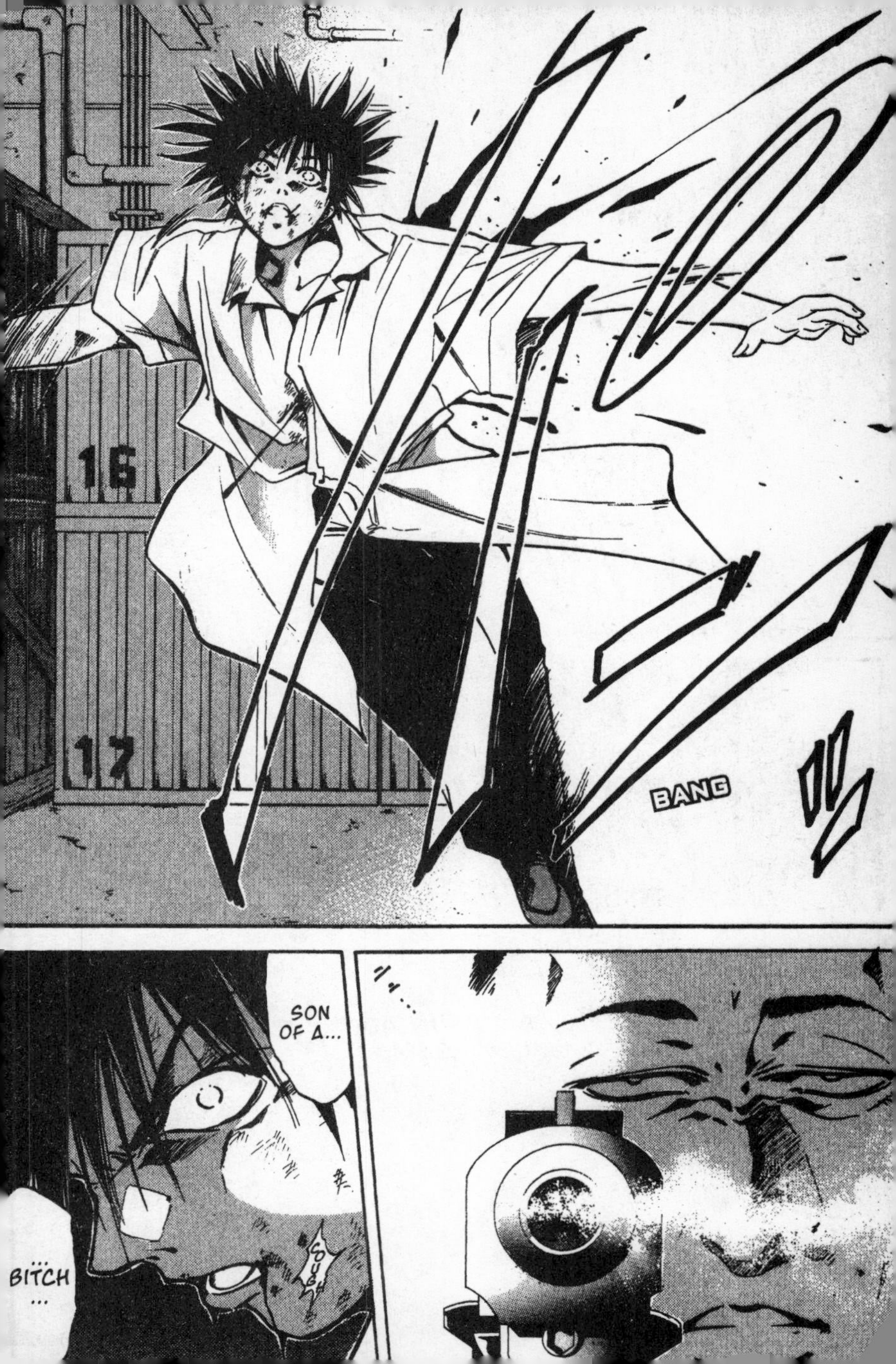
BANG
SON OF A...
COUGH
...BITCH...

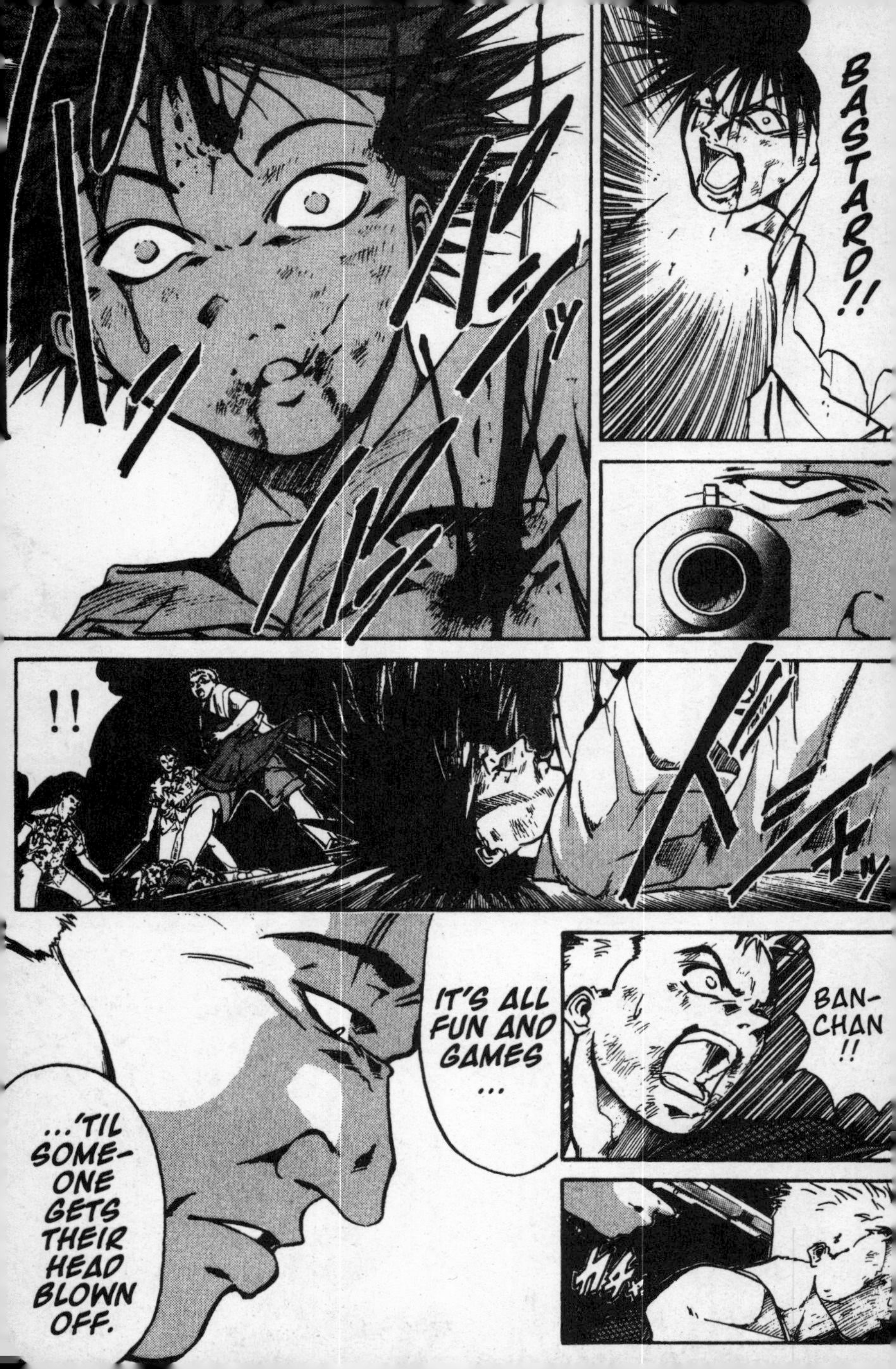
BASTARD!!
!!
BAN-CHAN!!
IT'S ALL FUN AND GAMES...
...'TIL SOME-ONE GETS THEIR HEAD BLOWN OFF.

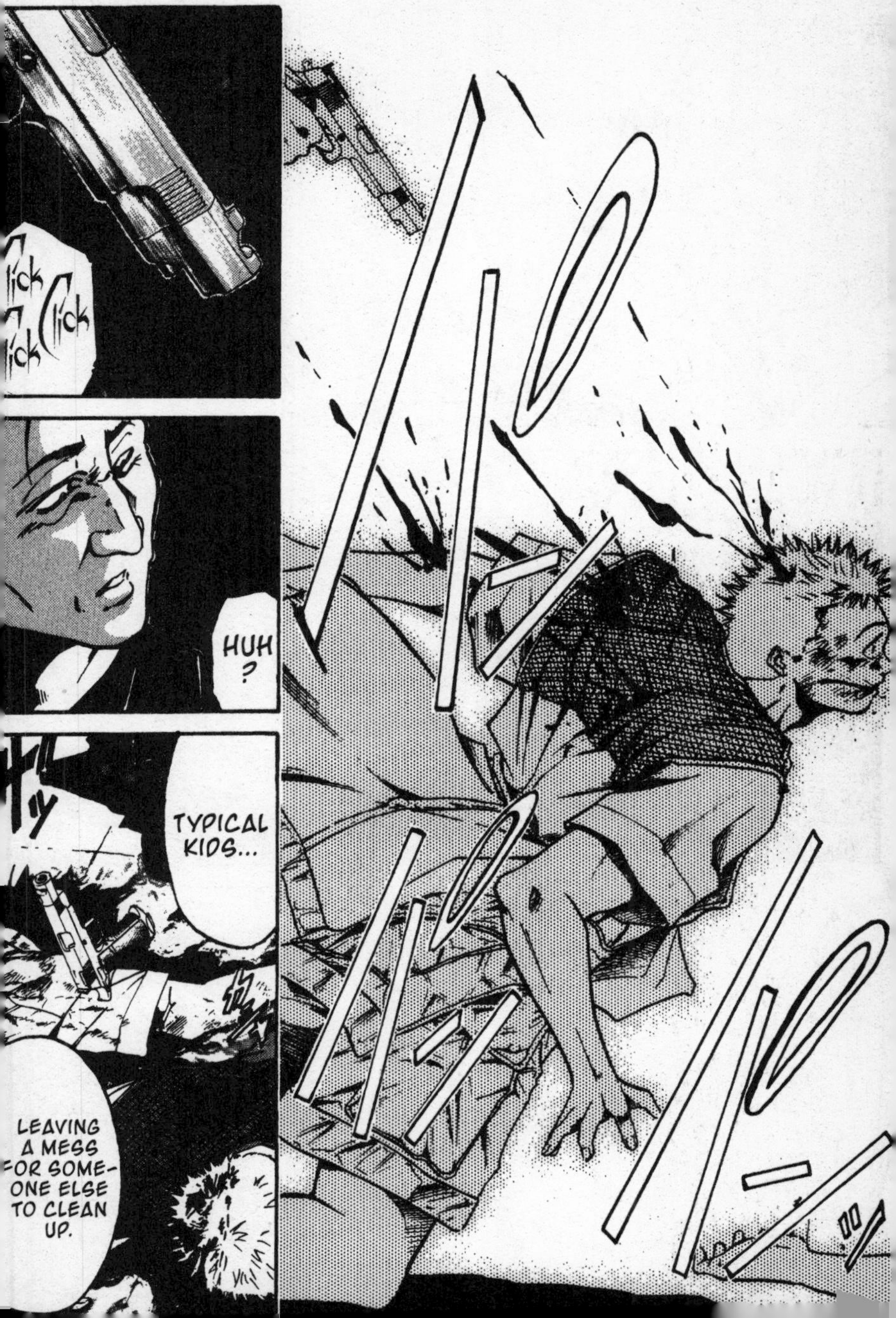
Click Click
Click
HUH?
TYPICAL KIDS...
LEAVING A MESS FOR SOME-ONE ELSE TO CLEAN UP.

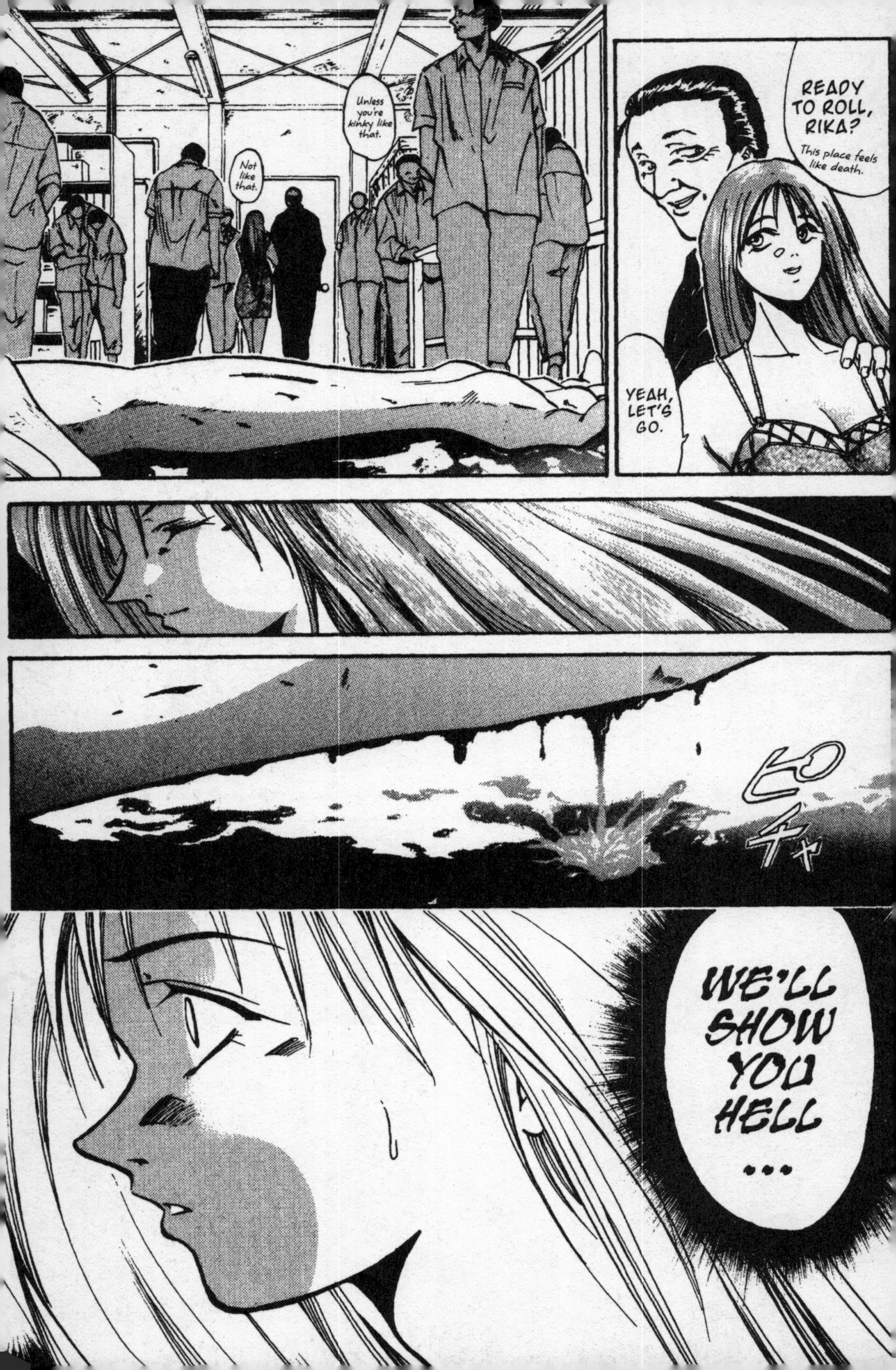
READY TO ROLL, RIKA?
This place feels like death.
YEAH, LET'S GO.
Unless you're kinky like that.
Not like that.
ピチャ
WE'LL SHOW YOU HELL ...

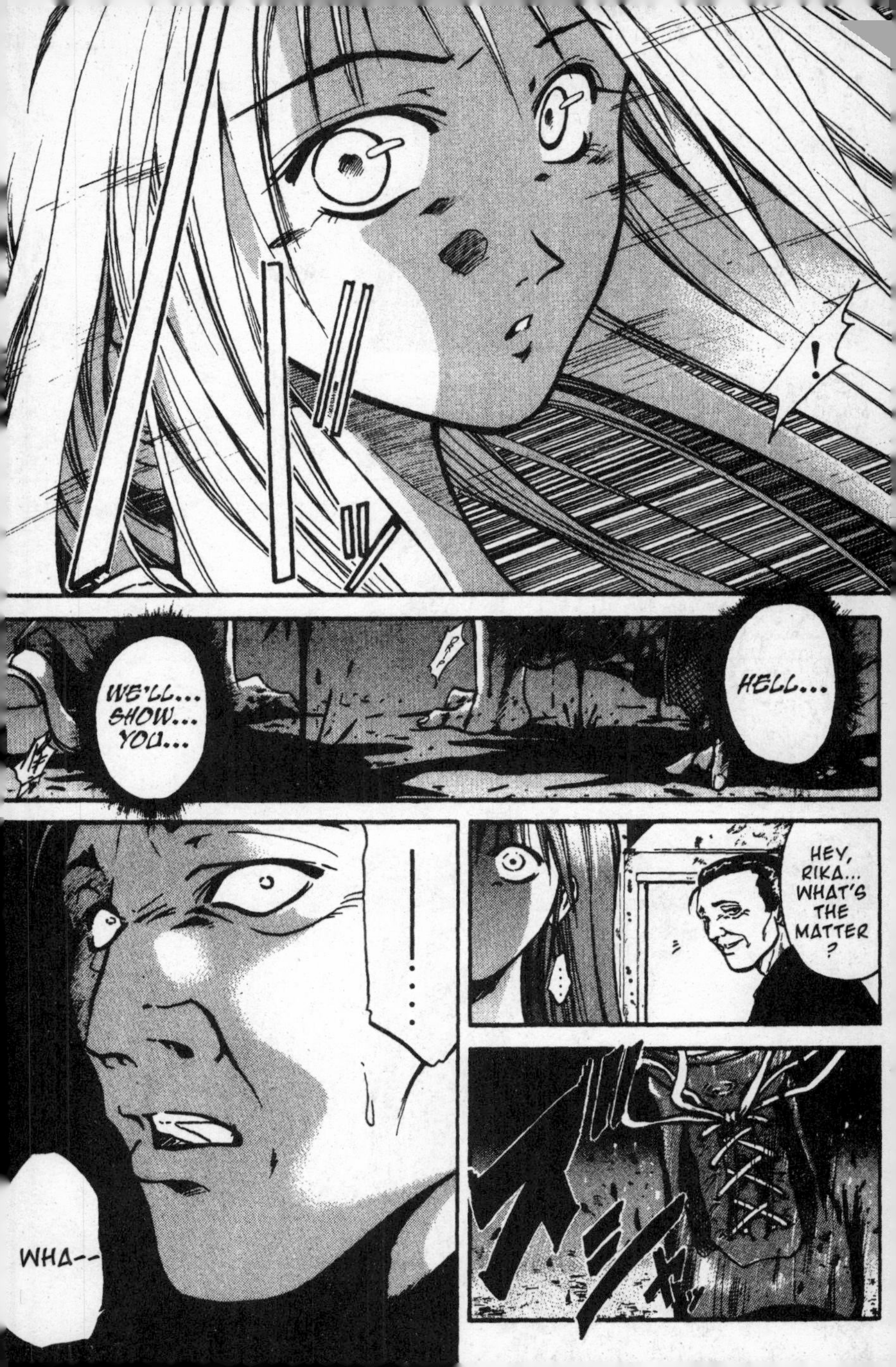
!
HELL...
WE'LL... SHOW... YOU...
HEY, RIKA... WHAT'S THE MATTER?
......
WHA--

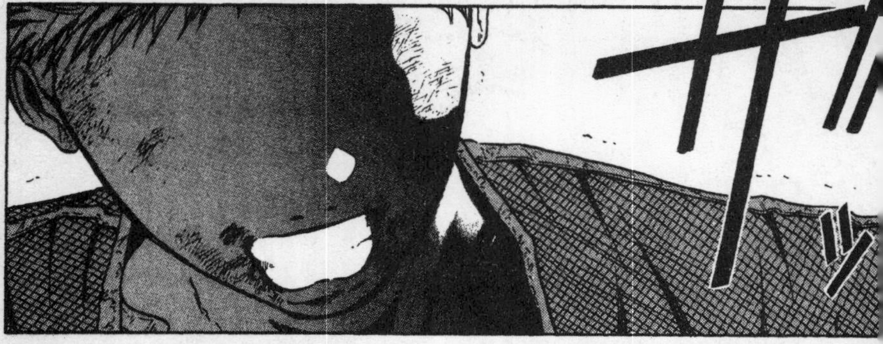
ザッ
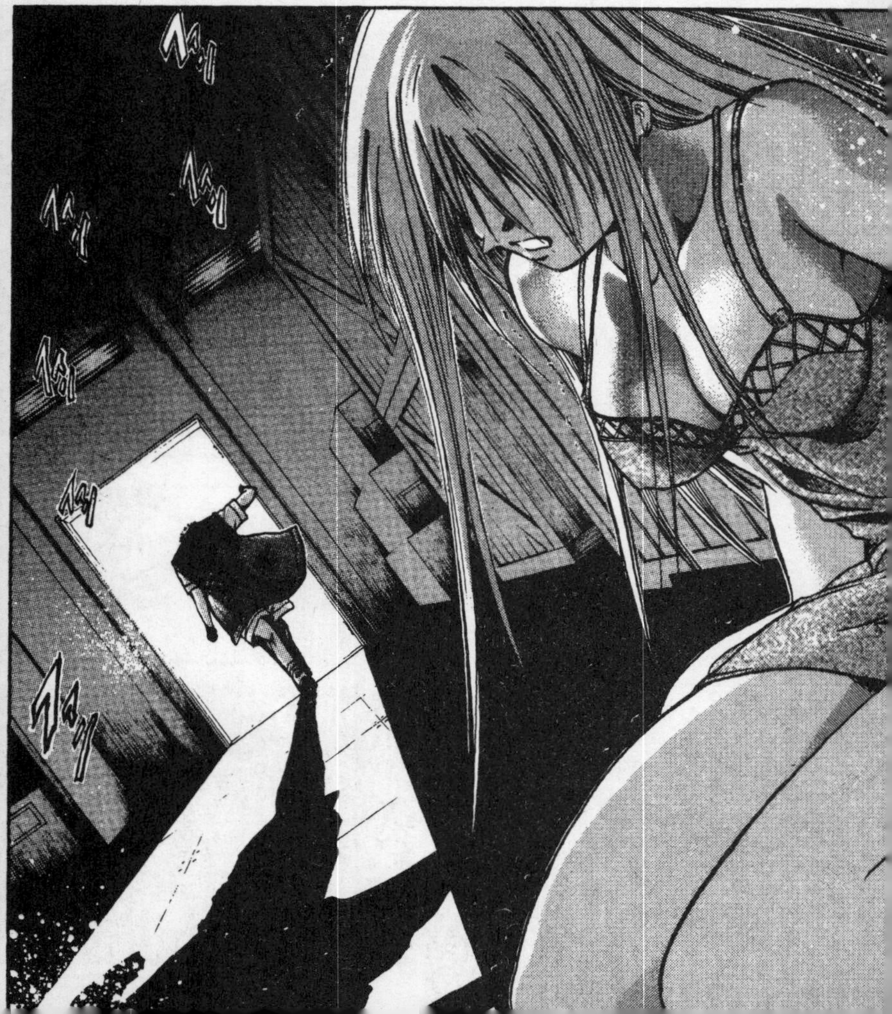

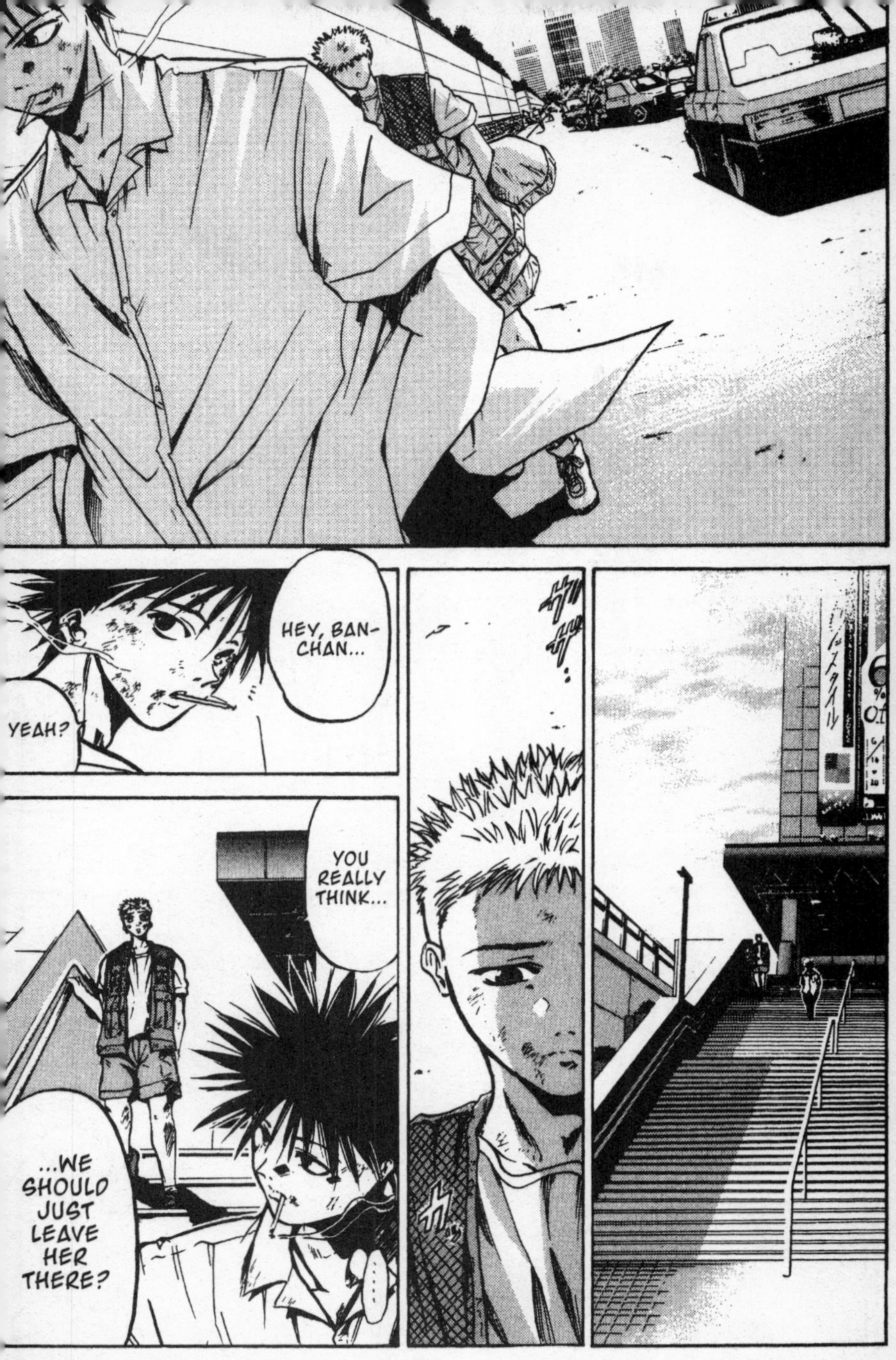
HEY, BAN-CHAN...
YEAH?
YOU REALLY THINK...
...WE SHOULD JUST LEAVE HER THERE?
.....

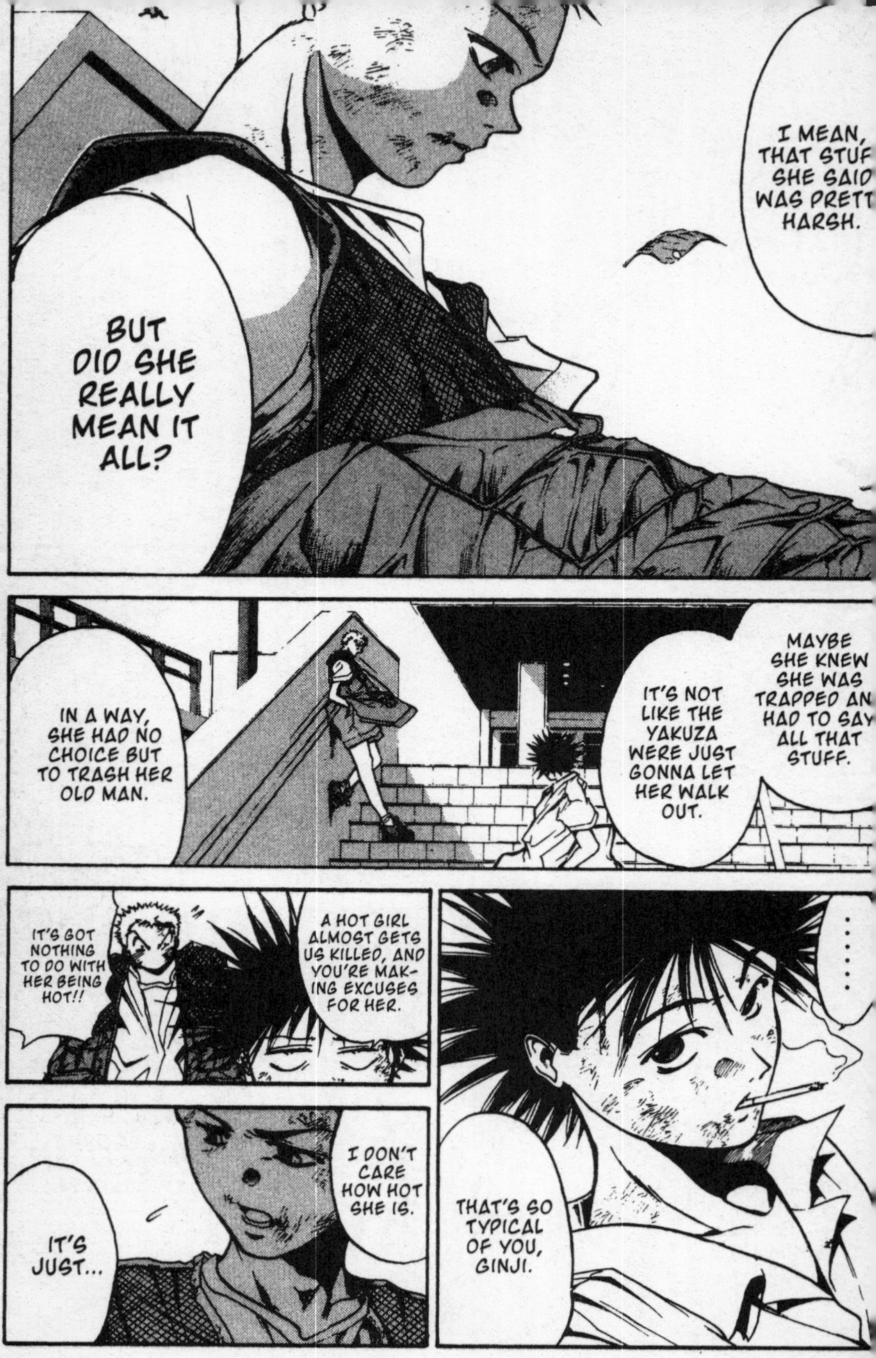
I MEAN, THAT STUF SHE SAID WAS PRETT HARSH.
BUT DID SHE REALLY MEAN IT ALL?
MAYBE SHE KNEW SHE WAS TRAPPED AN HAD TO SAY ALL THAT STUFF.
IT'S NOT LIKE THE YAKUZA WERE JUST GONNA LET HER WALK OUT.
IN A WAY, SHE HAD NO CHOICE BUT TO TRASH HER OLD MAN.
......
THAT'S SO TYPICAL OF YOU, GINJI.
A HOT GIRL ALMOST GETS US KILLED, AND YOU'RE MAKING EXCUSES FOR HER.
IT'S GOT NOTHING TO DO WITH HER BEING HOT!!
I DON'T CARE HOW HOT SHE IS.
IT'S JUST...

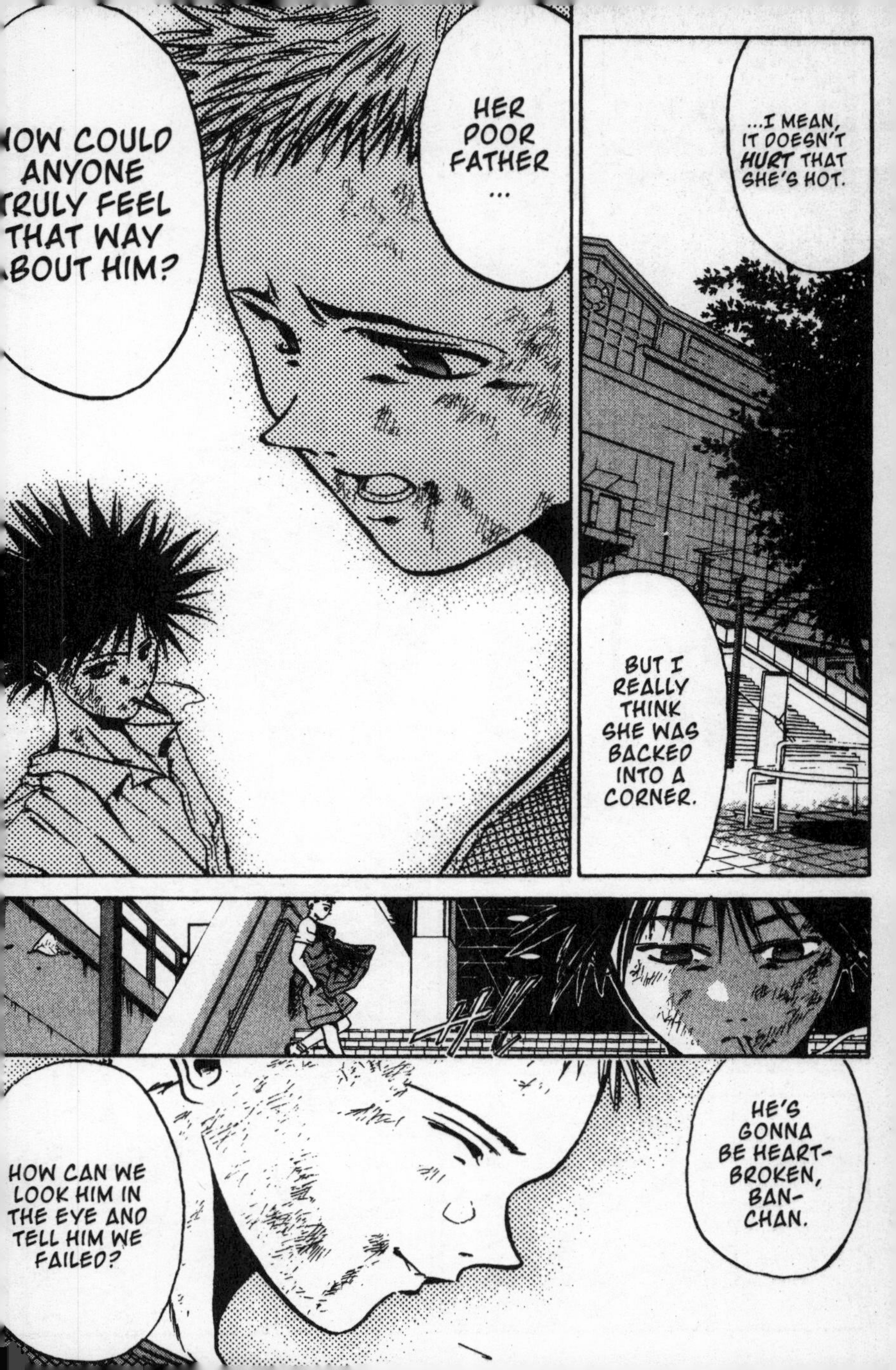
...I MEAN, IT DOESN'T *HURT* THAT SHE'S HOT.
BUT I REALLY THINK SHE WAS BACKED INTO A CORNER.
HER POOR FATHER ...
HOW COULD ANYONE TRULY FEEL THAT WAY ABOUT HIM?
HE'S GONNA BE HEART-BROKEN, BAN-CHAN.
HOW CAN WE LOOK HIM IN THE EYE AND TELL HIM WE FAILED?

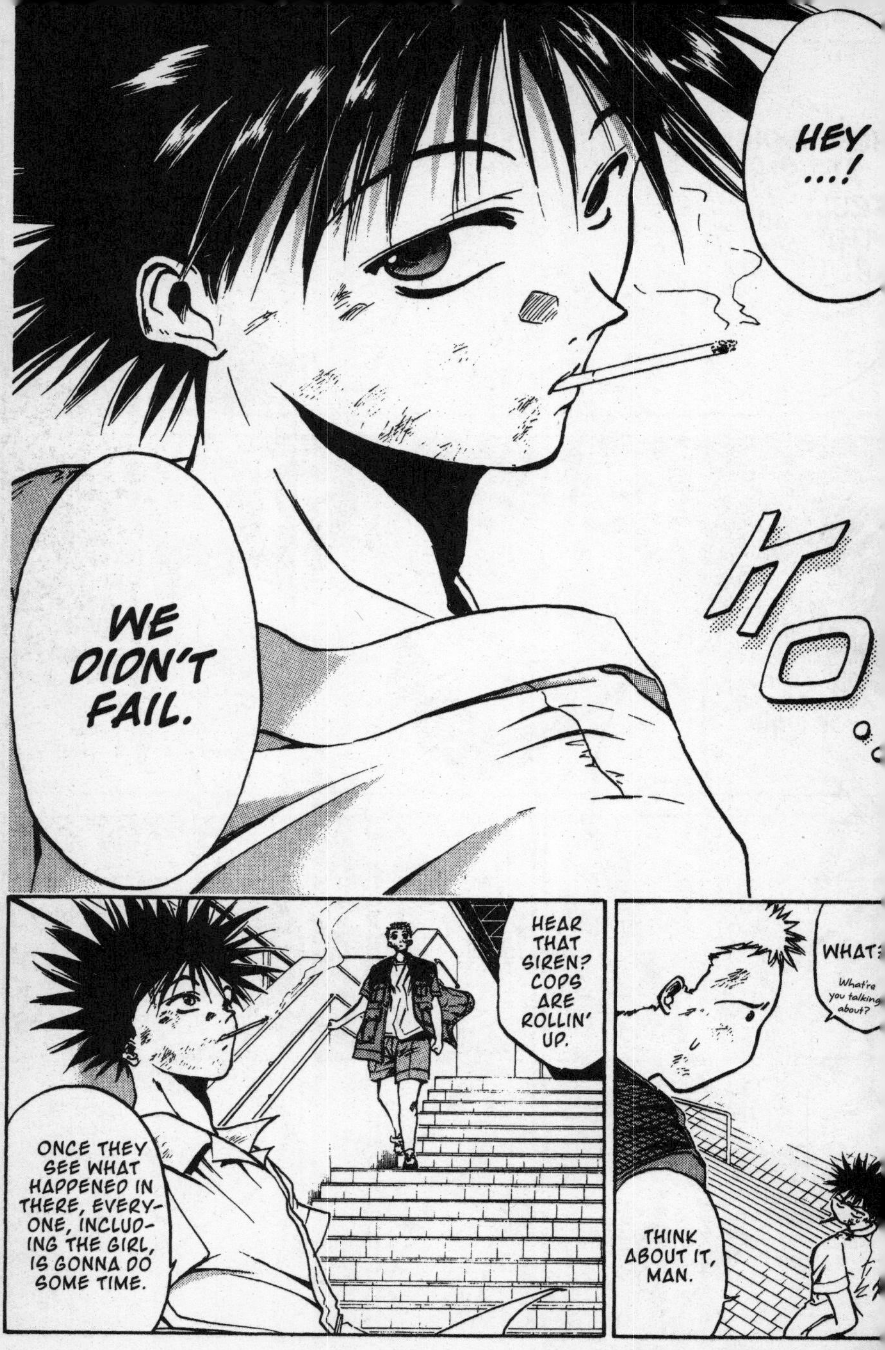
HEY ...!
KO
WE DIDN'T FAIL.
WHAT?
What're you talking about?
THINK ABOUT IT, MAN.
HEAR THAT SIREN? COPS ARE ROLLIN' UP.
ONCE THEY SEE WHAT HAPPENED IN THERE, EVERY-ONE, INCLUD-ING THE GIRL, IS GONNA DO SOME TIME.

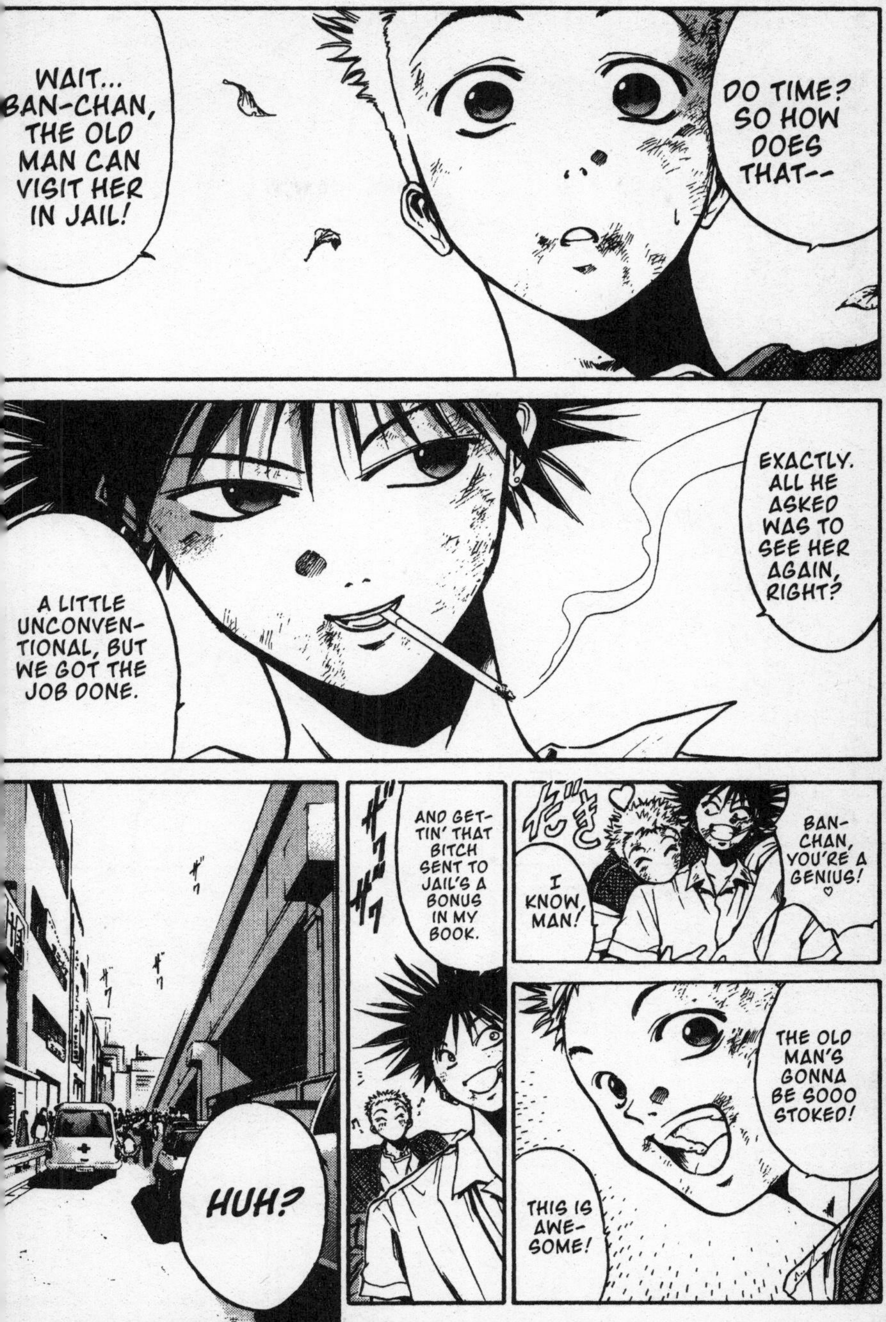
DO TIME? SO HOW DOES THAT--
WAIT... BAN-CHAN, THE OLD MAN CAN VISIT HER IN JAIL!
EXACTLY. ALL HE ASKED WAS TO SEE HER AGAIN, RIGHT?
A LITTLE UNCONVENTIONAL, BUT WE GOT THE JOB DONE.
BAN-CHAN, YOU'RE A GENIUS! ♡
I KNOW, MAN!
THE OLD MAN'S GONNA BE SOOO STOKED!
THIS IS AWESOME!
AND GETTIN' THAT BITCH SENT TO JAIL'S A BONUS IN MY BOOK.
HUH?

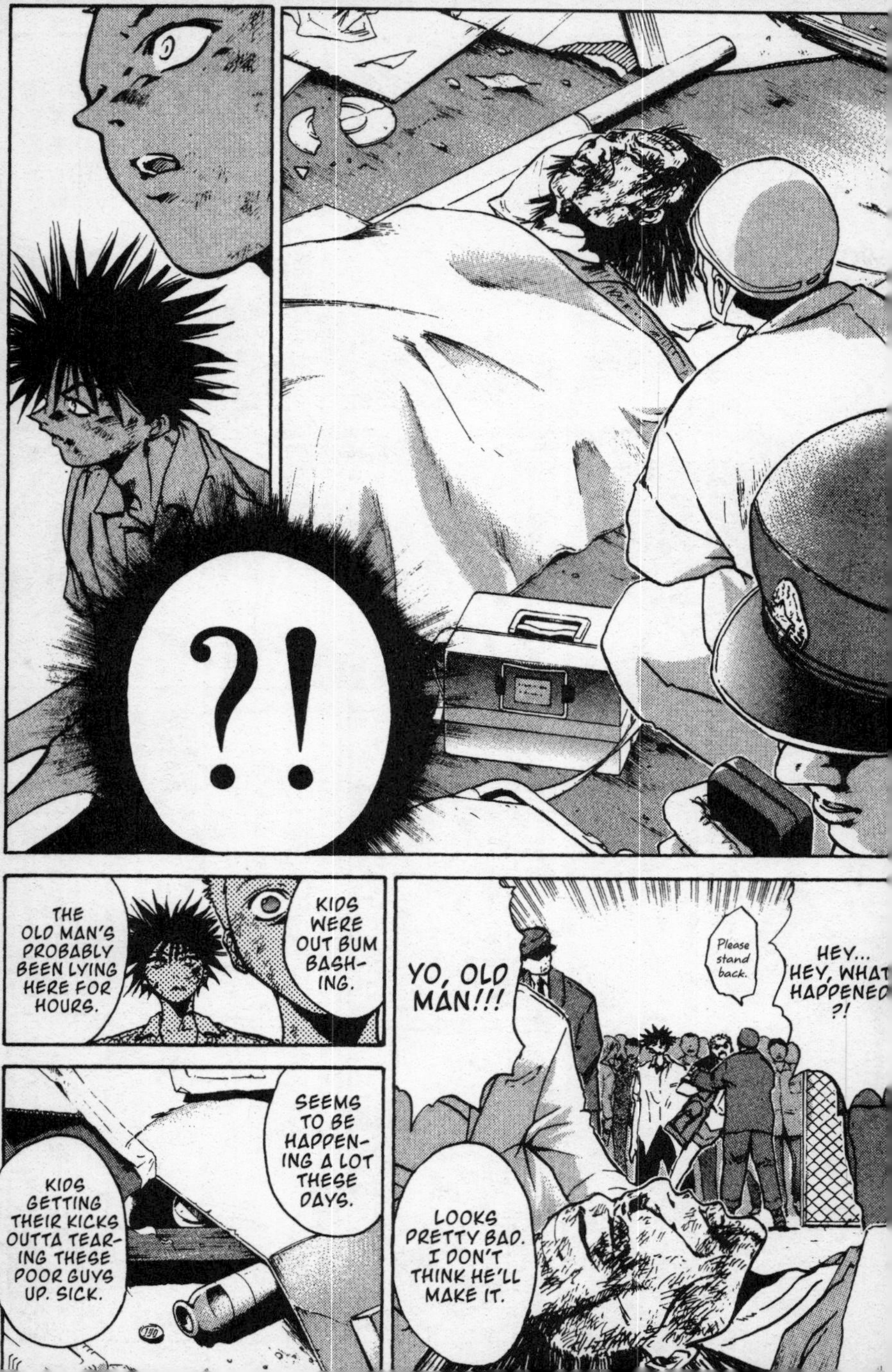
?!
HEY... HEY, WHAT HAPPENED?!
Please stand back.
YO, OLD MAN!!!
LOOKS PRETTY BAD. I DON'T THINK HE'LL MAKE IT.
KIDS WERE OUT BUM BASH-ING.
THE OLD MAN'S PROBABLY BEEN LYING HERE FOR HOURS.
SEEMS TO BE HAPPEN-ING A LOT THESE DAYS.
KIDS GETTING THEIR KICKS OUTTA TEAR-ING THESE POOR GUYS UP. SICK.

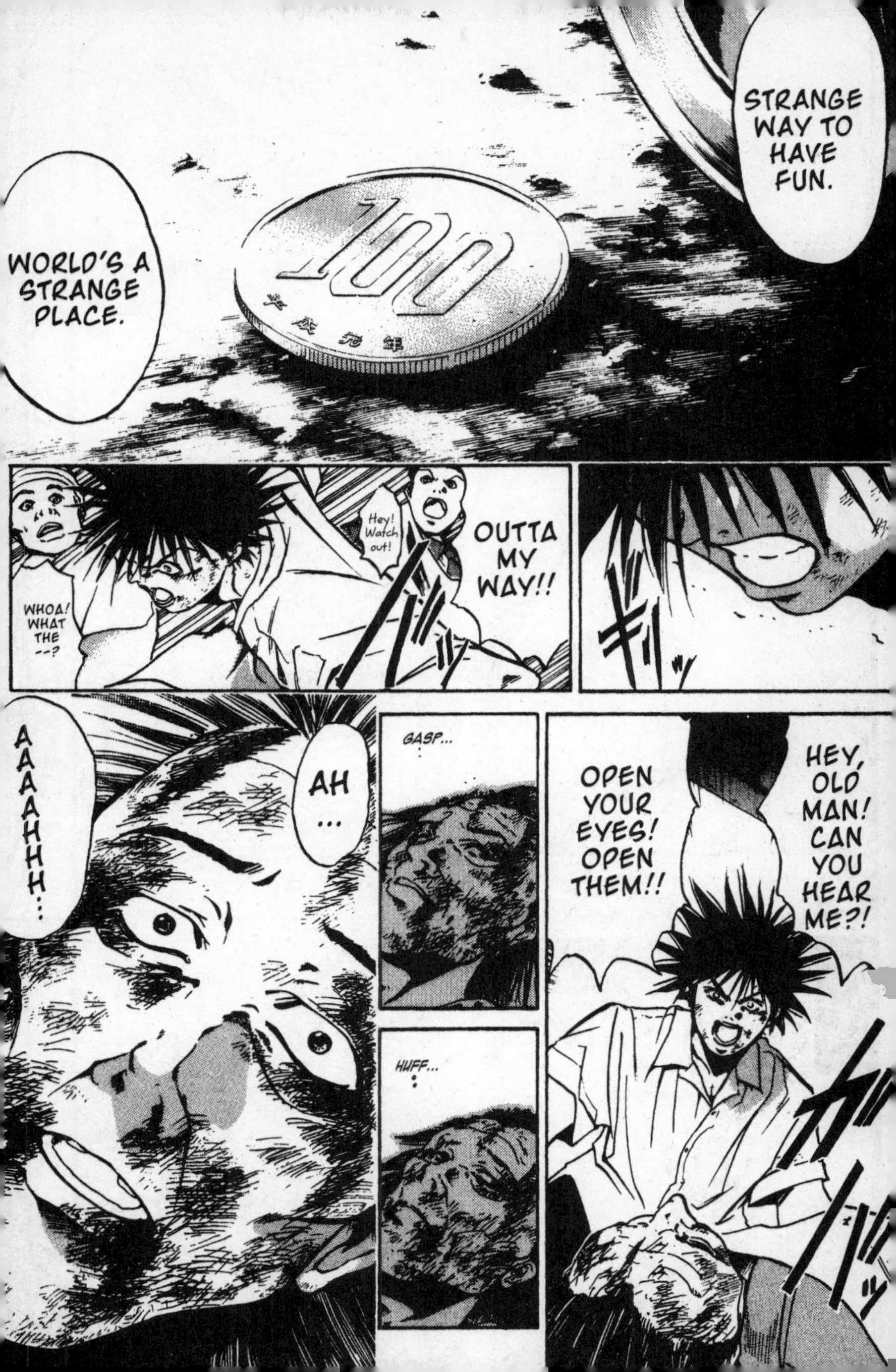
STRANGE WAY TO HAVE FUN.
100
WORLD'S A STRANGE PLACE.
OUTTA MY WAY!!
Hey! Watch out!
WHOA! WHAT THE --?
HEY, OLD MAN! CAN YOU HEAR ME?!
OPEN YOUR EYES! OPEN THEM!!
GASP...
HUFF...
AH ...
AAAAHHH...

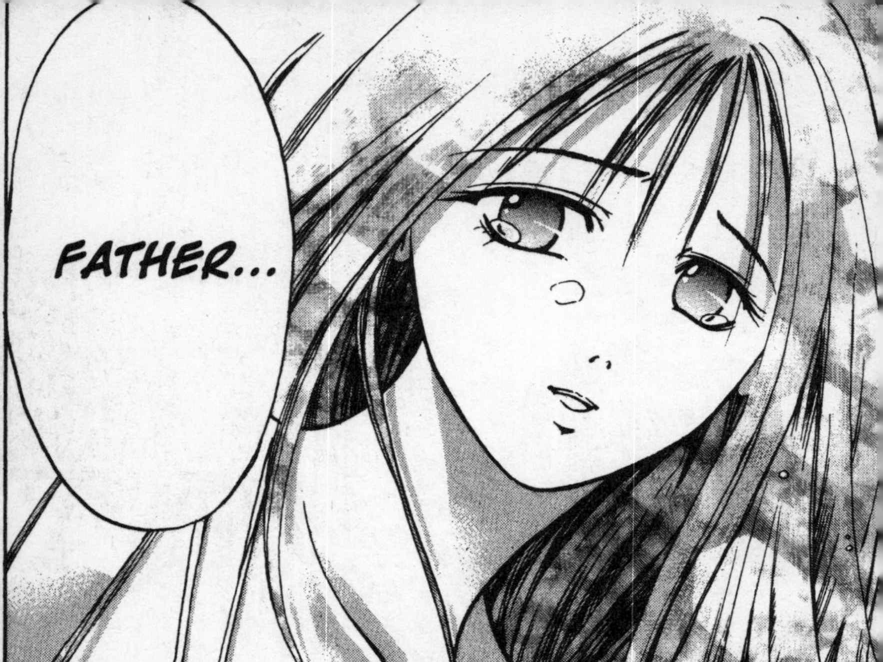
FATHER...
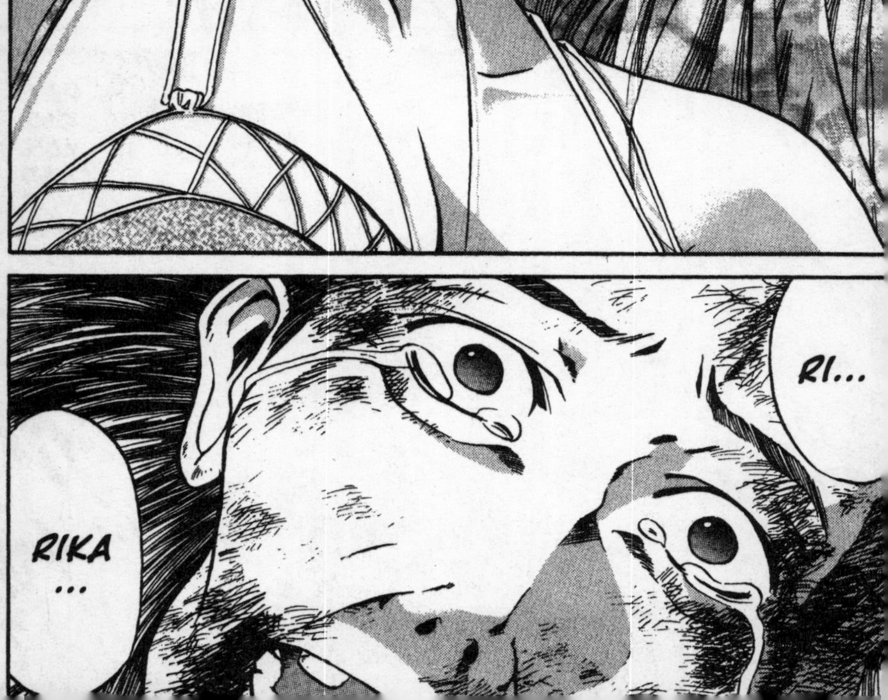
RI...
RIKA
...

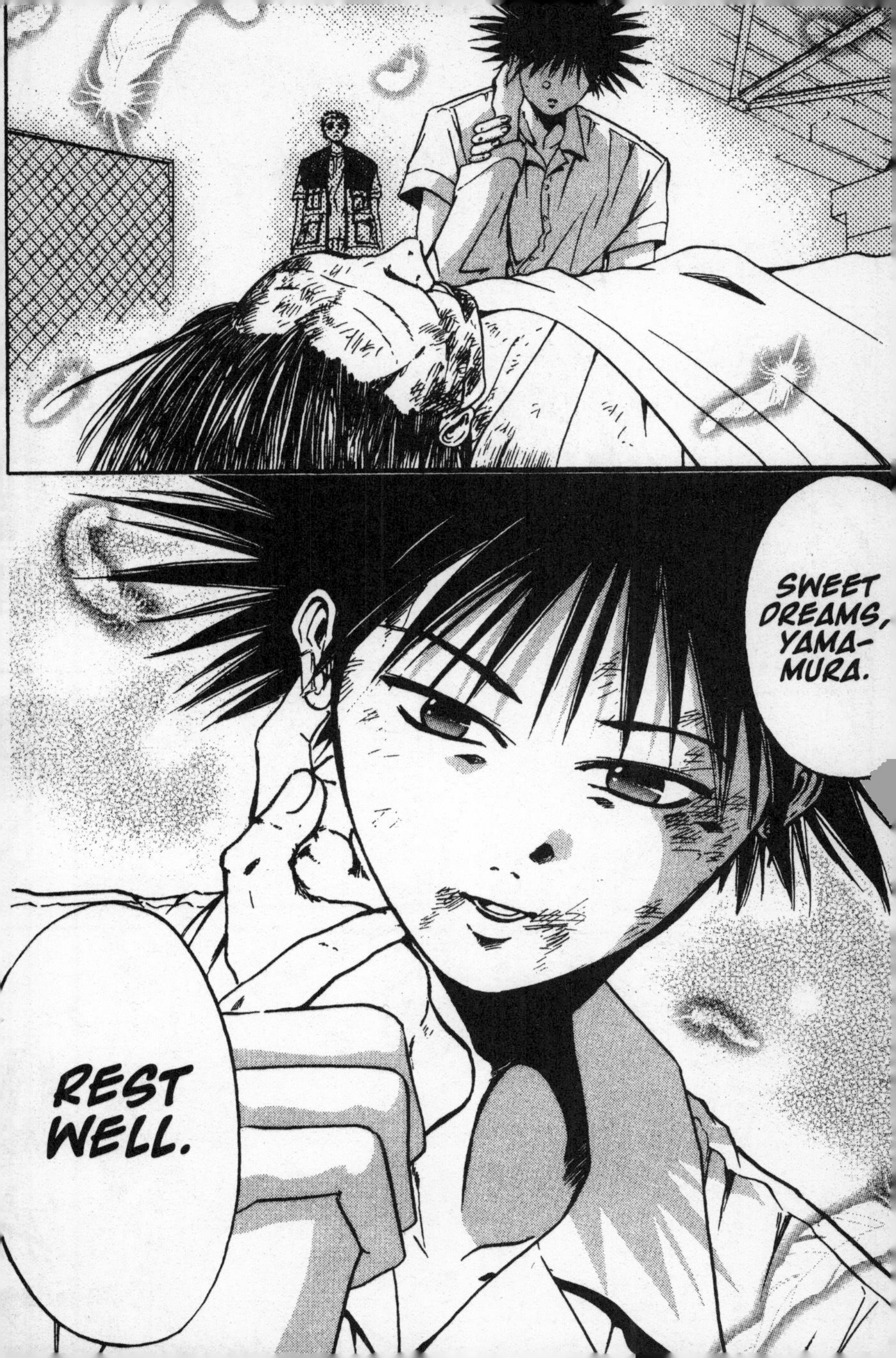
SWEET DREAMS, YAMAMURA.
REST WELL.

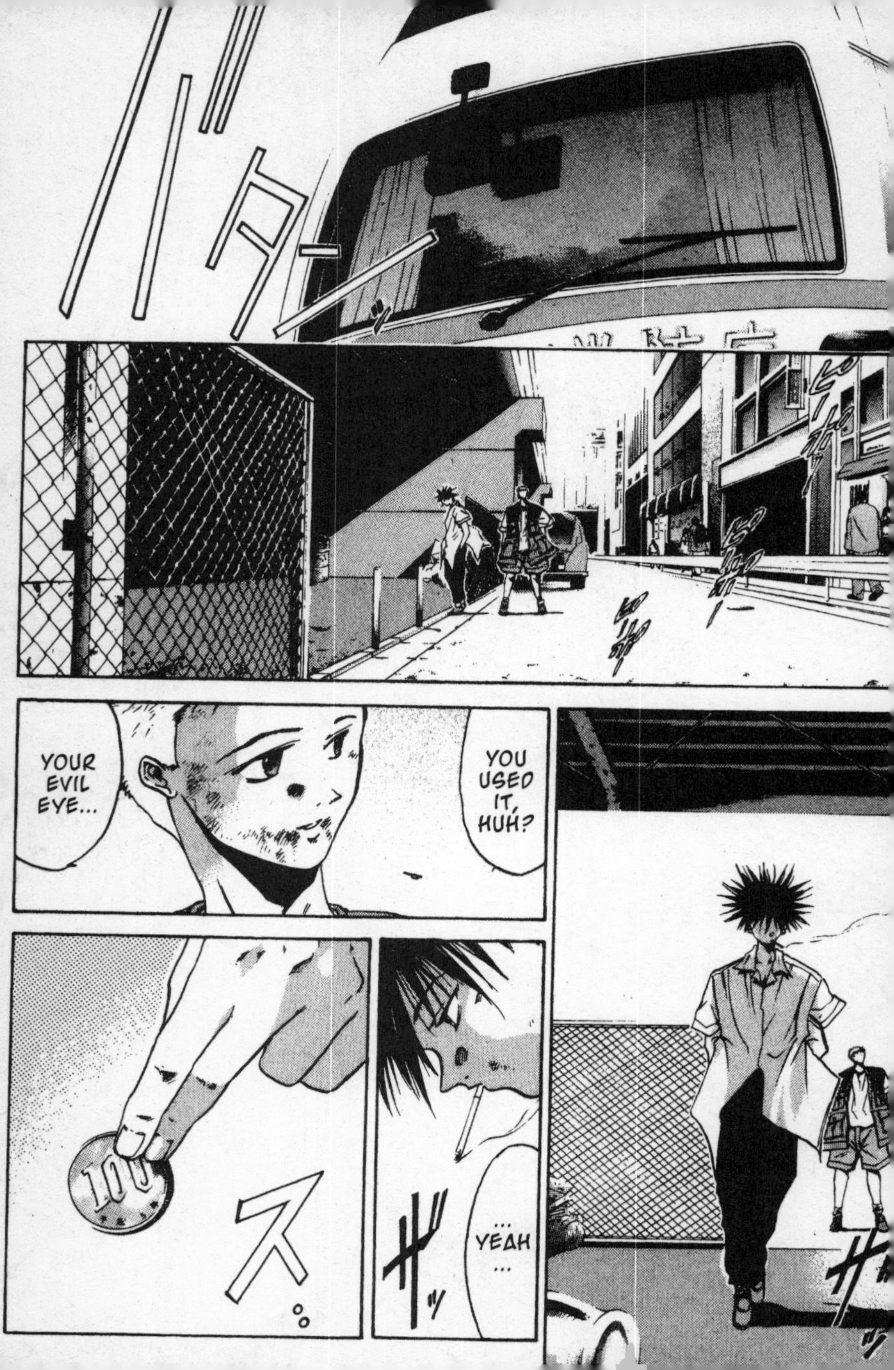
YOU USED IT, HUH?
YOUR EVIL EYE...
... YEAH ...

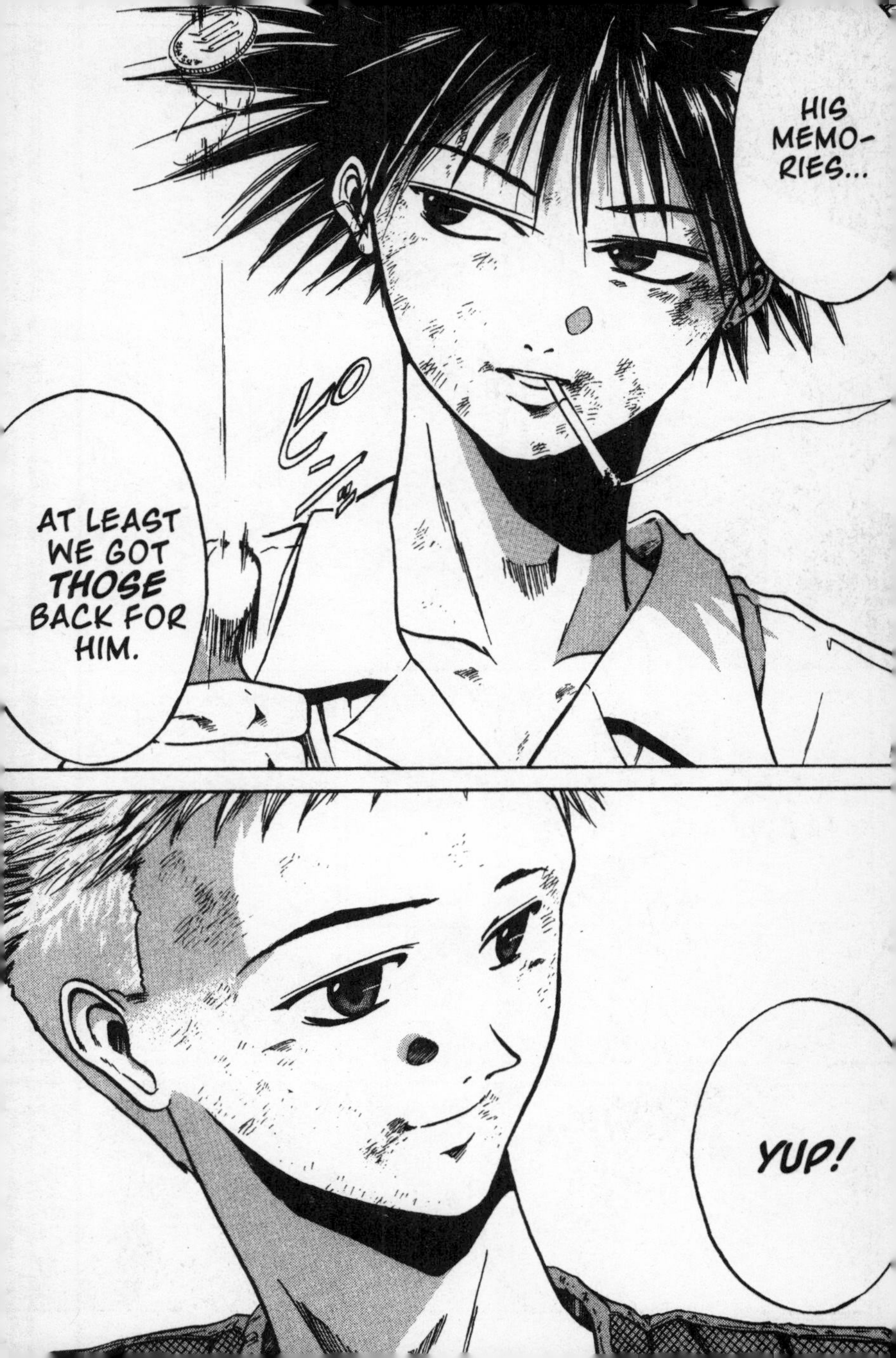
HIS MEMORIES...
AT LEAST WE GOT THOSE BACK FOR HIM.
YUP!

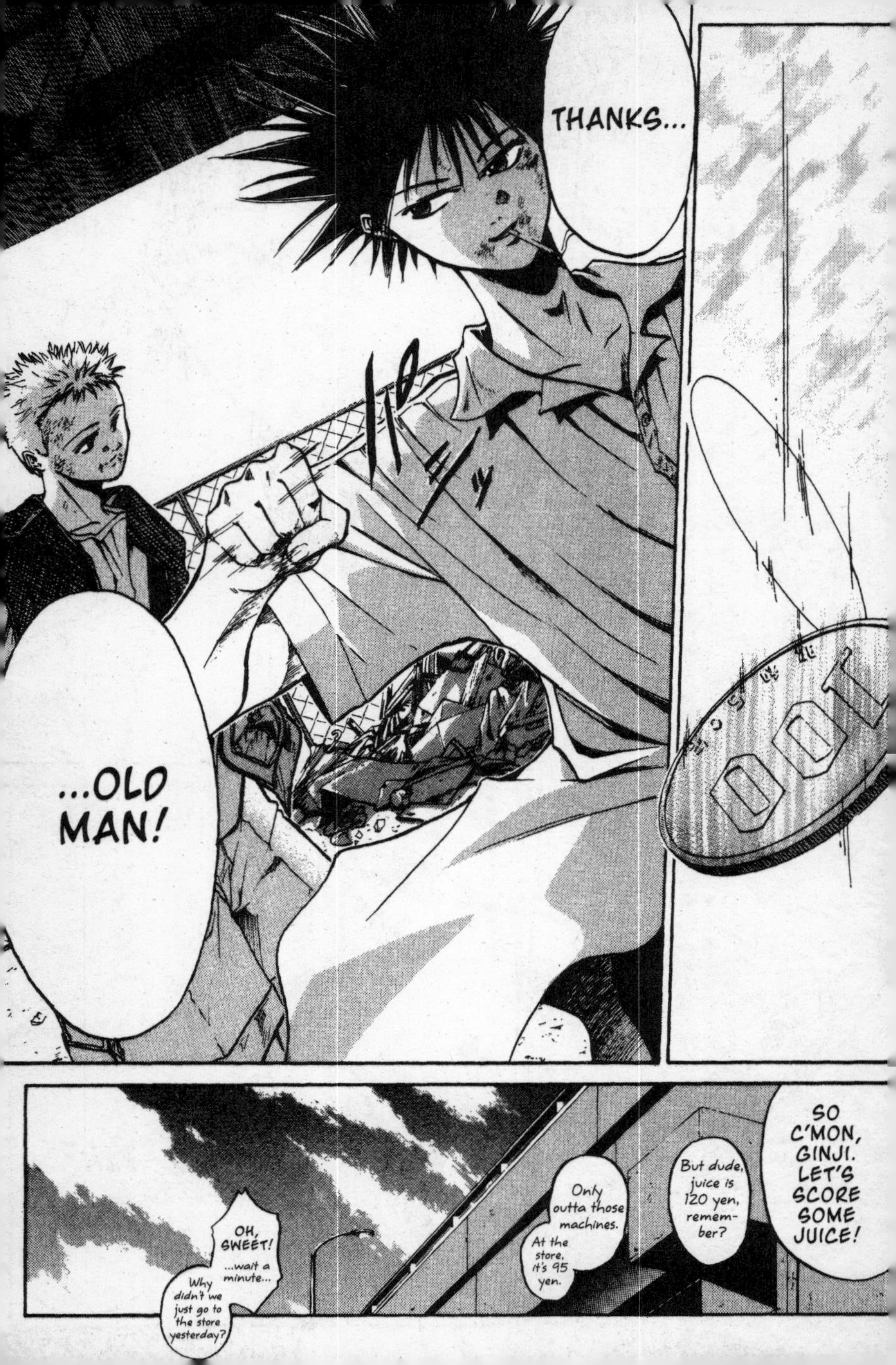
THANKS...
...OLD MAN!
SO C'MON, GINJI. LET'S SCORE SOME JUICE!
But dude, juice is 120 yen, remember?
Only outta those machines.
At the store, it's 95 yen.
OH, SWEET!
...wait a minute...
Why didn't we just go to the store yesterday?

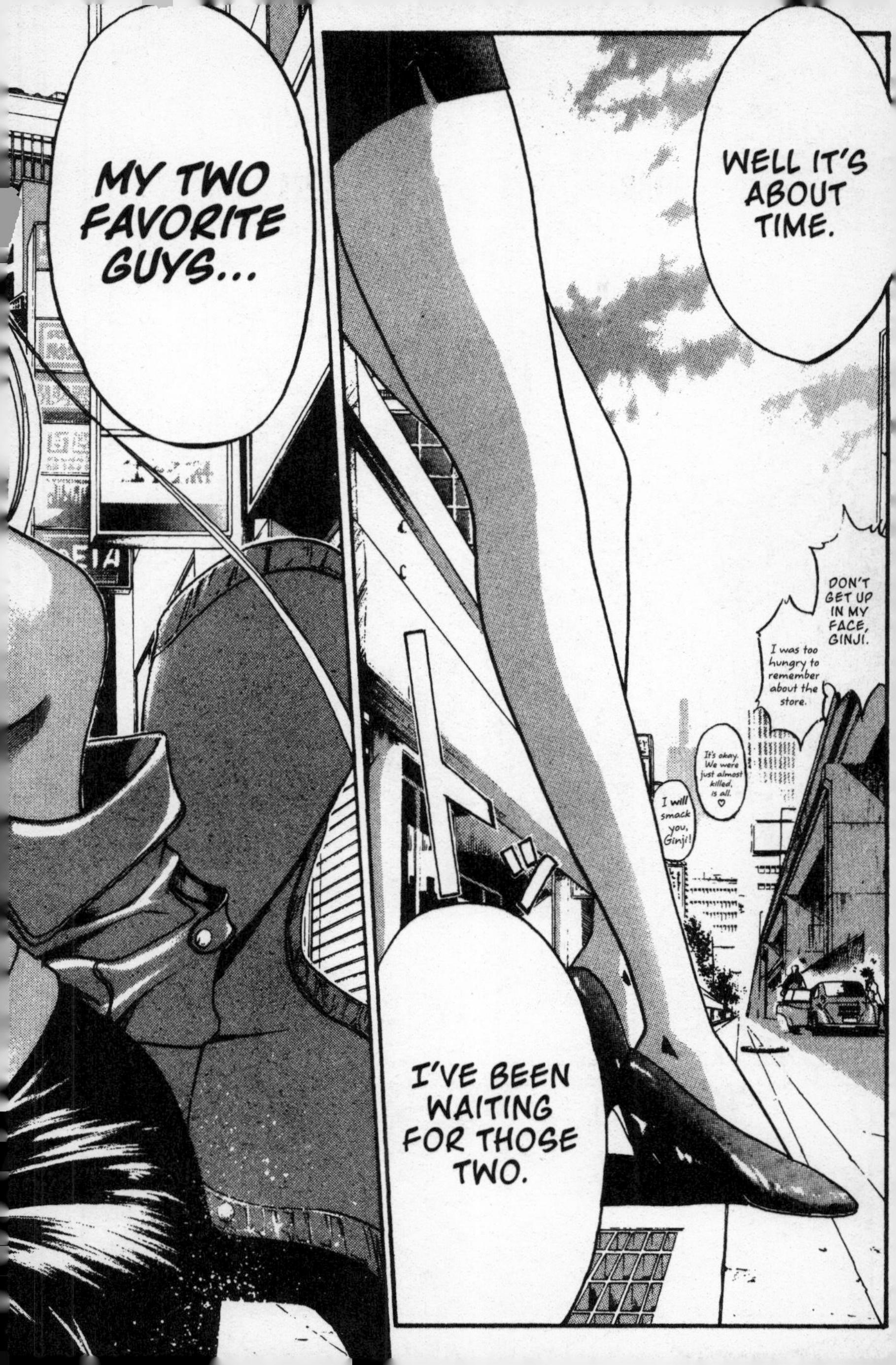
WELL IT'S ABOUT TIME.
DON'T GET UP IN MY FACE, GINJI.
I was too hungry to remember about the store.
It's okay. We were just almost killed, is all. ♡
I will smack you, Ginji!
I'VE BEEN WAITING FOR THOSE TWO.
MY TWO FAVORITE GUYS...

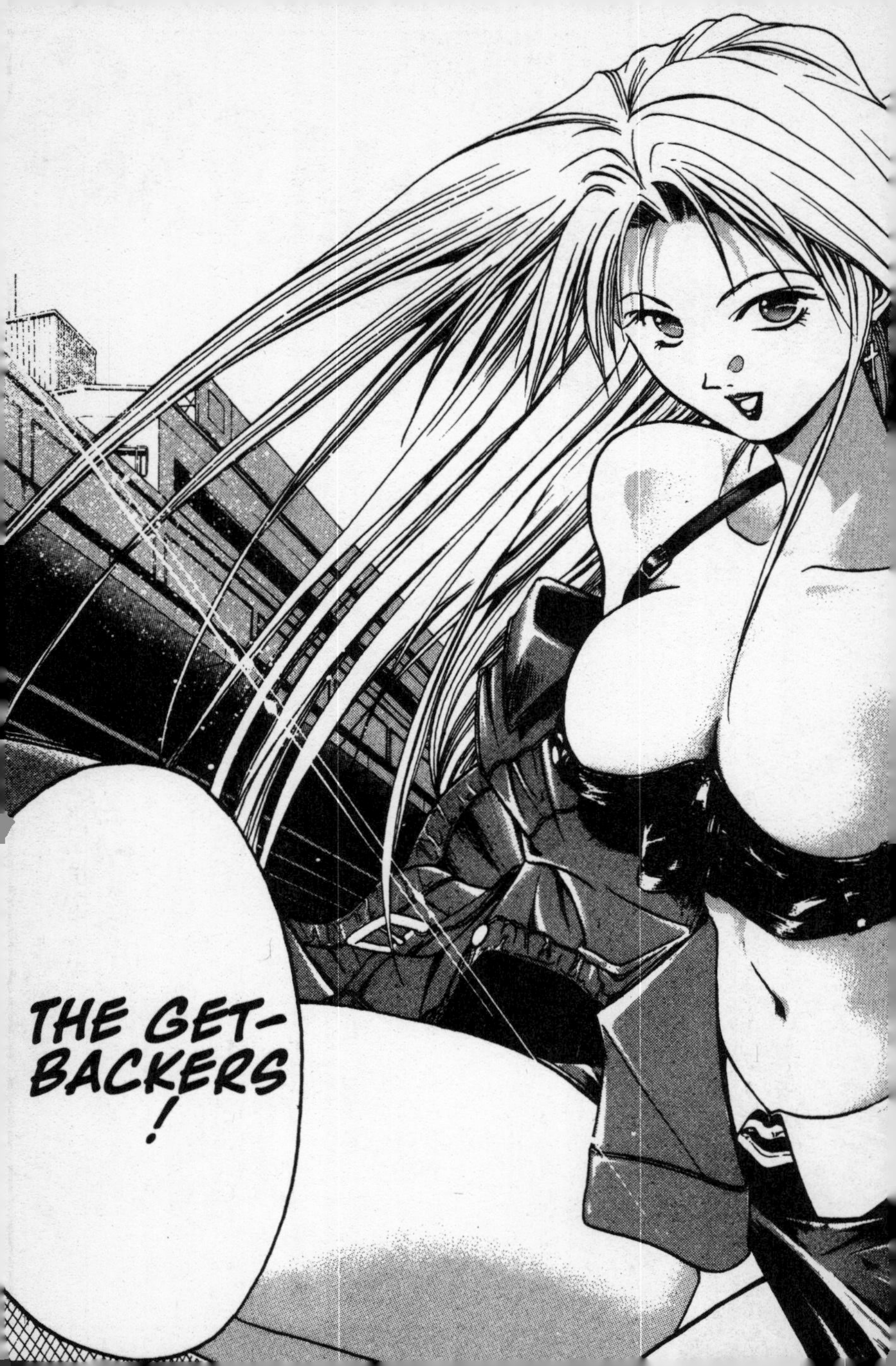
THE GET-BACKERS!

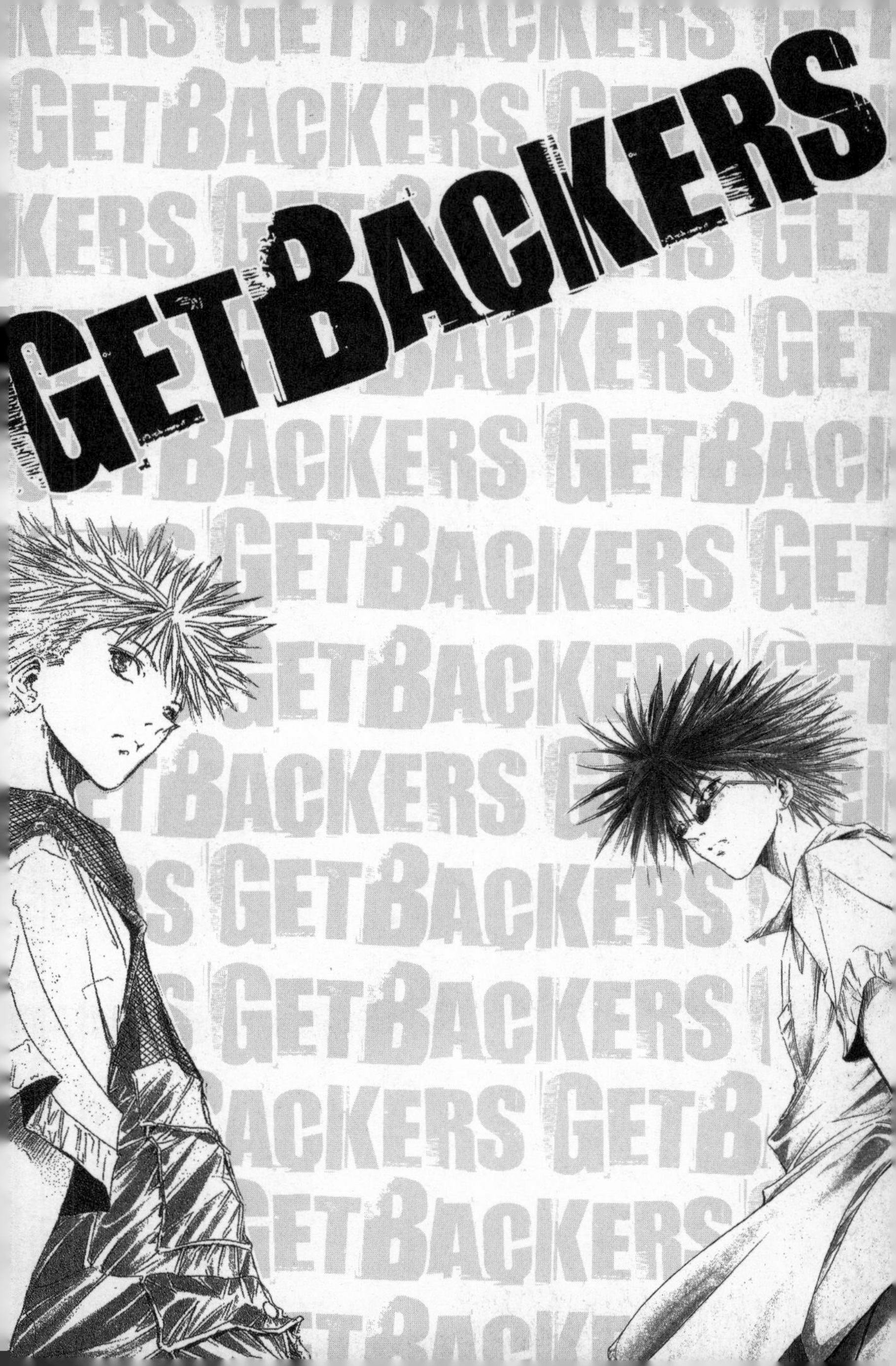
GETBACKERS

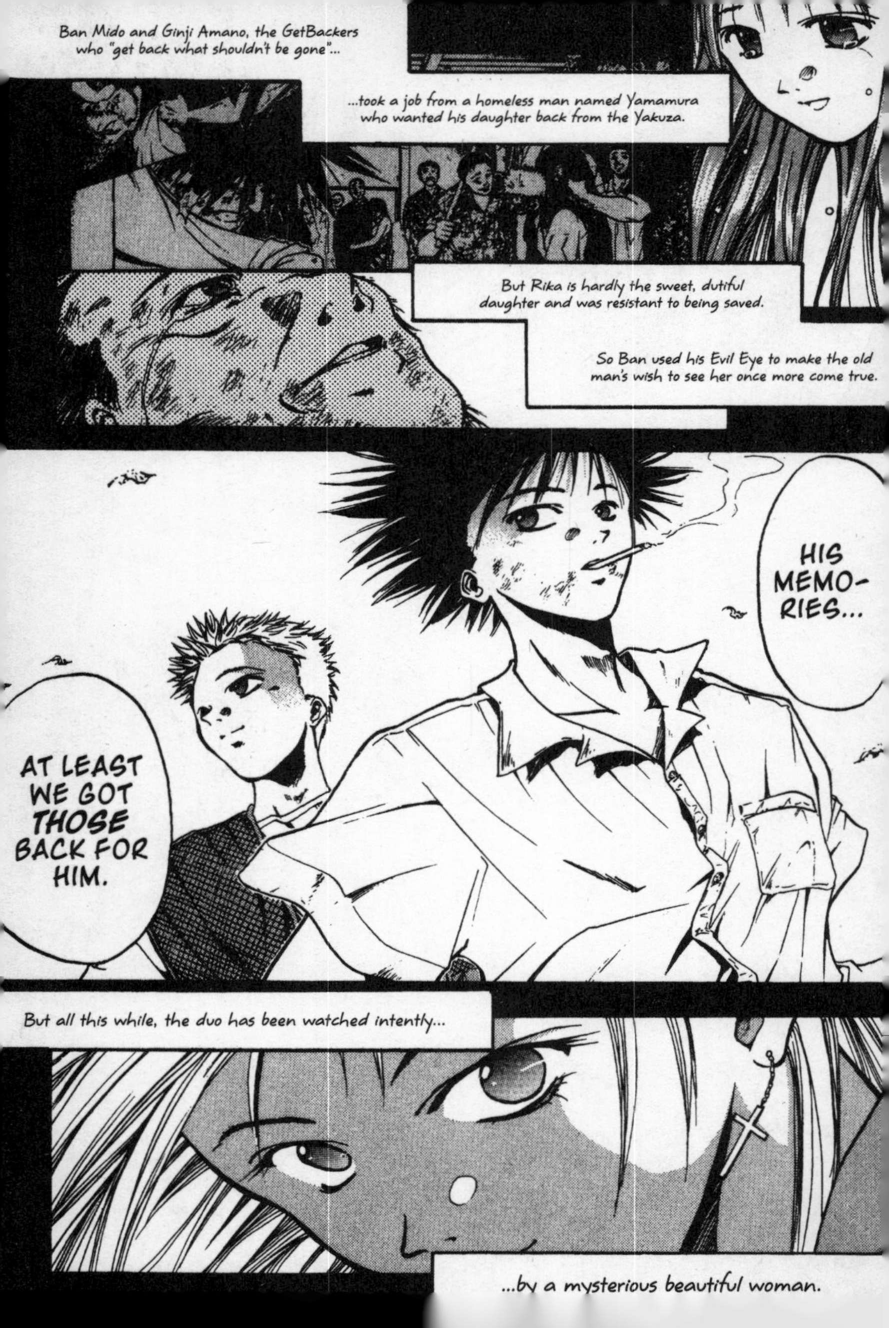
Ban Mido and Ginji Amano, the GetBackers who "get back what shouldn't be gone"...
...took a job from a homeless man named Yamamura who wanted his daughter back from the Yakuza.
But Rika is hardly the sweet, dutiful daughter and was resistant to being saved.
So Ban used his Evil Eye to make the old man's wish to see her once more come true.
HIS MEMORIES...
AT LEAST WE GOT THOSE BACK FOR HIM.
But all this while, the duo has been watched intently...
...by a mysterious beautiful woman.

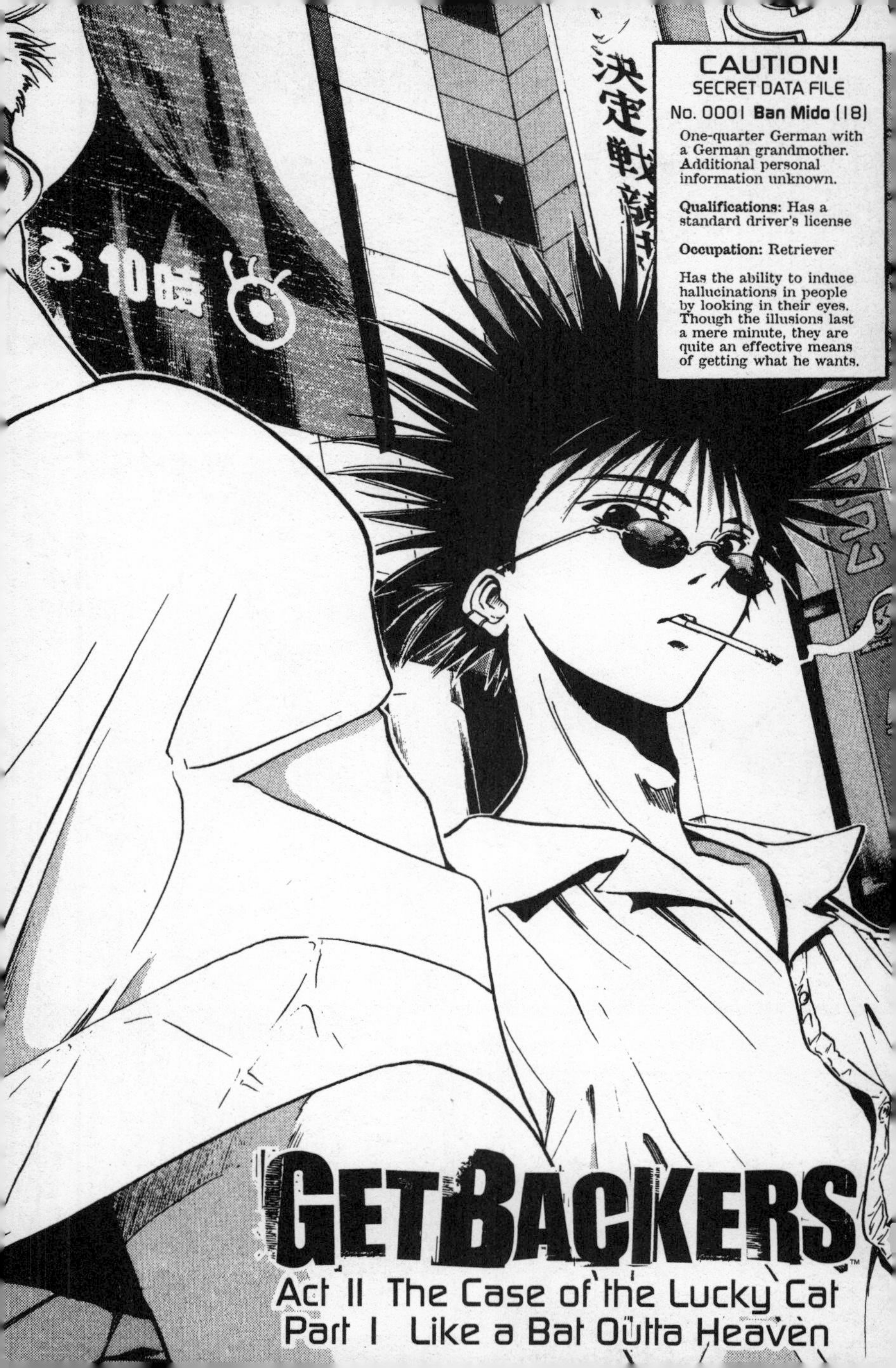
CAUTION!
SECRET DATA FILE
No. 0001 Ban Mido (18)
One-quarter German with a German grandmother. Additional personal information unknown.
Qualifications: Has a standard driver's license
Occupation: Retriever
Has the ability to induce hallucinations in people by looking in their eyes. Though the illusions last a mere minute, they are quite an effective means of getting what he wants.
GETBACKERS™
Act II The Case of the Lucky Cat
Part I Like a Bat Outta Heaven

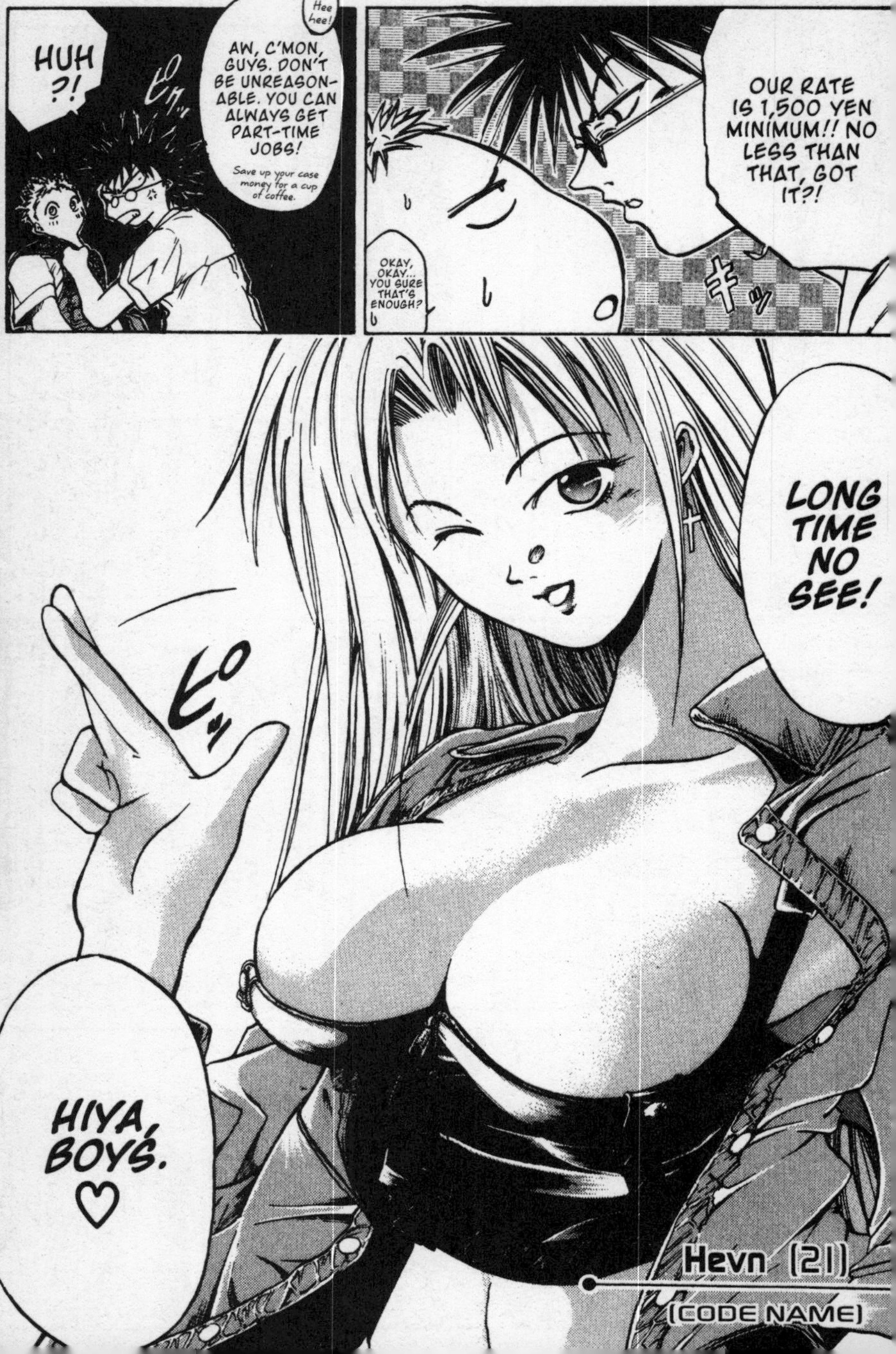
OUR RATE IS 1,500 YEN MINIMUM!! NO LESS THAN THAT, GOT IT?!
OKAY, OKAY... YOU SURE THAT'S ENOUGH?
Hee hee!
AW, C'MON, GUYS. DON'T BE UNREASONABLE. YOU CAN ALWAYS GET PART-TIME JOBS!
Save up your case money for a cup of coffee.
HUH ?!
LONG TIME NO SEE!
HIYA, BOYS. ♡
Hevn (21)
(CODE NAME)

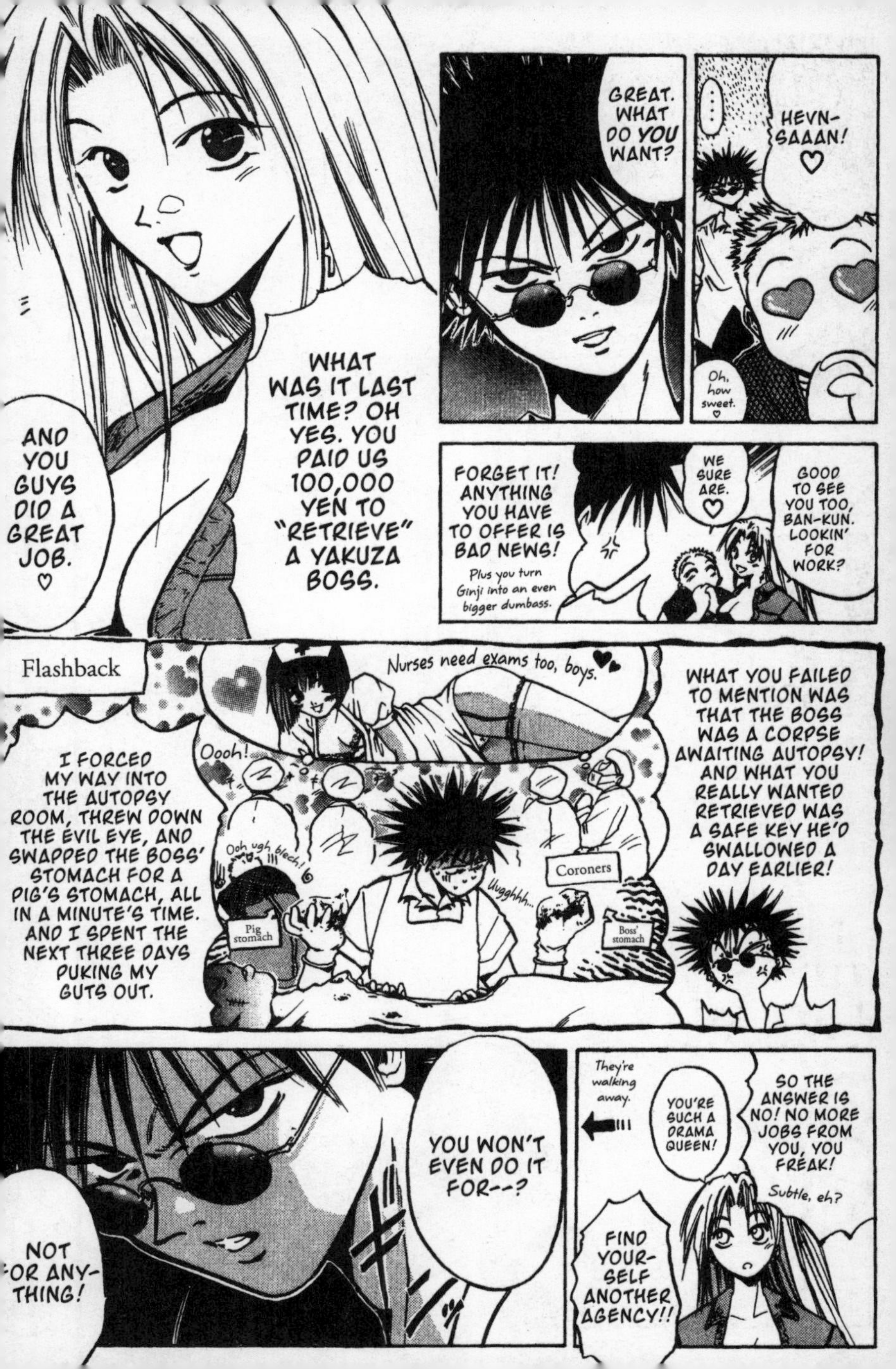
...
HEVN-SAAAN! ♡
Oh, how sweet. ♡
GREAT. WHAT DO YOU WANT?
GOOD TO SEE YOU TOO, BAN-KUN. LOOKIN' FOR WORK?
WE SURE ARE. ♡
FORGET IT! ANYTHING YOU HAVE TO OFFER IS BAD NEWS!
Plus you turn Ginji into an even bigger dumbass.
WHAT WAS IT LAST TIME? OH YES. YOU PAID US 100,000 YEN TO "RETRIEVE" A YAKUZA BOSS.
AND YOU GUYS DID A GREAT JOB. ♡
WHAT YOU FAILED TO MENTION WAS THAT THE BOSS WAS A CORPSE AWAITING AUTOPSY! AND WHAT YOU REALLY WANTED RETRIEVED WAS A SAFE KEY HE'D SWALLOWED A DAY EARLIER!
Nurses need exams too, boys.
Coroners
Uuggghh...
Boss' stomach
Oooh!
Ooh ugh blech!
Pig stomach
Flashback
I FORCED MY WAY INTO THE AUTOPSY ROOM, THREW DOWN THE EVIL EYE, AND SWAPPED THE BOSS' STOMACH FOR A PIG'S STOMACH, ALL IN A MINUTE'S TIME. AND I SPENT THE NEXT THREE DAYS PUKING MY GUTS OUT.
SO THE ANSWER IS NO! NO MORE JOBS FROM YOU, YOU FREAK!
Subtle, eh?
YOU'RE SUCH A DRAMA QUEEN!
They're walking away.
FIND YOURSELF ANOTHER AGENCY!!
YOU WON'T EVEN DO IT FOR--?
NOT FOR ANYTHING!

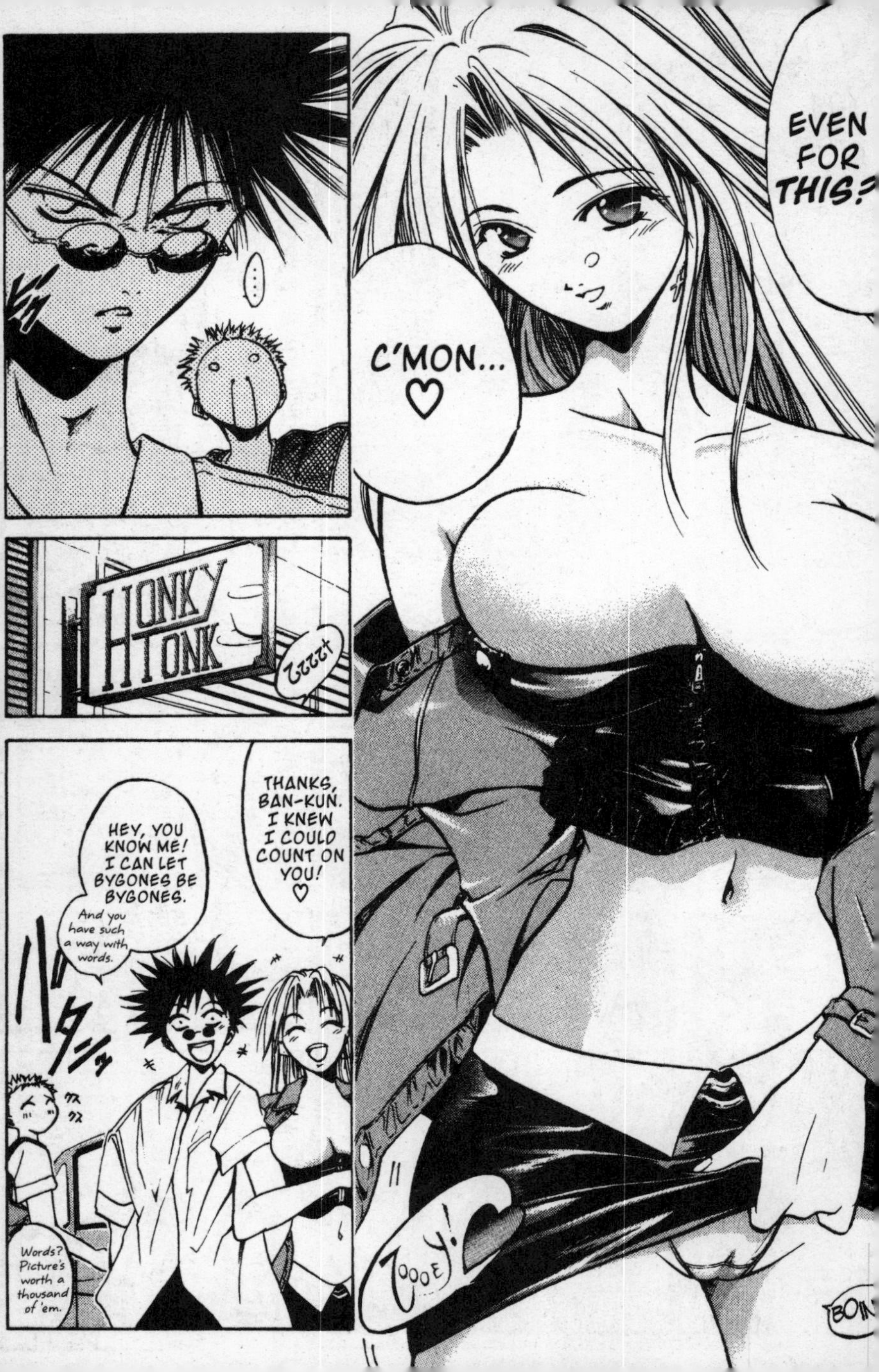
EVEN FOR THIS?
C'MON... ♡
BOIN
...
HONKY TONK
THANKS, BAN-KUN. I KNEW I COULD COUNT ON YOU! ♡
HEY, YOU KNOW ME! I CAN LET BYGONES BE BYGONES.
And you have such a way with words.
Words? Picture's worth a thousand of 'em.

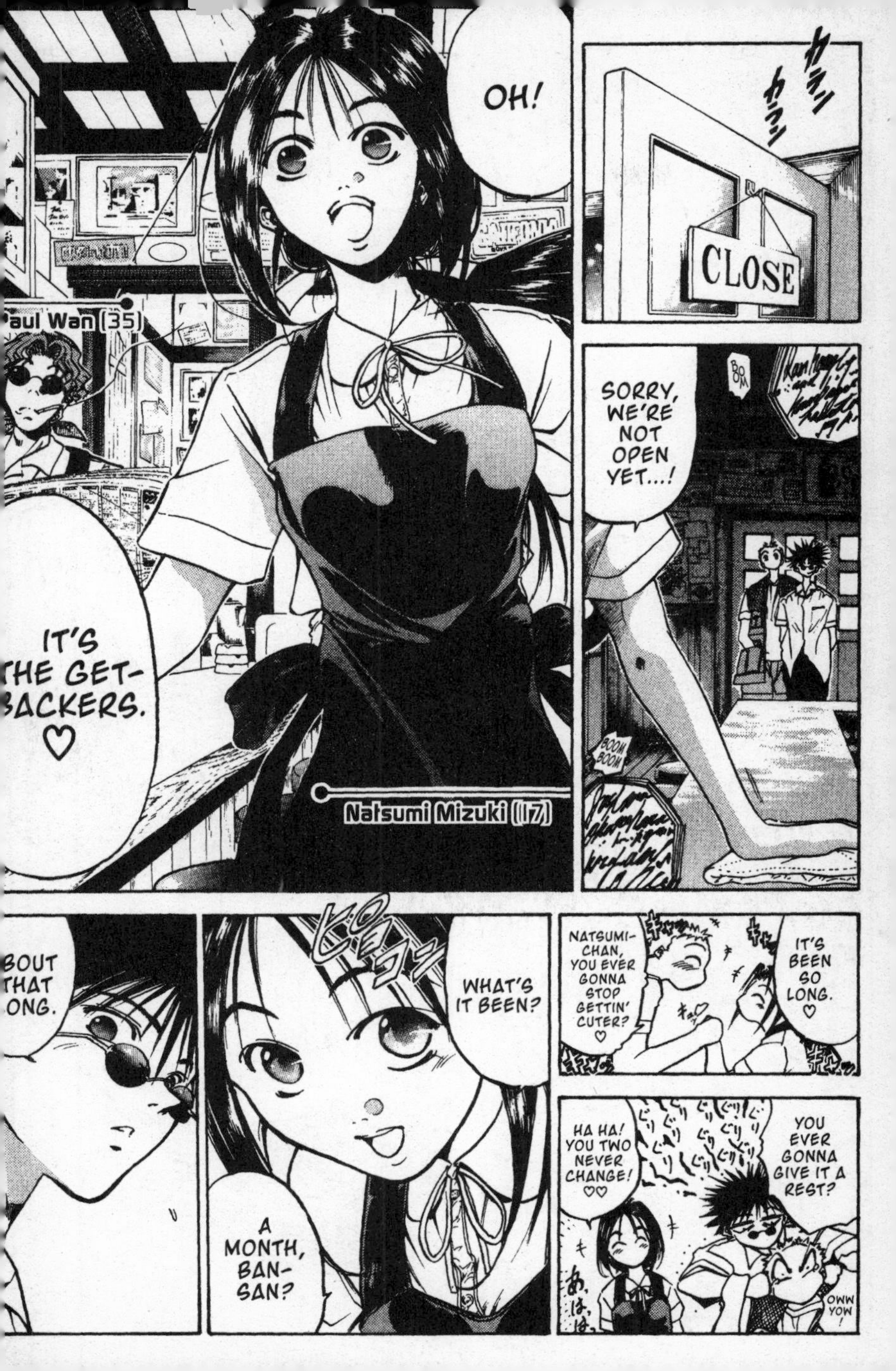
CLOSE
SORRY, WE'RE NOT OPEN YET...!
BOOM
BOOM BOOM
OH!
IT'S THE GET-BACKERS. ♡
Paul Wan (35)
Natsumi Mizuki (17)
IT'S BEEN SO LONG. ♡
NATSUMI-CHAN, YOU EVER GONNA STOP GETTIN' CUTER? ♡
YOU EVER GONNA GIVE IT A REST?
HA HA! YOU TWO NEVER CHANGE! ♡♡
OWW YOW!
WHAT'S IT BEEN?
A MONTH, BAN-SAN?
BOUT THAT ONG.

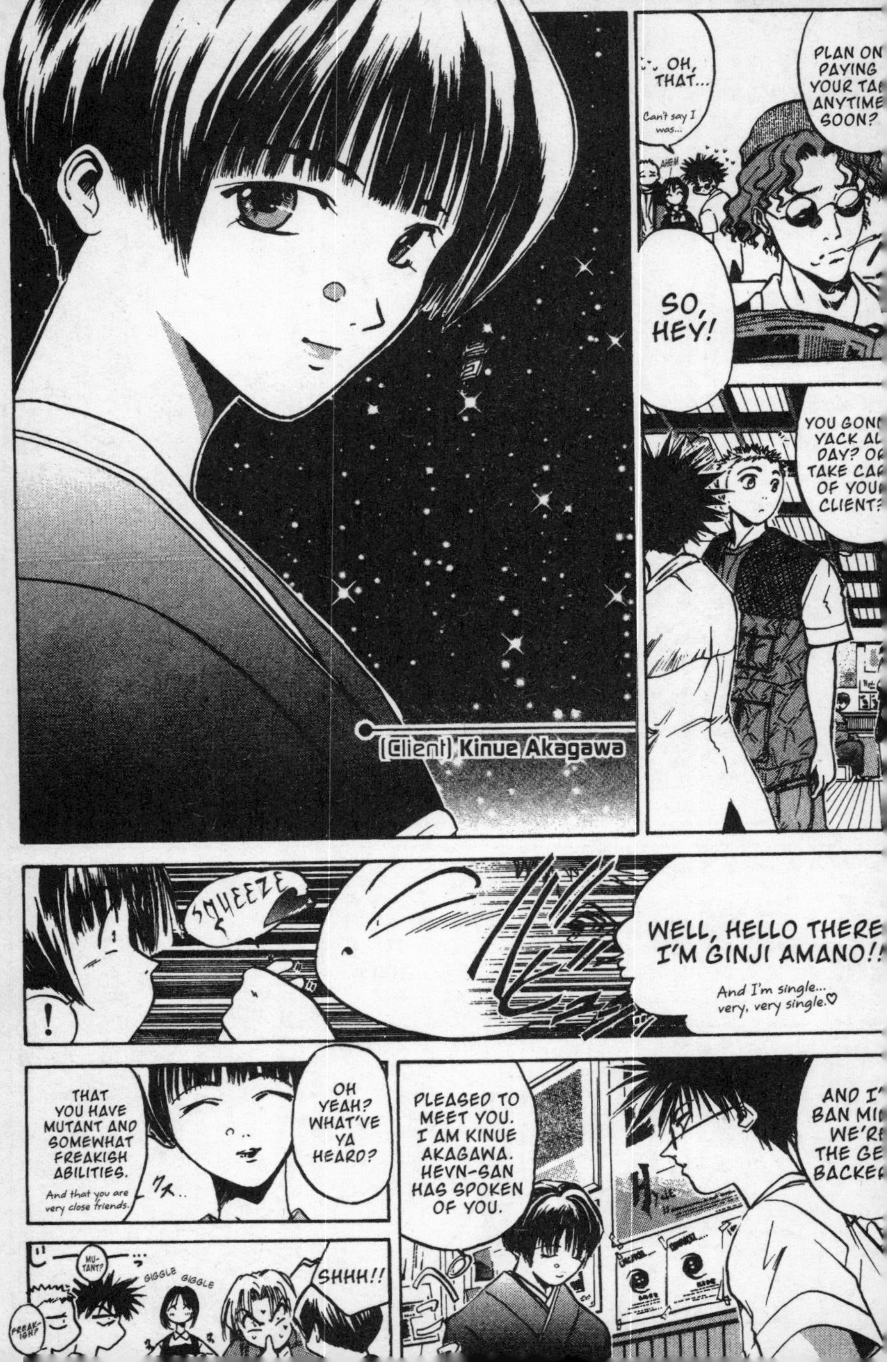
PLAN ON PAYING YOUR TA ANYTIME SOON?
... OH, THAT...
Can't say I was...
AHEM
SO, HEY!
YOU GONN YACK AL DAY? OR TAKE CAR OF YOUR CLIENT?
(Client) Kinue Akagawa
WELL, HELLO THERE I'M GINJI AMANO!!
And I'm single... very, very single.♡
SQUEEZE
!
AND I' BAN MI WE'R THE GE BACKER
PLEASED TO MEET YOU. I AM KINUE AKAGAWA. HEVN-SAN HAS SPOKEN OF YOU.
OH YEAH? WHAT'VE YA HEARD?
THAT YOU HAVE MUTANT AND SOMEWHAT FREAKISH ABILITIES.
And that you are very close friends.
SHHH!!
GIGGLE GIGGLE
MU-TANT?
FREAK-ISH?

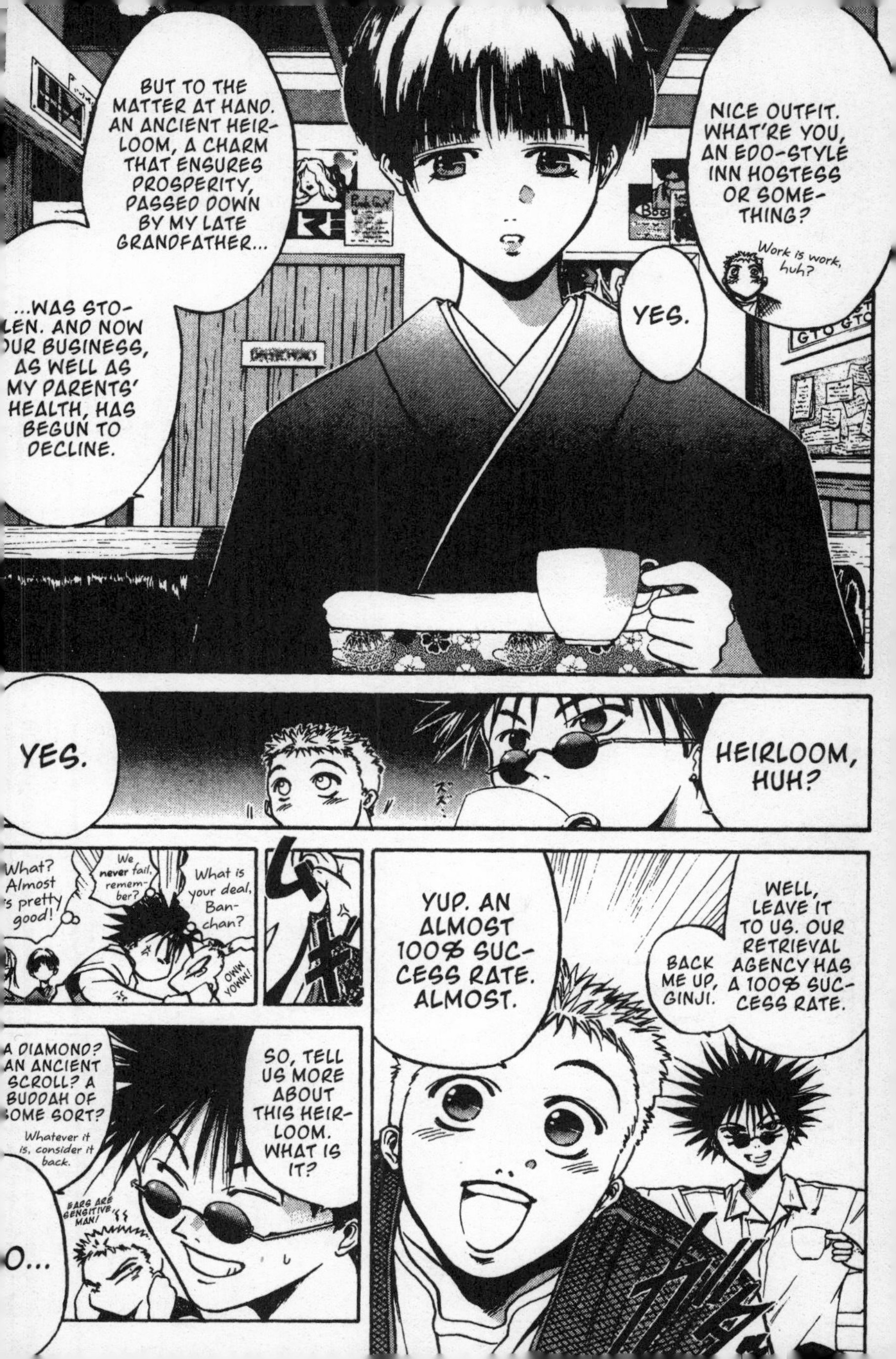
NICE OUTFIT. WHAT'RE YOU, AN EDO-STYLE INN HOSTESS OR SOMETHING?
Work is work, huh?
YES.
BUT TO THE MATTER AT HAND. AN ANCIENT HEIRLOOM, A CHARM THAT ENSURES PROSPERITY, PASSED DOWN BY MY LATE GRANDFATHER...
...WAS STOLEN. AND NOW UR BUSINESS, AS WELL AS MY PARENTS' HEALTH, HAS BEGUN TO DECLINE.
HEIRLOOM, HUH?
YES.
WELL, LEAVE IT TO US. OUR RETRIEVAL AGENCY HAS A 100% SUCCESS RATE.
BACK ME UP, GINJI.
YUP. AN ALMOST 100% SUCCESS RATE. ALMOST.
We never fail, remember?
What is your deal, Ban-chan?
What? Almost 's pretty good!
OWW YOWW!
SO, TELL US MORE ABOUT THIS HEIRLOOM. WHAT IS IT?
A DIAMOND? AN ANCIENT SCROLL? A BUDDAH OF OME SORT?
Whatever it is, consider it back.
EARS ARE SENSITIVE, MAN!
O...

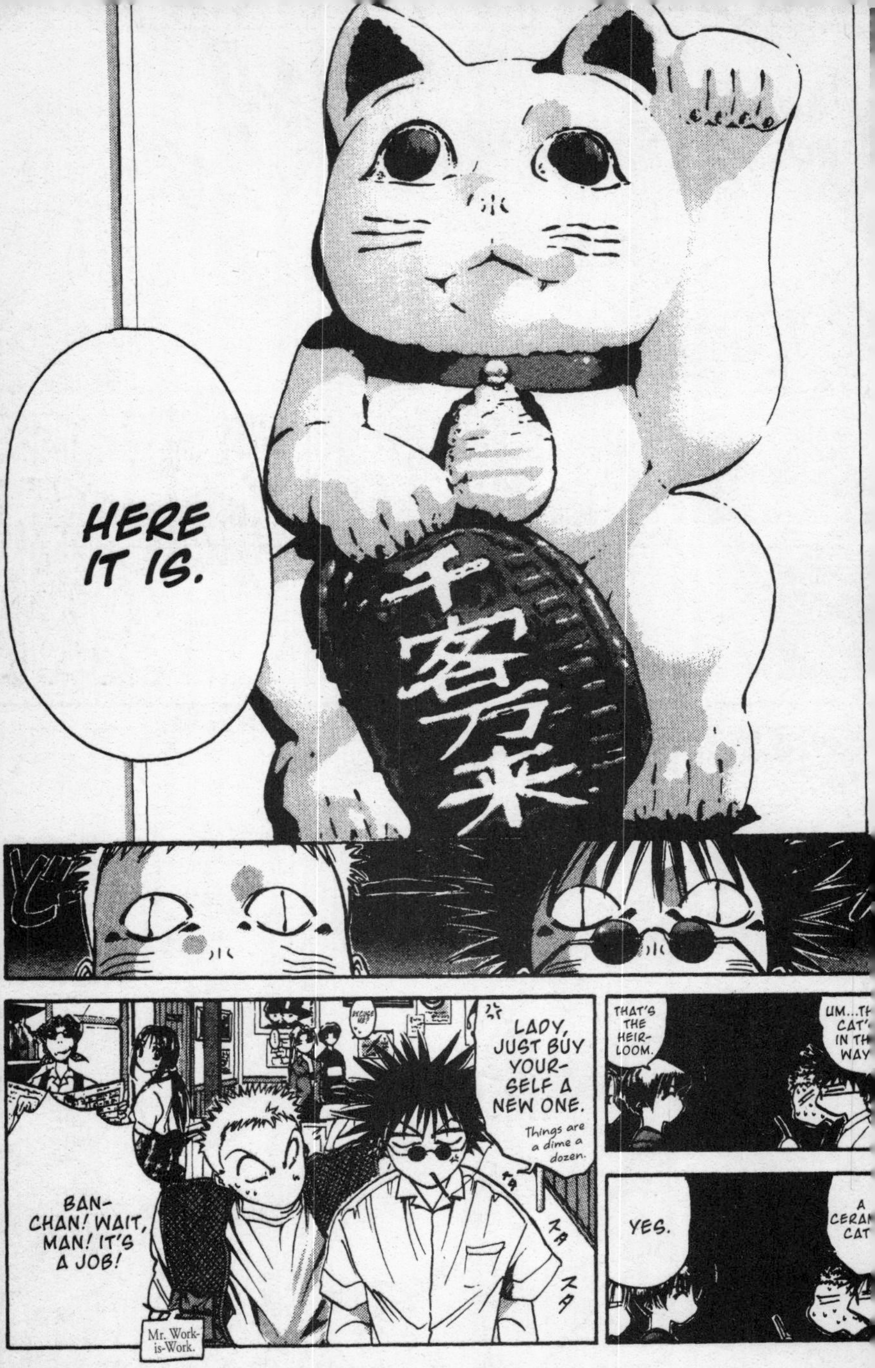
HERE IT IS.
THAT'S THE HEIR-LOOM.
YES.
LADY, JUST BUY YOUR-SELF A NEW ONE.
Things are a dime a dozen.
BAN-CHAN! WAIT, MAN! IT'S A JOB!
Mr. Work-is-Work.

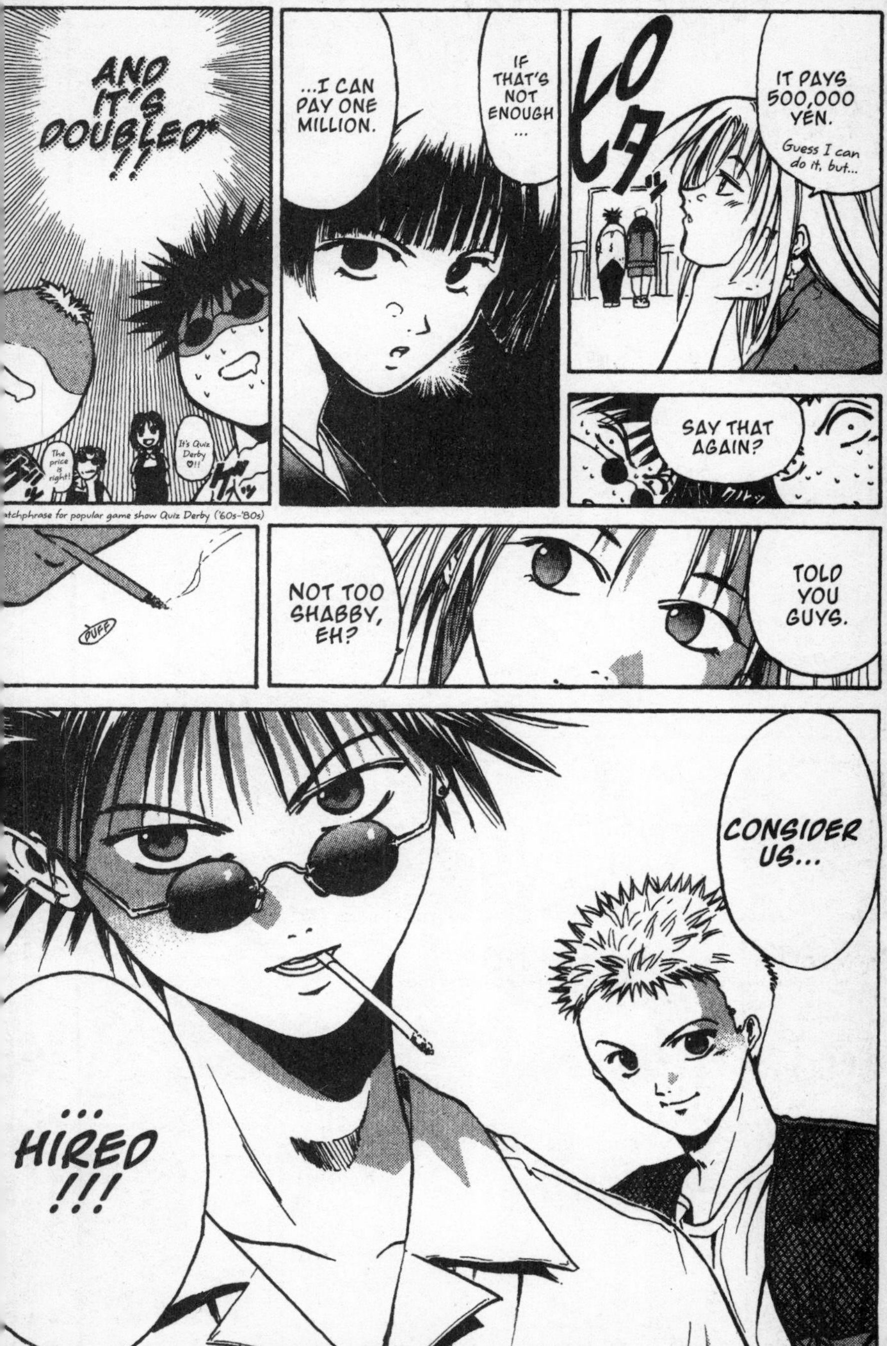
IT PAYS 500,000 YEN.
Guess I can do it, but...
SAY THAT AGAIN?
IF THAT'S NOT ENOUGH ...
...I CAN PAY ONE MILLION.
AND IT'S DOUBLED* !!
It's Quiz Derby ♡!!
The price is right!
TOLD YOU GUYS.
NOT TOO SHABBY, EH?
PUFF
CONSIDER US...
... HIRED !!!
atchphrase for popular game show Quiz Derby ('60s-'80s)

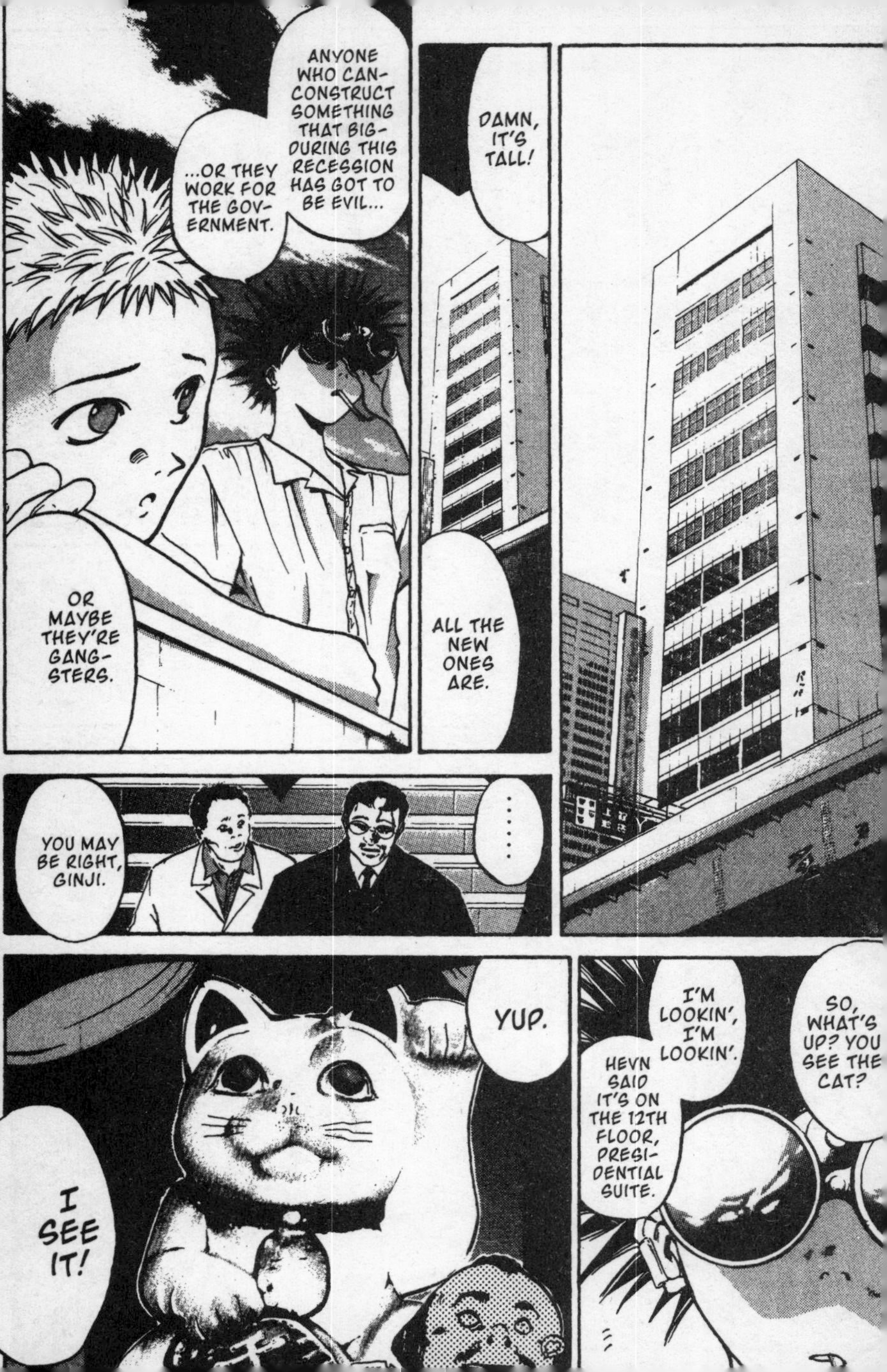
DAMN, IT'S TALL!
ALL THE NEW ONES ARE.
ANYONE WHO CAN-CONSTRUCT SOMETHING THAT BIG-DURING THIS RECESSION HAS GOT TO BE EVIL...
...OR THEY WORK FOR THE GOVERNMENT.
OR MAYBE THEY'RE GANGSTERS.
......
YOU MAY BE RIGHT, GINJI.
SO, WHAT'S UP? YOU SEE THE CAT?
I'M LOOKIN', I'M LOOKIN'.
HEVN SAID IT'S ON THE 12TH FLOOR, PRESIDENTIAL SUITE.
YUP.
I SEE IT!

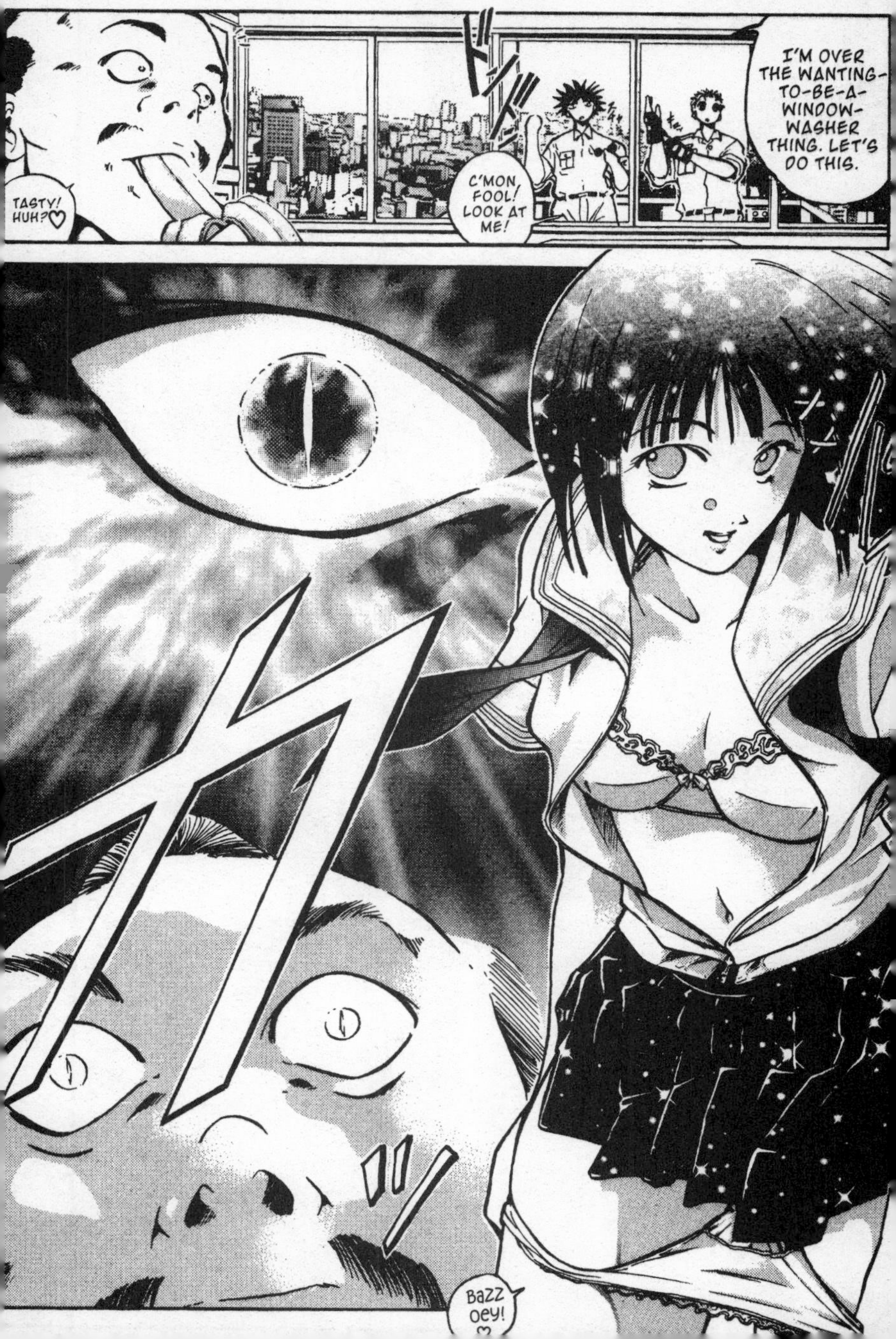
I'M OVER THE WANTING-TO-BE-A-WINDOW-WASHER THING. LET'S DO THIS.
C'MON FOOL! LOOK AT ME!
TASTY! HUH?♡
BaZZ oey! ♡

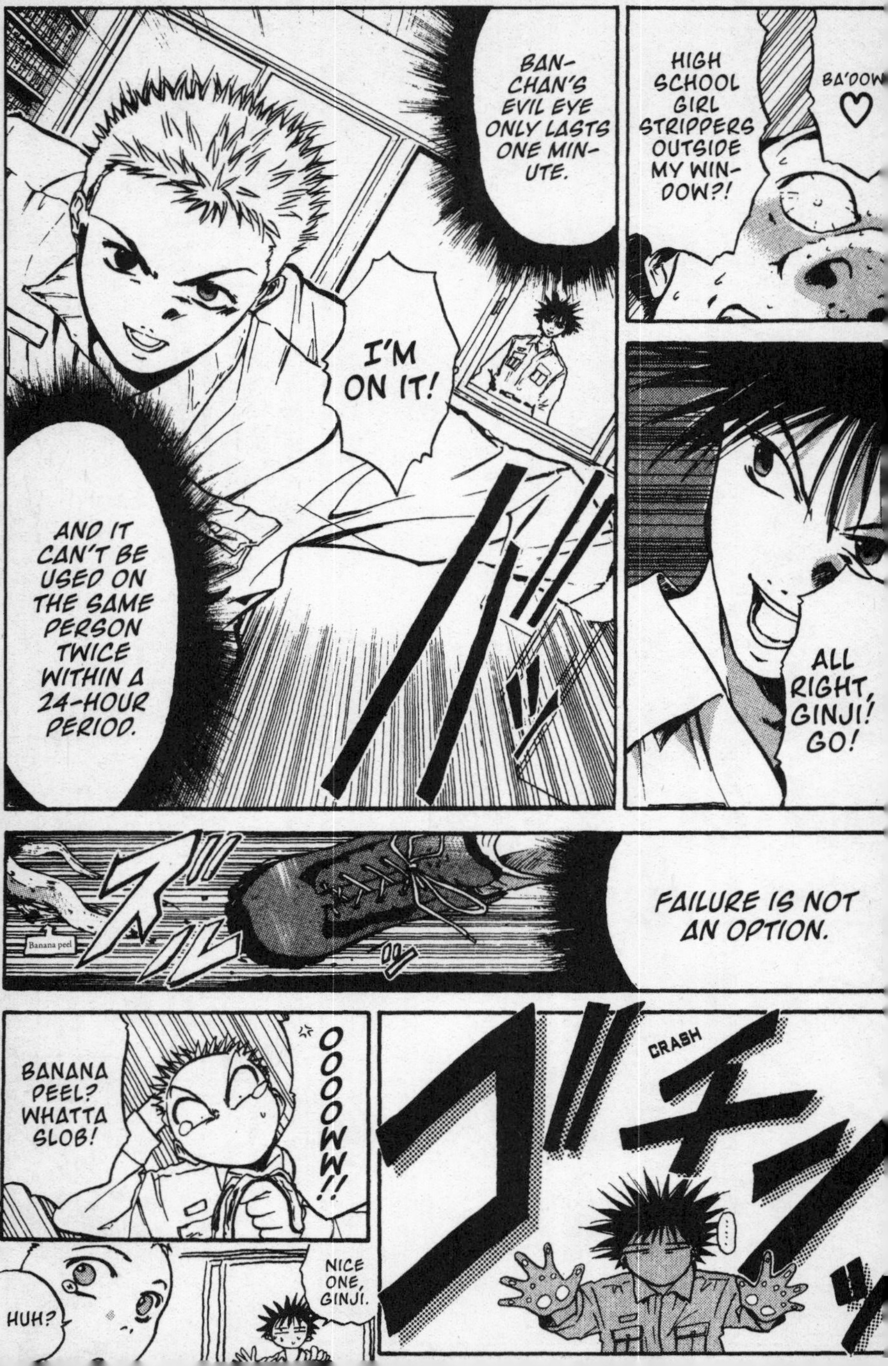
BA'DOW ♡
HIGH SCHOOL GIRL STRIPPERS OUTSIDE MY WINDOW?!
ALL RIGHT, GINJI! GO!
BAN-CHAN'S EVIL EYE ONLY LASTS ONE MINUTE.
I'M ON IT!
AND IT CAN'T BE USED ON THE SAME PERSON TWICE WITHIN A 24-HOUR PERIOD.
FAILURE IS NOT AN OPTION.
Banana peel
CRASH
OOOOOWW!!
BANANA PEEL? WHATTA SLOB!
NICE ONE, GINJI.
HUH?

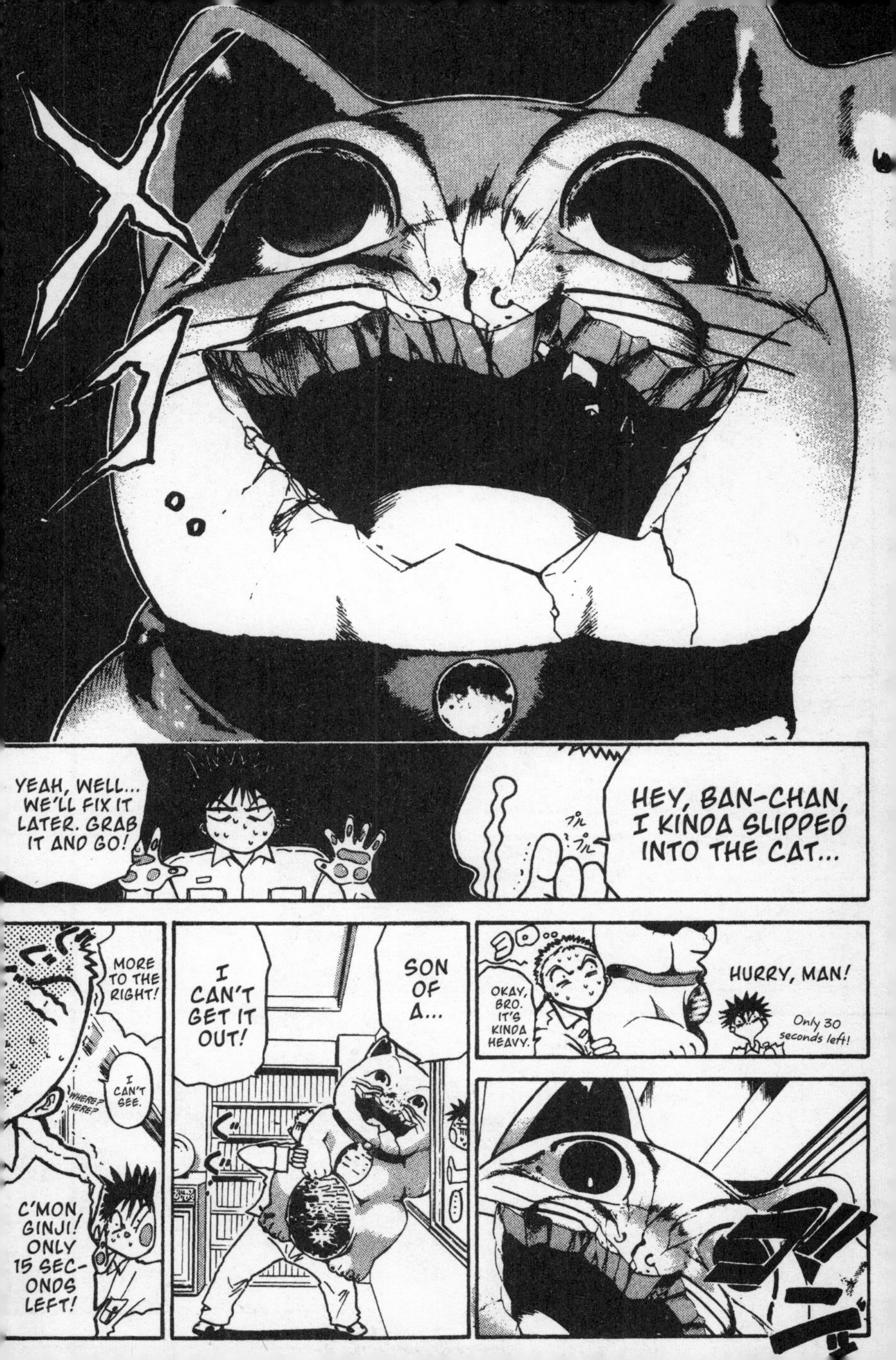
HEY, BAN-CHAN, I KINDA SLIPPED INTO THE CAT...
YEAH, WELL... WE'LL FIX IT LATER. GRAB IT AND GO!
HURRY, MAN!
Only 30 seconds left!
OKAY, BRO. IT'S KINDA HEAVY.
SON OF A...
I CAN'T GET IT OUT!
MORE TO THE RIGHT!
I CAN'T SEE.
WHERE? HERE?
C'MON GINJI! ONLY 15 SECONDS LEFT!

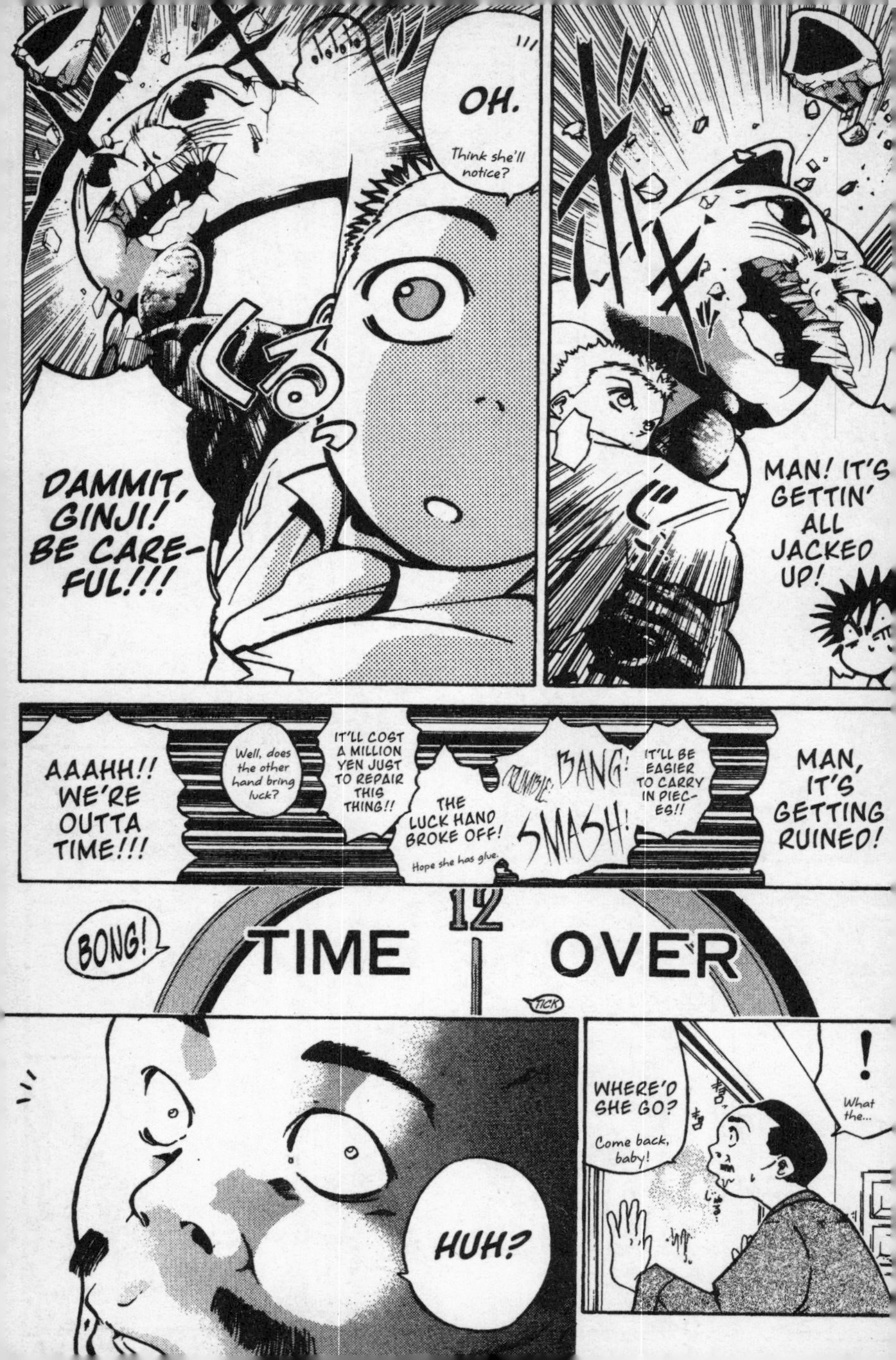
MAN! IT'S GETTIN' ALL JACKED UP!
OH.
Think she'll notice?
DAMMIT, GINJI! BE CARE-FUL!!!
MAN, IT'S GETTING RUINED!
IT'LL BE EASIER TO CARRY IN PIEC-ES!!
BANG!
CRUMBLE
SMASH!
THE LUCK HAND BROKE OFF!
Hope she has glue.
IT'LL COST A MILLION YEN JUST TO REPAIR THIS THING!!
Well, does the other hand bring luck?
AAAHH!! WE'RE OUTTA TIME!!!
BONG!
12
TIME OVER
TICK
!
What the...
WHERE'D SHE GO?
Come back, baby!
HUH?

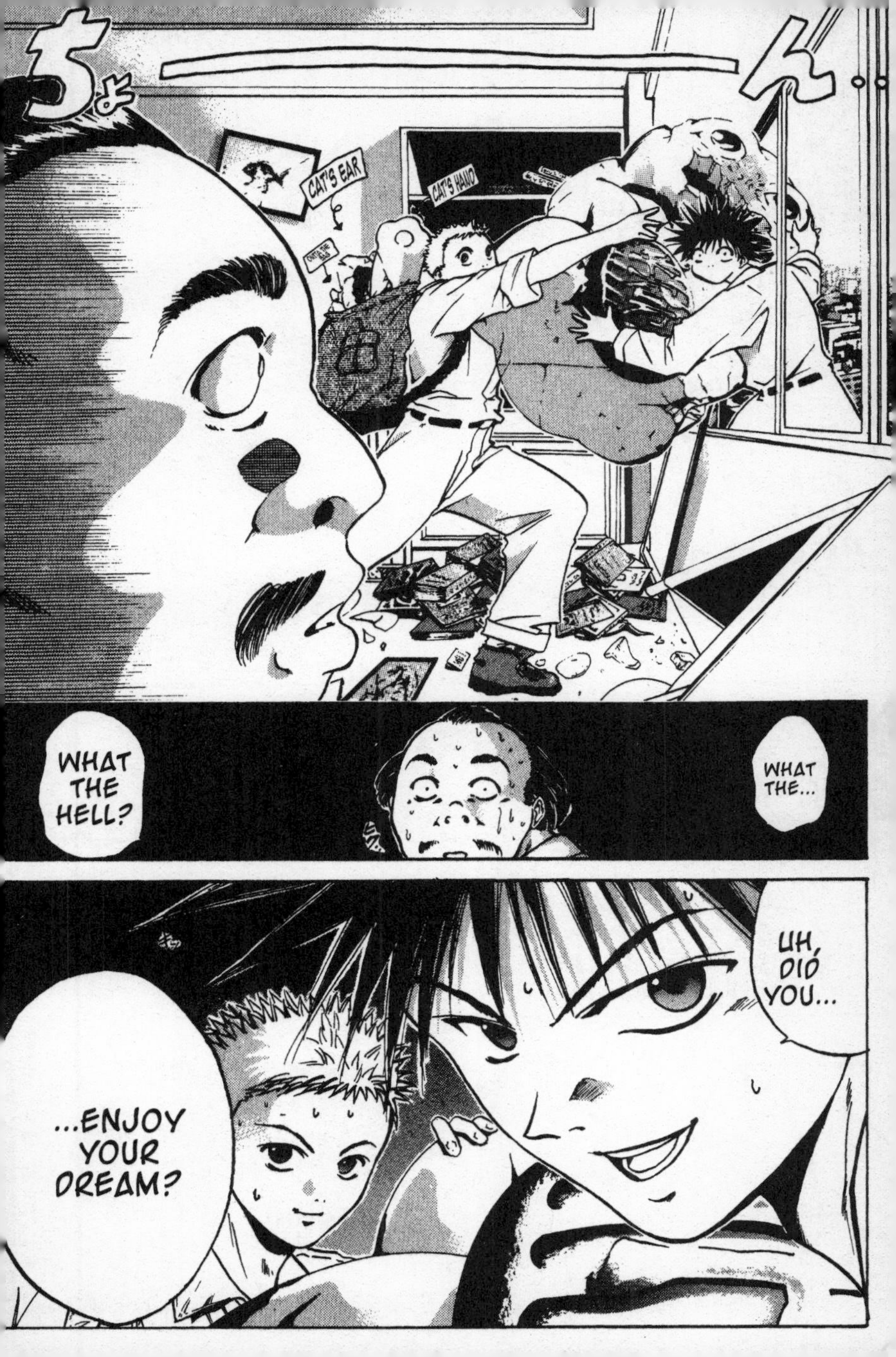
ちょ
ん..
CAT'S EAR
CAT'S HAND
WHAT THE...
WHAT THE HELL?
UH, DID YOU...
...ENJOY YOUR DREAM?

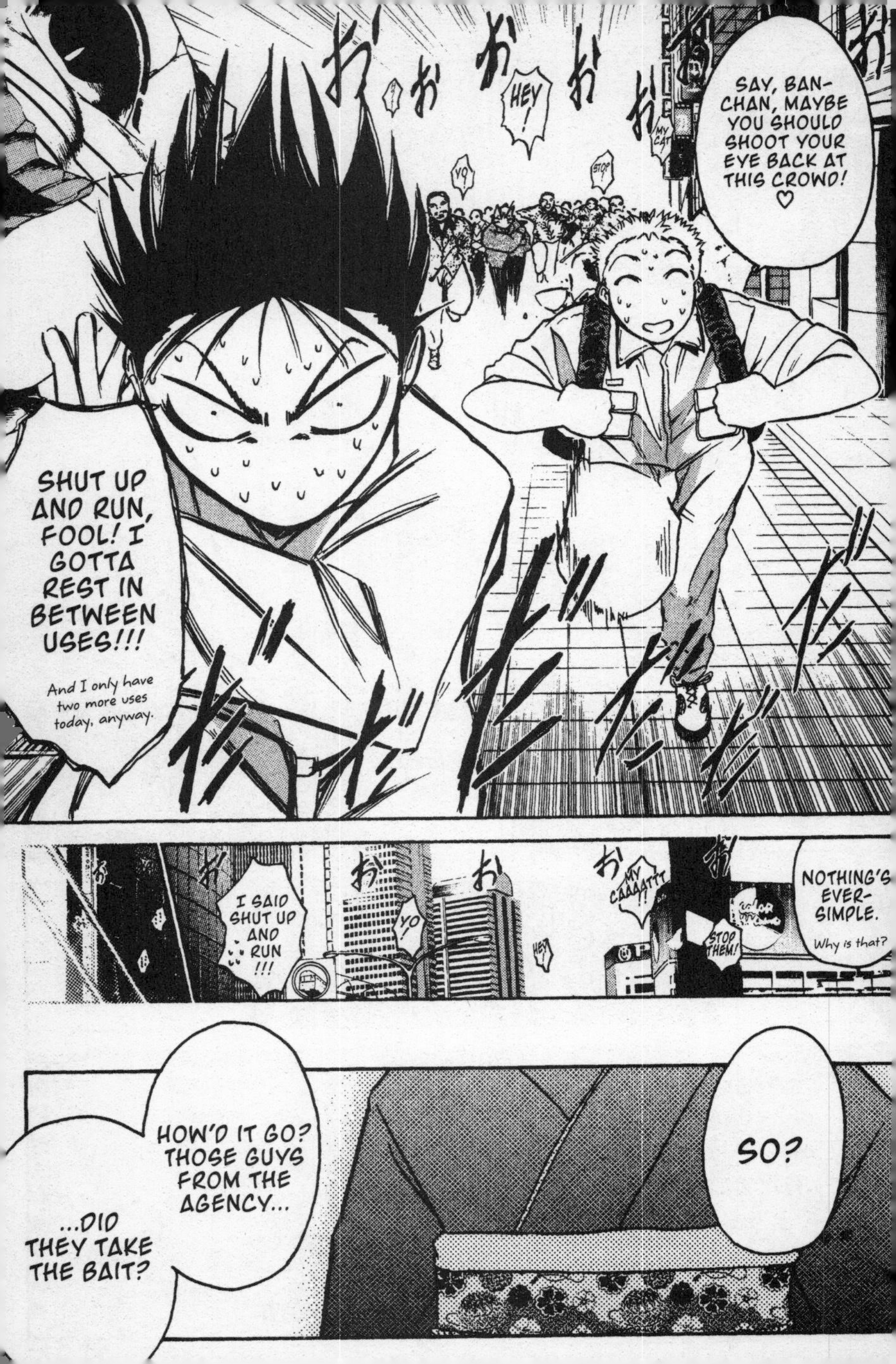
SAY, BAN-CHAN, MAYBE YOU SHOULD SHOOT YOUR EYE BACK AT THIS CROWD! ♡
MY CAT
STOP
HEY!
YO
SHUT UP AND RUN, FOOL! I GOTTA REST IN BETWEEN USES!!!
And I only have two more uses today, anyway.
NOTHING'S EVER-SIMPLE.
Why is that?
STOP THEM!
MY CAAAATTT!!
HEY
YO!
I SAID SHUT UP AND RUN!!!
SO?
HOW'D IT GO? THOSE GUYS FROM THE AGENCY...
...DID THEY TAKE THE BAIT?

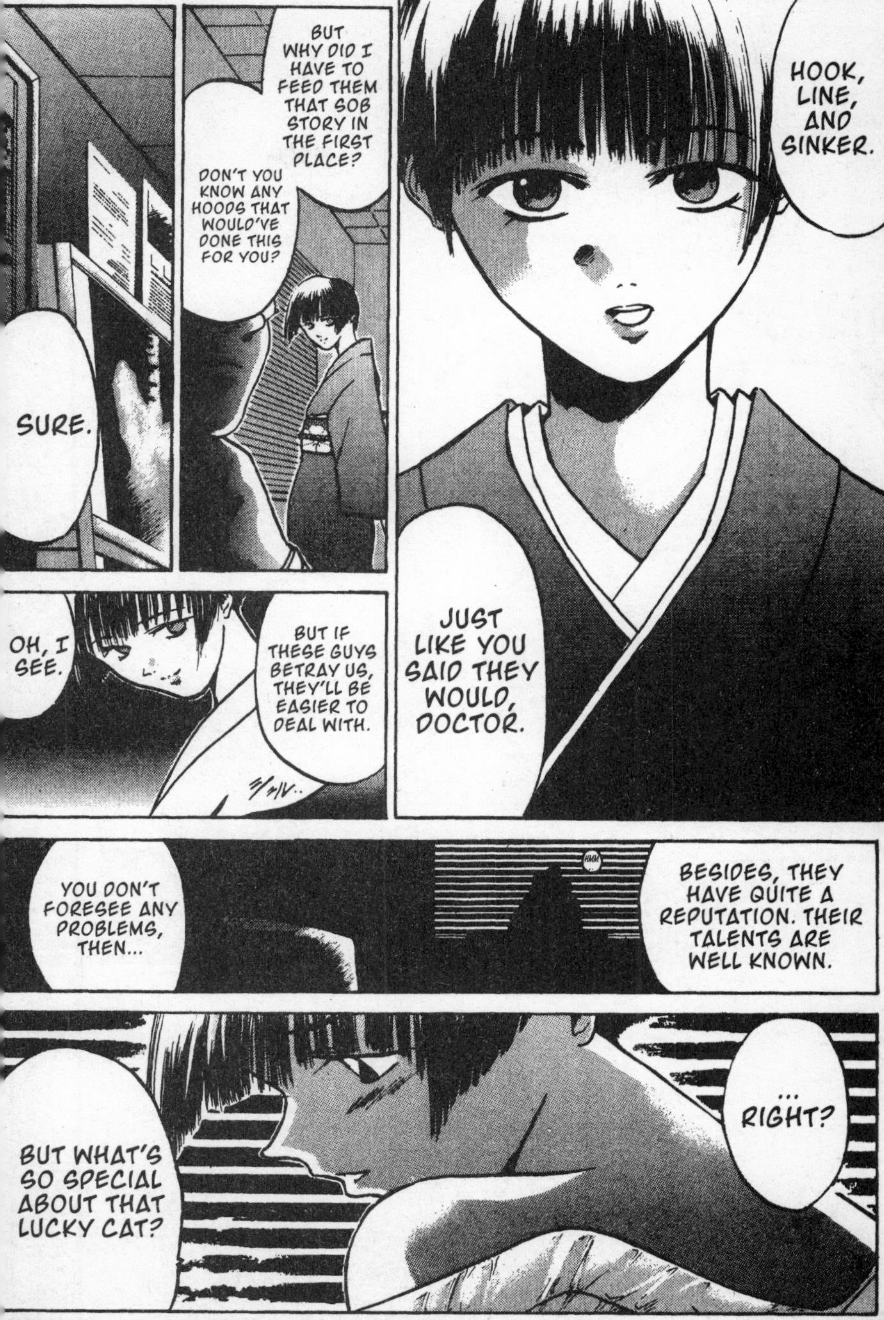
HOOK, LINE, AND SINKER.
JUST LIKE YOU SAID THEY WOULD, DOCTOR.
BUT WHY DID I HAVE TO FEED THEM THAT SOB STORY IN THE FIRST PLACE?
DON'T YOU KNOW ANY HOODS THAT WOULD'VE DONE THIS FOR YOU?
SURE.
BUT IF THESE GUYS BETRAY US, THEY'LL BE EASIER TO DEAL WITH.
OH, I SEE.
BESIDES, THEY HAVE QUITE A REPUTATION. THEIR TALENTS ARE WELL KNOWN.
HMM
YOU DON'T FORESEE ANY PROBLEMS, THEN...
... RIGHT?
BUT WHAT'S SO SPECIAL ABOUT THAT LUCKY CAT?

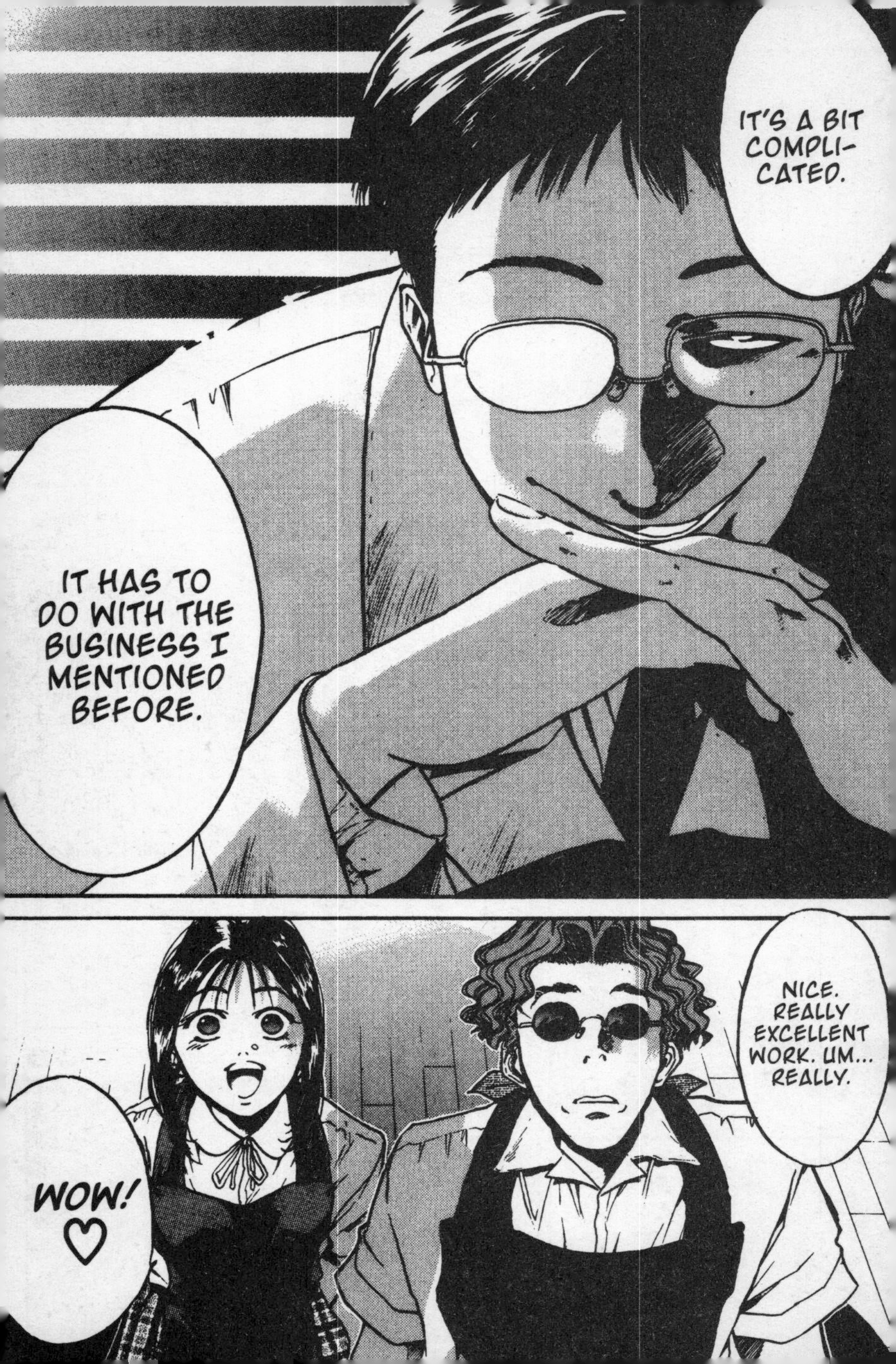
IT'S A BIT COMPLICATED.
IT HAS TO DO WITH THE BUSINESS I MENTIONED BEFORE.
NICE. REALLY EXCELLENT WORK. UM... REALLY.
WOW! ♡

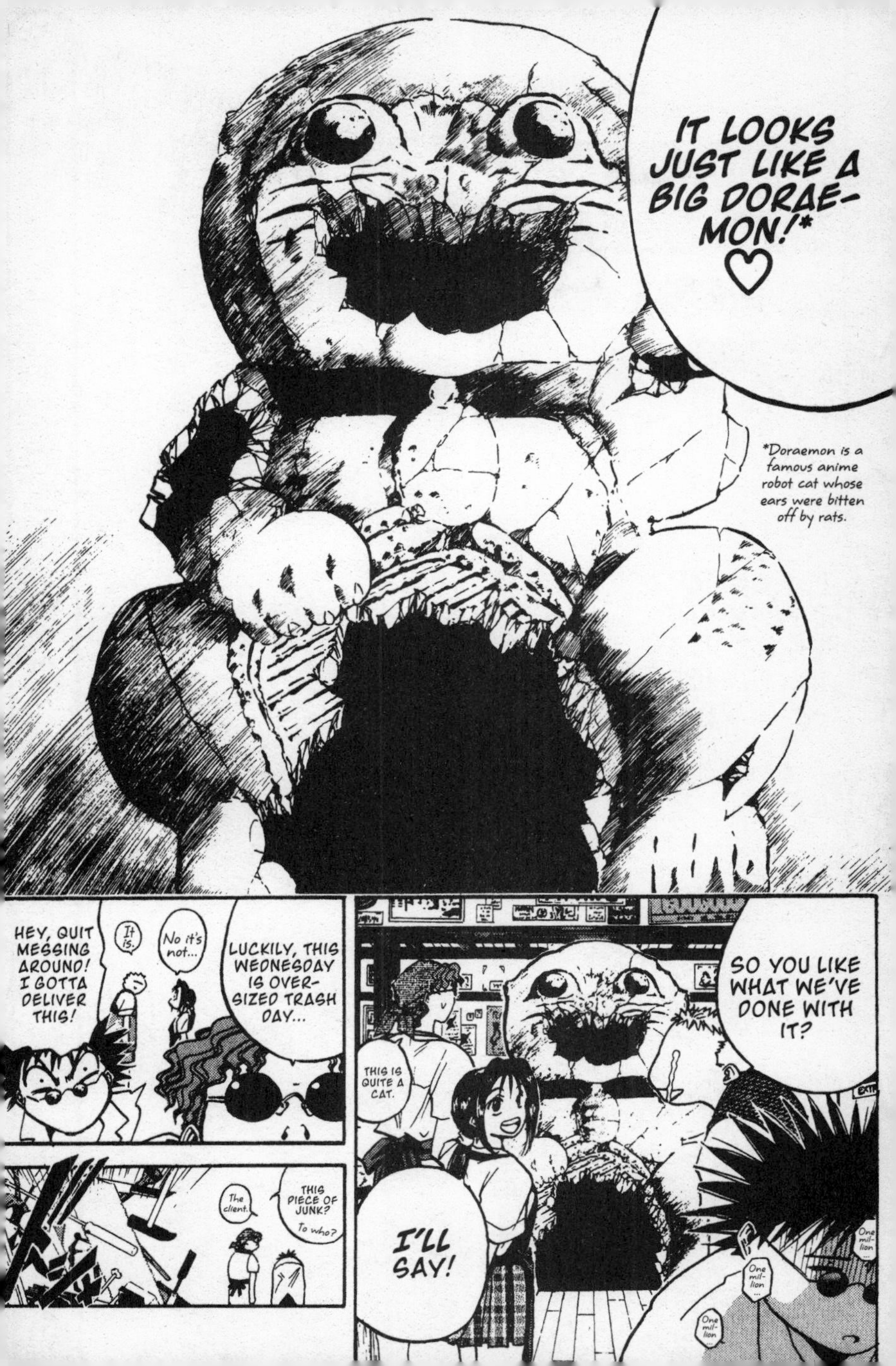
IT LOOKS JUST LIKE A BIG DORAE-MON!* ♡
LUCKILY, THIS WEDNESDAY IS OVER-SIZED TRASH DAY...
No it's not...
It is.
HEY, QUIT MESSING AROUND! I GOTTA DELIVER THIS!
THIS PIECE OF JUNK?
To who?
The client.
SO YOU LIKE WHAT WE'VE DONE WITH IT?
THIS IS QUITE A CAT.
I'LL SAY!
One mil-lion...
One mil-lion...
One mil-lion...

*Doraemon is a famous anime robot cat whose ears were bitten off by rats.

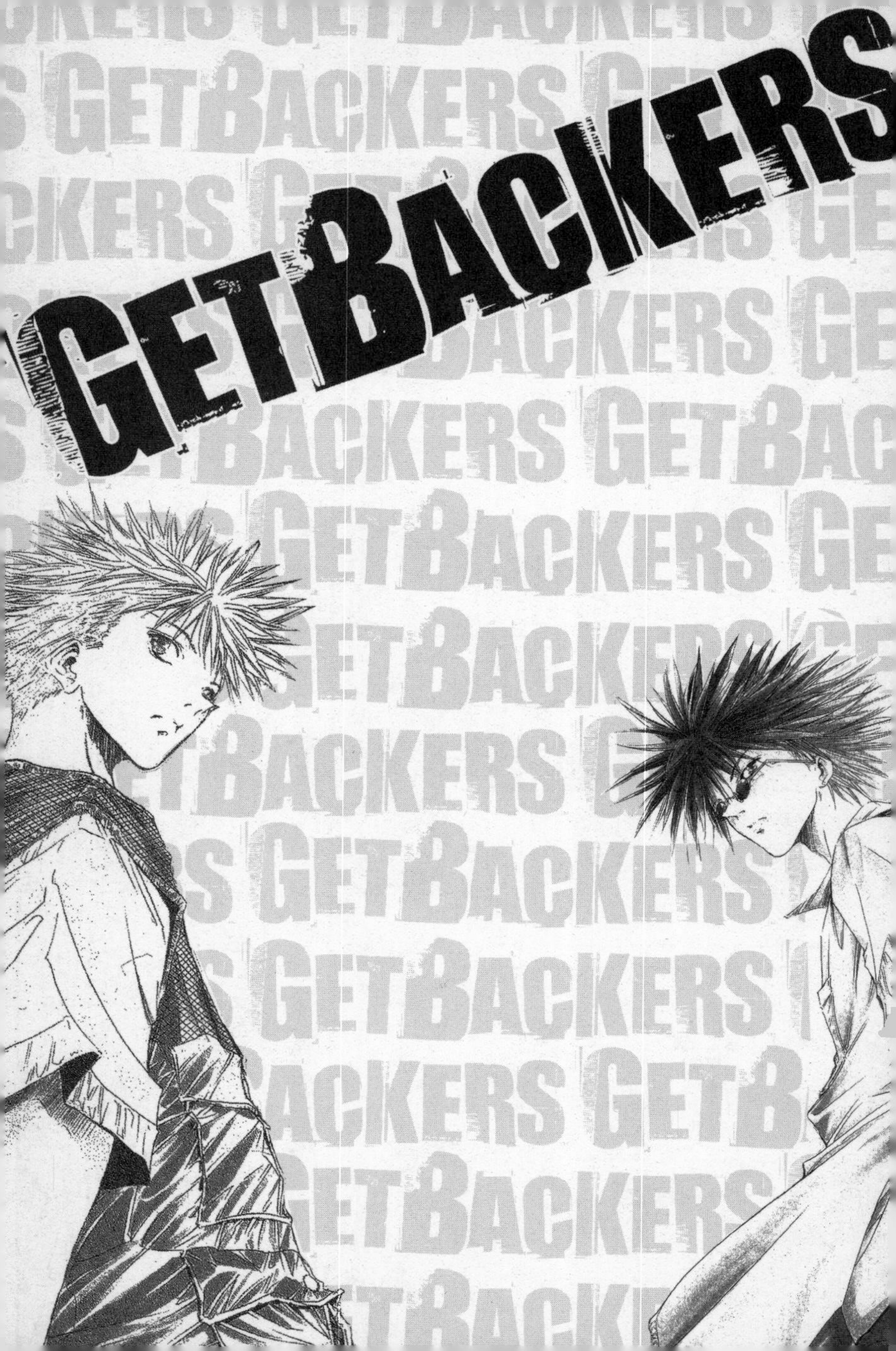
GETBACKERS

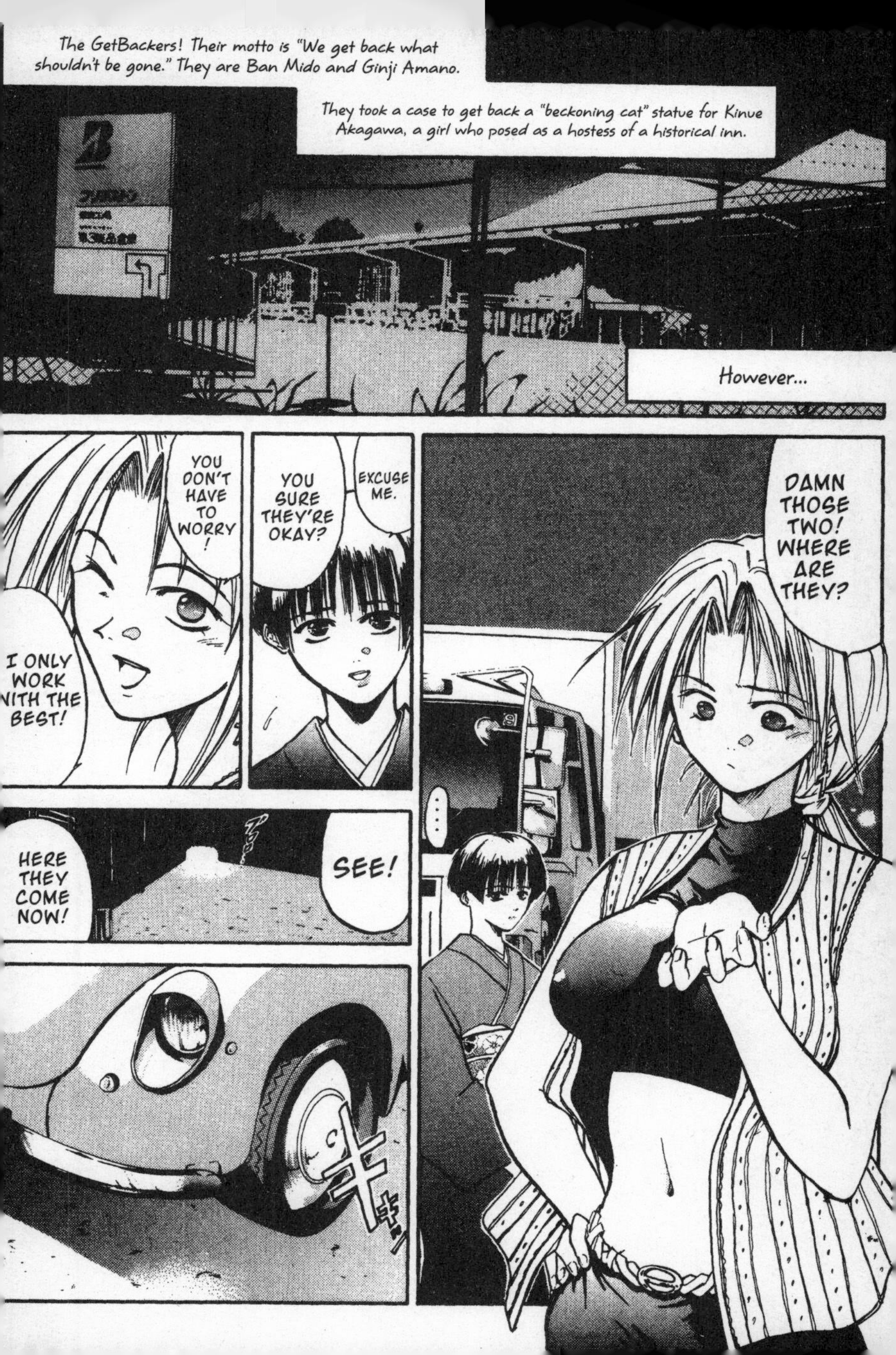
The GetBackers! Their motto is "We get back what shouldn't be gone." They are Ban Mido and Ginji Amano.
They took a case to get back a "beckoning cat" statue for Kinue Akagawa, a girl who posed as a hostess of a historical inn.
However...
DAMN THOSE TWO! WHERE ARE THEY?
...
EXCUSE ME.
YOU SURE THEY'RE OKAY?
YOU DON'T HAVE TO WORRY!
I ONLY WORK WITH THE BEST!
SEE!
HERE THEY COME NOW!

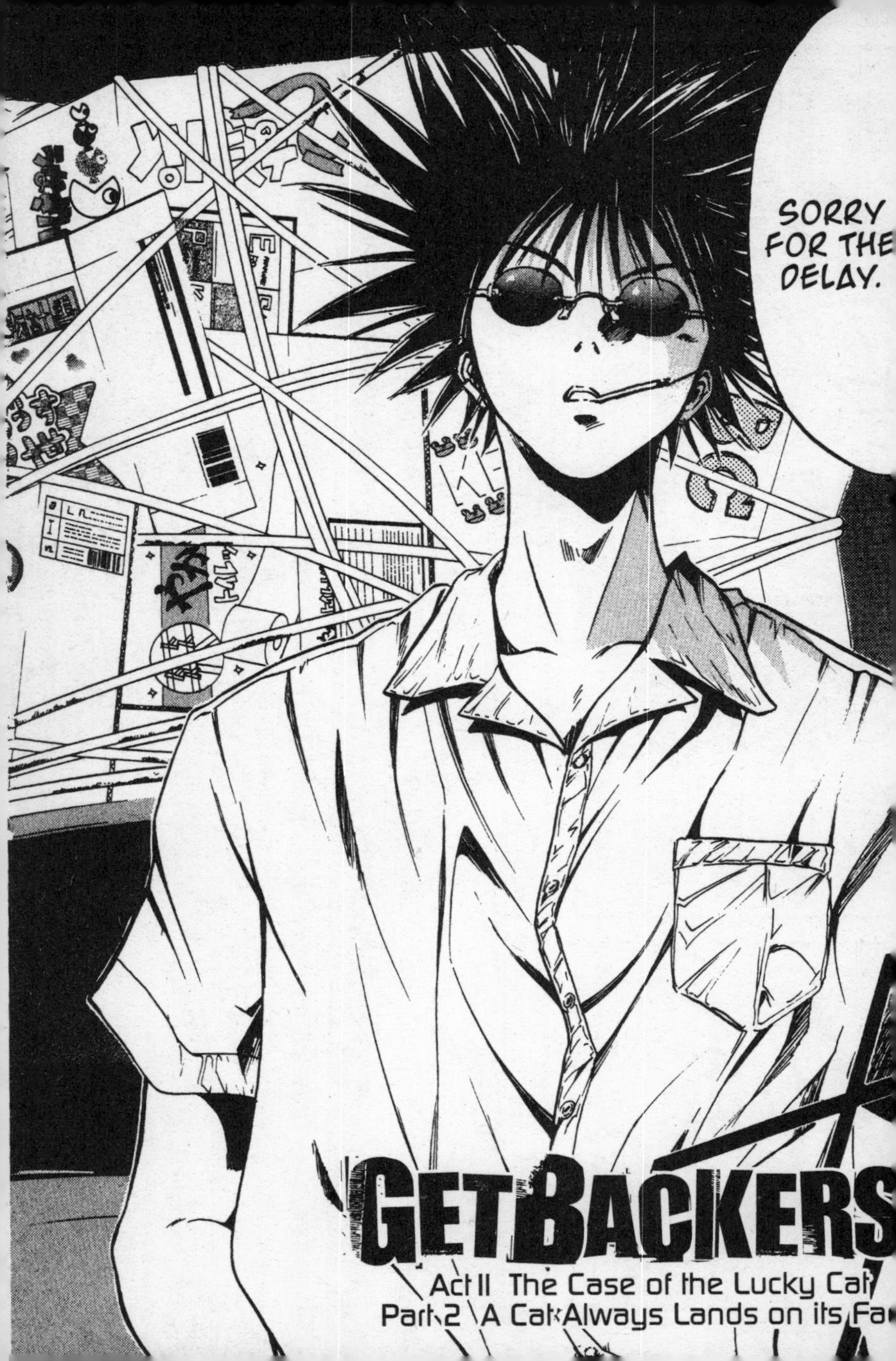
SORRY FOR THE DELAY.
GETBACKERS
Act II The Case of the Lucky Cat
Part 2 A Cat Always Lands on its Fa

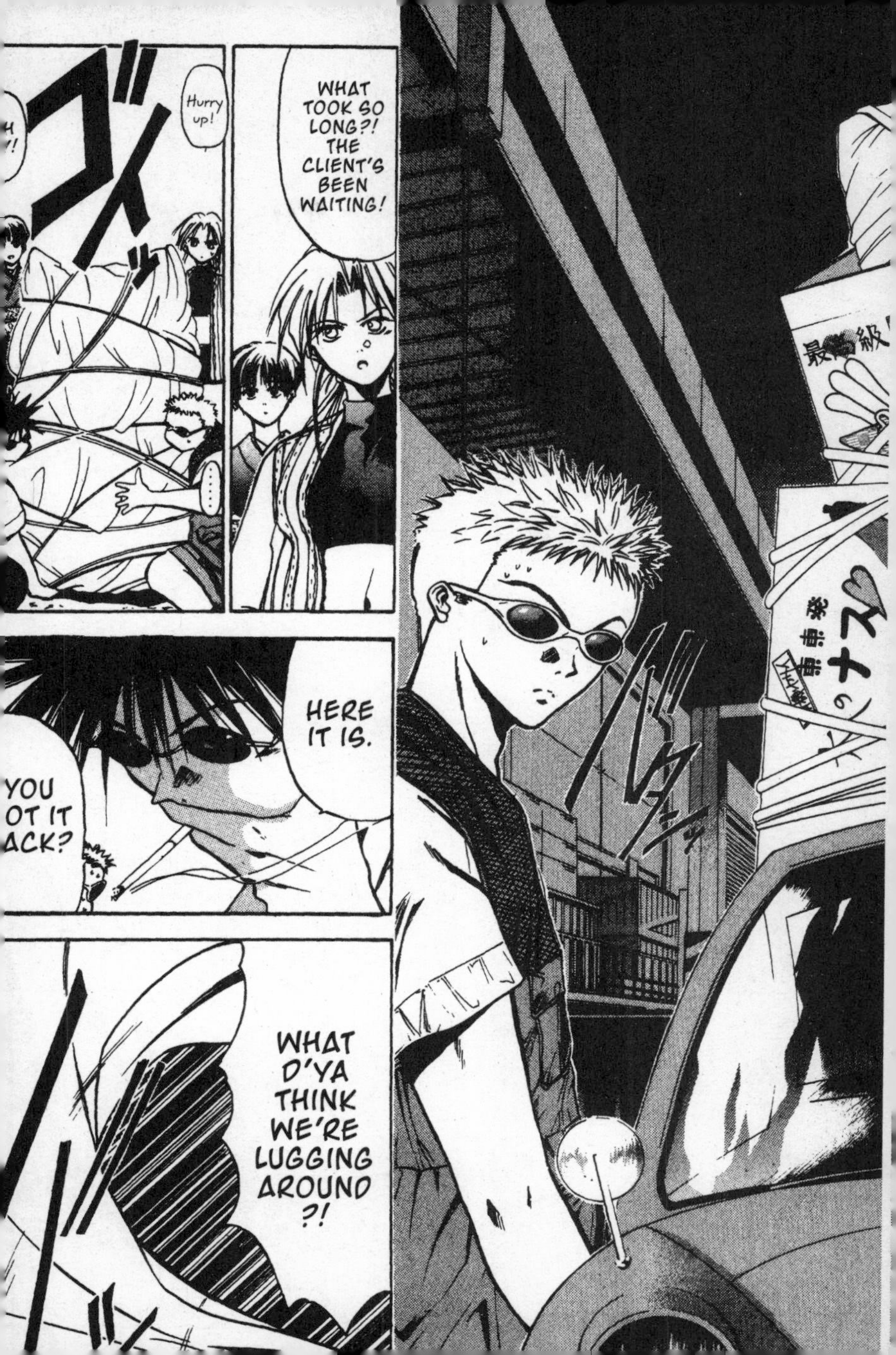
WHAT TOOK SO LONG?! THE CLIENT'S BEEN WAITING!
Hurry up!
HERE IT IS.
YOU OT IT ACK?
WHAT D'YA THINK WE'RE LUGGING AROUND ?!

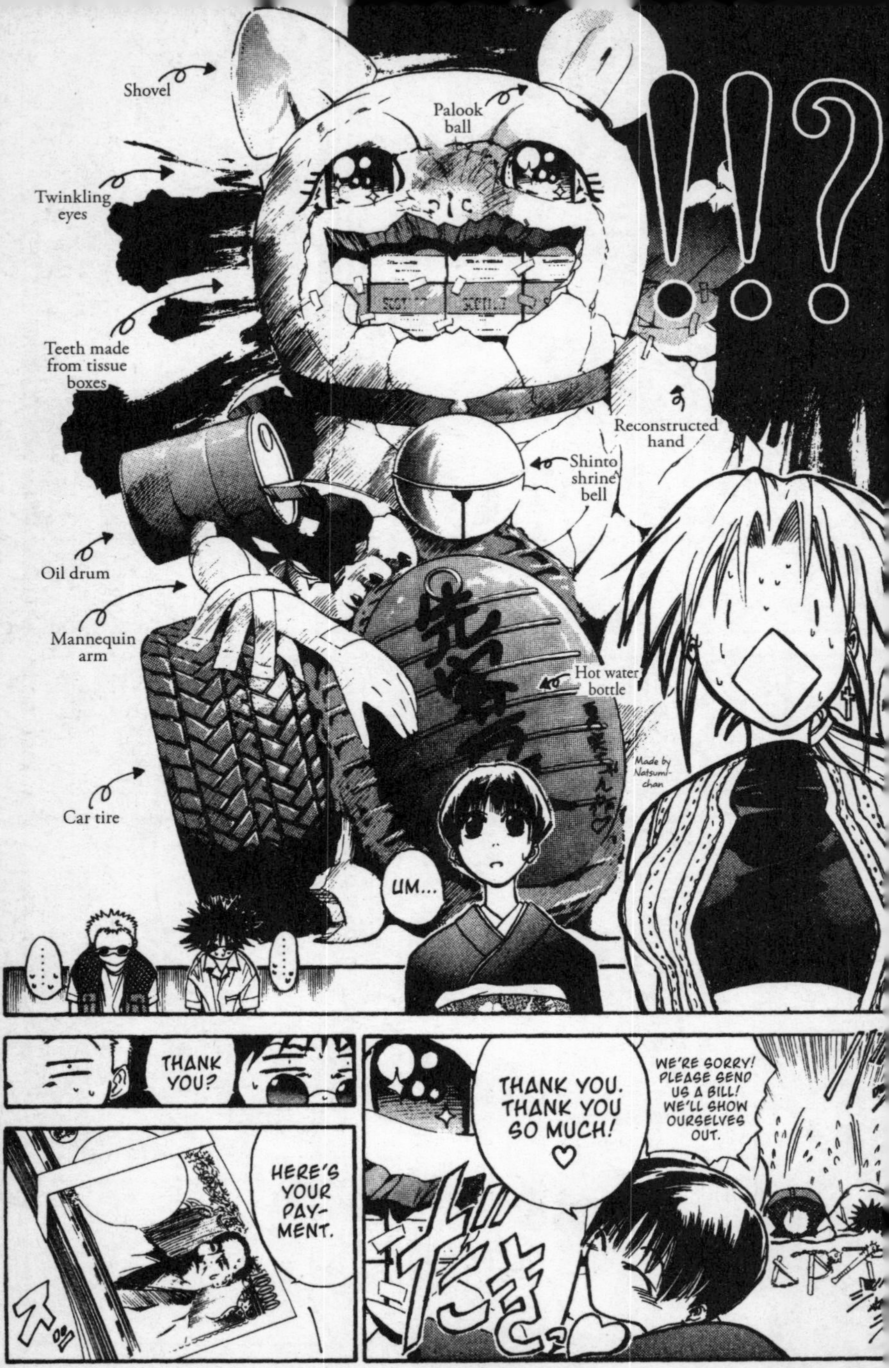

!!?
Shovel
Palook ball
Twinkling eyes
Teeth made from tissue boxes
Reconstructed hand
Shinto shrine bell
Oil drum
Mannequin arm
Hot water bottle
Made by Natsumi-chan
Car tire
UM...
THANK YOU?
HERE'S YOUR PAY-MENT.
THANK YOU. THANK YOU SO MUCH! ♡
WE'RE SORRY! PLEASE SEND US A BILL! WE'LL SHOW OURSELVES OUT.

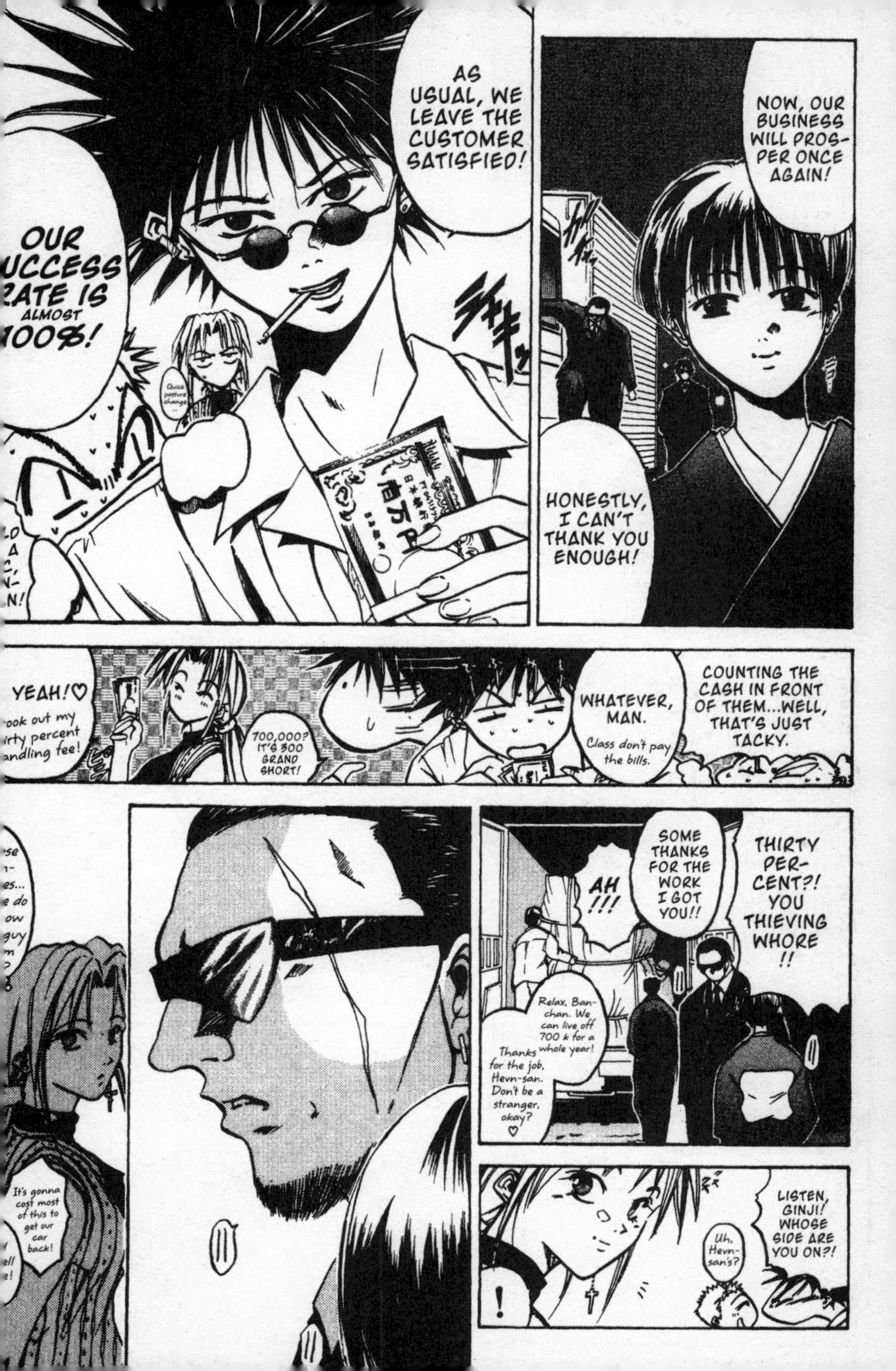
NOW, OUR BUSINESS WILL PROSPER ONCE AGAIN!
HONESTLY, I CAN'T THANK YOU ENOUGH!
AS USUAL, WE LEAVE THE CUSTOMER SATISFIED!
OUR UCCESS RATE IS ALMOST 100%!
Quick posture change...
COUNTING THE CASH IN FRONT OF THEM...WELL, THAT'S JUST TACKY.
WHATEVER, MAN.
Class don't pay the bills.
700,000? IT'S 300 GRAND SHORT!
YEAH!♡
rook out my irty percent andling fee!
THIRTY PER-CENT?! YOU THIEVING WHORE!!
SOME THANKS FOR THE WORK I GOT YOU!!
AH!!!
Relax, Ban-chan. We can live off 700 k for a whole year!
Thanks for the job, Hevn-san. Don't be a stranger, okay? ♡
LISTEN, GINJI! WHOSE SIDE ARE YOU ON?!
Uh, Hevn-san's?
!
It's gonna cost most of this to get our car back!

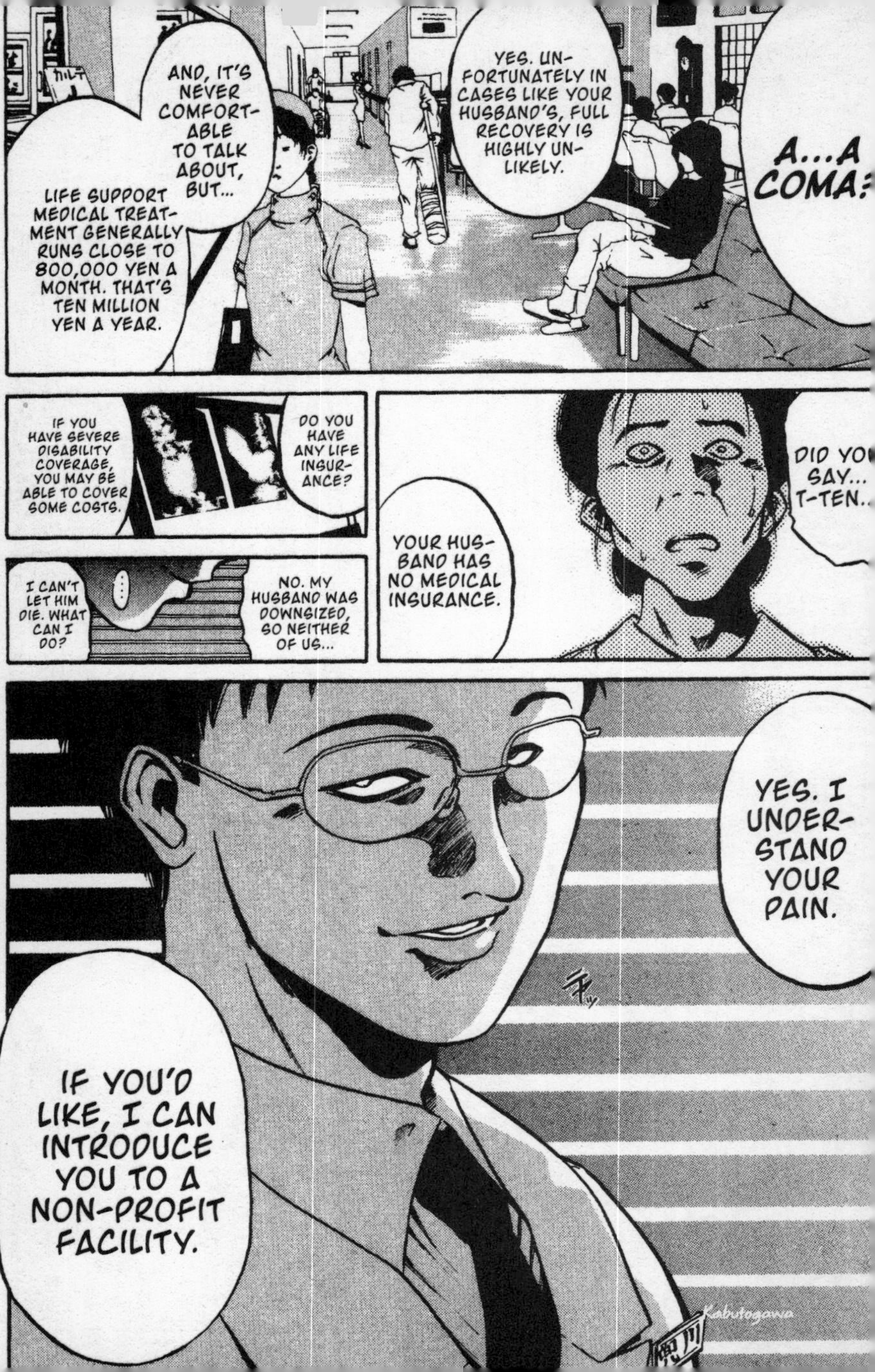
A...A COMA!?
YES. UNFORTUNATELY IN CASES LIKE YOUR HUSBAND'S, FULL RECOVERY IS HIGHLY UNLIKELY.
AND, IT'S NEVER COMFORTABLE TO TALK ABOUT, BUT...
LIFE SUPPORT MEDICAL TREATMENT GENERALLY RUNS CLOSE TO 800,000 YEN A MONTH. THAT'S TEN MILLION YEN A YEAR.
DID YOU SAY... T-TEN...
YOUR HUSBAND HAS NO MEDICAL INSURANCE.
DO YOU HAVE ANY LIFE INSURANCE?
IF YOU HAVE SEVERE DISABILITY COVERAGE, YOU MAY BE ABLE TO COVER SOME COSTS.
NO. MY HUSBAND WAS DOWNSIZED, SO NEITHER OF US...
...
I CAN'T LET HIM DIE. WHAT CAN I DO?
YES. I UNDERSTAND YOUR PAIN.
IF YOU'D LIKE, I CAN INTRODUCE YOU TO A NON-PROFIT FACILITY.
Kabutogawa

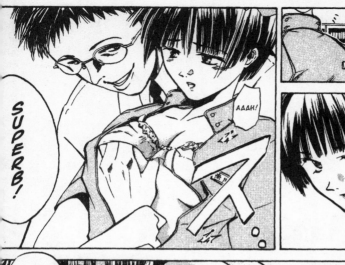

SUPERB!

AAAH!

HOW WAS IT, DOCTOR?

COME IN!

Ah--

Ah--

Knock Knock

D YOU ND THE ISK?

SO, HOW'D IT GO, SAMEJIMA?

NO. NO, WE DIDN'T.

• • • • •

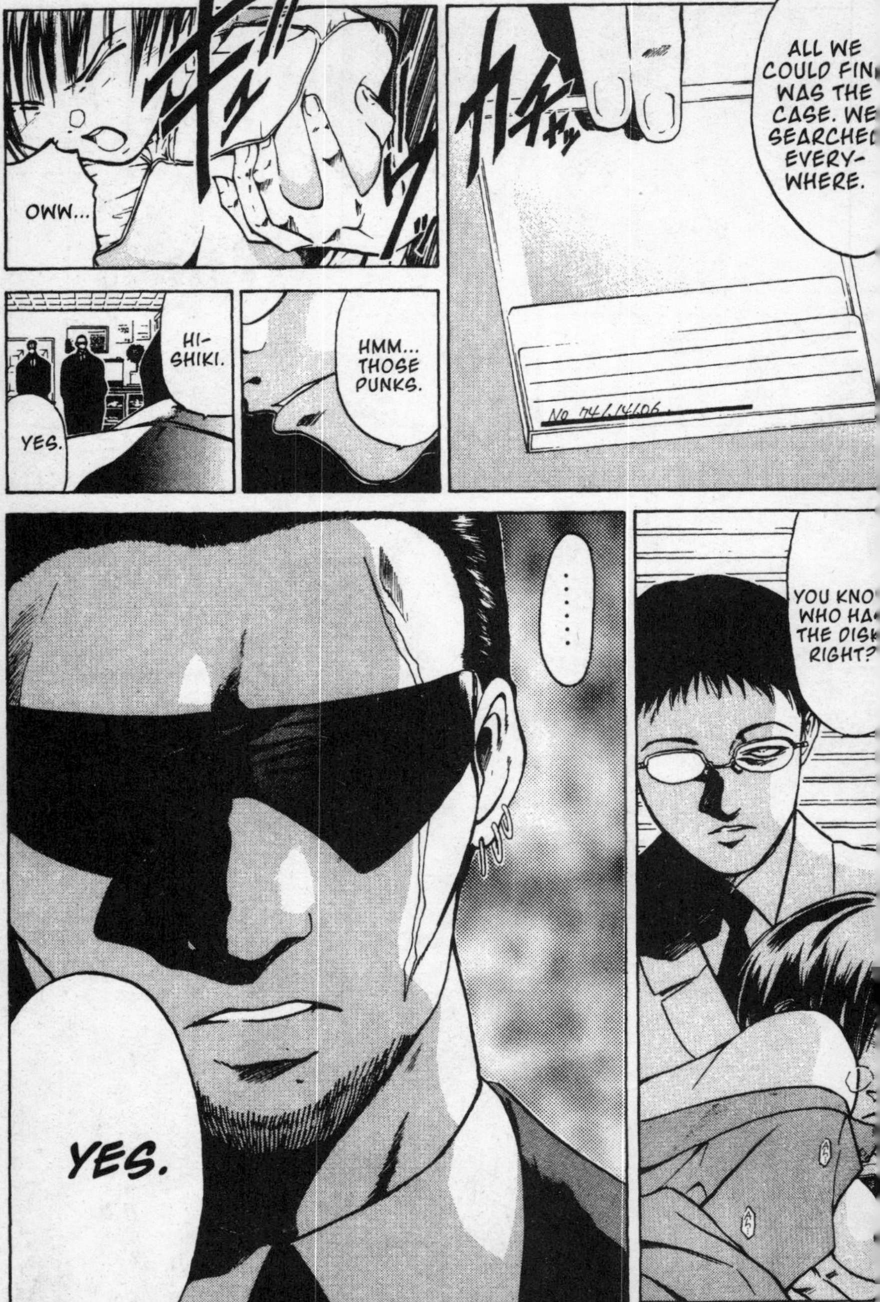
ALL WE COULD FIN WAS THE CASE. WE SEARCHE EVERY-WHERE.
OWW...
HMM... THOSE PUNKS.
HI-SHIKI.
YES.
YOU KNO WHO HA THE DIS RIGHT?
......
YES.

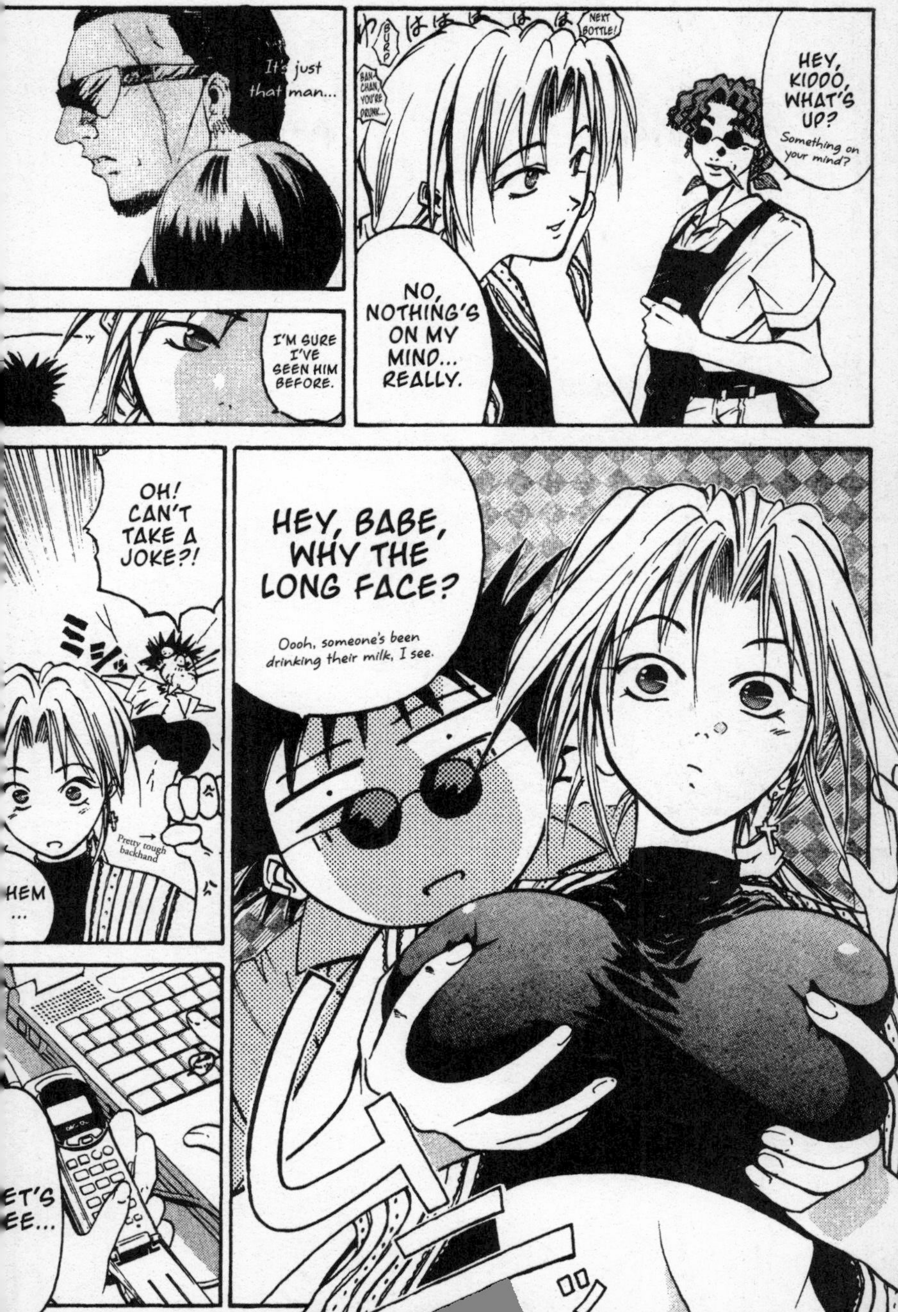
NEXT BOTTLE!
HEY, KIDDO, WHAT'S UP?
Something on your mind?
BURP
BAN-CHAN, YOU'RE DRUNK...
NO, NOTHING'S ON MY MIND... REALLY.
It's just that man...
I'M SURE I'VE SEEN HIM BEFORE.
HEY, BABE, WHY THE LONG FACE?
Oooh, someone's been drinking their milk, I see.
OH! CAN'T TAKE A JOKE?!
Pretty tough backhand
HEM ...
ET'S EE...

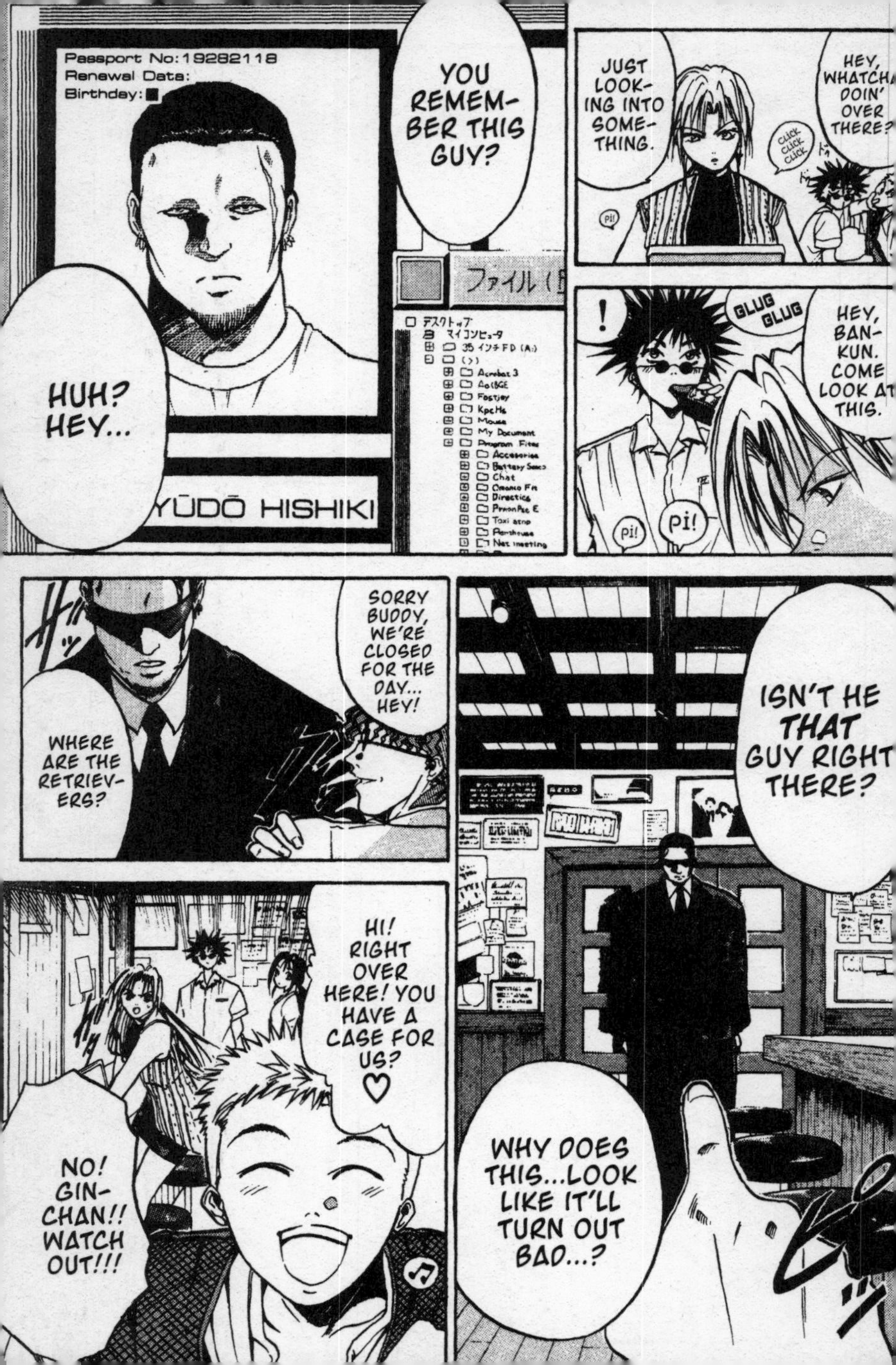
HEY, WHATCHA DOIN' OVER THERE?
CLICK CLICK CLICK
JUST LOOKING INTO SOMETHING.
pi!
HEY, BAN-KUN. COME LOOK AT THIS.
GLUG GLUG
!
pi!
pi!
YOU REMEMBER THIS GUY?
Passport No:19282118
Renewal Data:
Birthday:
YŪDŌ HISHIKI
ファイル
デスクトップ
マイコンピュータ
Acrobat 3
My Document
Program Files
Accessories
Chat
HUH? HEY...
ISN'T HE *THAT* GUY RIGHT THERE?
WHY DOES THIS...LOOK LIKE IT'LL TURN OUT BAD...?
SORRY BUDDY, WE'RE CLOSED FOR THE DAY... HEY!
WHERE ARE THE RETRIEVERS?
HI! RIGHT OVER HERE! YOU HAVE A CASE FOR US? ♡
NO! GIN-CHAN!! WATCH OUT!!!

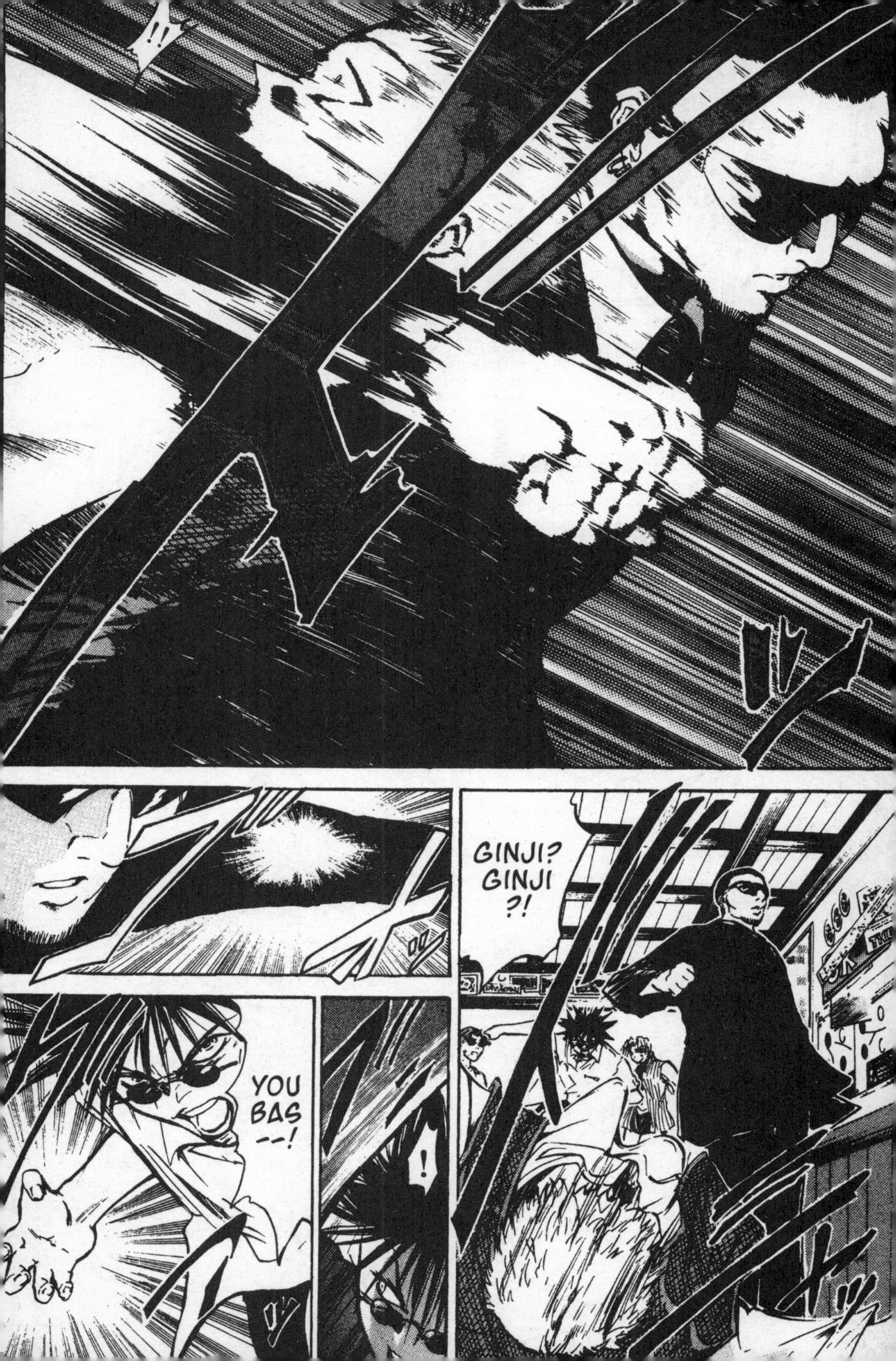
!!
GINJI? GINJI ?!
!
YOU BAS--!

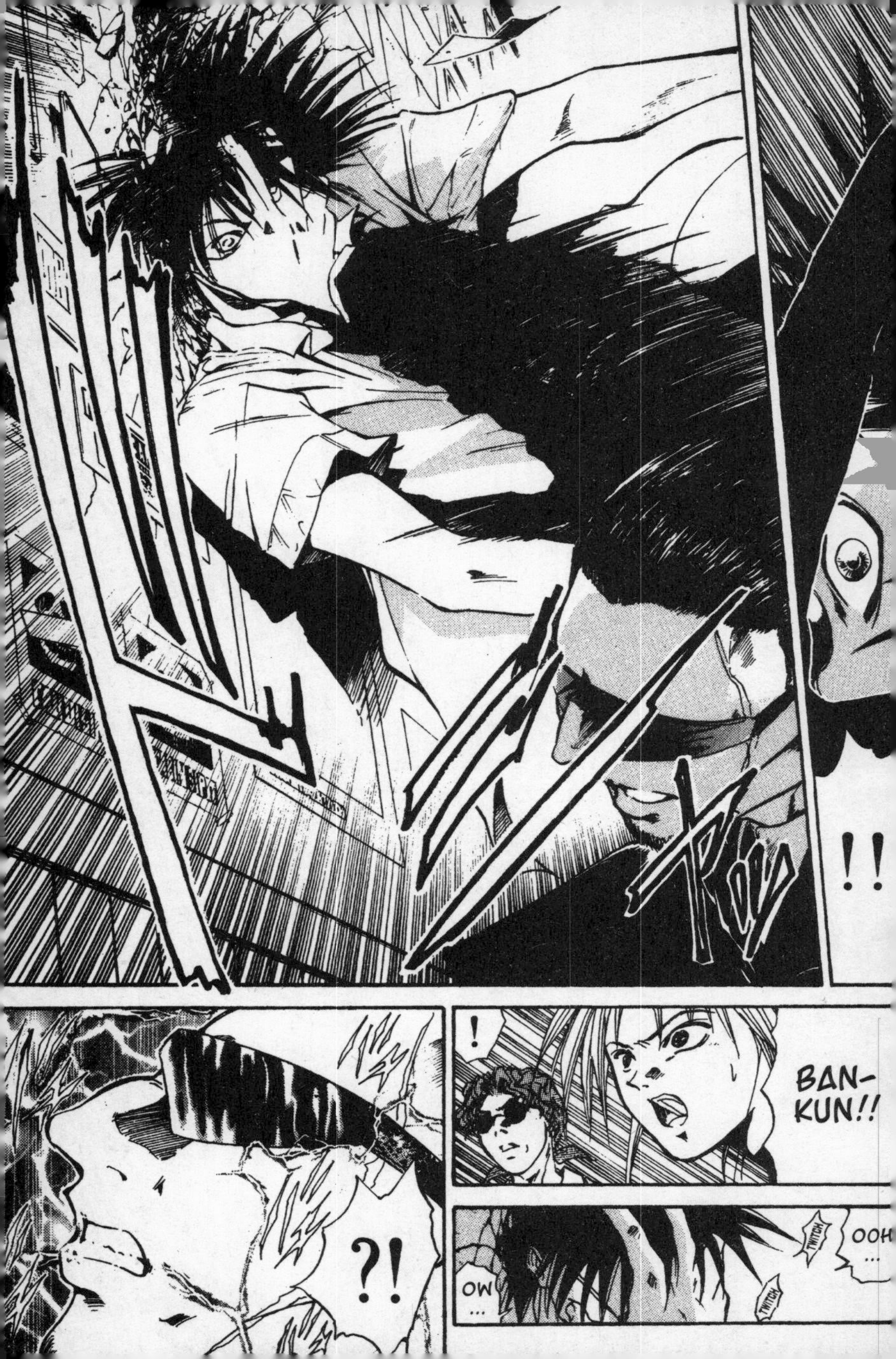
!!
!
BAN-KUN!!
?!
OOH ...
TWITCH
TWITCH
OW ...

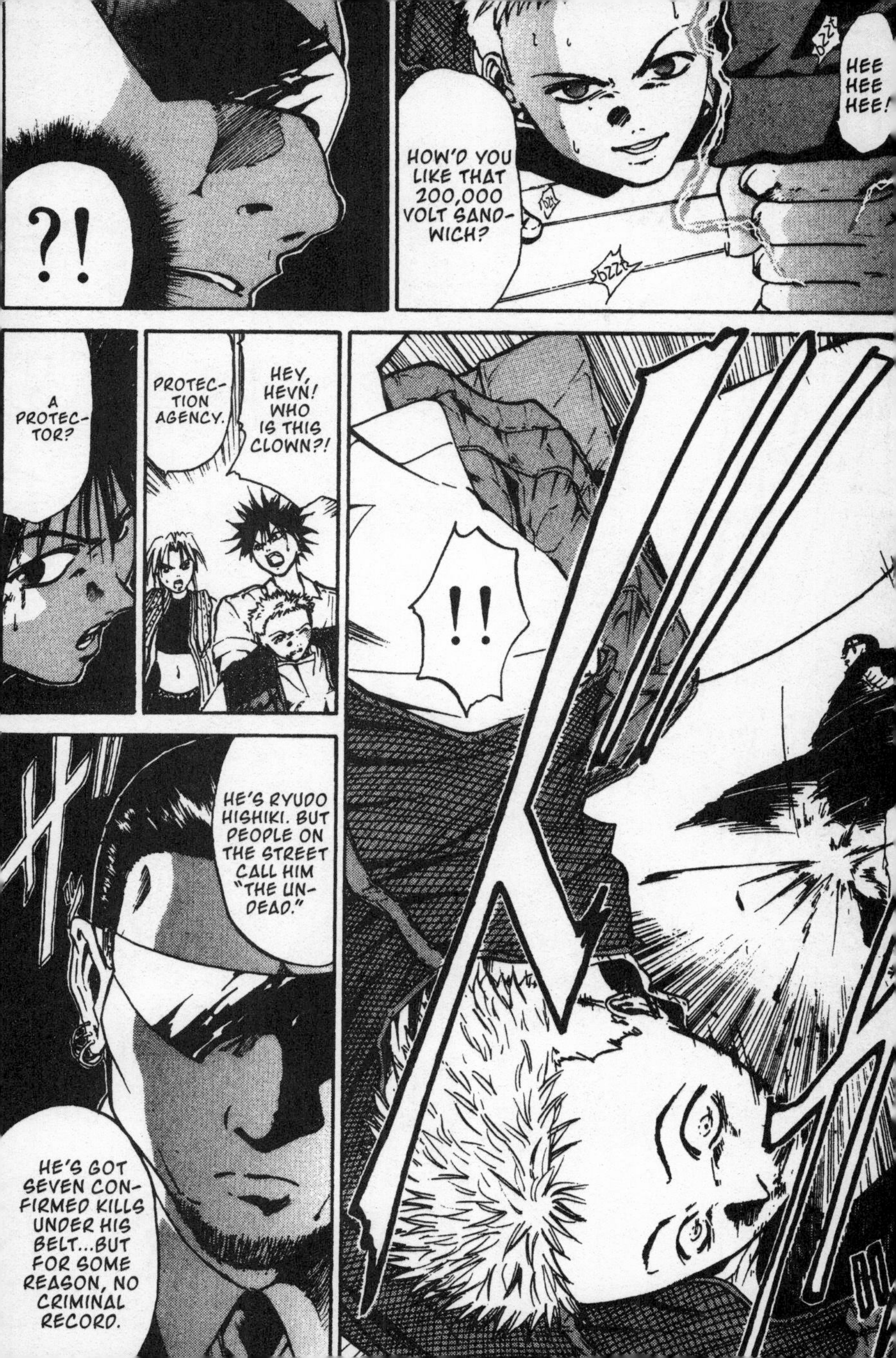

HEE HEE HEE!
bzz
HOW'D YOU LIKE THAT 200,000 VOLT SANDWICH?
bzz
?!
!!
HEY, HEVN! WHO IS THIS CLOWN?!
PROTECTION AGENCY.
A PROTECTOR?
HE'S RYUDO HISHIKI. BUT PEOPLE ON THE STREET CALL HIM "THE UNDEAD."
HE'S GOT SEVEN CONFIRMED KILLS UNDER HIS BELT...BUT FOR SOME REASON, NO CRIMINAL RECORD.

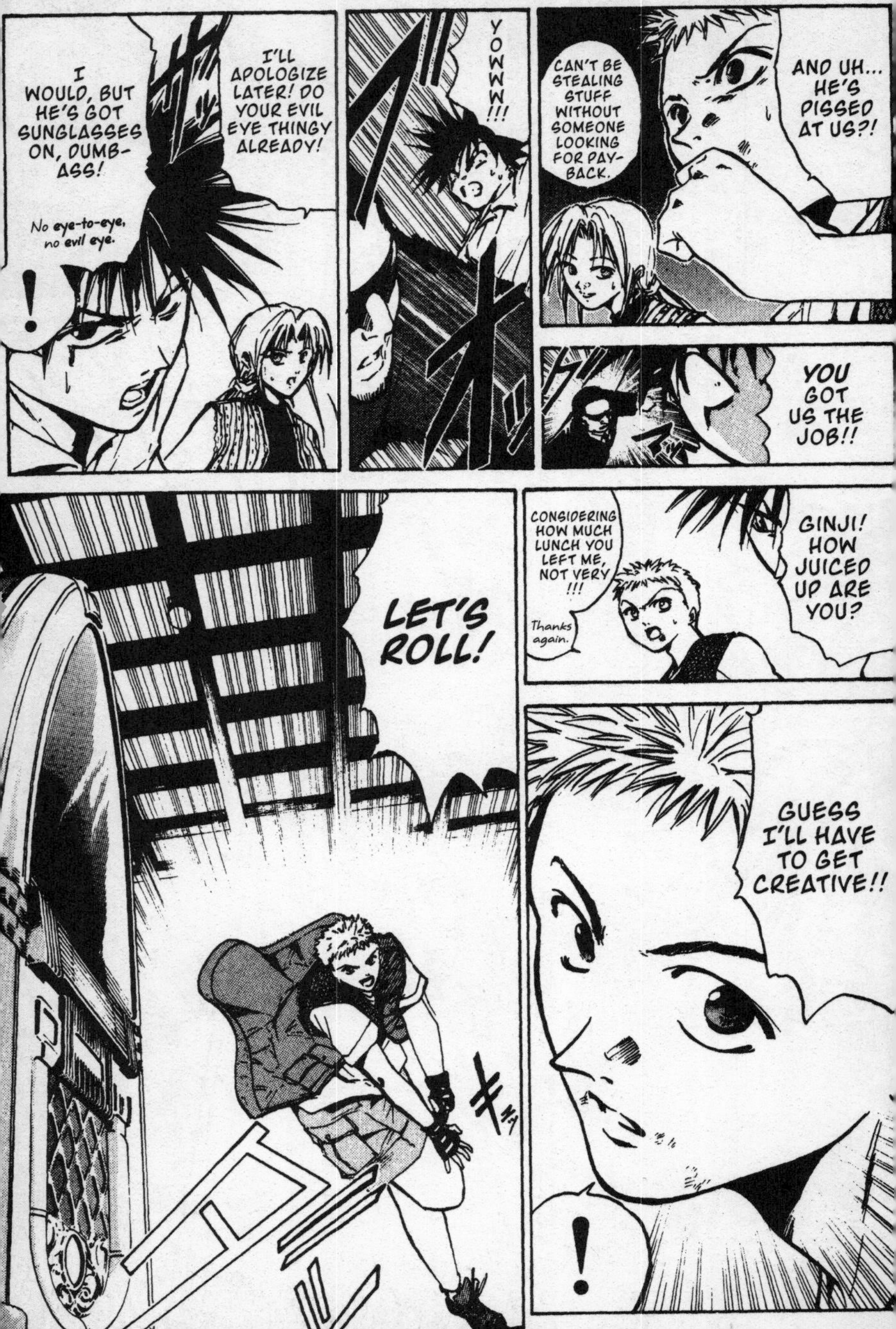
AND UH... HE'S PISSED AT US?!
CAN'T BE STEALING STUFF WITHOUT SOMEONE LOOKING FOR PAY-BACK.
YOU GOT US THE JOB!!
YOWWW!!!
I'LL APOLOGIZE LATER! DO YOUR EVIL EYE THINGY ALREADY!
I WOULD, BUT HE'S GOT SUNGLASSES ON, DUMB-ASS!
No eye-to-eye, no evil eye.
!
GINJI! HOW JUICED UP ARE YOU?
CONSIDERING HOW MUCH LUNCH YOU LEFT ME, NOT VERY!!!
Thanks again.
GUESS I'LL HAVE TO GET CREATIVE!!
!
LET'S ROLL!

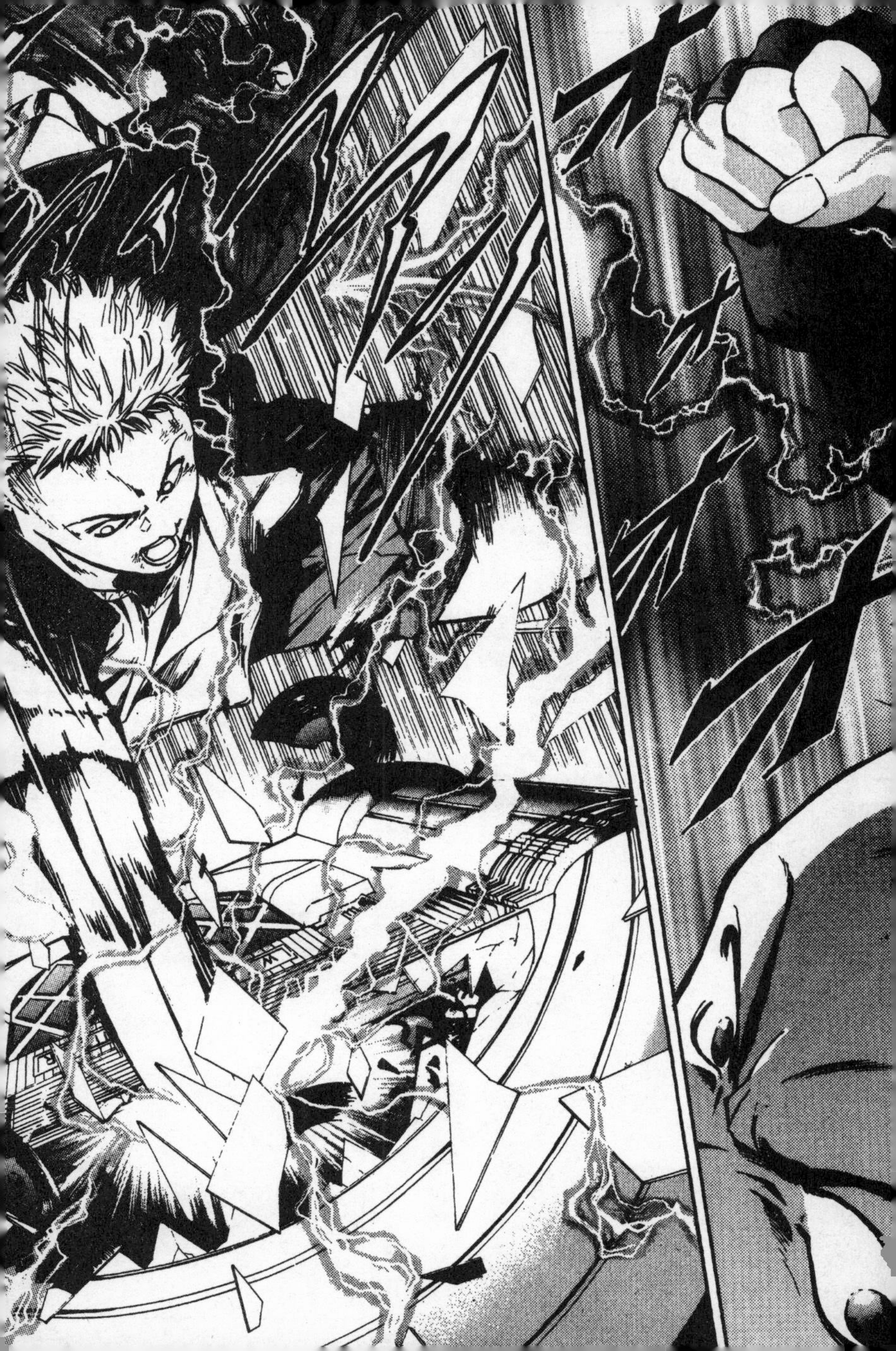

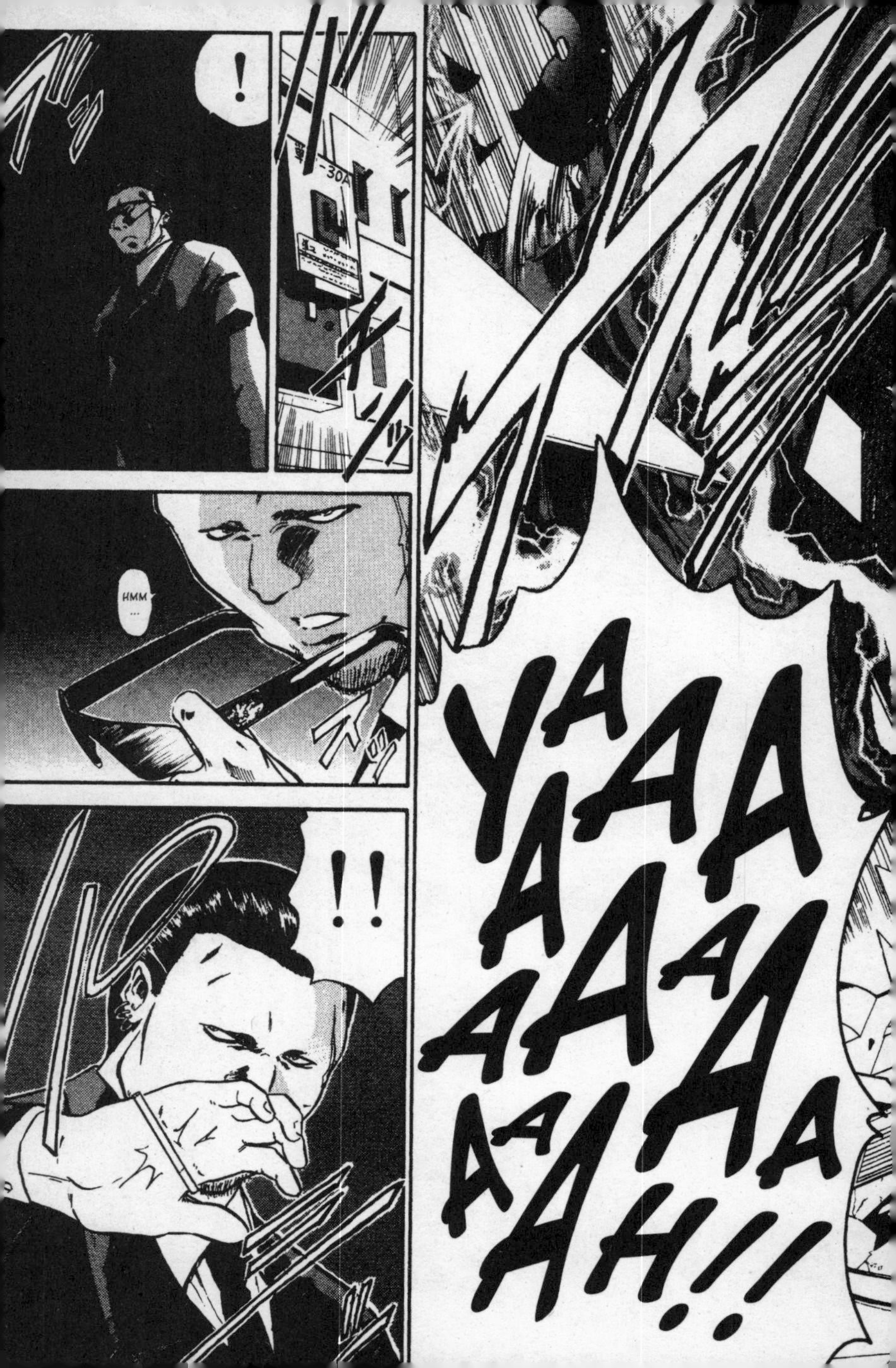
YAAAAAAAAAAAAAH!!
!
HMM ...
!!

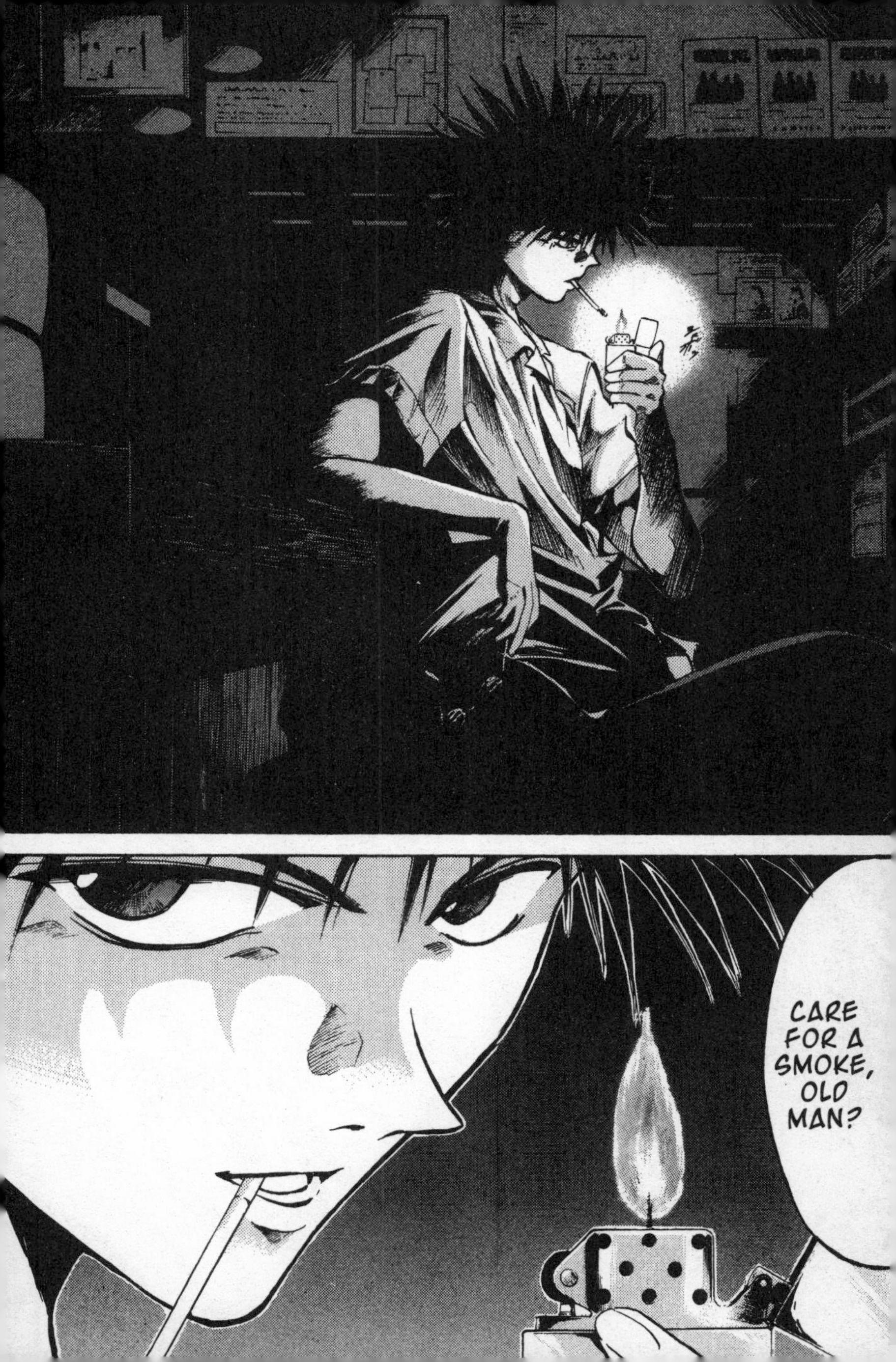
CARE FOR A SMOKE, OLD MAN?

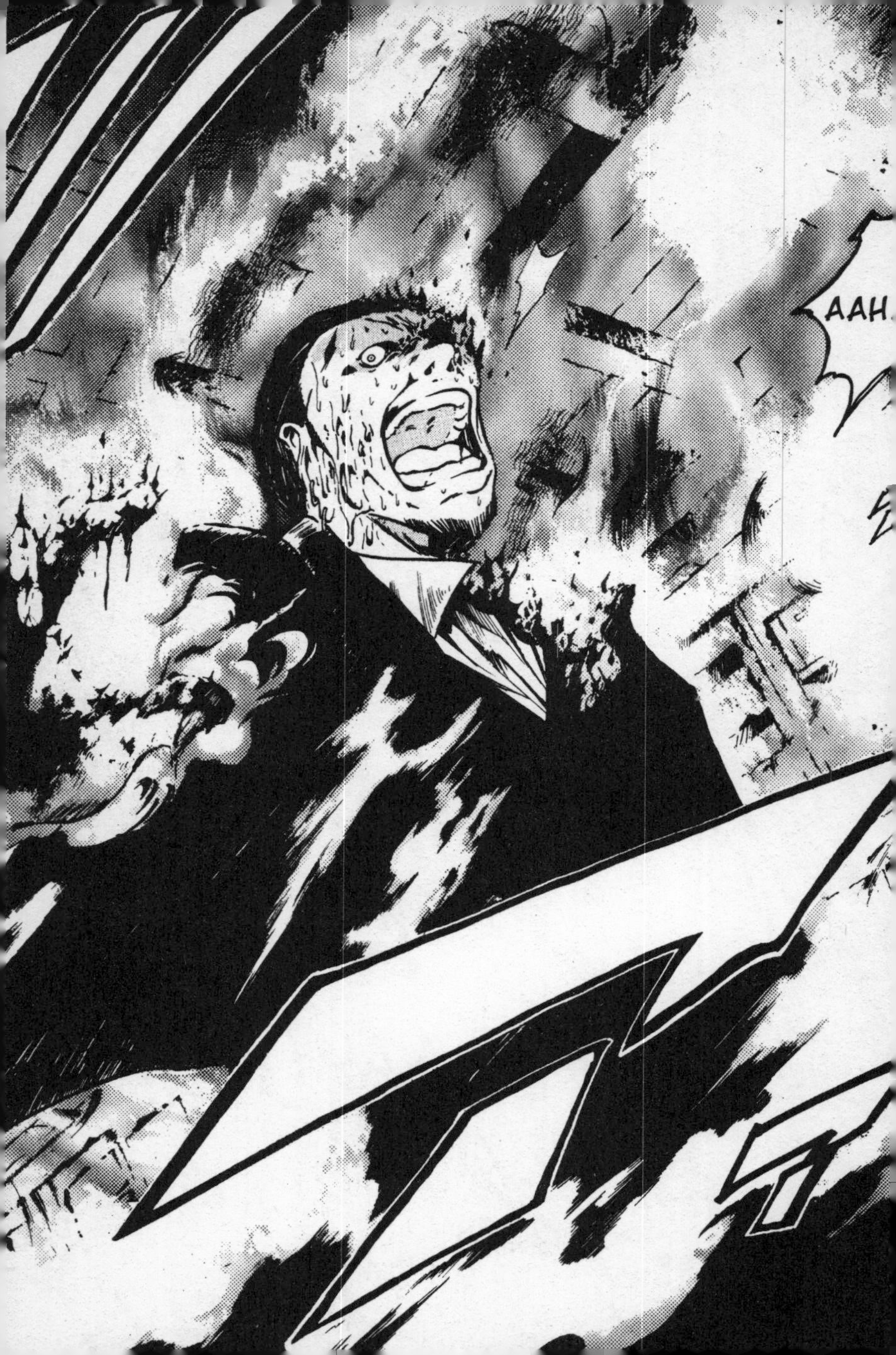
AAH...

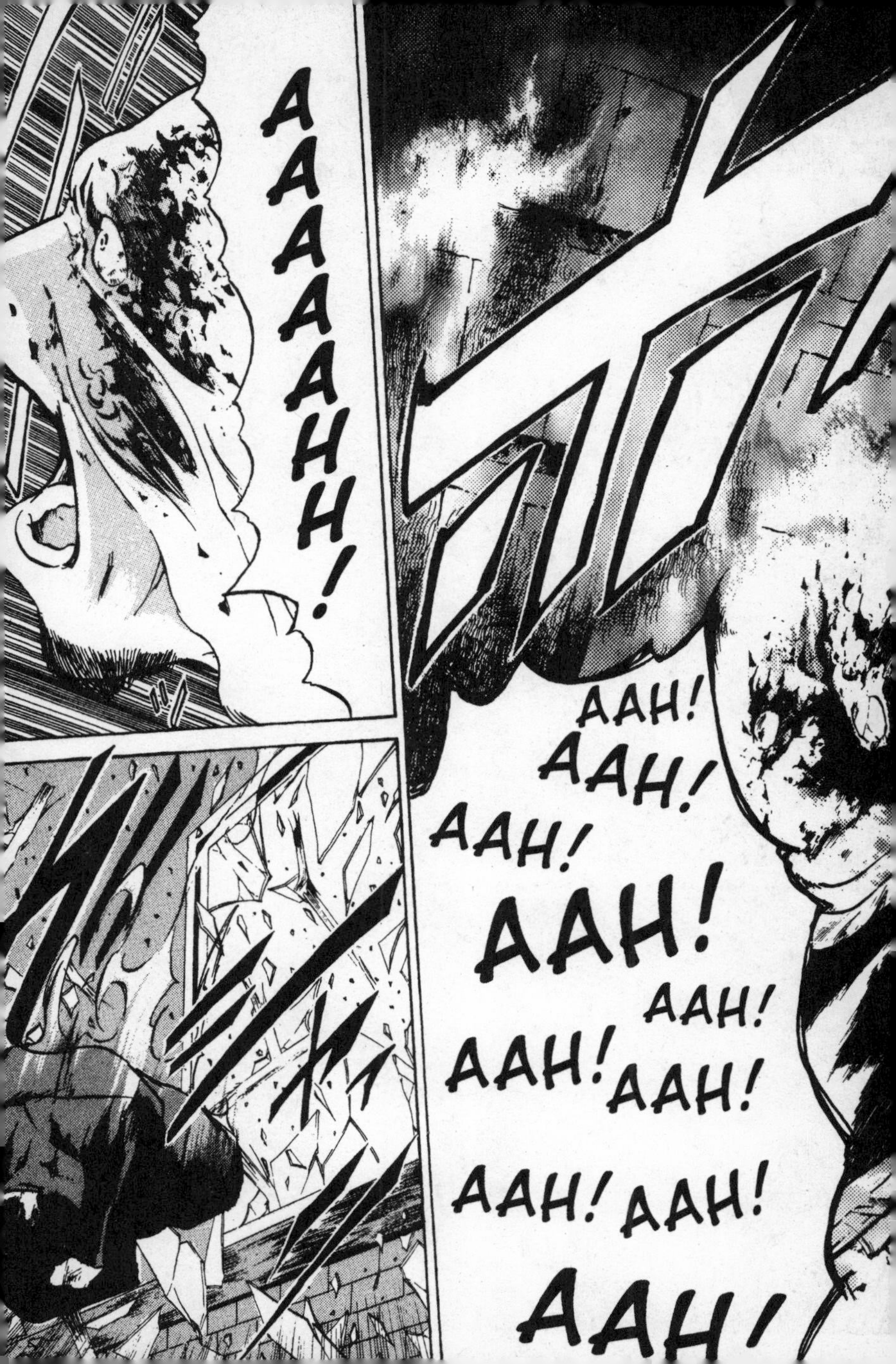
AAH!
AAH!
AAH!
AAH!
AAH!
AAH!
AAH!
AAH!
AAH!
AAH!
AAAAAAHH!

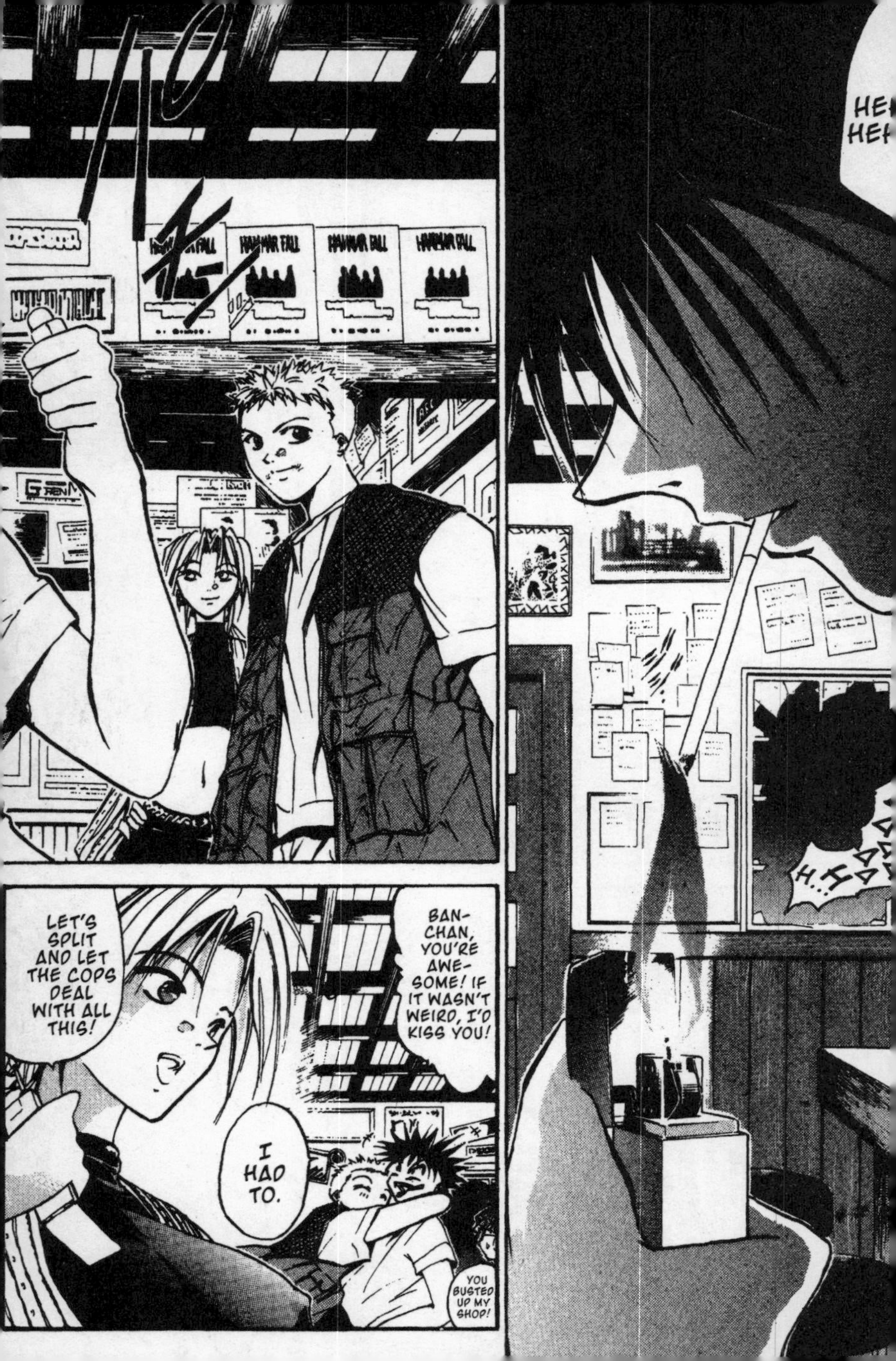
H..HAAAA
BAN-CHAN, YOU'RE AWESOME! IF IT WASN'T WEIRD, I'D KISS YOU!
LET'S SPLIT AND LET THE COPS DEAL WITH ALL THIS!
I HAD TO.
YOU BUSTED UP MY SHOP!

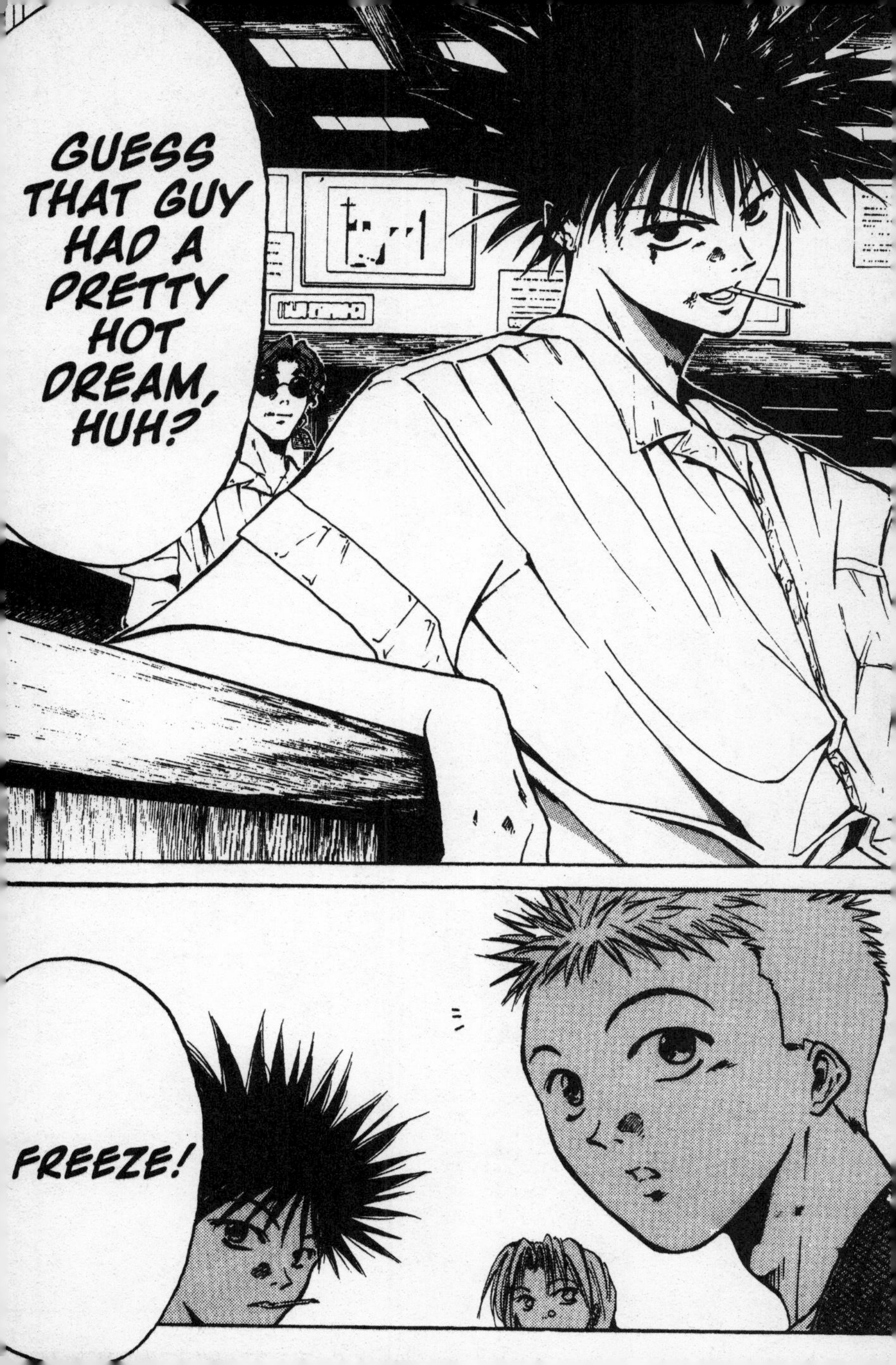
GUESS THAT GUY HAD A PRETTY HOT DREAM, HUH?
FREEZE!

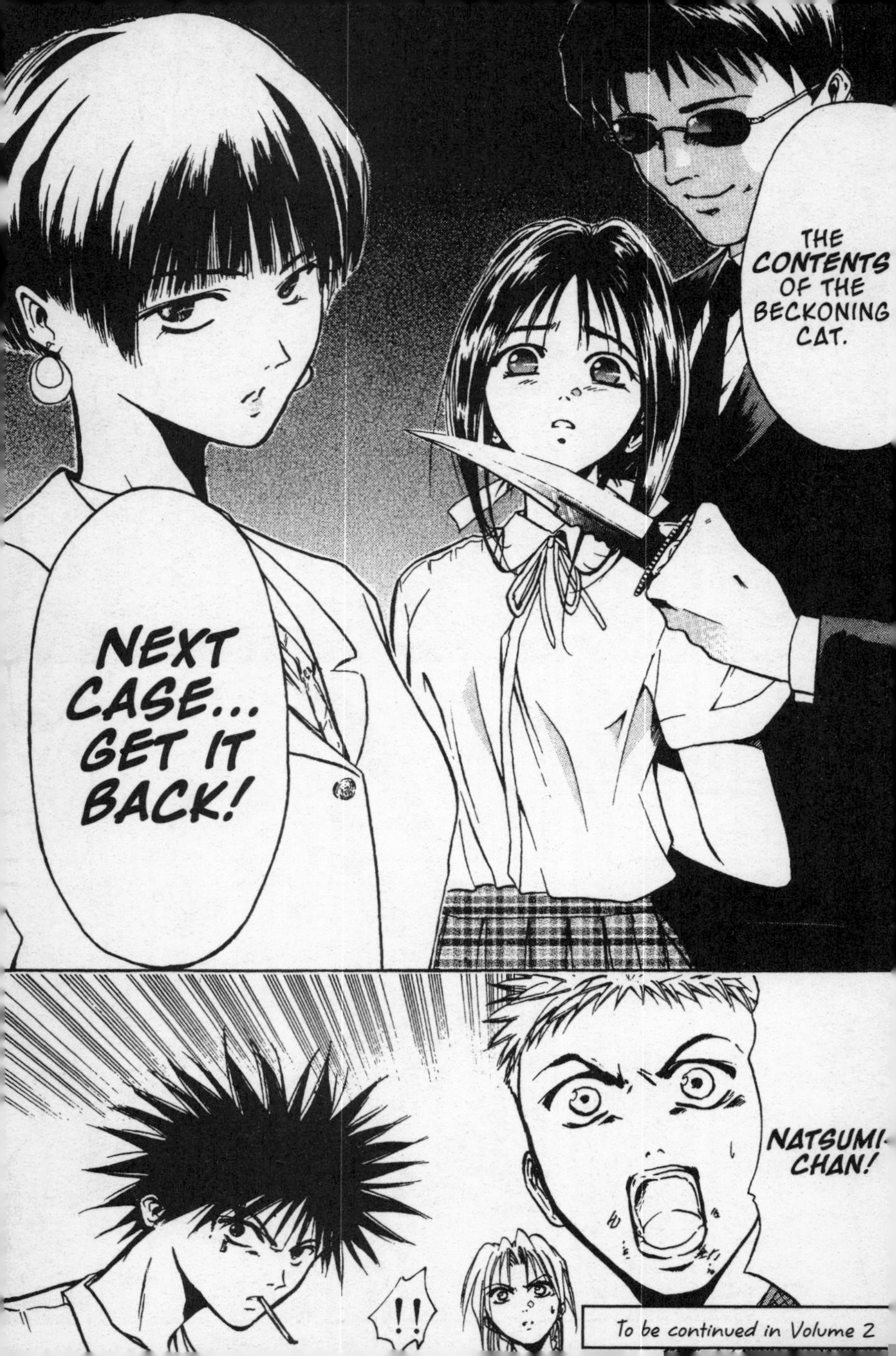
THE CONTENTS OF THE BECKONING CAT.
NEXT CASE... GET IT BACK!
NATSUMI-CHAN!
!!
To be continued in Volume 2

スタッフ紹介　SUPPORT STAFF

伊川 良樹　YOSHIKI IKAWA

土屋 奈朋　NAHO TSUCHIYA

大久保 篤　ATSUSHI ŌKUBO

榎並 博昭　HIROAKI ENAMI

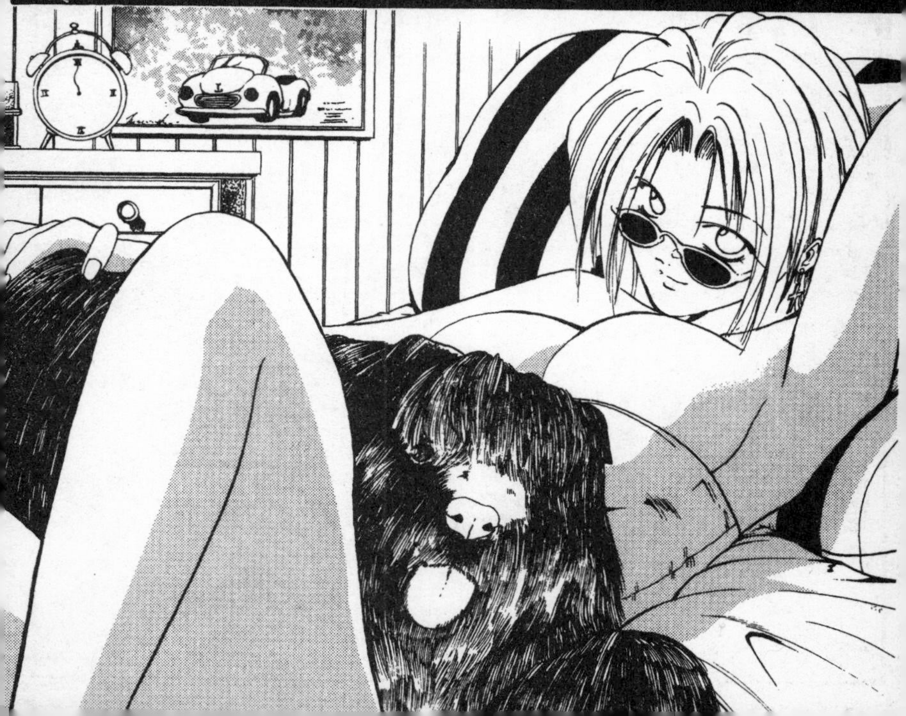

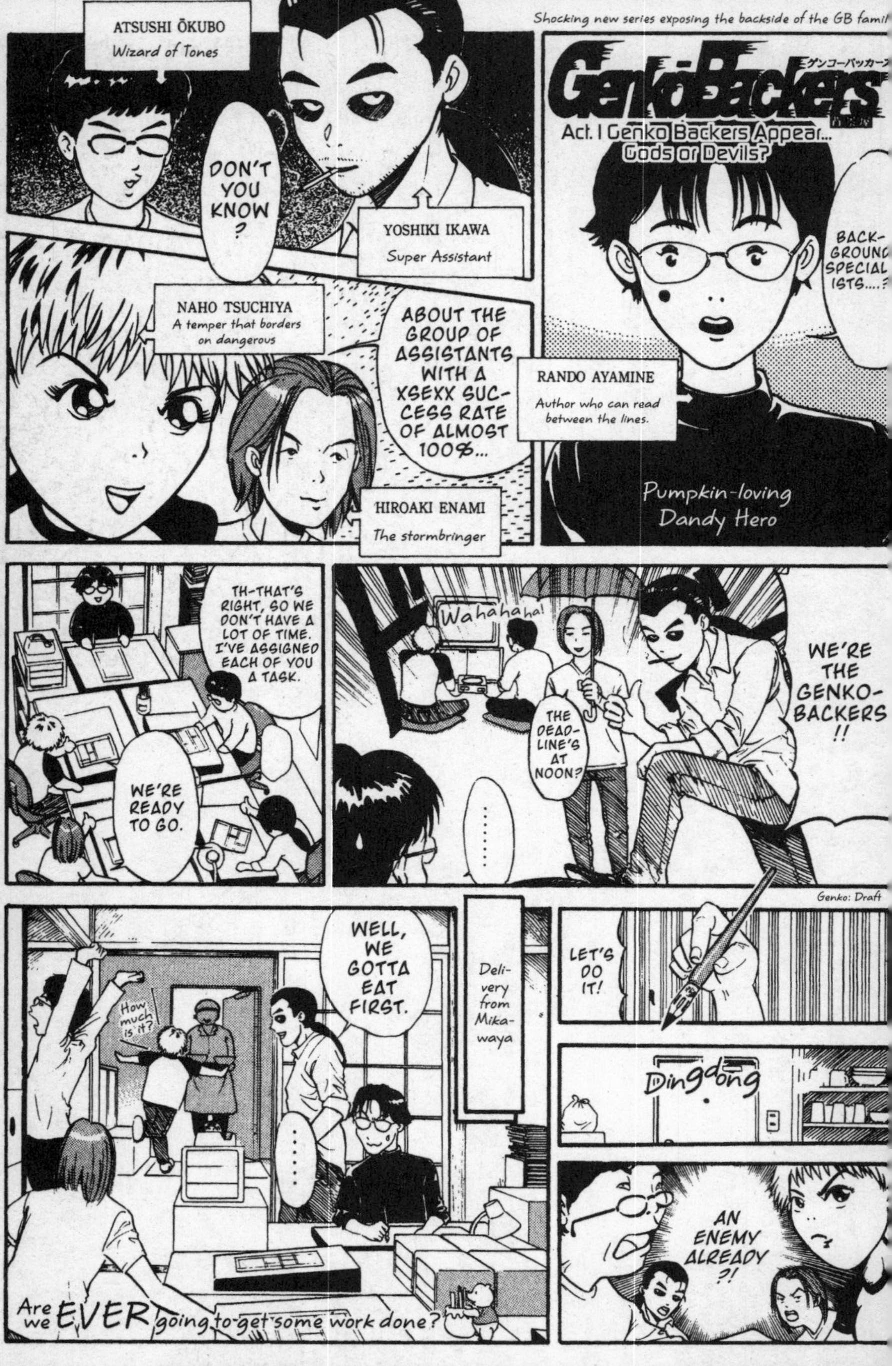
Shocking new series exposing the backside of the GB famil
GenkoBackers
ゲンコーバッカーズ
Act. I Genko Backers Appear... Gods or Devils?
BACK-GROUND SPECIALISTS....?
RANDO AYAMINE
Author who can read between the lines.
Pumpkin-loving Dandy Hero
YOSHIKI IKAWA
Super Assistant
ATSUSHI ŌKUBO
Wizard of Tones
DON'T YOU KNOW?
ABOUT THE GROUP OF ASSISTANTS WITH A XSEXX SUCCESS RATE OF ALMOST 100%...
NAHO TSUCHIYA
A temper that borders on dangerous
HIROAKI ENAMI
The stormbringer
WE'RE THE GENKO-BACKERS!!
Wahahaha!
THE DEADLINE'S AT NOON?
......
TH-THAT'S RIGHT, SO WE DON'T HAVE A LOT OF TIME. I'VE ASSIGNED EACH OF YOU A TASK.
WE'RE READY TO GO.
Genko: Draft
LET'S DO IT!
Dingdong
AN ENEMY ALREADY?!
Delivery from Mikawaya
WELL, WE GOTTA EAT FIRST.
How much is it?
......
Are we EVER going to get some work done?

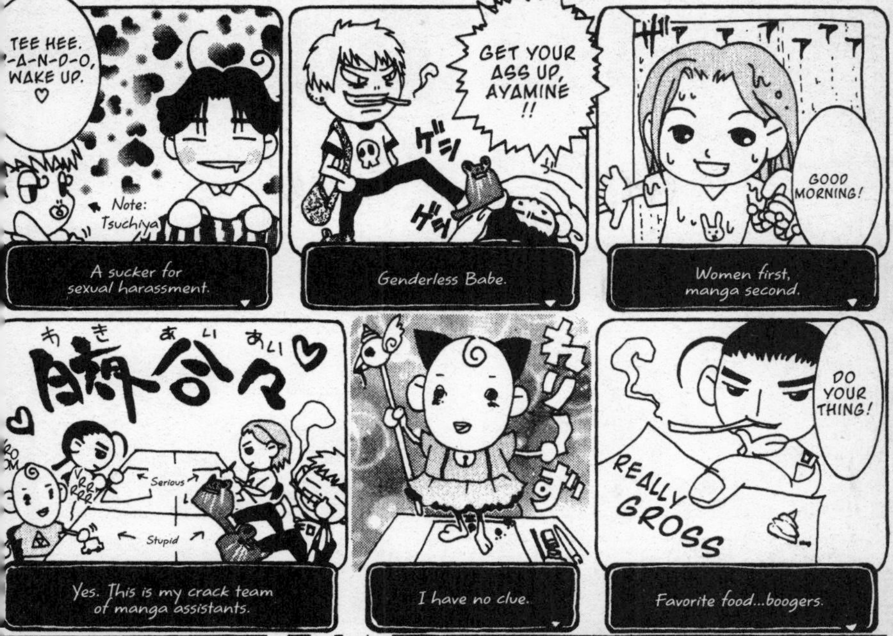
GOOD MORNING!
Women first, manga second.
GET YOUR ASS UP, AYAMINE !!
ゲシ
Genderless Babe.
TEE HEE. -A-N-D-O-O, WAKE UP. ♡
Note: Tsuchiya
A sucker for sexual harassment.
DO YOUR THING!
REALLY GROSS
Favorite food...boogers.
I have no clue.
Serious
Stupid
Yes. This is my crack team of manga assistants.

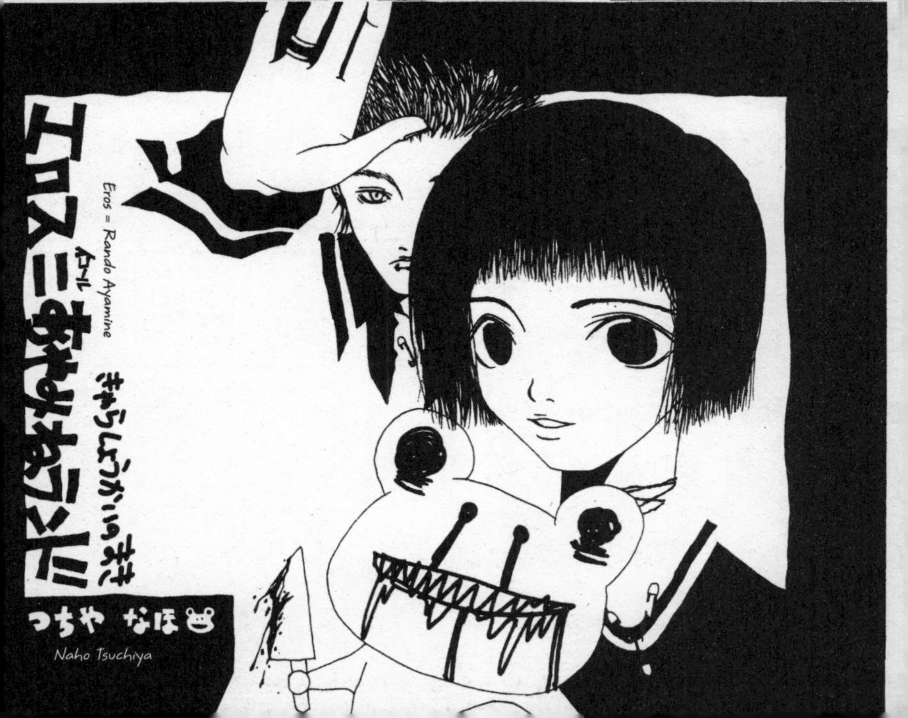
Eros = Rando Ayamine
つちや なほ
Naho Tsuchiya

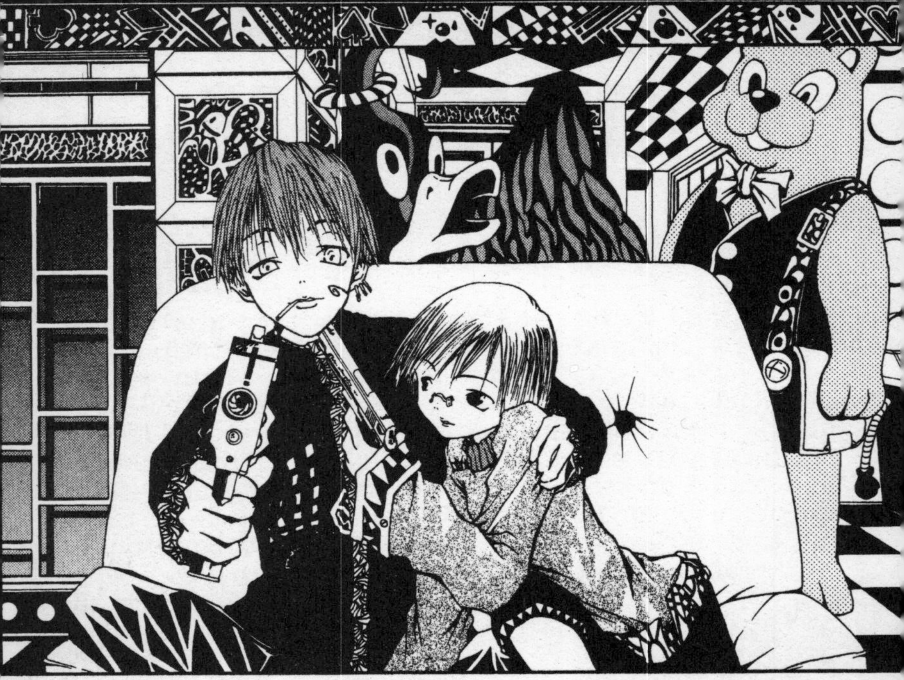

Senior Class B #8 Atsushi Okubo

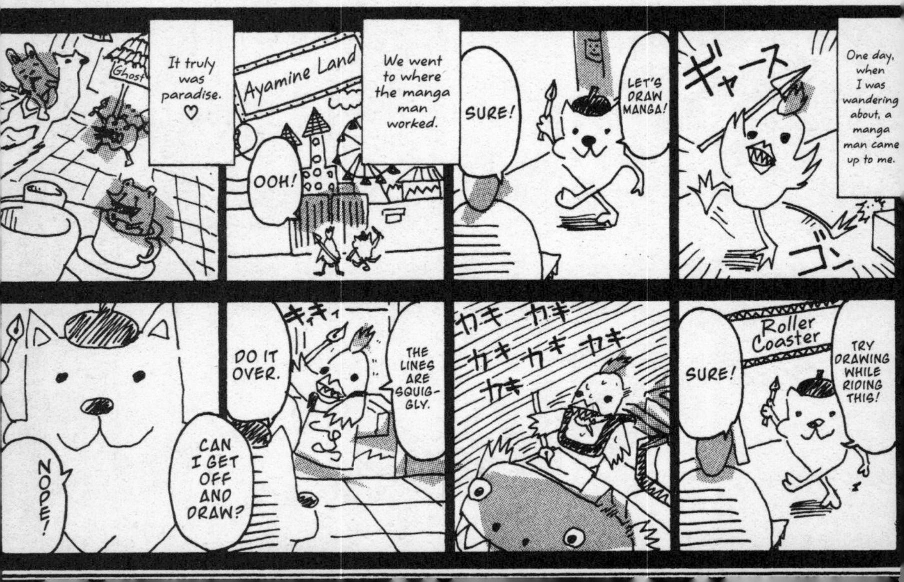
One day, when I was wandering about, a manga man came up to me.
ギャース
ゴン
LET'S DRAW MANGA!
SURE!
We went to where the manga man worked.
Ayamine Land
OOH!
It truly was paradise. ♡
Ghost
Roller Coaster
TRY DRAWING WHILE RIDING THIS!
SURE!
カキ カキ
カキ カキ カキ
カキ
キキィー
THE LINES ARE SQUIG-GLY.
DO IT OVER.
CAN I GET OFF AND DRAW?
NOPE!

In the next electrifying volume of

GETBACKERS

Clueless, duped and unconscious, the GetBackers are in a real pickle. But with the right people on their side, and supernatural powers at their disposal, they may be able to wiggle out of this pickle...that is unless their organs don't get sold off first by black market organ dealers, the fiends that knocked them unconscious and put them in this pickle in the first place. Of course Hevn, who led them to the fiends who put them in the pickle, is in a pickle of her own as the organ broker himself, Dr. Kabutogawa, unveils his lascivious intentions for her. Ah, life in a retrieval agency can be downright dangerous at times. Action, adventure and enough panty shots to shame even the dirtiest of old men in the next exciting volume of *GetBackers!*

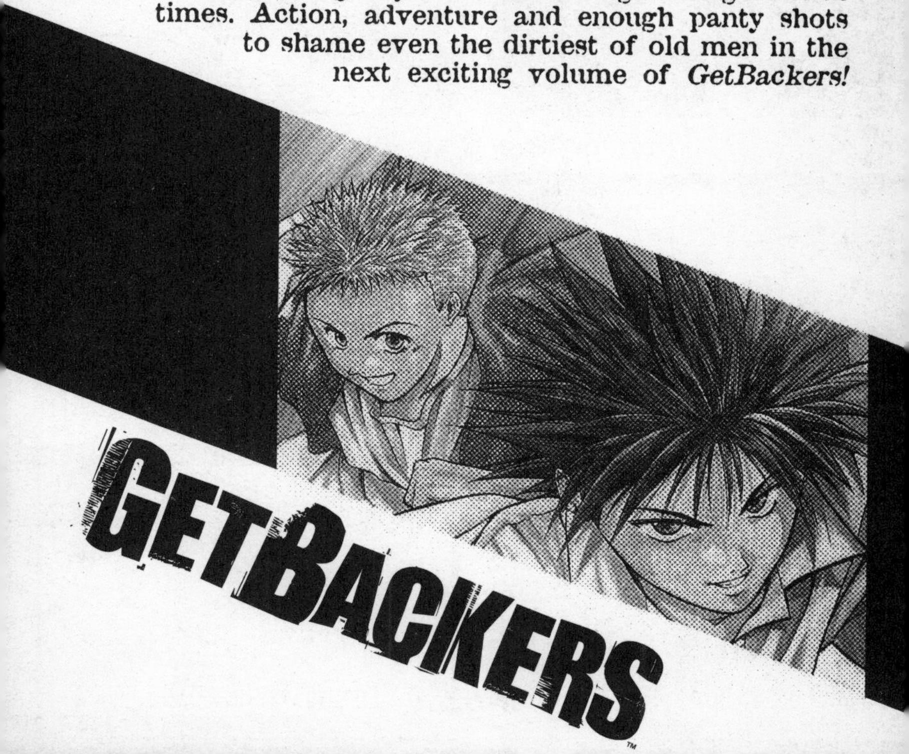
GETBACKERS

TOKYOPOP SHOP

THIS FALL, TOKYOPOP CREATES A FRESH, NEW CHAPTER IN TEEN NOVELS...

For Adventurers...

Witches' Forest:
The Adventures of Duan Surk

By Mishio Fukazawa
Duan Surk is a 16-year-old Level 2 fighter who embarks on the quest of a lifetime—battling mythical creatures and outwitting evil sorceresses, all in an impossible rescue mission in the spooky Witches' Forest!

BASED ON THE FAMOUS
FORTUNE QUEST WORLD

For Dreamers...

Magic Moon

By Wolfgang and Heike Hohlbein
Kim enters the enigmatic realm of Magic Moon, where he battles unthinkable monsters and fantastical creatures—in order to unravel the secret that keeps his sister locked in a coma.

THE WORLDWIDE BESTSELLING FANTASY
*THRILL*OGY ARRIVES IN THE U.S.!

POP FICTION

SHRINE OF THE MORNING MIST

BY HIROKI UGAWA

When the spirit world suddenly shifts out of balance, it's up to sisters Kurako, Yuzu and Tama to save us—but first they must get through their family drama.

FANTASY

T TEEN AGE 13+

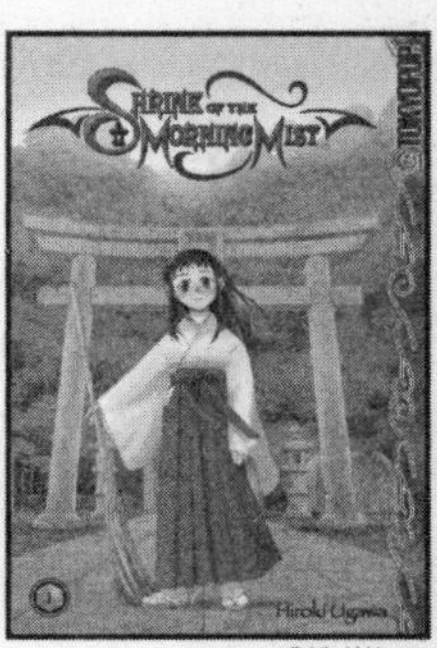
SHRINE OF THE MORNING MIST
TOKYOPOP
Hiroki Ugawa

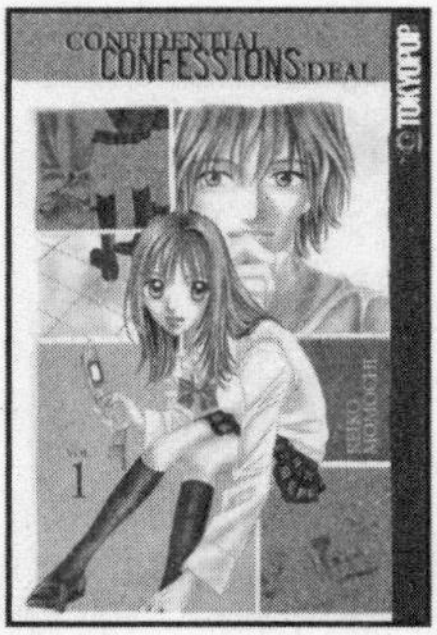
CONFIDENTIAL CONFESSIONS DEAI
TOKYOPOP
REIKO MOMOCHI
1

CONFIDENTIAL CONFESSIONS -DEAI-

BY REIKO MOMOCHI

In this unflinching portrayal of teens in crisis, silence isn't always golden...

DRAMA

OT OLDER TEEN AGE 16+

DEATH JAM

BY JEON SANG YOUNG

Muchaca Smooth is an assassin with just one shot to make it big!

ACTION

OT OLDER TEEN AGE 16+

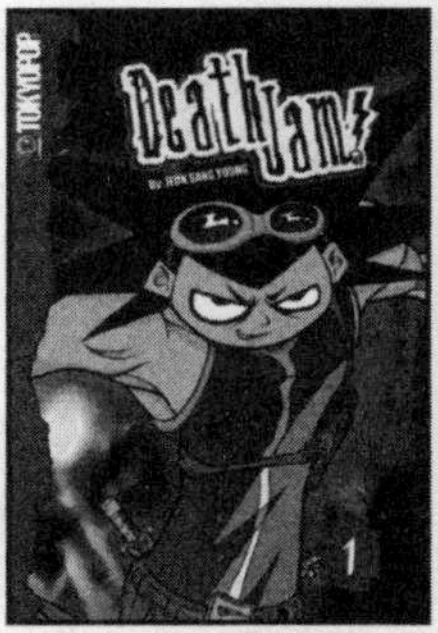
TOKYOPOP
Death Jam!
1

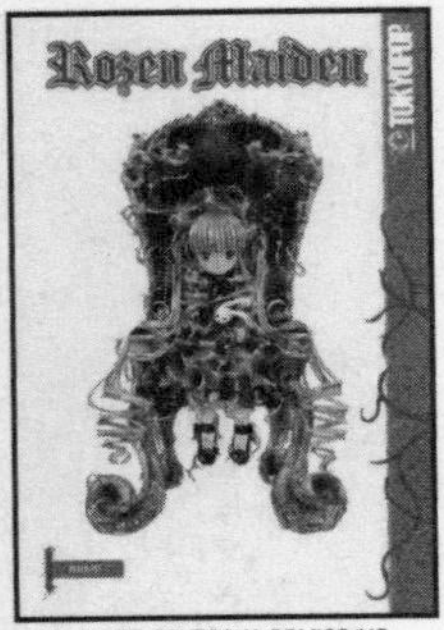
Rozen Maiden
TOKYOPOP
© PEACH-PIT, GENTOSHA COMICS INC.

ROZEN MAIDEN

BY PEACH-PIT

Welcome to the world of *Rozen Maiden* where a boy must enter an all-new reality to protect and serve a living doll!

FANTASY

T TEEN AGE 13+

From the creators of *DearS*!

BOYS OF SUMMER

BY CHUCK AUSTEN AND HIROKI OTSUKA

Just because you strike out on your first attempt at scoring with a girl doesn't mean you won't end up hitting a home run!

COMEDY

OT OLDER TEEN AGE 16+

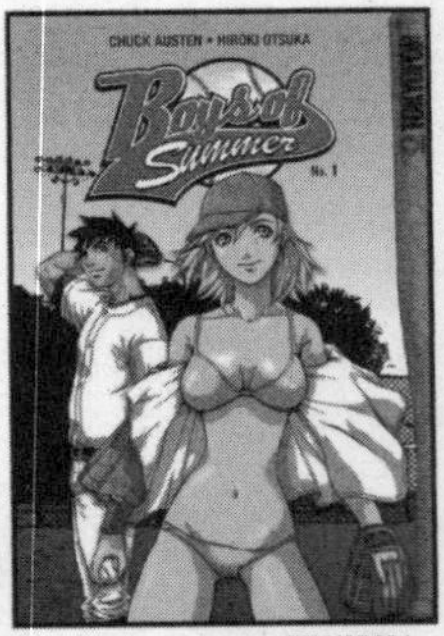
CHUCK AUSTEN • HIROKI OTSUKA
Boys of Summer
No. 1
TOKYOPOP
© Chuck Austen and TOKYOPOP Inc.

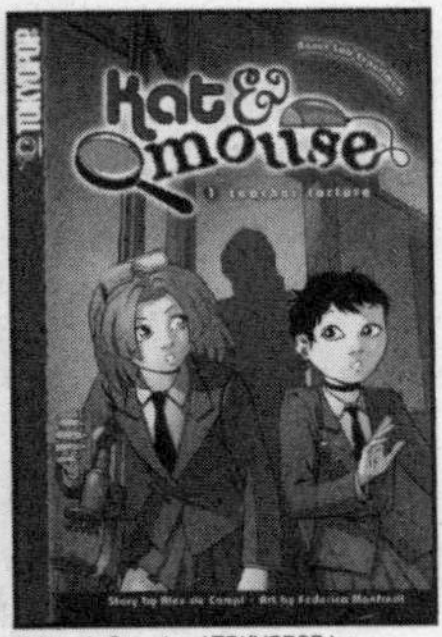
TOKYOPOP
Kat & mouse
© Alex de Campi and TOKYOPOP Inc.

KAT & MOUSE

BY ALEX DE CAMPI AND FEDERICA MANFREDI

When science whiz Kat teams up with computer nerd Mouse, bullies and blackmailers don't stand a chance!

MYSTERY

A ALL AGES

STOP!

This is the back of the book.
You wouldn't want to spoil a great ending!

This book is printed "manga-style," in the authentic Japanese right-to-left format. Since none of the artwork has been flipped or altered, readers get to experience the story just as the creator intended. You've been asking for it, so TOKYOPOP® delivered: authentic, hot-off-the-press, and far more fun!

DIRECTIONS

If this is your first time reading manga-style, here's a quick guide to help you understand how it works.

It's easy... just start in the top right panel and follow the numbers. Have fun, and look for more 100% authentic manga from TOKYOPOP®!

P9-BHY-989